059191

59

00007884

ESRI

D0528638

MICROECONOMIC SIMULATION MODELS FOR PUBLIC POLICY ANALYSIS

Volume 2

Sectoral, Regional, and General Equilibruim Models

Microeconomic Simulation Models for Public Policy Analysis

A 1978 conference sponsored by
The Institute for Research on Poverty
Mathematica Policy Research, Inc.
The National Science Foundation

This is a volume in the

Institute for Research on Poverty Monograph Series

A complete list of titles in this series appears at the end of this volume.

MICROECONOMIC SIMULATION MODELS FOR PUBLIC POLICY ANALYSIS

Volume 2

Sectoral, Regional, and General Equilibrium Models

Edited by

Robert H. Haveman
Institute for Research on Poverty
University of Wisconsin—Madison
Madison, Wisconsin

Kevin Hollenbeck
Urban Systems Research and Engineering
Washington, D. C.

THE ECONOMIC & SOCIAL
RESEARCH INSTITUTE LIBRARY
Recd. - 6 APR 1981
336

ACADEMIC PRESS
A Subsidiary of Harcourt Brace Jovanovich, Publishers

New York   London   Toronto   Sydney   San Francisco

This book is one of a series sponsored by the Institute for Research on Poverty
of the University of Wisconsin pursuant to the provisions of the
Economic Opportunity Act of 1964.

Copyright © 1980 by the Board of Regents of the University of Wisconsin System
on behalf of the Institute for Research on Poverty.
All rights reserved.
No part of this publication may be reproduced or transmitted in any form or by any means,
electronic or mechanical, including photocopy, recording, or any information storage and
retrieval system, without permission in writing from the publisher.

The views expressed in this book are those of the authors; they do not necessarily represent the
official views of the institutions with which the authors are affiliated.

ACADEMIC PRESS, INC.
111 Fifth Avenue, New York, New York 10003

United Kingdom Edition published by
ACADEMIC PRESS, INC. (LONDON) LTD.
24/28 Oval Road, London NW1   7DX

Library of Congress Cataloging in Publication Data
Main entry under title:

Microeconomic simulation models for public policy
    analysis.

    (Institute for Research on Poverty monograph series)
    "A 1978 conference, sponsored by the Institute for
Research on Poverty, Mathematica Policy Research, Inc.,
the National Science Foundation."
    Includes bibliographical references and index.
    CONTENTS: v. 1.   Distributional impacts.——v. 2.
Sectoral, regional, and general equilibrium models.
    1. Policy sciences——Mathematical models——
Congresses. 2. Microeconomics——Mathematical models——
Congresses. I. Haveman, Robert H. II. Hollenbeck,
Kevin. III. Wisconsin. University——Madison. Institute
for Research on Poverty. IV. Mathematica Policy Research, Inc.
V. United States. National Science Foundation. VI.
Series: Wisconsin. University——Madison. Institute for
Research on Poverty. Monograph series.
H22.M5   338.5'01'51   79—8866
ISBN 0—12—333202—8 (v. 2)

PRINTED IN THE UNITED STATES OF AMERICA

80 81 82 83   9 8 7 6 5 4 3 2 1

*We would like to dedicate this book to David Kershaw (1942-1979),
founder of Mathematica Policy Research,
supporter of and participant in this conference,
colleague and friend.*

*The Institute for Research on Poverty is a national center for research
established at the University of Wisconsin in 1966 by a grant from the
Office of Economic Opportunity. Its primary objective is to foster basic,
multidisciplinary research into the nature and causes of poverty and means
to combat it.*

*In addition to increasing the basic knowledge from which policies aimed at the
elimination of poverty can be shaped, the Institute strives to carry analysis beyond
the formulation and testing of fundamental generalizations to the development and
assessment of relevant policy alternatives.*

*The Institute endeavors to bring together scholars of the highest caliber whose
primary research efforts are focused on the problem of poverty, the distribution of
income, and the analysis and evaluation of social policy, offering staff members
wide opportunity for interchange of ideas, maximum freedom for research into
basic questions about poverty and social policy, and dissemination of their findings.*

mpr *Mathematica Policy Research, Inc. (MPR) was founded in 1968
to operate the nation's first large-scale social policy experiment,
the New Jersey Negative Income Tax Experiment. Since that time,
MPR has expanded considerably and now conducts social policy research, social
science experiments, and large-scale evaluation research in the areas of income security and welfare, health, housing, education and training, and microsimulation
modeling.*

*MPR has a staff of over 300 persons who specialize in economic, sociological,
and survey research, policy analysis, systems design and implementation, and national sample and specialized survey operations. The company has attracted a professional research and operating staff with a strong commitment to social change
through policy research in the public sector. Corporate headquarters and the Research, Survey, and Information Systems divisions are located in Princeton, New
Jersey. The Research Division also maintains an office in Madison, Wisconsin. MPR
Denver is located in Denver, Colorado, and the Policy Studies Division is located in
Washington, D.C.*

CONTENTS

LIST OF FIGURES   xi

LIST OF TABLES   xiii

LIST OF CONTRIBUTORS   xvii

PREFACE   xxi

CONTENTS OF VOLUME 1   xxix

MICRODATA MODELS OF THE MACROECONOMY

**1   Policy Explorations with the Transactions Model of the
      U.S. Economy**   3

Robert L. Bennett and Barbara R. Bergmann

A Short Description of the Transactions Model
Fitting the Model to Data for 1973-1975   22
Simulations of the Effects of Policy Changes   29
Future Directions for Research with the Transactions Model   38

Discussion   39

Donald A. Nichols

Discussion   44

Robert P. Strauss

2   **Experiments with Fiscal Policy Parameters on a Micro to Macro**
    Model of the Swedish Economy   49

    Gunnar Eliasson

    Introduction   49
    The Model   50
    Taxes, Business-Cycle Policy, and Industrial Structure: Applications of
    the Swedish Micro to Macro Model   68
    Conclusions and Plans for the Future   86

    Discussion   88

    Benjamin A. Okner

    Discussion   93

    Harold W. Watts

3   **Corporate and Personal Tax Integration in the United States:**
    Some Preliminary Findings   97

    Don Fullerton, A. Thomas King, John B. Shoven, and
    John Whalley

    Introduction   97
    Objectives of Tax Integration and the General Equilibrium Approach 98
    A General Equilibrium Model of the U.S. Economy and Tax System   101
    Representing the Tax Integration Plans in Model Equivalent Form   113
    Results   118
    Conclusion   124

    Discussion   125
    Nicholas M. Kiefer

    Discussion   128
    Jonathan R. Kesselman

    MICRODATA MODELS WITH REGIONAL AND/OR
        SECTORAL IMPACTS

4   **A Microeconomic Simulation Model for Analyzing the Regional**
    and Distributional Effects of Tax-Transfer Policy: An Analysis of
    the Program for Better Jobs and Income   137

    Robert H. Haveman, Kevin Hollenbeck, David Betson, and
    Martin Holmer

    Introduction   137
    The Structure of the Simulation Model   138
    The Program for Better Jobs and Income—The Basis for Analysis   140

Some Policy Implications 150
Caveats and Future Directions of Research 151

Appendices

Appendix A: The Detailed Structure of the Microeconomic
Simulation Model for Analyzing the Regional and Distributional
Effects of Tax-Transfer Policy
153

Appendix B: Simulated State Supplementation under the
Program for Better Jobs and Income 159

Discussion 163

Anne P. Carter

Discussion 168

Benjamin Chinitz

5   **Rehabilitating Central-City Housing: Simulations with The
Urban Institute Housing Model**
171

Larry Ozanne and Jean E. Vanski

Introduction 171
The Model 172
Data Bases Underlying the Model 180
Simulating Rehabilitation Programs 186
Summary, Conclusions, and Implications 203

Discussion 204

Bruce Hamilton

Discussion 208

Edgar O. Olsen

6   **IDIOM: A Disaggregated Policy-Impact Model of the U.S. Economy** 213

Stephen P. Dresch and Daniel A. Updegrove

Introduction 213
Implementing the Model 219
Directions of Substantive Model Development 221
An Application to Military Export Policy and Compensatory Alternatives 224
Appendix: A Mathematical Description of IDIOM 232

Discussion 243

Steven B. Caldwell

Discussion   246

James R. Hosek

AN APPRAISAL OF MICRODATA SIMULATION MODELS

7   Microdata Simulation: Current Status, Problems, Prospects   253

Kenneth J. Arrow

REFERENCES   267

INDEX   283

LIST OF FIGURES

1.1	Scheme of Portfolio Allocation for Households	15
1.2	Flow Chart Illustrating the Sequence of Decision Making Concerning Prices	16
1.3	Employment Subsidized under Alternative Wage Subsidy Schemes	37
2.1	Macro Delivery and Income Determination Structure of Swedish Model	53
2.2	Business Decision System (One Firm)	56
2.3	Production System (One Firm)	58
2.4	Ordering of Variables, Policy Parameters, and Coefficients of Entire Micro to Macro Model	62
2.5	Tax System	63
2.6	GNP Effects of Value-added and Payroll Tax Changes	72
2.7	Sector Effects on Industrial Output of Complete Change of Tax over Five-year Period	83
2.8	Relationship between Rates of Return (*RR*) and Growth in Output (*DQ*) of Individual Firms in the Market	84
2.9	Rates of Change in Nominal Wage Costs to Firms (*DW*) and Real Rates of Return (*RR*) after Inflationary Period in Investment Goods Sector	86
3.1	Outline of the Interrelation between Data Sets for the Model	104
4.1	A Schematic Flow Chart of the Simulation Model	140

LIST OF TABLES

1.1	Summary of Sequence of Events in a Round of the Transactions Model	6
1.2	Information Continually Updated and Available Concerning Each Fictional Firm during a Run of the Transactions Model	8
1.3	Information Continually Updated and Available Concerning Each Fictional Person during a Run of the Transactions Model	12
1.4	Market Participation in Transactions Model, by Sector	18
1.5	Cash Flows Between Sectors Occurring in the Transactions Model, by the Event Generating Them	20
1.6	Gross National Product	24
1.7	Unemployment Rates	25
1.8	National Income	26
1.9	Personal Income and Outlay	27
1.10	Interest Rates	28
1.11	Balance Sheet for Nonfinancial Firms	30
1.12	Results of Monetary and Fiscal Policy Experiments	32
1.13	Contrasting Results of Experimental Runs with Two Forms of Wage Subsidy, 1975 III-IV	37
1.14	Within-sample Forecast Accuracy of Bennett, Bergmann, and Data Resources Quarterly Models of the U.S. Economy, 1973-1975	46
2.1	Swedish Taxes	65
2.2	Sensitivity Analysis with Value-added and Payroll Taxes	73
2.3	Effect of Temporary Lowering of Value-added Tax by 3 Percentage Points, 2nd and 3rd Quarters 1974	77
2.4	"Budget Neutral" Changes Between Payroll and Value-added Tax Systems	79
3.1	Classification of Industries, Consumer Goods, and Consumer Groups Used in Model	102

3.2   U.S. Taxes and Their Treatment in the Model   106
3.3 f_i Proportion and Tax Rate on Tax on Capital (*CTR*) for
       Each Tax Scheme   117
3.4   Welfare Gains under Various Assumptions   119
3.5   Percentage Changes in Real Income after Income Taxes and
       Transfers by Consumer Group, for Each Tax Replacement   120
3.6   Percentage Changes in Relative Prices and Quantity Outputs
       by Industry, for Each Tax Replacement   122
4.1   Changes in Disposable Income from PBJI, by Income Source   141
4.2   Distribution of Change in Disposable Income by Income Class   143
4.3   Change in Disposable Income and Gross Output from PBJI,
       by Region   144
4.4   Ratios of Gross Output to Changes in Disposable Income and
       Induced Manpower Demand from PBJI, by Region   145
4.5   Net Change in Gross Output from PBJI and Federal Income
       Surtax, by Production Sector   147
4.6   Net Change in Induced Manpower Demand from PBJI and
       Federal Income Surtax, by Occupation   148
4.7   Earnings Class Net Impact Indicators from PBJI and Federal
       Income Surtax, by Region   149
5.1   Characteristics of Four Hypothetical Metropolitan Areas   182
5.2   No-Policy Simulation Results, Eight Cases, 1960-1970   185
5.3   Assumed Rehabilitation in 1960   188
5.4   Percentage Changes in Housing Services from the Stock under
       a Rehabilitation Program   192
5.5   Absolute Changes in Housing Services from the Stock under
       a Rehabilitation Program   195
5.6   Changes for Households under a Rehabilitation Program   198
5.7   Change in Housing Services from the Stock under a Combined
       Household-Assistance and Rehabilitation Program   201
5.8   Changes for Households under a Combined Housing-Assistance
       and Rehabilitation Program   202
6.1   National Model Outputs   215
6.2   Regional Model Outputs   218
6.3   1973 IDIOM National Income Accounts Calibration Procedures   220
6.4   IDIOM Parameter and Data Documentation   222
6.5   IDIOM Dimensionality   223
6.6   Arms Export Reduction by Industry   225
6.7   National Income and Product Impacts for Four Scenarios of
       Arms Export Reduction   226
6.8   Selected Effects of Arms Export Reduction on National
       Industry, Occupation, and Primary Materials   228

6.9   Regional and State Employment Impacts of Four Scenarios of
      Arms Export Reduction   229
6.10 Base National Model Variables and Parameters   234
6.11 Regional Model Variables and Parameters   238

LIST OF CONTRIBUTORS

KENNETH J. ARROW, Joan Kenney Professor of Economics and Professor of Operations Research, Stanford University, Stanford, California

RICHARD S. BARR, Assistant Professor of Management Science, Southern Methodist University, Dallas, Texas

HAROLD BEEBOUT, Director, Policy Studies Division, Mathematica Policy Research, Inc., 2101 L Street, N.W., Washington, D.C.

ROBERT L. BENNETT, Associate Professor of Economics, University of Maryland—College Park, College Park, Maryland

BARBARA R. BERGMANN, Professor of Economics, University of Maryland College Park, College Park, Maryland

DAVID BETSON, Economist, Office of the Secretary, Office of Income Security Policy/Research, Office of the Assistant Secretary for Planning and Evaluation, U.S. Department of Health, Education and Welfare, Washington, D.C.

GERARD M. BRANNON, Professor of Economics, Georgetown University, Washington, D.C.

STEVEN B. CALDWELL, Assistant Professor of Sociology, Cornell University, Ithaca, New York

ANNE P. CARTER, Professor of Economics, Brandeis University, Waltham, Massachusetts

BENJAMIN CHINITZ, Vice President for Regional Research, Abt Associates; Professor of Economics, SUNY—Binghamton, Binghamton, New York

LEONARD DRABEK, Economist, Manpower Analysis Branch, Health Resources Administration, U.S. Department of Health, Education and Welfare, Washington, D.C.

STEPHEN P. DRESCH, Chairman, Institute for Demographic and Economic Studies, Inc., 155 Whitney Avenue, New Haven, Connecticut

GUNNAR ELIASSON, President, Industrial Institute for Economic and Social Research (IUI), Grevgatan 34, Stockholm, Sweden

DON FULLERTON, Assistant Professor of Economics and Public Affairs, Woodrow Wilson School of Public and International Affairs, Princeton University, Princeton, New Jersey

HARVEY GALPER, Associate Director, Office of Tax Analysis, U.S. Treasury Department, Washington, D.C.

IRWIN GARFINKEL, Professor, School of Social Work, University of Wisconsin—Madison; Director, Institute for Research on Poverty, University of Wisconsin—Madison, Madison, Wisconsin

AMIHAI GLAZER, Assistant Professor of Economics, University of California, Irvine, Irvine, California

EDWARD M. GRAMLICH, Professor of Economics and Public Policy, University of Michigan, Ann Arbor, Michigan

DAVID GREENBERG, Economist, SRI International, Menlo Park, California

MARTIN GREENBERGER, Professor of Mathematical Sciences, The Johns Hopkins University, Baltimore, Maryland

BRUCE HAMILTON, Associate Professor of Political Economy, The Johns Hopkins University, Baltimore, Maryland

ROBERT HARRIS, Executive Vice President, The Urban Institute, 2100 M Street, N.W., Washington, D.C.

ROBERT H. HAVEMAN, Professor of Economics, University of Wisconsin—Madison; Fellow, Institute for Research on Poverty, University of Wisconsin—Madison, Madison, Wisconsin

KEVIN HOLLENBECK, Senior Analyst, Urban Systems Research and Engineering, 1120 19th Street, N.W., Washington, D.C.

MARTIN HOLMER, Economist, Office of the Secretary, Office of Income Security Policy/Research, Office of the Assistant Secretary for Planning and Evaluation, U.S. Department of Health, Education, and Welfare, Washington, D.C.

JAMES R. HOSEK, Economist, Rand Corporation, 1700 Main Street, Santa Monica, California

MICHAEL D. INTRILIGATOR, Professor of Economics, UCLA; Research Associate, Human Resources Research Center, Los Angeles, California

RICHARD KASTEN, Economist, Office of the Secretary, Office of Income Security Policy/Research, Office of the Assistant Secretary for Planning and Evaluation, U.S. Department of Health, Education, and Welfare, Washington, D.C.

JONATHAN R. KESSELMAN, Associate Professor, Department of Economics, University of British Columbia, Vancouver, B.C., Canada

NICHOLAS M. KIEFER, Assistant Professor of Economics, University of Chicago, Chicago, Illinois

LARRY J. KIMBELL, Director of Economics Models, UCLA Business Forecasting Project; Associate Professor, Graduate School of Mangement, UCLA; Research Associate, Human Resources Research Center, Los Angeles, California

A. THOMAS KING, Economist, Office of Economic Research, Federal Home Loan Bank Board, Washington, D.C.

JILL A. KING, Senior Researcher, Mathematica Policy Research, Inc., 2101 L Street, N.W., Washington, D.C.

MYLES MAXFIELD, JR., Research Economist, Mathematica Policy Research, Inc., 2101 L Street, N.W., Washington, D.C.

JOSEPH J. MINARIK, Research Associate, The Brookings Institution, 1775 Massachusetts Avenue, N.W., Washington, D.C.

DONALD A. NICHOLS, Professor of Economics, University of Wisconsin—Madison, Madison, Wisconsin

BENJAMIN A. OKNER, Senior Staff Economist, Office of Tax Analysis, U.S. Treasury Department, Washington, D.C.

EDGAR O. OLSEN, Associate Professor, Department of Economics, University of Virginia—Charlottesville, Charlottesville, Virginia

GUY H. ORCUTT, Professor of Economics and member of the Institution for Social and Policy Studies, Yale University, New Haven, Connecticut

LARRY OZANNE, Senior Research Associate, The Urban Institute, 2100 M Street, N.W., Washington, D.C.

FREDRIC RAINES, Associate Professor of Economics, Washington University, St. Louis, Missouri

SAMUEL A. REA, JR., Associate Professor of Economics, University of Toronto, Toronto, Canada

RICHARD RUGGLES, Professor of Economics, Yale University, New Haven, Connecticut

LOUISE B. RUSSELL, Senior Fellow, The Brookings Institution, 1775 Massachusetts Avenue, N.W., Washington, D.C.

P. ROYAL SHIPP, Senior Specialist in Income Maintenance, Congressional Research Service, Library of Congress, Washington, D.C.

JOHN B. SHOVEN, Associate Professor of Economics, Stanford University, Stanford, California

TIMOTHY M. SMEEDING, Assistant Professor of Economics, University of Utah; Visiting Research Associate, Institute for Research on Poverty, University of Wisconsin—Madison, Madison, Wisconsin

ROBERT P. STRAUSS, Professor of Economics and Public Policy, School of Urban and Public Affairs, Carnegie-Mellon University, Pittsburgh, Pennsylvania

MICHAEL K. TAUSSIG, Professor of Economics, Rutgers College, New Brunswick, New Jersey

J. SCOTT TURNER, Associate Professor of Management Science, Oklahoma State University, Stillwater, Oklahoma

RAYMOND UHALDE, Labor Economist, Office of the Secretary, U.S. Department of Labor, Washington, D.C.

DANIEL A. UPDEGROVE, Project Manager, EDUCOM Financial Planning Model, P. O. Box 364, Princeton, New Jersey

JACQUES VAN DER GAAG, Research Associate, Institute for Research on Poverty, University of Wisconsin—Madison, Madison, Wisconsin

JEAN E. VANSKI, Research Associate I, The Urban Institute, 2100 M Street, N.W., Washington, D.C.

HAROLD W. WATTS, Professor of Economics, Center for Social Sciences, Columbia University, New York, New York

RICHARD F. WERTHEIMER II, Senior Research Associate, The Urban Institute, 2100 M Street, N.W., Washington, D.C.

JOHN WHALLEY, Professor of Economics, University of Western Ontario, London, Ontario, Canada

DONALD E. YETT, Director of the Human Resources Research Center, Los Angeles, California; Professor of Economics, University of Southern California, Los Angeles, California

PREFACE

During the last decade, an increasing number of federal and state agencies have employed policy simulation experiments on microdata files in analyzing current and proposed legislation. While the primary objective of much social legislation is the redistribution of income, the intent of other public policies may focus on resource allocation and be largely divorced from objectives related to sectoral or household income distribution. However, no matter what their objectives, most policies will result in both a reallocation of resources and a redistribution of income. Benefits will be received and costs will be borne differentially by various regions, sectors, occupations, or income classes. It is the task of the policy analyst to identify the gainers and losers and, to the extent possible, quantify the changes in economic well-being to each group.

Many models have been developed whose purpose is to estimate detailed sectoral and income distributional impacts of various public policies. The original and most well known of the models for the analysis of sectoral impacts are the input-output models developed by Wassily Leontief (1951). These models are already a generation old and have been complemented in recent years by other applied microeconomic models whose objectives include distributional analysis. Yet the literature on this new generation of models is scant, despite the fact that in some instances there is heavy reliance on them for policy purposes.[1] Among the set of such models, microeconomic simulation models represent a relatively small but rapidly growing component.

Microeconomic Simulation Models: A Definition and History

Microeconomic simulation models are designed to simulate the effects of proposed changes in economic policy variables—prices, taxes, subsidies, regulations—on data bases containing observations of disaggregated components of one or more ma-

[1] Two recent reviews of recent models and their applications are Greenberger et al. (1976) and U.S. Environmental Protection Agency (1974).

jor sectors of the economy. The units of analysis may be households, individuals, firms, or industries. There is a natural two-part structure to all of these models consisting of a data base and the rules applied to, or operations performed on, the data base. Typically, these rules or operations are economic behavioral models which have been estimated from cross-sectional or longitudinal data.

These models have emerged as an important analytical tool for two reasons. First, they reflect the basic tenet of microeconomics that a complex entity composed of many components can best be explained and predicted through an analysis of its constituent parts. Second, rational decision making in policy formation requires information about the benefits and costs of proposed policies and the gainers and losers experiencing these impacts. Microeconomic simulation provides policymakers with the capability of examining the entire distribution of effects, not just an aggregate or a mean. It is not surprising, then, that the major line of development of these models has been in the area of direct income redistributional policy—income maintenance programs and the tax system.

Clearly, the first generation of microeconomic simulation models is found in the work of Guy Orcutt and his associates in the late 1950s (Orcutt, 1957, 1960; Orcutt et al., 1961). Following the Orcutt work, a number of microeconomic simulation models were developed, largely in an effort to analyze the distributional effects of the U.S. income support system. Some of these were developed in conjunction with government commissions (e.g., the President's Income Maintenance Commission), others were constructed at universities and research organizations, and, with a lag, still others were developed in government agencies. Because of their cost and complexity, public financial support was crucial in all of the efforts. Models of the AFDC Program, Social Security benefits, the Family Assistance Plan of the Nixon administration, and the entire public transfer system were developed in the late 1960s and early 1970s. Paralleling these efforts were studies that relied heavily on microdata to examine the incidence of the tax system. Recent work in the area of tax-transfer policies has proceeded in two directions—bringing additional data and innovative modeling techniques to bear in more comprehensive examinations of the distributional effects of tax-transfer policy and examining behavioral responses to the various social programs.

The distributional consequences of other policies have been analyzed with microeconomic simulation models as well—for example, in the fields of energy, housing, and health care delivery. Another interesting application of the techniques has been in the study of intergenerational transfers of wealth. Moreover, microeconomic simulation has been performed on other economic units besides the household and its members.

A number of production simulation models have recently extended the input-output and process analysis framework developed in the 1950s and 1960s. Typically not as data-intensive as their linear technology precursors, these models allow for richer behavioral assumptions. The types of analyses that have been undertaken include studies of industrial concentration, price inflation, and production planning.

Among the more recent advances in the field of microeconomic simulation have been models which integrate the household and production sectors of the economy. This has been accomplished in a number of ways: linking a household microdata base to a production model, using a fixed-point algorithm to solve for equilibrium prices and wages, and parametrizing "synthetic" household and production data.

The Microeconomic Simulation Conference and the Structure of the Volumes

Heretofore there has been no systematic review of these modeling efforts and their actual and potential uses in policymaking. Moreover, while many of these micromodels are similar in structure and objectives, there has been little communication among researchers involved in their construction. As a result, there has been substantial overlap of effort among the builders of the models, insufficient exploration of complementarities among the models, and almost no discussion of priorities in extending and updating the models.

To contribute to the remedying of these problems, a conference, "Microeconomic Simulation Models for the Analysis of Public Policies," was held in March 1978, in Washington, D.C. This conference was jointly sponsored by the Institute for Research on Poverty, Mathematica Policy Research, Inc., and the National Science Foundation. The purpose of the conference was to further communication among model builders with a view toward facilitating the exchange of information on model structure and construction and encouraging cooperation. A further purpose was to disseminate information to policymakers and the academic community on the use of microeconomic simulation models in specific policy applications. Finally, through the comments of individuals who were not themselves involved in the construction and use of such models, the conference provided an opportunity to allow the strengths and weaknesses of the various models to be appraised, the reliability of their results scrutinized, and the possibilities for interchanges of components presented.

Thirteen models were discussed at the conference. In addition, Kenneth J. Arrow reviewed the papers presented at the conference and prepared an overview evaluating the potentials and pitfalls of microeconomic simulation. These volumes include papers and discussants' comments on each model, as well as Professor Arrow's review. The papers are ordered in the same fashion as they were presented at the conference. Each paper is followed by the critique of the two conference discussants. The first discussion comment is directed to the technical characteristics of the model; the second focuses on the policy analysis which was performed with the model. The opportunity was offered to attendees of the conference to submit for publication comments about aspects of any of the papers that were not discussed at the conference. The Barr and Turner comments on the Minarik paper resulted from this offer.

The author of each paper was requested to address a common set of issues in preparing his or her paper. First, each paper was to include a description of the model and its operation, including the underlying data bases. Second, the results of applying the model to a particular federal policy or proposed policy, including an analysis of sectoral and income distributional results, were to be presented in sufficient detail to convey the power of the model. Finally, we asked each author to describe his or her plans for future development of the model. This organization is present in most of the papers.

The conference was organized into four general, but not mutually exclusive, subject areas. The first three papers (Minarik, Beebout, and Orcutt et al.) present extended microdata models for first-round distributional analysis; the next four papers (Maxfield, Betson et al., J. A. King, and Yett et al.) present microdata models that incorporate behavioral responses to the policies being simulated; the next three papers (Bennett and Bergmann, Eliasson, and Fullerton et al.) present microdata models of the macroeconomy; while the final three papers (Haveman et al., Ozanne and Vanski, and Dresch and Updegrove) describe microdata models with regional and/or sectoral impacts.

Microeconomic Simulation Modeling: Problems and Prospects

The papers discussed at the conference and presented in these volumes exhibit a wide range of approaches to microeconomic simulation. Some involve primarily the development of techniques to estimate the impact of policy measures on microdata points in a static context. In some of the static models, behavioral responses to price and income changes caused by the policy are imputed to microdata observations (say, households). Others use time-specific microdata as the basis for simulating demographic changes and their interaction with policy variables through time. These are dynamic models. In the class of dynamic models, some employ data points that are real observations taken from longitudinal surveys of households or businesses, while others employ data points that are constructed entities with but few characteristics meant to conform to real households or businesses. A number of the models are national in scope; others focus on portions of the national economy (e.g., the business sector, urban areas, the health care sector, or specific regions). Still others seek to estimate disaggregated impacts in which regions, industries, occupations, and income classes are distinguished, in addition to national totals. These models involve a number of sequential behavioral responses as the economic effects of a policy are spread throughout the economy. Finally, some of the models rely on complex algorithms for their solutions, while others are "solved" simply by imposing the rules or schedules of a postulated public program on the characteristics of the microdata observations.

To say anything meaningful regarding the problems of and prospects for such a diverse set of models is difficult. However, to the extent that all of these models rely on and manipulate microdata, they do share a common research approach with particular merits and difficulties. As is clear from the papers in the two volumes, through microdata-based models, richer analyses than were previously possible— involving simulated impacts of actual and proposed public policies on detailed demographic and income groups, industries, regions, and occupations—can be undertaken. These impact estimates can reflect behavioral responses to a program, the effect of the program and its induced responses through time, and the linkages and interdependencies that are inherent in the economic system. And, because the models are based upon microdata, estimates can be made of the impact of a policy change on narrowly defined sectors of the economy (regions, industries, occupations) and specific demographic and economic groups.

The benefits of such analyses are important to policymakers. To the extent that program costs depend upon the response of individuals to the income and incentive effects of the program, more reliable cost estimates are obtained. Similarly, to the extent that the merit of a program depends on who is benefited and who is hurt, and the extent of gains and losses, such systematic and detailed sectoral analyses are important in the design of programs and policies. The process of designing an efficient program is, by definition, one of considering the effects of various program characteristics on conflicting objectives, and trading off gains and losses among them so as to achieve a structure that optimizes some social objective function. Only through simulations based on microdata can the economic effects of various program sizes and characteristics be discerned, and only by discerning such impacts can programs be structured to achieve desired goals at least cost.

These analytic gains do not come without cost, however. The construction, estimation, operation, and updating of these models require very large research, computer, and survey costs. Because of their complexity, size, and especially, their reliance on microdata, the operational cost of a number of these models is likely to exceed that of some of the major national macroeconometric models.

As the papers make clear, the complexity of microdata and the computer-intensive technology inherent in simulation analysis make the research process in this area both time-consuming and frustrating. The potential for calculation and programming errors is very large, and because of the cumulative and linked nature of such models, errors discovered at an early stage require the recalculation of estimates developed in later stages. Similarly, minor restructuring of earlier parts of models (the potential for which is enormous) requires recalculation and often reprogramming of later stages in the analysis.

The problem of appropriately modeling behavioral responses to program, price, or income incentives is a further difficulty of microdata simulation efforts. For example, if the simulation effort requires estimates of labor supply responses to price and income incentives, the range of elasticity estimates available for inclusion in the model is very large. Under these circumstances, the simulation results from any particular specification are suspect, and the use of sensitivity analyses establishing reasonable bounds around the estimates is called for. Because this problem is so pervasive—involving not only individual response functions to program structures (e.g., labor supply, consumption, and migration relationships), but also coefficients describing input-output relationships, regional trade relationships, marginal output/labor requirements, and labor demand/earned income relationships—the reliance on sensitivity analyses has serious drawbacks. Not only does the sheer number of simulation estimates become unmanageably large, but the range of upper- and lower-bound estimates of the final variables of interest expands significantly. While there are means of controlling this growth, the ultimate interpretation of results is problematic.

A fourth problem should be noted: Efforts to expand the complexity of such models (for example, to include dynamic relationships and intertemporal changes in family or enterprise structure) run the risk of introducing debilitating computational difficulties. While additional efforts to refine a model always have potential benefits, if such efforts are carried sufficiently far, a high risk of establishing an unmanageably complex structure is encountered. The efforts required to simplify the structure of such a model so as to make it operational may be substantial.

A final and probably most difficult problem concerns the reliability of the underlying microdata. Most of the models rely on survey data, the weaknesses of which—misreporting, missing data, inadequate sample design—are well known. These problems may undermine the reliability of more aggregate analyses at least as much as microdata studies, but the need for the latter to deal with each of the numerous observations multiplies the difficulty of achieving estimates at all. This problem of reliability and the associated difficulty in interpreting results is even more severe in the case of synthetic data than in the case of survey-based data. To the extent that the rules of the simulations are based upon behavioral models estimated from observed data, the model results will be based upon statistical inference. However, serious analysis of the statistical properties of microsimulation estimates have not been undertaken by any of the model builders. Furthermore, virtually all of the extant models involve some amount of *ad hoc* manipulation of the data in order to achieve results, hence precluding any notion of model validity. Verification of model results should be high on the agenda of future research.

These, then, form a list of both potentials and problems. They can serve as a checklist of issues that a reader might keep in mind as the models presented in these volumes are scrutinized and appraised. Clearly, the overall appraisal of any model, or of the microeconomic simulation research method itself, will depend on the weights that individuals place on these various considerations, and these we cannot hope to supply. This study will have served its purpose, however, if it lays an objective basis for such an appraisal.

ACKNOWLEDGMENTS

Besides the participants, whose involvement was deeply appreciated, it takes the cooperation of many individuals in order to organize and administer a conference such as the one at which the papers and comments in these volumes were presented. First and foremost, the financial support and encouragement of the sponsoring institutions are gratefully acknowledged. The individuals at those institutions most directly responsible for committing that support were Irwin Garfinkel, of the Institute for Research on Poverty, David Kershaw, of Mathematica Policy Research, and James Blackman and Daniel Newlon, of the National Science Foundation. Nancy Carlisle, of the National Academy of Sciences, very capably handled the locational arrangements of the conference. Gale Maynard and Gini Martens are owed a large debt of gratitude for all their time and effort in the administration of the conference and in the preparation stages of these volumes. The success of the conference was due, in large part, to their efforts. Gale was ably assisted by Judy Penland, Perry Frank, and Constance Zuckerman. The editing of the manuscripts was done with great care and expertise by Elizabeth Uhr. No author, we are sure, would fail to attest to the improvements in both clarity and felicity which her work brought to their papers. The task of organizing the editing process, including communicating with both editors and authors, fell to Jan Blakeslee. She handled the many stages between manuscript submission and publication with a fine professional touch. Finally, the authors would like to thank Andrea, Jon, Beth, Sally, Kate, Jessica, and Dianne, whose last names are known by those for whom it matters.

Robert H. Haveman
Kevin Hollenbeck

CONTENTS OF VOLUME 1

EXTENDED MICRODATA MODELS FOR FIRST-ROUND
DISTRIBUTIONAL ANALYSIS

1   The MERGE 1973 Data File
    Joseph J. Minarik

    Discussion
    Timothy M. Smeeding

    Discussion
    Harvey Galper

    Submitted Discussion
    Richard S. Barr and J. Scott Turner

2   Food Stamp Policy Modeling: An Application of MATH
    Harold Beebout

    Discussion
    Richard Ruggles

    Discussion
    P. Royal Shipp

3   Microanalytic Modeling and the Analysis of Public Transfer Policies
    *Guy H. Orcutt, Amihai Glazer, Robert Harris, and
    Richard Wertheimer II*

    Discussion
    Samuel A. Rea, Jr.

    Discussion
    Michael K. Taussig

MICRODATA MODELS WITH BEHAVIORAL RESPONSE

4   Aspects of a Negative Income Tax: Program Cost, Adequacy of
     Support, and Induced Labor Supply Reduction
     Myles Maxfield, Jr.

     Discussion
     Fredric Raines

     Discussion
     Irwin Garfinkel

5   A Microsimulation Model for Analyzing Alternative Welfare Reform
     Proposals: An Application to the Program for Better Jobs and Income
     David Betson, David Greenberg, and Richard Kasten

     Discussion
     Raymond Uhalde

     Discussion
     Edward M. Gramlich

6   The Comprehensive Human Resources Data System: A Model for
     Estimating the Distributional Impacts of Energy Policies
     Jill A. King

     Discussion
     Martin Greenberger

     Discussion
     Gerard M. Brannon

7   The HRRC Health Care Sector Simulation Model
     *Donald E. Yett, Leonard Drabek, Michael D. Intriligator,
     and Larry J. Kimbell*

     Discussion
     Jacques van der Gaag

     Discussion
     Louise B. Russell

REFERENCES
INDEX

MICRODATA MODELS OF THE MACROECONOMY

1

POLICY EXPLORATIONS WITH THE TRANSACTIONS MODEL OF THE U.S. ECONOMY

Robert L. Bennett
Barbara R. Bergmann

The Transactions Model has been designed as an instrument for the study of problems and policies heretofore studied with the aid of conventional macroeconomic models.* The microeconomic specification of the model makes possible the depiction of policies in a far more realistic fashion than is feasible in simultaneous equations models. It enables us also to study the effects of any policy on the distribution of income and assets at the same time we are studying its macroeconomic effects. The first part of this paper gives a somewhat cursory description of the model as it stands;[1] next the process of fitting the model to quarterly U.S. macrodata for the years 1973-1975 is explained and the goodness of fit is displayed. The results of a number of counterfactual runs of the model for the period 1973-1975 are then presented. In these latter runs, various government actions are represented as being different from what they historically were. In one set of runs varying monetary and fiscal policies are tried. In others the effects of various forms of wage subsidies are explored.

A SHORT DESCRIPTION OF THE TRANSACTIONS MODEL

The Transactions Model consists entirely of explicit descriptions of decision making and the consequent simulated actions of individual decision makers. The model's "action" on the macroeconomic level is built up exclusively from the record of the "action" on the microeconomic level by "adding up" the microeconomic results into the macroeconomic results numerically by computer.

*We acknowledge support from the Computer Science Center of the University of Maryland. Some of the materials incorporated in this work were developed with the financial support of the National Science Foundation Grant 77-14693.

[1] For a more complete description, see Bennett and Bergmann (1978).

3

The Transactions Model has the following characteristics:

1. The model has been designed primarily to elucidate phenomena and policy options in macroeconomics. Production, employment and unemployment, inflation, productivity, investment in capital goods, money markets, and portfolio management are among the subjects of interest.

2. Not only decisions, but also interactions among individual decision makers in the economy are explicitly represented. The interaction of individual decision makers takes the form of transactions between individual buyers and sellers in which goods, services, or claims are exchanged against money, at prices announced by individual actors. Thus, the monetary and "real" sides are integrated in the model's simulated economy precisely as they are in the actual economy.

3. Each time a transaction occurs, its effect on simulated macroeconomic variables—nominal GNP accounts, flow-of-funds accounts, and so on—is recorded. The price at which the transaction occurs is also recorded, so that it may be reflected in the simulated GNP deflator.

All of the usual macroeconomic variables are thus simulated by the model on a basis consistent with the portrayed action on the microeconomic level.

4. The decision makers represented in the model—firms producing different kinds of goods and services, financial firms, governments, the monetary authority, and workers who are also consumers and asset holders—are subject to constraints on their behavior deriving from technological requirements and the size of real and financial stockpiles. Constraints imposed by governmental policies (such as unemployment insurance requirements, interest rate maxima, and the like) are also observed. Each individual decision maker's "experience" and situation in the simulated economy are kept track of by means of numerous microeconomic variables whose values enter into the decision-making process and affect the constraints on behavior. Where the application of policy instruments to an individual depends on that individual's history (such as the dependence of unemployment insurance eligibility on employment history), this can be portrayed in a simple manner.

5. The model is cast in a form designed to be useful for purposes of discussions of economic policy in the United States. In all of its magnitudes, it is a "scale model" of the U.S. economy. Parameters have been set so that the simulated macroeconomic time series output of the model tracks the macroeconomic time series generated by the U.S. economy for 1973-1975. Each business firm represents an industrial sector in the U.S. economy. The model's labor force (which starts out at 800 persons and grows in the course of the simulation) matches that of the U.S. labor force in distribution by sex, marital status, and occupation.

The data used to set initial conditions and to fit the model's parameters include the national income accounts (both the income and product sides), the GNP deflators, the flow-of-funds data, unemployment rates, the *Current Population Reports* (for the distribution of labor force characteristics), Standard and Poor's, and others.[2] Seasonally adjusted data were used, as unadjusted data were not available for all magnitudes.

The Transactions Model is written in the form of a computer program and associated files of data on the U.S. economy. The program controls the creation of the initial microeconomic and macroeconomic conditions, it schedules and regulates the behavior of the decision makers, and it produces as output time series of simulated macroeconomic results.

The first step in a run of the model is the assignment to each individual decision maker of characteristics and attributes, some of which will remain fixed in the course of the run, and others of which will change as simulated economic activity progresses. For a firm, an example of a fixed attribute is the type of product produced and a vector of input-output coefficients; for a worker-consumer, fixed attributes are sex, marital status, and broad occupational group. Attributes of business firms that vary as the action proceeds include the current price of output, amount of inventory held, number of employees by type, quantity and characteristics of capital goods, and a complete accounting of assets and liabilities by type, including money. A worker-consumer's attributes that vary include financial assets and liabilities by type, car ownership, homeownership, employment status, average past expenditures. The initial conditions on the microeconomic level are set so as to conform to U.S. macroeconomic conditions at the beginning of the calendar quarter in which the run is to start.

A scale factor is used to bring the magnitudes generated by the miniature simulated economy up to the level of magnitudes generated by the U.S. economy, the ratio of the actual U.S. labor force to the simulated labor force in the period in which the simulation starts. The scale factor—88.1 million : 800 for the runs beginning 1973 I (first quarter)—does not change in the course of the simulation and is used for all magnitudes: numbers of persons, physical outputs, flows of funds, value of production, income.

After the creation of the initial conditions, a scheduling program takes over, which arranges for economic events to occur in a fixed sequence. The economic events include decision making and actions based on the decisions that have been taken. Most of the events involve two actors in an interaction whose results must be in accord with the wishes of both. An example of a set of events depicted in the model is the consumption decisions of a consumer, followed by interactions between that consumer and a firm during which the consumer makes purchases from the firm and money flows from the consumer's cash account to the firm's. Another example of a set of events is a decision by a firm to increase its liquidity, followed by an interaction between the firm and a bank, in which a loan might be granted, money created and credited to the firm's cash account, and a schedule of repayments of interest and principal set up.

---

[2]We are currently in the process of incorporating information on the distribution of interest-paying and dividend-paying assets from the IRS *Statistics of Income* into our initial conditions.

A full set of all the actions within the repertoire of the decision makers occurring in a prescribed sequence is called a "round." All of the usual kinds of activities that bear on the macroeconomic performance of the economy in the short and medium run are represented in a round: production and hiring, wage and price set-

Table 1.1
Summary of Sequence of Events in a Round of the Transactions Model

Event
1. Tentative production decisions by firms.
2. Hiring and weekly hours decision by firms.
3. Layoffs, resignations; search by firms and governments for workers, and by workers for jobs; hirings.
4. Wage rate setting by firms for each occupation.
5. Production, affecting firms' inventories.
6. Cost accounting by firms, computation of taxes owed.
7. Price setting by each firm for its product.
8. Inter-industry purchases by firms of flow inputs.
9. Payment of taxes by firms to governments.
10. Investment decisions and capital goods purchases by firms from those firms producing capital goods.
11. Decisions concerning housing stock by real estate firm.
12. Events which give rise to inputed items in GNP but no flow of funds.
13. Payment of wages by firms and governments.
14. Transfer payments to unemployed.
15. Receipt by individual workers of property income.
16. Payment of income and social security taxes by workers to government.
17. Payments by workers on mortgages and bank loans.
18. Home and car ownership decisions by workers.
19. Other consumption decisions; purchases of goods and services.
20. Portfolio management decisions and activities by consumers.
21. Government purchases of goods and services from firms.
22. Rest-of-the-world sales to and purchases from firms.
23. Government debt management decisions and actions.
24. Finance and liquidity decisions by nonfinancial firms; actions through bank and financial intermediary.
25. Financial intermediary adjustments of cash position.
26. Monetary authority decisions and actions on open market.
27. Bank reactions to reserve position: setting of loan policy; discounts with monetary authority; selling or buying open market securities.
28. Financial intermediary readjustments of cash position.
29. Setting of current consumer loan rate, business loan rate, mortgage and savings accounts interest rates by bank.
30. Current bill and bond rate set by financial intermediary.
31. Payment by government and firms of interest on existing obligations at original rate to financial intermediary.
32. Payment of interest to firms on their holdings of bonds and bills by financial intermediary.

ting, government procurement, the creation and sale of financial claims by business firms, the government, and worker-consumers, the payment to worker-consumers for their services as factors of production, the making of transfer payments, and sales of consumer and investment goods, as well as intermediate goods. These are listed in Table 1.1 in the order they occur in each round.

The Time Frame of the Model

A quarter of a year of calendar time in the U.S. economy is represented in the Transactions Model by twelve complete rounds of events, and a month by four. As the rounds proceed, macroeconomic magnitudes affected by the events are changed appropriately. National income accounts are continually built up in this way, and at the end of each cycle of twelve rounds the program arranges for the printing out of simulated quarterly national accounts, brought up to the scale of the U.S. economy by an unchanging multiplicative factor. Unemployment rates can be printed monthly.

In conventional macroeconomic models, the basic period of the analysis generally is taken to be identical with the shortest period for which all the data are available (the "data period"), and the system is solved anew for each data period. This use of the simultaneous equations formulation can be thought of as an adaptation to the fact that available data on economic activity are averaged out or aggregated over time periods which are so long that the actors must be seen as reacting more than once within a data period to actions of others which occur within the same period. Within a calendar quarter, for example, there is time for a fall in production to cause a reduction in consumption which will in turn react back on production. The simultaneous solution of a set of behavioral equations which specify such reactions purports to represent the stable situation after all of these actions and reactions have taken place and behavior has settled down into a pattern in which all actions are mutually consistent in the sense that they can remain at constant levels.[3]

In the Transaction Model, the fact that within a data period there can be multiple interactions among the actors is dealt with in a different way, which we believe to provide somewhat greater realism. We have done away with the identity of the data period and the basic period of analysis, and have disaggregated the data period into shorter periods, taking as the basic period of analysis a time interval so short that it is plausible to represent each actor as revising each type of decision only once during each basic period. We have chosen to represent each calendar quarter as being made up of 12 such basic periods; the basic period thus corresponds approximately to a week of real time. Within each basic period, a complete round of economic events is scheduled.

---

[3] If we were to try to think concretely (perhaps some might say, to the point of mistaken concreteness) of what kind of an actual economic system might be exactly represented by an empirical quarterly simultaneous equations model, it would have to be an economy where the law requires that a "tatonnement" take place before ordinary business hours on the first day of each quarter and further requires that activity proceed at the steady pace thus determined for all the rest of the days of the quarter.

Table 1.2
Information Continually Updated and Available Concerning Each Fictional Firm during a Run of the Transactions Model

Materials Requirements

AIO(KFIRM,IFIRM)
Physical units of the product of firm KFIRM required as input for the production of one unit of the product of firm IFIRM.

AIOCAP(KFIRM,IFIRM)
Units of output of KFIRM required to put in place a new "machine" for the use of IFIRM.

Capital Stock

OPUT(IFIRM,JVIN)
Maximum output producible on all of the machines of vintage JVIN in a week if workers are on a standard workweek.

OPUTS(IFIRM,JVIN)
Maximum output producible on all of the structures of vintage JVIN in a week if workers are on a standard workweek.

CAPCY(IFIRM)
Maximum currently available capacity for output in a standard workweek.

ONEW(IFIRM)
Output producible with one unit of new machine.

ONEWS(IFIRM)
Output producible with one unit of new structures.

STARTC(IFIRM)
Backlog of firm's orders to the construction industry.

STARTM(IFIRM)
Backlog of firm's orders for machines.

VIN(IFIRM)
Marginal vintage of machines currently used.

VINS(IFIRM)
Marginal structure vintage.

Labor Requirements and Usage

EMPFIX(IFIRM)
Number of employees on the "fixed" staff.

RLAB(IFIRM,JVIN)
Number of employees required to cooperate with all machines of vintage JVIN.

RLABS(IFIRM,JVIN)
Number of employees required to cooperate with all structures of vintage JVIN.

FLABOR(LCASTE,IFIRM)
RLABOR(LCASTE,IFIRM)
Proportion of employees of the fixed and variable staffs respectively who are required to be of occupation LCASTE.

HRS(IFIRM)
Ratio of weekly hours to standard workweek.

WAGEF(LCASTE,IFIRM)
Weekly wage paid by IFIRM to average worker in occupation LCASTE, adjusted for weekly hours.

PRTAX(IFIRM)
Current period's payroll tax liability.

DESEMP(IFIRM)
Desired employment of "variable" employees.

EMP(IFIRM)
Total current employment.

XLNEW(IFIRM)
Labor required to cooperate with one unit of new machines.

XLNEWS(IFIRM)
Labor required to cooperate with one unit of new structures.

Sales, Production, and Inventories

SALE(IFIRM)
Current weekly sale, in physical units.

AVSALE(IFIRM)
Moving average (with geometric weights) of weekly sales.

Table 1.2 (continued)

EXPORT(IFIRM)	Firm's share of total U.S. constant dollar exports.
GOVBUY(IFIRM)	Firm's share of constant dollar sales to the federal government.
GOVBYL(IFIRM)	Firm's share of constant dollar sales to state and local governments.
ORDERS(KFIRM, IFIRM)	IFIRM's order backlog of KFIRM's product.
DPROD(IFIRM)	Current desired weekly production.
XPROD(IFIRM)	Actual weekly production.
XINV(JFIRM,IFIRM)	Quantity of output of product of JFIRM held as inventory by IFIRM.
PINV (JFIRM,IFIRM)	Inventory of JFIRM's product held at end of last period by IFIRM.
INVEN(IFIRM)	= 1 if IFIRM's product is held as inventory; 0 otherwise.
SHPROD(IFIRM)	Additional quantity firm desired to produce, but could not because of capacity, labor or input shortage.
SHORT(IFIRM)	Quantity of product demanded but not sold because of inventory deficiency.
CAPSHT(IFIRM)	Output which was not produced because of capacity shortage.

Other Cost, Price, and Profit Information

CAPCO(IFIRM)	Depreciation allowance, weekly.
TAXIND(IFIRM)	Rate of indirect taxes on value of firm's output.
CORP(IFIRM)	Proportion of firm's computed profit subject to corporate income tax.
XINTER(IFIRM)	Interest payments weekly on firm's debt.
ACOST(IFIRM)	Average cost of units of output currently produced.
XMCOST(IFIRM)	Marginal cost at current level of output.
P(IFIRM)	Current price of firm's output.
PLAST(IFIRM)	Price of firm's output in last period.
PI(IFIRM)	Acquisition price of the average unit of IFIRM's current inventory.
PO(IFIRM)	Average price of unfilled orders for IFIRM's product.
PROFIT(IFIRM)	Profits on current week's output.
PMARG(IFIRM)	Customary profit margin over average cost.

Financial Assets

CASH(IFIRM)	Size of firm's demand deposits.
BBONDS(IFIRM), BILLS(IFIRM)	Maturity value of open market securities held.

Financial Liabilities

BLOANS(IFIRM,IMAT)	Bank loans maturing in period IMAT.
BONDS(IFIRM,IMAT)	Maturity value of bonds outstanding maturing in period IMAT.
BONSEL(IFIRM)	Desired weekly sale of the firm's bonds.

The construction of an entirely recursive model (recursive with respect to the basic period of analysis rather than the data period) does more than advance somewhat the cause of realism. It also saves us from the surely tedious and perhaps infeasible chore of simultaneously solving all the behavioral equations. Put another way, the elimination of simultaneity (in the sense of multiple intra-period reactions) frees us to postulate realistic behavioral rules for the actors (if we know any) and realistically described government policies without having to worry that the mathematics of the solution process will be too difficult.

The Firms

Private production in the simulated economy has been divided into twelve industries[4] and one firm assigned to each industry. Table 1.2 gives a list of the items of information kept track of during a run, for each firm.

A physical unit of output of each industry is defined as the amount of that product which could have been bought in the starting period of the simulation for one dollar. Thus, the price of a physical unit produced by a particular industry starts out at $1.00 but changes as the simulation proceeds in accordance with simulated developments in that particular industry. Prices in the model are analogous to wholesale prices in the U.S. economy, with a trade margin tacked on.

Physical units of capital goods, called "machines," are also defined so as to sell for $1.00 in the starting period. A machine is specialized to the industry in which it is used, and for each using industry is defined as an appropriately weighted combination of physical quantities of the outputs of eight of the twelve industries. The physical quantities of the goods which make up a machine used by a particular industry are assumed not to change through time, although the cost does, as prices of the output of the eight industries change. Each machine is assumed to be "born" with a particular labor requirement and a particular rated output associated with it. As the machine ages these characteristics do not change until the machine goes out of service, which occurs at the end of a fixed period.

A firm's capital goods are differentiated by quarterly acquisition date; the more recently produced physical units of capital goods are assumed to have better output-labor ratios than the older units, with a higher-rated output per machine and a lower amount of labor required for a machine to produce its rated output. The rates of change of the output capabilities and labor input requirements for physical units of newly produced capital goods are among the basic parameters of the model, since they are an important component of productivity change. Firms order new capital goods each round, and these are delivered over the subsequent 30 rounds.

Purchases by one firm of the outputs of others for noncapital inputs to cur-

---

[4]The industries are (1) agriculture, forestry, and fisheries; (2) mining; (3) contract construction; (4) automobile manufacturing; (5) other durable manufacturing; (6) nondurable manufacturing; (7) transportation, communication, electric, gas and sanitary services; (8) wholesale and retail trade; (9) other services (including hospitals, private schools, and other nonprofit institutions); (10) real estate; (11) banks and savings institutions; and (12) other finance and insurance institutions.

rent production (so-called flow inputs) are governed by the 1967 Input-Output Table, and are taken to be unchanging over the time period of the simulation and unaffected by capital goods purchases.

A firm's variable costs include payroll costs (which depend on wage levels and staffing patterns for the firm's machines), materials inputs purchased from other firms, and payroll and sales taxes. Its fixed costs include depreciation, payroll for managerial and clerical workers, and interest on its debt.

The firm's short-run average cost curves are influenced by the presence of substantial fixed costs and rising marginal cost. Larger outputs cause the firm to bring into production successively older vintages of capital goods with smaller output/labor ratios. A firm's simulated cost curve shifts whenever the prices of labor and flow inputs change; it also shifts downward when investment results in the acquisition of new capital goods, which are always more cost-saving than the average of the old capital stock.

Worker-Consumer Asset Holders

As a run of the model starts, the labor force consists of 800 persons, divided into four occupational groups. As the run proceeds, people enter and leave the labor force.

Members of the labor force of the simulated economy are assigned to one of four broad occupational groups whose relative sizes and sex composition are derived from U.S. data: (1) professional, technical, managerial, and administrative workers, (2) clerical and sales workers, (3) crafts workers and operatives, and (4) service workers and laborers. In the present version, an individual cannot change occupational group. When new individuals enter the labor force they are assigned to an occupational group and have no assets. Persons not in the U.S. labor force who are in families that include labor force members are not directly represented in the model; consumer expenditures are made and assets held by labor force members on their behalf. Families containing no members of the labor force are represented collectively and receive transfer payments, which they use exclusively for purchasing consumption goods.

Table 1.3 gives the items of information for each individual in the model. Characteristics of individuals that have great influence on their economic functioning but are not now explicitly represented in the model include age and educational attainment. We identify two-earner families, which assemble assets and liabilities and pay taxes as a unit. Those families that are represented as owning their own homes make appropriate mortgage and tax payments. The value of the housing services of owned homes is included in the simulated GNP accounts, but there is no corresponding flow of funds.

The Financial Firms

Two of the model's firms, the "bank" and the "financial intermediary," have the special function of providing financial services to the other actors—the worker-consumer, the other business firms, and the governments. At the end of each round

Table 1.3
*Information Continually Updated and Available Concerning Each Fictional Person during a
Run of the Transactions Model*

Unchanging Personal Characteristics	
ISEX	Sex
ISPOUS	Identity of spouse (= 0 if unmarried, = −1 if married, but spouse not in labor force, = "address" of spouse if latter is in labor force).
ICASTE	Occupation (1-4).
IDIS	Skill level within occupation.
ISTIG	= 1 if at a disadvantage in being hired when unemployed; = 0 otherwise.
OWNCAR	= 1 if person has possibility of car ownership, 0 otherwise.
Labor Force Status	
LF	= 1 if in labor force, = 0 otherwise.
IEMPST	= identity of employer if person is employed, = 0 otherwise.
IUDAT	Date of last accession or separation.
IELIGW	Unemployment insurance eligibility, in weeks.
UI	= 1 if currently receiving unemployment insurance, = 0 otherwise.
Financial Status[a]	
HCASH	Money held in checking account.
SAVACC	Value of savings account deposits.
HBONDS	Maturity value of bonds held.
AMORT	Weekly payment due on consumer loans.
ISTART	Starting date of current consumer loan arrangements.
AMORTG	Weekly payment due on home mortgage.
INMORT	Starting date of mortgage.
Others[a]	
IDGAGE	Date of last new car purchase.
EXP	Moving average of consumer expenditures (geometric weights).

[a]In the case of labor force participants who are married to each other, the variables representing their financial status are consolidated into one.

they set the interest rates that will apply to newly issued debt in the subsequent round.

The bank gives bank loans on request to all of the nongovernmental actors, up to a limit on outstanding stock of loans for each actor. All of the cash held by the model's actors is a liability of the bank (as are all the savings deposits), and cash is created by payments from the bank to other actors, and destroyed by the reverse. The bank must observe reserve requirements, and it changes interest rates on new bank loans in accordance with its reserve position. Among its assets, the bank holds mortgages (which arise when worker-consumers buy houses), government bills and bonds (which arise when a government runs a deficit or rolls over existing debt), and loan instruments (which arise when other actors take out bank loans).

The financial intermediary makes a market in "open market securities" by buying all it is offered and making all requested sales. It announces higher interest rates on newly issued securities when supply of an instrument exceeds demand enough so that the size of its holdings of that instrument exceeds that which it wishes to hold, and lowers interest rates in the opposite case.

The Government Sectors

Three actors in the model represent the government sectors: a federal government, a state/local government, and a monetary authority.

The model's federal government collects personal income taxes each round from the worker-consumers by setting rules for exempted income and applying a (linear) schedule of marginal rates to nonexempted income. It also collects excise, corporate profit, and payroll taxes. It employs some of the labor force, makes purchases from the firms, and makes unemployment insurance payments and other transfer payments. When it runs a deficit it issues new bonds and bills which are sold for cash to the financial intermediary, through which they are sold to the other actors. Bills and bonds coming due are paid off or rolled over. The operation of the consolidated state/local government is similar to that of the federal, with some differences in function and on an appropriately different scale.

The monetary authority conducts open market operations by transactions with the financial intermediary. It also sets a reserve ratio and a maximum interest rate for savings accounts. The monetary authority also influences the amount of the bank's discounting by setting a discount rate, and it controls a parameter which influences the proportion of reserve deficiencies the bank covers by discounting.

Decision Making in the Transactions Model

The delineation of decision making in the present version of our model derives in an eclectic manner from the economic and business literature, and we lay claim to very little originality in this respect. At this point, it is worth emphasizing that any piece of decision-making machinery currently in the model can easily be entirely replaced by another piece of machinery which makes the decision in question in a qualitatively different way. The ease of doing this is derived from the recursive structure of the model, which eliminates simultaneous solution processes.

Consumers (after the payment of taxes and installments due on debt) decide on the allocation of the remainder of their income as between purchases of goods and services and purchases of financial assets. They are portrayed as desiring to save a fraction of their "discretionary income," and desiring not to make sudden large changes in their consumption of goods and services:

$$EXPD = \max \begin{cases} \min \begin{cases} SUBSIS \\ EXP \end{cases} \\ A(63) * EXP + (1 - A(63)) * [(YDIS - SUBSIS) * (1 - SRATE) + SUBSIS] \end{cases} \tag{1}$$

where *EXPD* is desired expenditure, *EXP* is a moving average of past expenditures, *YDIS* is wage and property income remaining after tax and debt payments, *SRATE* is the proportion of equilibrium discretionary income the consumer would like to use to buy financial assets, and *SUBSIS* is the cost of a market basket of goods constituting a "subsistence" requirement; computed as

$$SUBSIS = \sum_{IFIRM = 1}^{15} A(IFIRM + 100) * P(IFIRM) \tag{2}$$

where *P(IFIRM)* is the current price changed by *IFIRM* for its product. The *A(I)* are fitted parameters.

In allocating their purchases, consumers in the model follow a Stone-Geary linear expenditure system, and purchase from *IFIRM* a physical quantity:

$$BUY = A(IFIRM + 100) + A(FIRM + 120) * \max \begin{cases} (EXPD - SUBSIS)/P(IFIRM) \\ 0 \end{cases} \tag{3}$$

Although all consumers are assumed to have the same tastes, they spend differing amounts because of their differing assets, differing incomes, and differing expenditure histories.

In their portfolio management, consumers follow the scheme indicated in Figure 1.1. After a certain (low) level of assets has been reached, cash holdings at the end of the round are subject to an upper limit that depends on customary expenditure levels and the interest rate on savings accounts. There is a limit on savings accounts which is governed similarly, and all assets above these limits are invested in open market securities. The size of the portfolio each consumer has to manage depends, of course, on the sum of his previous savings decisions. The purchase of cars and homes is handled explicitly, as is the debt creation and repayment associated with such purchases.

Business firms set prices at the beginning of each round and sell to all customers at that price (see Figure 1.2). One of their goals is to maintain historic profit margins, so that if

$$\frac{P(IFIRM) - ACOST(IFIRM)}{ACOST(IFIRM)} < PMARG(IFIRM) = A(88) * \frac{PROFIT(IFIRM)}{SALE(IFIRM)} * P(IFIRM)$$

$$+ [1 - A(88)] * PMARG(IFIRM)_o \tag{4}$$

where *PMARG* is the average profit margin the firm has experienced, then the firm raises its price by a fixed percentage,

$$P(IFIRM) = P(IFIRM)_o * [1 + A(90)]. \tag{5}$$

The firms set output for each round to allow inventory to approach a desired

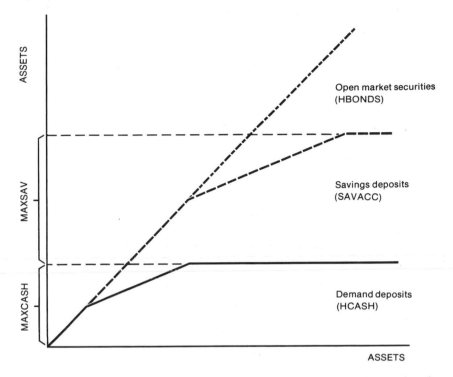

Figure 1.1. *Scheme of portfolio allocation for households. MAXCASH is a function of weekly outlays and interest rates on savings accounts. MAXSAVE is a function of weekly outlays and interest rates on savings accounts and open market securities.*

ratio to recent sales. They set wage increases based on changes in profits and the cost of living, and on unemployment rates:

$$
\begin{aligned}
WAGE(IFIRM,LCASTE) = {} & WAGE(IFIRM,LCASTE)_o \\
& * [1 + A(178) * CPICH \\
& + A(180) * \max \begin{cases} PROFIT(IFIRM) - PROMAX(IFIRM) \\ 0 \end{cases} \\
& + A(179) * URATEC(LCASTE) + A(48) * URATE],
\end{aligned} \tag{6}
$$

where *CPICH* is the change in the endogenously derived consumer price index, *PROMAX(IFIRM)* is maximum profits previously recorded, and *URATE* and *URATEC* are average and occupational unemployment rates respectively.

For the blue-collar occupations, wages are adjusted to reflect the workweek:

$$
\begin{aligned}
WAGE(IFIRM, JCASTE) = {} & WAGE(IFIRM,JCASTE)_o * \left\{ 1 + A(139) * [HRS(IFIRM)_o - 1] \right\}, \\
& JCASTE = 3, 4.
\end{aligned} \tag{7}
$$

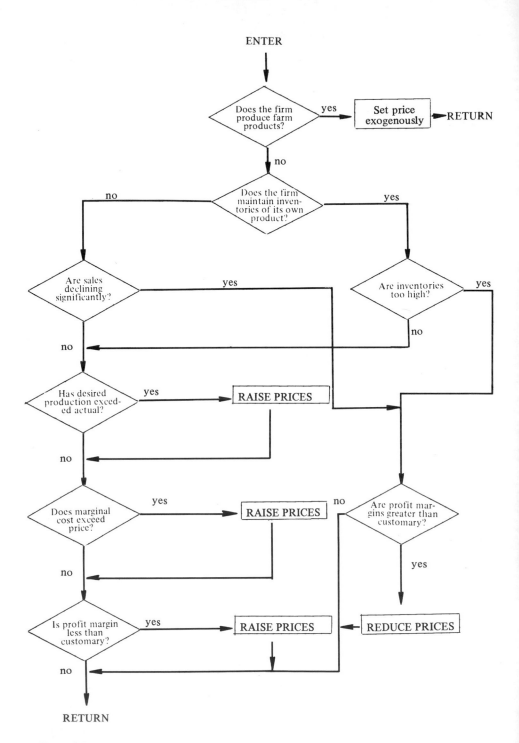

ENTER

Does the firm produce farm products? — yes → Set price exogenously → RETURN

no

Does the firm maintain inventories of its own product?

no / yes

Are sales declining significantly? — yes

Are inventories too high? — yes / no

no

Has desired production exceeded actual? — yes → RAISE PRICES

no

Does marginal cost exceed price? — yes → RAISE PRICES

Are profit margins greater than customary? — no / yes

no

Is profit margin less than customary? — yes → RAISE PRICES ← REDUCE PRICES

no

RETURN

Figure 1.2. *Flow chart illustrating the sequence of decision making concerning prices.*

Firms set desired employment by a lagged adjustment to production, making adjustments in weekly hours to achieve man-hour targets for the current round. Business firms' portfolio management and borrowing activities depend on their cash inflow from sales, cash outflow for wages, purchases of inputs and capital goods, and dividend payments. Like consumers, they are pictured as being sensitive to relative rates of return.

In making decisions about investment in newly produced capital goods, firms forecast future sales and compare the labor costs of operation of their older equipment (*LCO*) with the labor costs (*LCN*), interest cost (*RCOST*), and depreciation (*DEP*) chargeable on newly available equipment.

It will be advantageous to shift the production of output currently produced or prospectively to be produced on currently owned machines of *JVIN* to newly purchased machines if

$$LCO > \frac{OPUT(IFIRM,JVIN)}{ONEW(IFIRM)} \ * \ (LCN + DEP + RCOST) \ * \ A(IFIRM + 30). \qquad (8)$$

Thus, investment depends on the size and productivity of the stock of equipment on hand, on current and expected production (which determines the identity of the oldest machine used in the absence of investment), interest rates, prices of capital goods, speed of improvement in the characteristics of new machines, and current wage levels.

Expectations of the future are shown as entering into those decisions from which considerable damage is possible if the future is very different from the present, such as decisions to invest (or not to invest) in long-lived financial and real assets which may prove costly, according to how economic conditions materialize after the decision is made. In such cases, forecasts of future conditions become an ingredient in decision making. The actors in the present version of the model are represented as using very simple forecasting techniques. Firms considering capital outlays make forecasts of demand for their output at current prices using the rate of growth they have experienced in the recent past, if it has been positive. The expected future rate of inflation enters into portfolio management in terms of willingness to borrow or lend long.

"Markets" in the Transactions Model

Market participation by the actors in the Transactions Model are summarized in Table 1.4, where each horizontal line represents participation of each type of actor as buyer and/or seller in each of the markets for a good or financial claim. Prices in each of these markets are set once in a round, and all transactions for an entire round proceed at that price. Inventories serve as buffer stocks, allowing for differences in supply and demand in the short run.

For goods and services produced by nonfinancial firms, prices are normally set by producers on a cost-plus basis, and firms then sell all demanded at that price. A shift upward in a firm's average cost curve may be followed by a price adjustment. This in turn leads to a reduction in quantity demanded, depending on the

Table 1.4
Market Participation in Transactions Model, by Sector

Sector	Input Markets		Final Demand Markets				Financial Markets										
							Long-Term Claims					Short-Term Claims					
	Labor Services	Inter-Firm Purchases	Consumer Goods	Fixed Capital	Net Exports	Govt. Purchases	Corporate Bonds	Fed. Govt. Bonds	State & Local Bonds	Mortgages	Equities	Treasury Bills	Bank Loans	Money	Time & Svgs. Deposits	Discounts & Advances	Bank Reserves
Households																	
Labor force households	S		D				D	D	D		D	D	D	D	D		
Other households			D			S		D	D	S	D	D	D	D	D		
Nonfinancial Businesses																	
Agriculture, forestry & fisheries	D	DS	S	D	DS	S	DS	D	D		S	D	D	D			
Mining	D	DS	S	D	DS	S	DS	D	D		S	D	D	D			
Contract construction	D	DS	S	DS	DS	S	DS	D	D		S	D	D	D			
Automobile manufacturing	D	DS	S	DS	DS	S	DS	D	D		S	D	D	D			
Other durable manufacturing	D	DS	S	DS	DS	S	DS	D	D		S	D	D	D			
Nondurable manufacturing	D	DS	S	DS	DS	S	DS	D	D		S	D	D	D			

Transportation, communication, electric, gas and sanitary services	D	DS	S	DS	DS	S	DS	D	D	S	D	D	D
Wholesale and retail trade	D	DS	S	DS	DS	S	DS	D	D	S	D	D	D
Other services	D	DS	S	D	DS	S	DS	D	D	S	D	D	D
Real estate	D	DS	S	D	DS	S	DS	D	D	S	D	D	D
Financial Businesses													
Banks & savings institutions	D	DS	S	D	DS	S	DS	D	D	S	D	S	S
Other finance & insurance	D	DS	S	DS	DS	S	DS	D	D	S	D	D	D
Governments													
Federal (including government enterprises)	D	DS		DS	DS	DS	D	S	D	S			D
State & Local (including government enterprises)	D	DS	S	DS	DS	DS	D	D	S	D		D	D
Rest-of-world	DS	DS	S	DS	DS	S	DS	D	D	DS	DS	D	D
Federal Reserve			S				DS	D	D				S	S

Note: S and D indicate participation on the supply and demand side, respectively. For financial claims, those on the demand side may sell already existing claims in their possession, but only those on the supply side may create new ones.

Table 1.5
Cash Flows Between Sectors Occurring in the Transactions Model, by the Event Generating Them

from ⟍ to	Nonfinancial Business	Households	Government	Financial Intermediaries	Banks & Savings Institutions	Monetary Authority	Rest-of-World
Nonfinancial businesses	Investment goods 10 purchases	Consumer goods & svcs. Consumer debt I&A[a]	Govt. goods & svcs.	Investment goods 10 purchases Home purchases[b] Home repairs[b] Govt. sec. I&A[a,b] Bus. bond issues[b]	Investment goods 10 purchases Bank loans		Exports
Households	Wage payments New consumer loans		Wage payments Transfer payments	Wage payments New consumer loans Home mortg. issues[b] Dividends[b] Govt. sec. I&A[a,b] Bond I&A[a,b]	Wage payments New consumer loans		
Governments (including government enterprises)	10 purchases Sales taxes Profit taxes Soc. ins. taxes	Consumer goods & svcs. Income taxes Soc. ins. taxes	10 purchases Fed grants-in-aid to S/L govt.	10 purchases Sales taxes Profit taxes Soc. ins. taxes Home taxes[b] Home mortg. I&A[a,b] Govt. sec. I&A[a,b]	10 purchases Sales taxes Profit taxes Soc. ins. taxes		Exports

Financial intermediaries	10 purchases Dividends[b] Bond I&A[a,b] Govt. sec. purch.[b] Bus. bond purch.[b]	Consumer svcs. Cons. debt I&A[a] Home purchases[b] Home repairs, taxes[b] Home mortg. I&A[a,b] Bond purchases[b]	Govt. goods & svcs. Govt. sec. I&A[a,b] Home mortg. purch.[b] Govt. sec. purch.[b]	10 purchases	10 purchases Dividends[b] Bank loans Home mortg. purch.[b] Govt. sec. purch.[b] Bus. bond purch.[b]	Govt. sec. purch.[b]	Exports Govt. sec. purch.[b] Bus. sec. purch.[b] Bond I&A[a]
Banks & savings institutions	10 purchases Bank loan I&A[a]	Consumer goods & svcs. Cons. debt I&A[a] Deposits to svg. accts.	Govt. goods & svcs.	10 purchases Bank loan I&A[a] Home mortg. I&A[a,b] Govt. sec. I&A[a,b] Bus. bond I&A[a]	10 purchases	Discounts	Exports Bank loan I&A[a]
Monetary authority				Govt. bond I&A[a,b]	Discounts I&A[a]		Foreign exch. sales
Rest-of-world	10 purchases	Consumer goods & svcs.	10 purchases Govt. transfers Govt. purchases	10 purchases Govt. sec. I&A[a,b] Bus. sec. I&A[a,b] Bond issues[b]	10 purchases Bank loans	Foreign exch. purch.	

[a] I&A stands for "interest and amortization payments."

[b] Cash payments which accrue to financial intermediaries in their capacity as agent for the account of others, or are made by them in that capacity.

21

price elasticity for the product, and on what changes in other prices have been occurring. Changes in costs in the simulated economy also affect the demand for goods through their effects on incomes.

Wage changes are made by firms, with no bargaining by workers. The demand for labor in the present version of the model is only in the medium run affected by wages. In the very shortest run, the demand for labor is based on the labor necessary to produce desired output using the existing stock of capital equipment, with desired output being based on sales and inventory levels. However, higher labor costs affect prices, which affect total demand and the distribution of demand among products. Higher wages encourage the purchase of larger quantities of the new, more labor-saving capital equipment which, when it is put in place, has the effect of reducing the amount of labor required to meet a given production target.

As noted above, the markets for financial claims are run along lines perhaps more congenial to neoclassical theory, with the financial intermediary making the market. Each interest-bearing financial claim represented in the model has as an attribute the original interest rate it promised to pay. Thus, changes in interest rates for newly issued securities announced by the financial intermediary affect the prices at which older securities are traded.

Transactions and the Flow of Funds

Every sale engaged in by individual actors in the simulated economy involves the passing of commodities or claims from one decision maker to another and the passing of demand deposits in the opposite direction. Each transaction is accomplished by a subroutine named TRANS, which is called into action whenever any decision maker wants to buy anything from any other decision maker. TRANS is the principal means by which the interactions of decision makers are depicted, and it is also the principal means by which "action" on the microlevel is made to contribute to the GNP and the flow-of-funds accounting.

TRANS is used whenever money changes hands—for the purchase of commodities, labor, financial assets, as well as for the payment of taxes, and the making of government transfer payments. It is the consistent use of this "naturalistic" mechanism that makes possible the automatic integration of real and nominal GNP accounts and the flow-of-funds accounts. TRANS also ensures that all stocks (of money, financial claims, or of goods) are built up or drawn down in accordance with the flows that the actors decide shall occur. Table 1.5 contains a list of the events in the course of the simulation that generate cash flows between one type of actor and another.

FITTING THE MODEL TO DATA FOR 1973-1975

The parameters of the model were set by a process which searched for that set of values which minimized the square root of the sum of squared percentage errors (hereafter the standard percentage error or SPE) in simulating certain selected macroeconomic series during the 1973-1975 period. This period witnessed very large fluctuations in most of the macroeconomic variables that are of interest, and turning points for some of them, and achieving a good fit in the relevant variables during such a period is a more stringent test than a good fit during a period in which there were either small or monotonic changes. Most of the data which we used for fitting were available only quarterly: we cumulated the simulated flow variables over the quarters and for simulated stock variables we used the end-of-period figures. Several variables were available monthly, and for some of these, particularly interest rates, we fitted to the monthly series.

In searching for sets of parameter values, a process somewhat analogous to single equation fitting techniques was used to get a first approximation. For each parameter, a macrodata series was identified as the one on which that parameter would have its first-order effect, and all parameters which affected a particular macro series were fitted at the same time, using exogenous values for other magnitudes. For example, parameter $A(63)$ in Equation (1) above has its first-order effect on consumption. In running the model to search for values for this parameter which give low errors in simulating consumption, we constrained investment and wage setting to follow the path they actually took in the U.S. economy over the period, replacing equations (6-8) above with computer routines which achieved that. After all parameters had been given values by the "single equation" technique, the whole model was rerun to ensure that the interaction of the parts gave a good overall fit. At this stage, any parameter value which created serious errors in simulated values of variables on which it had a second-order effect was adjusted.

In all runs of the model, including the ones reported in this paper, the values used are the simulated ones rather than the correct ones; after setting up the initial conditions, we make no mid-course corrections. Thus, the errors of the series which are reported below include all cumulative effect of errors.

Table 1.6 shows the simulated and actual values for gross national product, its major components, and the GNP deflator. The mean values of the simulated and actual GNP series are quite close, and the SPE is 1.5%. The series for government expenditures in Table 1.6 includes net exports. Both government expenditures and net exports are set exogenously in the real values, and the errors noted in Table 1.6 result largely from errors in the price series. For personal consumption expenditures the mean value of the simulated series is a little low, while the SPE is a respectable 1.6%.

Fixed investment is simulated quite closely to the actual series, with the mean values almost identical and a SPE of 2%. The two components of fixed investment—investment in plant and equipment and investment in residences—had somewhat greater variance. The simulated mean for residential investment was 5% below the actual mean, and the SPE was 8.4%. Investment in plant and equipment, on the other hand, had an error of the mean of only 1.5% and a SPE of 2.6%.

Most of the variance in GNP is explained by errors in tracking changes in inventories. The pattern of changes in inventory is reasonably accurate—the turning

Table 1.6
Gross National Product (billions of dollars at annual rate)

Year	Quarter	GNP		Personal Consumption Expenditures		Change in Inventory		Fixed Investment		Government Expenditures & Net Exports		GNP Deflator	
		Simulated	Actual	Simulated	Actual	Simulated	Actual	Simulated	Actual	Simulated	Actual	Simulated	Actual
1973	I	1280	1265	800	787	12	12	202	199	267	267	104	103
1973	II	1312	1288	814	801	22	15	206	203	271	269	106	105
1973	III	1332	1317	824	818	20	15	206	205	282	279	109	107
1973	IV	1344	1355	834	833	10	29	205	202	295	290	111	109
1974	I	1375	1373	852	853	8	13	205	204	309	303	113	112
1974	II	1396	1399	876	879	11	13	204	206	306	302	116	115
1974	III	1427	1432	895	907	18	7	202	206	313	311	118	118
1974	IV	1428	1449	894	911	12	10	199	202	324	327	120	122
1975	I	1460	1446	931	933	−6	−22	197	195	338	341	123	125
1975	II	1531	1482	969	960	5	−30	195	194	361	358	125	126
1975	III	1560	1549	975	987	17	−2	196	199	372	365	127	128
1975	IV	1550	1588	972	1012	9	−4	194	206	376	375	129	130
Mean		1416	1412	886	890	11	5	201	202	318	316	117	117
SPE		.0151		.0156		2.9741		.0207		.0118		.0120	

Note: This table presents the simulated values of each variable in a column to the left of the actual values. Following the quarter values in a column is the mean value for the 1973-1975 period. The standard percentage error is given last.

Table 1.7
Unemployment Rates (percentage)

Year	Quarter	Civilian		Professional		Clerical		Crafts		Laborer		Hours	
		Simulated	Actual	Simulated	Actual	Simulated	Actual	Simulated	Actual	Simulated	Actual	Simulated	Actual
1973	I	4.9	4.9	2.5	2.5	4.6	4.6	5.4	5.5	6.6	6.5	1.0	1.0
1973	II	4.9	4.9	2.5	2.6	4.6	4.6	5.4	5.4	6.6	6.4	1.0	1.0
1973	III	4.8	4.8	2.5	2.4	4.8	4.6	5.2	5.5	6.3	6.3	1.0	1.0
1973	IV	5.2	4.8	2.5	2.5	4.7	4.4	6.2	5.5	y.7	6.4	1.0	1.0
1974	I	5.7	5.0	2.5	2.5	5.1	4.7	7.5	5.9	6.9	6.5	1.0	1.0
1974	II	5.8	5.1	2.5	2.5	5.0	4.6	7.8	5.9	7.3	6.8	1.0	1.0
1974	III	5.7	5.6	2.7	2.7	5.9	5.1	5.6	6.7	8.3	7.3	1.0	1.0
1974	IV	6.3	6.7	3.0	3.2	6.2	5.7	6.8	8.8	8.7	8.1	1.0	1.0
1975	I	7.5	8.1	3.4	3.8	6.6	6.7	9.7	11.2	9.2	9.6	1.0	1.0
1975	II	7.9	8.7	3.4	3.9	7.0	7.1	10.4	12.5	9.6	10.1	1.0	1.0
1975	III	7.9	8.6	3.5	3.9	7.0	6.9	10.2	12.0	10.1	10.2	1.0	1.0
1975	IV	8.2	8.5	3.5	4.0	7.2	7.1	10.3	11.2	10.7	10.5	1.0	1.0
Mean		6.2	6.3	2.9	3.0	5.7	5.5	7.6	8.0	8.1	7.9	1.0	1.0
SPE		.0760		.0719		.0638		.1672		.0572		.0270	

Note: This table presents the simulated values of each variable in a column to the left of the actual values. Following the quarter values in a column is the mean value for the 1973-1975 period. The standard percentage error is given last.

25

Table 1.8

National Income (billions of dollars at annual rate)

Year	Quarter	National Income		Compensation of Employees		Rental Income		Proprietors' Income		Corporate Profits		Net Interest	
		Simulated	Actual	Simulated	Actual	Simulated	Actual	Simulated	Actual	Simulated	Actual	Simulated	Actual
1973	I	1058	1027	769	771	24	22	107	86	114	101	44	47
1973	II	1069	1048	786	790	24	21	103	91	109	98	47	47
1973	III	1091	1070	810	807	22	21	102	95	104	98	54	49
1973	IV	1101	1099	829	828	19	22	98	98	99	99	55	51
1974	I	1104	1110	854	846	18	21	87	91	90	96	56	55
1974	II	1114	1122	875	867	17	21	81	85	84	88	57	62
1974	III	1118	1145	893	890	17	21	78	86	71	82	60	66
1974	IV	1128	1152	904	902	16	21	78	86	67	74	62	69
1975	I	1176	1145	920	904	18	22	96	81	78	69	65	69
1975	II	1250	1178	941	913	20	22	113	87	107	87	67	70
1975	III	1265	1229	956	935	21	22	105	95	114	105	69	70
1975	IV	1255	1260	966	963	19	23	96	97	103	105	71	72
Mean		1144	1132	875	868	20	22	95	90	95	92	59	61
SPE		.0260		.0129		.1508		.1410		.1093		.0656	

Note: This table presents the simulated values of each variable in a column to the left of the actual values. Following the quarter values in a column is the mean value for the 1973-1975 period. The standard percentage error is given last.

Table 1.9
Personal Income and Outlay (billions of dollars at annual rate)

Year	Quarter	Personal Income		Personal Taxes		Disposable Personal Income		Personal Consumption Expenditures		Personal Interest		Personal Saving	
		Simulated	Actual	Simulated	Actual	Simulated	Actual	Simulated	Actual	Simulated	Actual	Simulated	Actual
1973	I	1028	1012	146	145	882	867	800	787	21	19	61	60
1973	II	1054	1038	151	147	904	891	814	801	21	20	68	70
1973	III	1080	1064	155	153	925	912	824	818	21	21	81	73
1973	IV	1097	1095	157	158	940	938	834	833	21	21	86	83
1974	I	1108	1110	158	161	950	948	852	853	20	21	78	74
1974	II	1133	1137	161	167	973	969	876	879	20	22	77	69
1974	III	1156	1173	164	174	992	998	895	907	20	23	77	69
1974	IV	1174	1194	165	178	1009	1016	894	911	20	23	95	82
1975	I	1223	1203	170	179	1053	1024	931	933	20	22	102	68
1975	II	1278	1230	145	142	1133	1088	969	960	20	22	144	106
1975	III	1284	1265	184	174	1100	1091	975	987	20	23	104	81
1975	IV	1286	1300	183	180	1103	1120	972	1012	20	23	111	85
Mean		1158	1152	162	163	997	988	886	890	20	22	90	77
SPE		.0167		.0385		.0174		.0156		.0952		.2277	

Note: This table presents the simulated values of each variable in a column to the left of the actual values. Following the quarter values in a column is the mean value for the 1973-1975 period. The standard percentage error is given last.

Table 1.10
Interest Rates (percentages)

Year	Quarter	Government Bonds		Mortgages		Treasury Bills		Business Loans	
		Simulated	Actual	Simulated	Actual	Simulated	Actual	Simulated	Actual
1973	I	6.0	6.2	8.8	8.7	5.6	6.1	8.5	8.8
1973	II	6.2	6.3	9.2	9.0	6.5	7.2	9.5	10.5
1973	III	6.4	6.4	9.7	10.4	7.5	8.5	11.6	13.8
1973	IV	6.7	6.4	10.4	10.0	8.5	7.4	13.5	13.6
1974	I	6.9	6.8	11.5	9.9	9.2	8.0	14.8	12.4
1974	II	7.1	7.0	11.9	10.8	8.6	8.1	14.5	16.2
1974	III	7.0	7.3	11.6	11.8	7.8	8.4	12.9	16.8
1974	IV	6.9	6.8	10.9	10.8	7.9	7.2	11.9	14.7
1975	I	6.9	6.7	11.0	9.9	7.4	5.5	10.5	11.1
1975	II	6.7	6.9	10.8	10.3	6.4	5.2	9.2	9.9
1975	III	6.5	7.3	10.7	11.1	6.3	6.4	8.7	11.0
1975	IV	6.4	7.2	10.7	10.6	6.0	5.5	8.5	10.2
Mean		6.6	6.8	10.6	10.3	7.3	6.9	11.2	12.4
SPE		.0497		.0728		.1491		.1451	

Note: This table presents the simulated values of each variable in a column to the left of the actual values. Following the quarter values in a column is the mean value for the 1973-1975 period. The standard percentage error is given last.

points are tracked rather well. But the magnitudes of the swings are somewhat erratic, indicating an area for improvement of the model in the future.[5]

Table 1.7 shows the model's performance with respect to unemployment rates for the civilian labor force and each of our four occupations. The simulated and actual means of the civilian unemployment rate are almost identical and the standard percentage error is 7.6%. As one would expect, there is somewhat less accuracy in fitting the unemployment rates of the different occupations, but the SPE is large (17%) only for crafts workers.

It is seen in Table 1.8 that on the income side of the national accounts the fit is good for compensation of employees and reasonably good for net interest, but in the fit for other property income series there is considerable room for improvement. Possibly a large part of the errors in the property income accounts results from the model's failure to shift income among periods for tax purposes in the way in which this was done in the real world. This weakness carries over from the business income series to the personal income series shown in Table 1.9. The series on personal saving has a distressingly large SPE of 23%, and one can see that the bulk of this error occurs in 1975. Obviously this is an area in which improvement needs to be made. The model's fit with respect to major interest rates is shown in Table 1.10. One can see at a glance that the fit is much better for the long-term (bond and mortgage) rates than for the short-term (treasury bill and bank loan) rates. As an example of the fit of the flow-of-funds output simulated by the model, Table 1.11 presents simulated balance sheet material for the nonfinancial firms, as compared with the actual data from the flow-of-funds accounts.

SIMULATIONS OF THE EFFECTS OF POLICY CHANGES

Specific Assumptions for Counterfactual Runs

In this section, we discuss how the model may be adapted to study varying policies, and examine our early explorations in the simulation of policy results.

All of the policy simulations we present here are based on reruns of the 1973-1975 period, with some aspect(s) of government policy altered to differ from historic policy. When modeling counterfactual situations, our usual intention is that one element of policy be changed, and that all the other elements of policy be unchanged. However, the translation of an "unchanged policy" into the numerical values of the relevant variables is sometimes problematical.

Many of our experiments involve changing fiscal policy in some way while holding monetary policy unchanged. Initially we thought that an unchanged

---

[5]The simulated firms set desired inventories at a half year's worth of a moving average of sales. Firms then produce enough each round to service current sales plus enough to close 1.7% of the gap between actual inventory and desired inventory. This formulation proved to give unstable results in running the policy experiments. Pending a more fundamental reworking of decision making with respect to inventories, we have added a limit on inventory accumulation, so that firms are programmed to be unwilling to allow the size of their inventories to lie above an 8% growth path running through actual inventories in January 1973.

Table 1.11

Balance Sheet for Nonfinancial Firms (end of period figures in billions of dollars)

Year	Quarter	Cash		Consumer Credit		Treasury Bills		Bonds (Assets)		Bank Loans		Bonds (Liabilities)	
		Simulated	Actual	Simulated	Actual	Simulated	Actual	Simulated	Actual	Simulated	Actual	Simulated	Actual
1973	I	51	54	36	34	2	3	171	175	149	158	512	510
1973	II	52	54	35	35	2	3	178	182	155	168	526	519
1973	III	51	54	34	35	2	2	182	185	157	174	539	534
1973	IV	51	55	35	39	2	2	187	189	162	180	554	549
1974	I	52	54	34	37	2	−1	197	204	168	187	568	568
1974	II	54	53	35	38	2	−1	205	213	176	201	582	582
1974	III	56	53	35	39	2	−1	214	215	183	205	596	601
1974	IV	56	56	36	41	2	2	218	223	184	210	610	618
1975	I	58	55	36	41	2	3	226	228	186	201	623	632
1975	II	62	54	37	41	2	5	239	233	200	199	636	635
1975	III	63	55	37	41	2	3	246	233	206	196	649	643
1975	IV	62	58	38	44	2	3	251	243	208	197	661	658
Mean		56	55	36	39	2	2	209	210	178	190	588	587
SPE		.0756		.0938		1.5252		.0280		.0879		.0087	

Note: This table presents the simulated values of each variable in a column to the left of the actual values. Following the quarter values in a column is the mean value for the 1973-1975 period. The standard percentage error is given last.

monetary policy could be characterized as an unchanged quantity of bank reserves. We soon found that this gave implausible results, so we now define an unchanged monetary policy to be the same quantity of excess (or deficient) reserves as prevailed in the factual situation. When either monetary or fiscal policy is changed in a counterfactual run of the model, we apply the changed assumption to the sum of counterfactual required reserves plus actual excess reserves. One might argue that the use of actual excess reserves also fails to capture the monetary policy which the Federal Reserve would look on as an unchanged policy in a specific counterfactual situation, but in order to model a more complex response we would have to have a completely endogenous Federal Reserve, and that is beyond the scope of our present experiments.

Our exogenous monetary authority also swerves from the historical past to some extent whenever our financial intermediary finds itself with excessive inventories of government securities or with inventories insufficient to accommodate purchases by other sectors. In this case, the monetary authority absorbs or provides the securities under repurchase agreements. These repurchase agreements do not affect the bank's decision making directly, but the financial intermediary adds these to its actual excess supply or demand for the securities in setting interest rates.

In counterfactual runs that do not explicitly involve changing government purchases or compensation of employees, we use exogenous real values and endogenous prices and wages. Endogenous wages for the governments are their exogenous wage rates times the ratio of endogenous to exogenous private wages.

The stocks of financial assets held by the government are set at their exogenous levels even in counterfactual situations by allowing the government to vary its liabilities. For imports of goods and services we use exogenous real values and exogenous import prices in all cases. Exports of goods and services are exogenous in the real values at endogenous prices of the exporting industry. Stock market prices, which enter into our consumption function, are exogenous in the runs presented here.

Experiments with Variations in Monetary and Fiscal Policy

Our first experiment is to measure the effects on macroeconomic variables of some different monetary and fiscal policies than those which prevailed in the 1973-1975 period. The changes in fiscal policy were a 5% surtax and a 5% reduction in federal personal income taxes. The changes in monetary policy were a 5% variation either way in the growth rate of bank reserves. In all cases the changed policy was applied from January 1, 1973, through December 31, 1975.

The specific amounts of the changes in policies were chosen so as to lie just within the bounds of reasonable debate at the end of 1972. At that time the civilian unemployment rate was slightly above 5% and the annual rate of inflation was between 5% and 6%. Those who are usually preoccupied with rates of inflation might well have argued for either or both of a 5% reduction in the annual growth of

Table 1.12
Results of Monetary and Fiscal Policy Experiments

Combinations of Tax and Monetary Policies		Civilian Unemployment Rate (%)	GNP Deflator (1972=100)	Govt. Bond Rate (%)	GNP (1972 prices)	Deviations from Base-Line Run (*billions of dollars*)			
						Cumulative Govt. Deficit from end of 1972			Corporate Profits
Tax	Money					Federal	Local	Combined	
				1973 IV					
1. Low	Easy	4.9%	110	6.4%	24	2	0	2	6
2. Actual	Easy	5.2	111	6.4	− 6	1	0	1	− 3
3. High	Easy	5.3	111	6.4	− 12	− 4	0	− 4	− 7
4. Low	Actual	4.9	111	6.6	18	2	0	2	7
5.[a] Actual	Actual	5.2	111	6.7	0	0	0	0	0
6. High	Actual	5.2	111	6.7	− 11	− 4	0	− 4	− 5
7. Low	Tight	4.9	111	6.7	12	2	0	2	7
8. Actual	Tight	5.2	111	6.8	− 5	1	1	2	0
9. High	Tight	5.2	111	6.8	− 10	− 4	0	− 4	− 3

					1974 IV					
1.	Low	Easy	5.5	120	5.5	40	1	– 2	– 1	5
2.	Actual	Easy	6.2	120	5.8	8	3	0	3	9
3.	High	Easy	6.5	120	5.6	0	–11	0	–11	–12
4.	Low	Actual	5.8	120	6.7	31	8	– 7	1	15
5.*a*	Actual	Actual	6.3	120	6.9	0	0	0	0	0
6.	High	Actual	6.9	121	7.2	– 27	– 3	– 5	– 8	–10
7.	Low	Tight	6.0	120	8.0	18	9	– 1	8	20
8.	Actual	Tight	6.9	121	8.7	– 45	7	2	9	– 2
9.	High	Tight	7.4	121	8.9	– 54	6	– 1	5	– 5

					1975 IV					
1.	Low	Easy	5.0	123	4.2	220	–34	–13	–47	94
2.	Actual	Easy	6.8	126	4.7	85	– 3	– 7	–10	26
3.	High	Easy	7.8	129	4.6	16	–32	– 4	–36	4
4.	Low	Actual	6.0	127	5.8	114	– 6	–17	–23	59
5.*a*	Actual	Actual	8.2	129	6.4	0	0	0	0	0
6.	High	Actual	9.4	130	6.5	– 44	4	–13	– 9	–19
7.	Low	Tight	7.3	128	9.1	29	7	– 5	– 2	50
8.	Actual	Tight	10.6	132	12.4	–175	47	9	56	–43
9.	High	Tight	11.1	132	12.7	–198	51	11	62	–52

*a*Base line.

33

bank reserves and/or a 5% increase in personal income taxes. Those who look more to the unemployment rate for their policy prescriptions might conceivably have advocated a 5% increase in the annual growth of bank reserves and/or a 5% reduction in personal income taxes. The actual growth rate in the M1 money stock in 1973 was near 6% and for M2 was near 9%. The reduction of 5% in the growth of bank reserves would move these approximately to 1% and 4%, and it is difficult to imagine that someone would recommend an even more restrictive monetary policy. It is likewise difficult to imagine the recommendation of a monetary policy for 1973 that would raise the rate of growth of M1 above 11% or the growth of M2 above 14% as was possible with our easier monetary policy. While many observers might have recommended increasing personal income taxes by more than 5% (in order to try to balance the federal budget), it is difficult to imagine a recommendation for a reduction greater than 5% in the face of the substantial inflation of the period.

This experiment involved running the model nine times to simulate all possible combinations of the policies described above: (1) a base-line run with neither of the policies changed, (2) four runs with one of the policies changed in one direction and the other unchanged, (3) two runs with both policies changed in the same direction, and (4) two runs with the policies changed in opposite directions.

Of the many variables available in our model for evaluating the effects of the various policy combinations, we have chosen the following six: (1) the civilian unemployment rate, (2) the GNP deflator, (3) real GNP, (4) the federal government deficit, (5) the local governments' deficit, and (6) corporate profits. Table 1.12 presents the results of running the model with nine combinations of monetary and fiscal policies. The results are shown for the fourth quarter of each of the years of the run, so that one can get some idea of the differential lags involved in responses to the various policies.[6] These data can also be used to indicate the elasticity of the target variables with respect to changes in policy. Finally, one can use data like these to assist in the choice of optimum policy combinations.

None of the policy combinations produces a significant effect on prices after only one year, but all combinations with lower taxes reduce the unemployment rate .3 percentage points. The range of the observations on unemployment after one year is 4.9% to 5.3%, after two years is 5.5% to 7.4%, and after three years becomes 5.0% to 11.1%. The range for real GNP in billions of 1972 dollars at an annual rate in the fourth quarter of 1973 was $-12 to $24; for 1974-IV was $-54 to $40; and for 1975-IV was $-98 to $220. This same time pattern is evident for the government deficits and corporate profits—minor impacts after one year, but quite significant changes after three.

Monetary policy appears in the model to work more slowly than fiscal policy. With the actual monetary policy and varying counterfactual fiscal policies the unemployment rate varies .3 points in the first year, 1.1 after two years, and 3.4 after three years. When monetary policy is varied with the actual fiscal policy, the unemployment rate evidences no impact after one year, a range of .7 points after two, and a range of 3.8 percentage points after three years. Thus, the second- and third-

---

[6]The assumed changes in taxes are applied immediately to taxable receipts during 1972, rather than applied in a lump sum at the beginning of 1973.

year impacts of our hypothetical policy changes on unemployment and inflation are roughly comparable, the first-year impact of fiscal policy is substantially stronger.

The price responses to the policy changes are rather modest—the simulated inflation continues regardless of policy. However, with Draconian measures of a tax increase plus tight money, the model simulates a slight increase in the inflation rate, and a slight decrease for the most stimulative combination tried. This result is due to the cost-plus nature of the pricing decisions. Although wages rise faster in periods of lower unemployment, causing cost curves to shift upward, this is apparently more than compensated for in the current version of the model by a greater spreading of fixed costs in periods of higher production, and by induced investment, which is cost saving in nature.

Using Table 1.12 one can calculate the approximate change in the unemployment rate, price level, and real GNP per unit change in each of the policy variables by itself. After three years with the actual fiscal policy, a 5% increase in the growth rate of bank reserves results in a 6.8% unemployment rate and a 5% reduction results in 10.6%. Thus a change in the growth rate of bank reserves of one percentage point results in a change in the opposite direction of .38 percentage points in the unemployment rate. Using the same method to calculate the response of the unemployment rate to the tax change, one finds that a one percentage point change in the federal personal income surtax changes the unemployment rate in the same direction by .34 percentage points. The three-year response of the GNP deflator to unit percentage point changes in the policies is .3 points for the tax change and −.6 for the monetary policy (the tighter monetary policy results in higher prices after three years). A one-point change in bank reserves results after three years in approximately $26 billion change in the same direction in GNP in 1972 prices at an annual rate, while a one-point change in taxes changes GNP in the opposite direction by $16 billion.

Our experiment indicates that in the face of uncertainty with respect to the course of monetary policy during the 1973-1975 period, the fiscal policy maker by lowering taxes could have improved the economy's performance substantially at moderate cost to the government—both federal and local. However, there is some indication from the results of this experiment that the fiscal policy maker might not have done badly by leaving taxes unchanged, if given an assurance of an easier monetary policy.

Wage Subsidy Experiments

In the first of two experiments with wage subsidies, the federal government was programmed to give a credit on the corporate profits tax of a portion of the wages of newly hired persons, with no restriction as to the personal characteristics of the hirees who would qualify. This kind of program is now considered by some as a desirable counterpart to the investment tax credit. In this simulation, we allowed a tax credit equal to 20% of the wage of persons who have been on the firm's payroll for less than a year. However, the number of persons covered was not allowed to exceed the net increase of the firm's work force over a base period.[7] In the second experiment, employers were given a tax credit of 20% on the first-year wages of persons who were marked as "hard to employ" and who had been unemployed for at least two months at the time of hiring. No requirement for net increase in employment was made in this case.

The way the model customarily runs, no direct employment effect could occur from either of these subsidy policies. The labor/output ratio for each vintage of capital goods is fixed, and firms are programmed to gear employment to desired output and to gear desired output to sales and inventory status.[8] There would be an indirect effect on employment, as the tax credit would increase dividends, although with some lag, which would increase aggregate demand. There would be a direct effect on the rate of price increase, as we have programmed firms to adjust average cost downward to take account of the tax rebate when considering price increases.

In evaluating the "employment growth subsidy," another source of downward bias inherent in the model is the fact that we have represented only one firm per industry. An industry having net losses in employment would in reality contain firms which would qualify for a subsidy if there were disparate movements in employment within the industry. In order to deal with this problem (which is by no means unique to this model) a substantive study of the distribution of employment changes by firm over the course of the cycle would be necessary, something which could presumably be done with Bureau of Labor Statistics monthly establishment microdata on employment.

In all runs of the model, including the base-line run reported earlier, 10% of the labor force members in all occupations were marked out as "hard to employ." In the job search simulated in the model, unemployed labor force members are chosen at random to "come for an interview" by a firm which has vacancies. Unless the special subsidy is in effect, a worker who is marked as hard to employ is turned down by the employer at 50% of the interviews to which he is called. When the wage subsidy is in effect, those marked as hard to employ are treated as other workers are (i.e., offered a job if called to an interview and of a needed occupation) if his value of the variable *IUDAT*, which records the round in which he left employment or entered the labor force, is smaller than *ITIME*, the variable which records the current date, by at least 8 rounds.

Figure 1.3 contrasts the extent of subsidized employment in the two experiments and makes it clear that, even allowing for the model's downward biases, a program of subsidizing employment growth is going to have little impact. The program of subsidizing the hard to employ, assuming that the subsidy does motivate behavior like that which we have programmed our simulated firms to follow, has

---

[7]The base period used for all the months of 1973 was January 1, 1973. For later months, the base period was taken to be one year previous to the current period. In the actual simulation, employment of a firm during the base period after 1973 was estimated by a geometrically weighted moving average centered at the base period to conserve memory spaces.

[8]In the medium run, wage levels affect investment, which affects demand, but also affects labor requirements for given output. In running these wage subsidy experiments, however, employers used the standard wage in the computations leading to investment decisions.

Figure 1.3. *Employment subsidized under alternative wage subsidy schemes.*

greater promise. The primary effect is of course the reduction of unemployment among the hard-to-employ. After the program has been in effect three years, the unemployment rate of such persons is only 1.6 points higher than that of the entire labor force. Although the hard-to-employ constitute 10% of the labor force, only 2.1% of the labor force is on subsidy after three years because the subsidy is assumed to last only one year for each individual, and the hard-to-employ are assumed to have the same separation rate as other workers.

In the subsidized employment growth, the program literally dies away to nothing in 1975, as the growth of aggregate demand ebbs. Since the price effects and the fiscal effects of any wage subsidy program are conditional on employers' hiring of subsidized workers, the employment growth subsidy is not likely to generate sizable effects of this sort. The effects of the two programs are further contrasted in Table 1.13.

Table 1.13
Contrasting Results of Experimental Runs with Two Forms of Wage Subsidy, 1975 III-IV

Employment Variables	Employment Growth Subsidy	Subsidy to Hard-to-Employ
% workers under subsidy	0.4%	2.1%
Unemployment rate of hard-to-employ	12.8%	9.0%
Unemployment rate, all workers	7.6%	7.4%
Direct cost (*billions of dollars annually*)	0.7	4.5
GNP price deflator as % of base-line deflator	99.6%	99.2%

FUTURE DIRECTIONS FOR RESEARCH
WITH THE TRANSACTIONS MODEL

The reader of this paper will have perhaps formed the impression that there are a number of ways in which the model might undergo improvement. First and foremost, we are looking to an improved method of parameter search which will produce better fits, and also, in providing a "hands-off" search methodology, insulate us from suspicions of choosing parameter values so as to make some particular conclusion emerge. Particular parts of the specification which need improvement include the specification of the behavior of inventory accumulation, a greater incorporation of expectations into decision making, and better specification of wage change behavior.

We believe that we have amply demonstrated the feasibility of building a complete macroeconomic model entirely on the basis of specifications of microbehavior. In doing so, we have also demonstrated the feasibility of integrating the analysis of the flow of funds with the analysis of transactions on income and product account. In addition, we have shown that a microsimulated model can be used to study policies which are specified in considerable detail, with the policy description itself integrated into the structure of the model. It seems to us evident that such developments are not only feasible but highly desirable in terms of the cogency of macroeconomic modeling.

DISCUSSION

Donald A. Nichols

One of the difficulties of presenting the results of a simulation model of this kind is that the model generates such a rich set of data that it's very difficult to choose what is to be summarized for a presentation. This is in great contrast to the presentation of a theoretical paper, where one makes some explicit assumptions at the outset, then derives the conclusions that follow directly from those assumptions, and then presents those conclusions completely. Here, the simplifying assumptions that a theorist makes at the outset have to be made at the end, when deciding which of the statistics are the most interesting to report, and which of the characteristics of this rich complex set of data are the most interesting ones to report. The reporting, therefore, of simulations of this kind is much more awkward than it is of a theoretical issue.

As a result, this paper contains many tables of statistics, and these presumably summarize what are surely roomfuls of statistics back at College Park. Often papers of this kind are unfairly criticized for some omission when in fact the variable was not omitted at all but simply left on the cutting-room floor. A problem, then, with models of this kind is that they generate too many data—not only too many data to present, but sometimes too many for even the authors to digest.

This is a microeconomic model of the macroeconomy. Aggregate statistics— GNP, the unemployment rate, the rate of inflation—are computed by adding up a batch of microcomponents. These microcomponents include not only households and firms, but governments and banking sectors. These microcomponents are not econometric estimates based on microdata; they are instead what is called *synthetic*.

In this model, the synthetic components are chosen to satisfy two criteria: One, their aggregated versions are supposed to make some empirical sense. That is, the authors look at the sum of the output of all their microcomponents to see how closely it tracks real GNP. They use some statistical tests to determine which of the various alternative microparameter values yield macro data that best replicates a chosen period of history.

The second criterion is simply that the microcomponents must have some intuitive appeal. While this criterion makes some sense, it should be emphasized that the microcomponents are not observations of firms that are tested econometrically against firm data. The microcomponents are, really, synthetic.

The components are not really firms, but industries. They are chosen to replicate various groupings of the two digit classification of industries for the U.S. economy. Each component behaves according to a set of rules, not specified in this version of the paper. Most sectors are designed to behave as would firms, however. They look at costs and determine prices through a markup equation. Decision rules are given for product and labor market actions, and these rules make more sense for a competitive firm than for a monopoly industry.

The different components interact in a recursive model. The decision taken by one sector becomes part of the environment for the next sector. And so, when one industry chooses to expand, by the time the next industry looks at the environment, there's a lower unemployment rate and a smaller number of workers to choose from.

Now let me ask, Why would one construct a model of this kind? One answer is that it might yield a better macro explanation of history. It is this issue that the authors have emphasized in their paper. Let me suggest some others.

The decision to use a recursive rather than a simultaneous model was due in this case to a belief on the part of the authors that the world is recursive. One of the motives for simulating equilibrium in the way they have is to capture that recursive nature. Yet this characteristic of the model is not fully exploited.

For example, the large econometric models are not very good at capturing processes that take a very short amount of time. One process which takes an extremely short time is the purchase of goods or the purchase of securities—in short, the use of money. Money is treated in the econometric models as a homogeneous, amorphous glob that you want a little more of when output is big and you want a little less of when interest rates are high. But the actual fact that forms the basis of money and banking courses is that you don't hold money for its own sake but to get rid of. Money is desirable because it can be spent, and individual money balances go up and down wildly. This characteristic of money is something that macromodels cannot capture very well. And so there is some advantage in going to a micromodel to do this. I should note that other micromodels of the financial sector have been built that have modeled the flow of funds from one bank to another, but they differed from the present model in that transactions are modeled explicitly here.

In this model, a synthetic trading mechanism is established in which transactions are recorded. For every purchase of an automobile, of a house, of a security, money changes hands; it is moved from one account to another and the huge program that runs this simulation keeps track of where the money is and where it has gone. A major usefulness, then, of a model of this kind would be in examining such a process, and thereby getting at something that cannot be gotten at through conventional econometric models. But the authors have not pursued this possibility. I think they should devote more of their efforts to examining the effects of government actions that affect the transactions process and less on examining the effects of conventional monetary and fiscal policies. Their model has no advantage for examining the latter policies.

Questions I would find interesting are the following: What happens to the effectiveness of monetary policy as the time it takes to complete a transaction is shortened? What happens to velocity when checks clear in half a time period? This model may not be able to provide quantitative answers to these questions, but it could yield some useful insights. The authors have constructed a laboratory machine of the transactions process, and their efforts should be judged on those grounds. Instead they have chosen to be judged as any other econometric model.

Transactions are not the only process that occurs faster than the three-month interval that constitutes a time period in most macroeconometric models. The hire-fire-quit decision and the existence of frictional unemployment is another. This model could shed light on that process as well. Similarly, issues concerning inventories could be analyzed to advantage in a model of this kind. The authors, however, have not exploited the potential of the model to consider these questions.

A second area where a model of this kind might be used to advantage is where distributions matter. If one is interested in the behavior of the tail of a distribution for example—as in the case of unemployment—then something is lost by using a model that considers only the means of distributions. This model, I think, should concentrate more on those areas where distributions matter and less on those areas where they don't.

Finally, where aggregations of nonlinear relations are to take place, I would think a model of this kind would have an advantage. The authors have not shown us that their model exploits these possibilities. They have not presented the tables or distributions that might be interesting to see in a variety of places. Instead, they present only the means of the distributions, and I take this as evidence that they have not concerned themselves with issues other than predicting the means.

In fairness to the authors, I should add that since this model is a first, one reason to construct it was simply to see whether in fact it was possible to construct such a thing. Can this bumblebee really fly? From this perspective the results of this exercise are not an improved understanding of the real world, but an improved understanding of the possibilities for a new tool for research. Like the first automobile, the fact that it runs is of interest in itself rather than the question of whether it's better than a horse for the purpose of transportation. From this perspective, the effort is a resounding success. The authors have clearly demonstrated that the model works, and we, as a result, have learned something about the possibility of using this technique.

However, the second question must also be addressed. And in this case, I must say that I don't think this model beats the horse. That is, in terms of its usefulness for policy or for any kind of experiment one might want to run to try to learn what the real economy is like, I would still turn to the existing models, rather than to this one.

The major reason for this is the lack of empirical reliability of this model because of the unknown properties of the estimation process. The authors do not report how many microparameters were varied in an attempt to explain how many variables for how many time periods. They note the statistical criterion used to choose among alternative values, but the concept of significance in a statistical sense is ignored. In fact, the estimating procedure is to change parameter values by hand until the macrovariables track the time values for the years 1973-1975. This does not permit the calculation of conventional statistics of the significance of the coefficients.

To a policymaker the choice of the 1973-1975 period also causes problems. This was a period of great unrest in macroeconomics; none of the econometric models that existed prior to 1973 predicted well the inflation and recession that came along at that time. This model, however, does explain that period. But since the model is not fine-tuned to data before that period, it is not a fair test to compare this to the econometric models and ask, Did this explain the 1973-1975 period better?—because in fact, the model was calibrated to the 1973-1975 period. It is not calibrated on the pre-1973 data and then permitted to predict the 1973-1975 period.

When you look at the tables that are presented in the text, there is a very impressive, tight relation between the outputs of the model and the outputs of the real economy; but this is probably due to the fact that this is the time period over which the model was calibrated, rather than to some superior predictive ability on the part of this model over the conventional macromodel. The paper does not consider the predictive ability of the model.

I found the reporting of the experiments difficult to follow. Some interesting quantitative statistics are presented, but not fully interpreted, while others are ignored. That is, no multipliers are given that would correspond to what a macroeconomist would look for. You can compute them only roughly and approximately from the statistics that are presented. They will tell you that if the money supply goes up 1% extra a year for these three years, what would happen to the unemployment rate, or something like that. And, from looking at these computations, I was impressed that the model does seem to come up with some of the same quantitative relationships as found in the econometric models, despite the fact that the methodology is very different and the criterion for calibrating and choosing parameters is very different.

I was troubled, however, by my reaction to these exercises. When I asked myself to judge the model and its policy conclusions my reaction was to check to see if the policy conclusions of this model were similar to what I thought I already knew. I asked myself, "Do these multipliers make sense?" I did not say, "If the conclusions of this model are different, I will reject what I have previously believed."

This indicates that I do not have enough faith in the methodology that was used compared to what is used in more conventional models to permit these exercises to cause me to change my mind. If my mind is to be changed, I must see a more rigorous estimation procedure and some sterner statistical tests.

Let me close by saying that I am impressed by the tremendous effort that has gone into this model, that the tightness of fit presented in the tables in the paper is truly remarkable, that I feel there are great possibilities for models of this kind in the future with major potential advantages over existing models, and that the authors have done us all a great service by exploring these possibilities extensively. Unfortunately for the authors, a massive and ambitious undertaking of this kind is much easier to criticize than a narrower, less ambitious effort. Fortunately for us, the possibility of being criticized has not kept them from proceeding.

DISCUSSION

Robert P. Strauss

Introduction

Large-scale econometric models of the U.S. economy have been used for some time by the executive agencies in their development of macroeconomic policy. With the inception of the Congressional Budget Control and Impoundment Act of 1974,[1] the Congress has become an active user of various econometric models which are commercially available (e.g., the quarterly models sold by Data Resources, Inc., Wharton Econometric Forecasting Associates, and Chase Econometrics). To date, however, large-scale microsimulation models of the economy, which through aggregation permit macroforecasts, have not been widely used for policy purposes.

The Bennett and Bergmann Transactions Model is an important contribution in the area of microsimulation because it was developed with the avowed purpose of allowing one of "add up" micromarkets to obtain macroresults. As such, it permits one to examine the aggregate effects of intervention in particular markets, a characteristic not easily available with the various macromodels. Other novel features of the model include an attempt to employ more realistic assumptions about firm-level or industry-level behavior (e.g., markup pricing); it is temporally disaggregated and entirely sequential (rather than simultaneous) in its characterization of decisions in the economy; and it provides for detailed occupational and educational characteristics of the labor force.

In the following remarks I shall address two dimensions of the Bennett and Bergmann model: (1) the use of their microsimulation model vis-à-vis econometric models as an aggregative predictive tool, and (2) an analysis of their counterfactual scenarios.

The Bennett and Bergmann Transactions Model as a Predictive Tool

Model construction normally is thought to be motivated by two concerns: to achieve or obtain predictions of the future and to understand better the behavior

---

[1] Public Law 93-344.

under consideration. The latter is usually thought to involve hypothesis testing and possibly answering the question, Why did it occur? Yet the two purposes are related, and in fact one can argue that the test of understanding is indeed predictive accuracy. Moreover, the usual classical statistical techniques (e.g., t-tests for statistical significance of particular model coefficients) used to test hypotheses about model structure are directly related to the forecasting ability of the model.

Policy analysis, which here is taken to mean the prediction of endogenous behavior under current law (e.g., taxes, spending, regulatory environment, etc.) and under changes in current law (e.g., tax cuts, etc.) necessarily relies heavily on economic models to achieve predictions.

For the policymaker, a natural question to ask is how the predictive content of the Transactions Model compares to various other aggregate macromodels. Three comments are involved here: whether the model is *a priori* likely to be a superior macroforecasting device; whether, as a result of the manner in which Bennett and Bergmann have estimated their model, it is likely to be an accurate forecasting device; and finally, whether, as an empirical proposition, the model predicts better than a representative aggregate macromodel.

With respect to the question of the *a priori* superiority of a micromodel for macroforecasting purposes, it is not obvious that macroforecasting needs will be better served by aggregating the results of a microsimulation model. To be sure, it would be desirable to know that individual markets can be modeled and cumulated to achieve greater accuracy than afforded by aggregate macromodels; however, there is a long tradition in economic theory, from the fallacy of composition to the effects of aggregation (e.g., Grunfeld and Grilliches, 1960), which argues that this need not be so. Of course, macroforecasting for policy purposes frequently involves an analysis of the effects of a targeted policy instrument on a particular market or industry. Here, the microsimulation approach should be a useful addition to the forecaster's tool kit. However, in aggregate terms, the case for relying on a microsimulation model remains to be made vis-a-vis relying on macromodels.

Perhaps the most unusual aspect of the Bennett and Bergmann microsimulation approach is the eschewing of traditional econometric estimation procedures. Specification and parameter values are obtained through the use of *a priori* information as well as substantial trial and error. Upon inspection, the trial and error approach used looks very much like a type of regression analysis.

Bennett and Bergmann state that they calibrate their model by minimizing the square root of the sum of squared percentage errors. We may write this as[2]

$$\min \sqrt{\Sigma_t \ [(\hat{Y}_t - Y_t)/Y_t]^2} \tag{1}$$

where $\hat{Y}$ is a forecast generated by model, presumably the result of a prior aggregation procedure, and Y is an actual, historical observation at time t. The forecast is

---

[2] Bennett and Bergmann are unclear whether this criterion is applied per equation, or as an *overall* criterion. However, if there are no across-equations constraints in parameters, then the two approaches should yield identical estimates.

generated by picking parameters and multiplying them by pertinent exogenous variables (X_t) which are also observed per equation.

Ordinary least square (OLS) minimizes a similar (but different) expression:

$$\min[\Sigma_t (Y_t - \hat{Y}_t)^2]$$ (2)

Ignoring the radical in Equation (1), we see the difference between Equation (1) and Equation (2) is the normalization by the historical data point, Y_t.

The use of (1) rather than (2) or some conventional variant of (2) might appear to be justified on intuitive grounds. That is, since (1) may represent the authors' loss function with respect to forecast errors, it would seem appropriate to use the same criterion to obtain parameters with which to subsequently forecast. Unfortunately, this sort of symmetry need not hold, and, in fact, Johnston (1974) has demonstrated for the case of quadratic prediction error loss functions that the manner in which one should estimate one's model is invariant to the user's choice of prediction error loss functions. Johnston's results argue for the use of usual econometric estimation procedures in lieu of Equation (1) and suggest Bennett and Bergmann may have obtained their parameters in a manner which does not best serve their prediction purposes.

Bennett and Bergmann report on the accuracy of their model within their sample period (1973 IV to 1975 IV); however, they do not report results of post-sample forecasts, although historical data are readily available for comparisons. While the within-sample forecast accuracy displayed in tables 1.6-1.11 of the paper is impressive, it is instructive to compare the results of the model to those from a quarterly aggregate macromodel. Table 1.14 relates Bennett and Bergmann's within-sample (for the period 1973 I to 1975 IV) forecast accuracy to that of Data Resources, Inc. quarterly model over the same period for three representative macro-variables: nominal GNP, the civilian unemployment rate, and corporate profits. DRI's GNP forecast error as measured by the mean square relative error, which is parametrically analogous to the calibration criteria of the Transactions Model, is 25% smaller, the DRI unemployment rate forecast error is 3.4% smaller, and the

Table 1.14
Within-Sample Forecast Accuracy[a] of Bennett, Bergmann[b] and Data Resources[c] Quarterly Models of U.S. Economy, 1973-1975

Models	GNP	Unemployment Rate	Corporate Profits
Bennett, Bergmann	.0151	.0770	.1093
DRI	.0121	.0745	.0966
% Bennett, Bergmann error over DRI	24.8%	3.4%	13.1%

[a] $\sqrt{\frac{1}{n}\sum_{t=1}^{12}[(Y_t - \hat{Y}_t)/Y_t]^2}$

[b] Derived from Tables 1.6, 1.7, and 1.8 in this chapter.

[c] Comparison of DRI dynamic simulation, DYNA78A, to observed data, May 1978 simulations.

DRI corporate profits forecast error is 13.1% smaller than Bennett and Bergmann's forecast errors. Of course, the forecasting differences reflect differences in specification, estimation technique, and period over which the parameters were estimated. Nonetheless, the within-sample difference in predictive accuracy, using Bennett and Bergmann's type of criteria, between their model and the DRI model is quite striking.

Analysis of the Counterfactual Scenarios of the Transactions Model

Bennett and Bergmann simulate their model through three different sets of policy environments: (1) a fiscal-monetary set of simulations with a ± 5% tax surcharge constituting the fiscal policy, and a ± 5% change in bank reserves constituting the monetary policy; (2) a 20% reduction in indirect business taxes; and (3) a wage subsidy via a 20% tax credit for new employees. All simulations are performed over the 1973-1975 sample period to contrast with the observed pattern of the macroeconomy.

The effects of the various fiscal-monetary simulations are in the directions one might expect: a tax cut with constant monetary policy increases real GNP in each year; under an easy money policy the tax cut raises GNP even more, and under a tight money policy less.

The magnitude of the effects are, however, rather startling. Under the tax cut, federal personal taxes are cut 5%; on national income accounts basis, that would have been about $5.4 billion in 1973. *Real* GNP by the fourth quarter of 1973 is $18 billion higher than actual GNP, and by fourth quarter of 1975, real GNP is $114 billion higher. A tax cut combined with easy money policy would have raised real GNP by $220 billion. The corresponding nominal figures would be about 13% higher in fourth quarter 1975.

The implied multipliers are huge compared to those in the econometric models. For example the Chase quarterly model has a 3 quarter real GNP multiplier for individual tax cuts of 1.23, and a 9 quarter GNP multiplier of 1.6; the DRI quarterly model has a 4 quarter real GNP multiplier for individual tax cuts of 1.4, and an 8 quarter real GNP multiplier of 2.0. The Transactions Model's simulation results suggest a 3 quarter real GNP multiplier of 3.4, and an 8 quarter real GNP multiplier of 5.8. It is difficult to imagine that these effects, admittedly during a tumultuous time in the U.S. economic history, would actually occur.

The results of the wage subsidy program are also in the direction one might expect; the targeted tax credit for those "hard-to-employ" appears to be more effective in decreasing the unemployment rate than the general tax credit. The Transactions Model is more versatile than the various quarterly models in being able to analyze possible policy initiatives.

Summary

The Transactions Model is an ambitious and interesting approach to the macroprediction problem. Because it is disaggregated and entertains more "realistic" assumptions than available macromodels, it holds out to the policymaker an impressive set of advantages.

However, at this stage of its development, I believe it would be premature to argue that it be used in lieu of available quarterly models. The model may suffer from being improperly estimated, and on a within-sample period basis, does an inferior job of tracking important macrovariables when compared to a commonly used, aggregative quarterly macromodel. In addition, the predictive power of the model needs to be established beyond the 1973-1975 sample period.

2

EXPERIMENTS WITH FISCAL POLICY PARAMETERS ON A MICRO TO MACRO MODEL OF THE SWEDISH ECONOMY

Gunnar Eliasson

INTRODUCTION

The Swedish micro to macro model was originally conceived as a device to study inflation at the micro market level and the relationships between inflation, profits, investment, and growth.* To accomplish this, we needed to specify the decision process at the firm level. A realistic short- and long-run supply determination of the individual firm was considered necessary. We needed explicitly modeled market mechanisms rather than rigid aggregation functions only. In fact, the micro to macro approach would make very little sense without an explicit market process. We needed quite elaborate short period-to-period feedback links through the markets to picture price-volume interactions. Finally, we had to bring everything up to the macro, national accounts, level for three reasons:

1. The complete micro to macro data-base system had to be consistent at the macro level. For this, substantial modifications of existing macro data bases assembled by the Swedish Central Bureau of Statistics were necessary. Lack of complete micro data information required that we fill in the holes with "synthetic" information in the form of "chopped up" aggregates.

2. Since we have had to gather the micro (firm) data ourselves, we have begun with a 100% synthetic firm micro data base that adds up to correct totals to get a head start with both experiments and calibration (we prefer that term to "estima-

*The project would have been impossible without the generous back up of technical skills from IBM Sweden, a partner in this research venture.

Several persons have been actively involved in this project at various times. In particular I would like to mention Gösta Olavi, IBM Sweden, who has provided indispensable and efficient support on the mathematical and programming side, as well as Louise Ahlström and Thomas Lindberg, at IUI, who have been responsible for putting together and adjusting the data base to the format of the model.

tion") of the model. This synthetic data base is being gradually replaced by real-firm data for completing the model.

3. Some important test variables will be historic time series on macro aggregates, like GNP, industrial investments, and others (see tables 2.3 and 2.4).

With this model properly set up, one will find that it is possible to study problems other than the ones mentioned above. More particularly we have added two quite general objectives: to study the "conflict" between short-term allocative efficiency and the stability of the entire system (or long-term efficiency), and to study the effects on industrial structure from exogenous influences such as relative price changes in world markets and technology changes.

Short-term allocative efficiency refers to the speed at which volume adjustments occur in response to market price signals. Long-term efficiency or stability depends upon how reliable these short-term market signals are for long-term decision making and/or how they are corrected and interpreted by individual firms, especially in the context of investment decisions. It follows that the more orderly is market price formation, the more reliable are price signals. However, the ups and downs in relative and absolute prices in the model depend on volume responses to past relative and absolute price changes and other factors. We will be able to watch the consequences of this when we replace the Swedish payroll tax completely with a value-added tax in one of the experiments to be reported on below.

Structural changes in the micro specified sectors occur endogenously in response to relative price changes in the sense that a number of coefficients in a corresponding macro model, like capital and labor elasticities in the production function, export price elasticities, and so on, would *not* be constant.

The empirical part of this paper, which reports a series of experiments on tax parameter changes, will illustrate part of this potential. Before this, however, we will give a verbal and diagrammatical presentation of the entire model. Emphasis is placed on the handling of the tax system in the model. We will also give some statistical highlights of the Swedish tax system.

THE MODEL

At the macro level the Swedish micro to macro model appears as a 10-sector, quarterly Leontief-Keynesian system, complemented with a quite sophisticated household (nonlinear) expenditure system with habit formation and saving being determined simultaneously with overall spending.[1] A macro monetary sector is fully integrated with the rest of the model. Four of the 10 sectors hold a number of individual firms, which compete with one another in the product, labor, and money markets.

---

[1] A complete mathematical specification of an earlier simpler version of the model and a partial mathematical write-up of the model used here are found in Eliasson (1976b).

Over time the economy operates under a "soft" exogenous, upper technology constraint. New, superior technology is brought in by way of endogenous investment. Hence economic growth is endogenous. Rates of return of individual firms, determined endogenously, are key variables in determining investment and growth.

Two basic ideas underlie this project. First, we are not interested in predicting more detail. Our concern is with understanding behavior at the macro level in the first place. We believe that more micro information is called for to explain macro behavior properly. Hence, we also need to study and to know the covariance structure of our micro units (firms), especially when it comes to getting our micro specifications right. We expect a realistic micro-founded model to possess macro properties that are not exhibited by conventional macro models. If we think our assumptions are right, we should put a corresponding belief in the realism of these unconventional properties. Right or wrong is a genuine empirical question, and the only truly scientific response to it is to go out and check.[2] The reader will have the opportunity to decide for himself as he proceeds.

Second, we believe that entering more information by more detailed breakdown of sectors tends to cut across decision units in a very arbitrary way and very soon meets with impossible problems in statistical measurement. Rather, we have opted for choosing the decision unit (the firm) as the economic agent and the observation unit. This makes it possible to model market processes explicitly at the micro level and to join micro and macro theory in a very natural way. Above all, however, this approach opens up a wealth of high-quality statistical micro information for direct use in improving our understanding of economic phenomena at the macro level.

The micro firm model is a generalized planning-realization model that is a combination of the well-known Cyert and March (1963) and Modigliani and Cohen (1961) models and some later elaborations of these ideas by myself (Eliasson, 1969). It also draws heavily on empirical information on business economic planning systems in U.S. and European firms (Eliasson, 1976a). If the firm model is simplified far enough it collapses into the classical model of one firm that is a unit with one production function facing a set of prices given from the outside. One novelty in this model is that the actions of all firms together in labor and product markets determine prices in a sequential manner. Since the model cannot be solved for these prices each period, there exists no equilibrium position of the economy where all firms have edged themselves into input-output combinations where marginal conditions are fulfilled. Rather, if they try too hard or if the market pushes them too hard (i.e., if the market allocation mechanism is too fact and efficient), the system becomes unstable.

On the output side the model simulates life cycles of individual firms (production, employment, prices, wages, profit and loss statements, cash flow balances,

---

[2]This means that the next stage of model development will be predominantly devoted to enlarging and refining the micro data base. See below.

balance sheets, etc.) according to the definitions we prescribe. On the production side there is a complete GNP breakdown on 10 sectors with an explicit aggregation from micro to macro in the four sectors inhabited by real firms. There is also a conventional breakdown of the GNP components from the demand side. All real transactions are traced on the money side and complete financial accounts are printed out for control purposes. At this time financial flows do not yet exert a feedback effect on the real side through an endogenous interest determination and/or through financial "quantity" constraints.

The model as it now stands can be loaded with data from any industrialized country[3] provided the statistical information required at this stage is available and provided some primary production sectors like agriculture do not play a heavy role in the economy. To explain how close to or how far from a representation of Swedish reality we are, we have to be more explicit.

Macro System

Figure 2.1 exhibits the macro flows of the model as it now stands. The production system makes up the center of the diagram. The four sectors RAW, IMED, DUR, and NDUR (see notes to Figure 2.1), are inhabited by individual firms in a way to be described in the next section. These sectors account for most of industrial output. Of the remaining sectors, the service sector and the government sector are indicated by Z and GOV respectively and are treated as ordinary macro input-output sectors in the model. Five additional input-output sectors are explicit in the same way in the model. These sectors—agriculture, mining, oil, construction, and electricity generation—are all placed in the box OTHER production. Output in these sectors is endogenously determined in an indirect way through total demand (i.e., there is no capacity constraint), exhibited to the right in Figure 2.1.

Total demand is determined by wages and salaries and dividends and so on in the consumption or expenditure system from the left in the upper part of the diagram. Total production is added up at the bottom of the diagram and the total system, finally, is supplied with imports from the left-hand part. The import and export rates of each market move over time in response to the domestic and foreign price differentials. At the export side this takes place at the level of the individual firm (see below).

There is an explicit micro (between firms) labor market (upper part of Figure 2.1) and an explicit product market between firms and between firms and households (middle and left-hand part of Figure 2.1). The market processes are explained in more detail below.

Total household demand is determined in a macro Stone-type expenditure system with a Friedman-type permanent income specification by adding up (a) wage payments in each individual firm; (b) wage payments for each of the other production sectors; (c) transfer payments; and (d) capital income. Then, income taxes are

[3] See, e.g., Albrecht (1978a), who has entered U.S. macro data into the Swedish model.

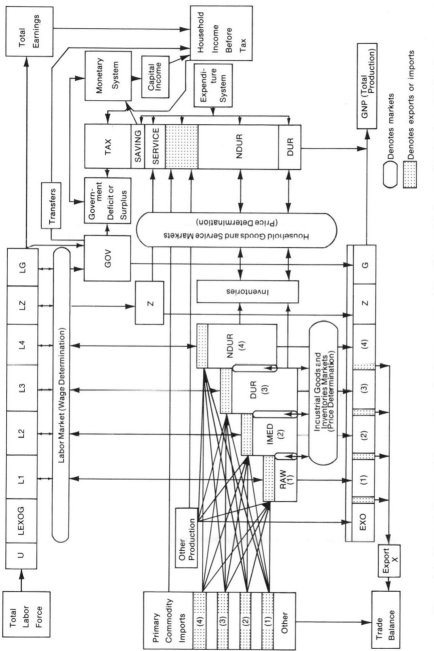

Figure 2.1. *Macro delivery and income determination structure of Swedish model. Sectors (Markets): 1. RAW = Raw material production; 2. IMED = Intermediate goods production; 3. DUR = Durable household and investment goods production; 4. NDUR = Consumer, nondurable goods production.*

subtracted to get disposable income. In this expenditure system, saving is determined simultaneously with consumption. There is a nonlinear tradeoff over time
between saving and purchases of household durable goods in which the real return
to saving and the unemployment situation play a crucial role. Furthermore, the
household savings plan is guided by a desire to maintain a certain real cash balance,
determined by household income and modified by the situation in the labor market
(precautionary motive) and the real rate of return to saving. Space does not allow
us to present more detail here.[4]

Government demand is indirectly exogenous in the sense that government
employment is entered exogenously. We then use the share of total government
purchases and final demand from the Swedish input-output tables to derive total
government demand. We should observe here that the government includes state
and local governments. It also includes the obligatory, supplementary pension
scheme, a circumstance that is of importance for the tax experiments to be reported
on below. In this sense the government sector includes what in Sweden is called
the "consolidated public sector."

The tax system will be described in more detail below. The model is planned
to include a monetary system in the near future. The empirical applications reported
below do not incorporate monetary effects. For this reason we abstain from presenting the monetary sector here.

The Firm Decision Model (Micro)

The novel part of this model is the business-firm sector and the way it combines through markets with the macro structure. In this section we will give a brief
presentation of the individual-firm model. To a large extent it draws on an earlier
interview study of business planning practices (Eliasson, 1976a).

Each of the four markets holds a variable number of firms. The data of all
firms add up to the total from Swedish national accounts statistics. This means that
after "real" firms have been entered into the data base, there always remains a dummy in each market (the difference between the market total and the sum of firms).
This dummy either remains and is treated as one firm or is split into several synthetic
firms (see later paragraph on data base).

For the time being there is only one price in each market. We have entered
this simplification for practical reasons. There is no way to collect price data on the
products of individual firms. This means that firms technically compete with one
another with their profit margins.[5] In the labor market, on the other hand, wage
levels can differ among firms. We assume, however, that labor is homogenous. Until
labor input has been made heterogenous at some later phase, this means that each
firm has its own homogenous wage level each period and that uneven income distributions for micro specified sectors, that can be reproduced for each period if we
so wish, depend on a slow and imperfect labor market arbitrage.

---

[4] The reader is referred to Eliasson (1976b).
[5] We plan to enter explicit market imperfections at some later time.

Figure 2.2 gives a view of the individual-firm model. At starting time, each firm is initialized with its own set of historical data and a set of data that describe its position at a point in time referred to as the positional data matrix. We call this process "initialization," as displayed on the left-hand side of Figure 2.2. The historical input vector consists of sales, market prices, wages, and profit margins.

In the EXP module, historical prices, wages, and sales are translated into expectations for the next year and the next quarter. Price and wage expectations remain fixed during each quarter. Sales expectations only serve as a first trial step in the search for a production plan each quarter.

Similarly, in the profit-targeting module, historic profit margins are translated into profit-margin targets for the next period. Profit targets can be revised from quarter to quarter. We have, however, entered the predominant practice among firms to try to stay within their annually budgeted profit targets throughout the budget year by making revisions very slowly. Similarly, profit targets are modeled to change quite slowly from year to year, while sales, price, and wage expectations may shift more rapidly in response to sudden changes in exogenous variables.

We have used conventional smoothing formulae with linear and quadratic error correction devices in the expectations and profit-targeting modules. The quadratic correction has been entered to allow for a tendency to risk aversion in markets where prices fluctuate a lot.[6] These modules have presented many problems in numerical specification. In the long run, however, we hope to be able to draw directly on internal firm data for a subsample of firms.

The firm model has deliberately been designed to mimic internal planning processes in a business firm. The use of profit-margin targets based on historic profit-margin targets performance for instance reflects frequent business practice. The

---

[6] Simplifying somewhat, the expectations function looks as follows:

$$HIST(\tau) = \lambda_1 *HIST(\tau) + (1 - \lambda_1) * \tau$$
$$HIST(DEV) = \lambda_2 * HIST(DEV) + (1 - \lambda_2) * [\tau - EXP(\tau)]$$
$$HIST(DEV2) = \lambda_3 *HIST(DEV2) + (1 - \lambda_3) * [\tau - EXP(\tau)]^2$$
$$EXP(\tau) = HIST(\tau) + a * HIST(DEV) + \beta * \sqrt{HIST(DEV2)}$$

where $0 \leq \lambda_i \leq 1$

$$DEV = [\tau - EXP(\tau)]$$
$$DEV2 = [\tau - EXP(\tau)]^2$$

*represents a multiplication sign, and := is "make equal to" in Algol. Expectations on τ, called $EXP_{(\tau)}$, are generated out of the firms' own experience as determined by the conventional smoothing formulae combined with a quadratic learning function.

So far we have tried once to estimate some of the individual firm coefficients above and several other coefficients by direct interviewing of executive staff people in one very large Swedish firm. The results turned out very successful in terms of improving historic tracking performance of data for the same firm. Further efforts of this kind are currently planned. To this has been added the possibility to impose an exogenous adjustment of expectations in individual firms. The profit-targeting function used in the model is very similar in form to $HIST_{(\tau)}$ above. The possibility of adjusting targets exogenously has also been added here as well as a device used sometimes in formalized profit-targeting systems in U.S. firms, namely always to raise targets slightly above what has been arrived at in the budgeting process (the maintain or improve principle, MIP) (Eliasson, 1976a, 236 ff.). For further detail on specification see Eliasson (1976b).

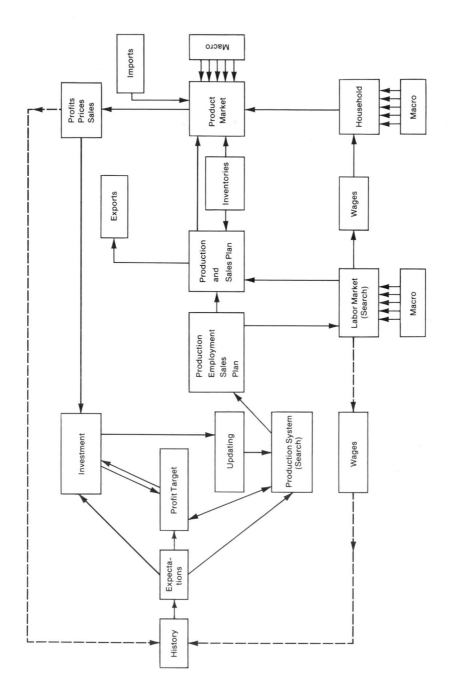

Figure 2.2. *Business decision system (one firm).*

stepwise decision sequence in Figure 2.2, furthermore, very much captures the iterative planning-realization-reporting round of the budget process. The model exhibits the common method of *not* carrying the iterations around several times each period to approximate profit maximization but rather stopping when profit margins compatible with long-term profit performance of the past are met. Another typical feature is to conclude the planning sequence at the left-hand side of Figure 2.2 with an internally inconsistent decision (budget) to be "corrected" in the realization phase or the next planning round.[7] The profit-margin target replaces the profit-maximizing assumption when it comes to determining, among other things, the output volume each period. The model allows a grading of the intensity by which the firm tries to improve its profit position each period. We can, if we so wish, approximate profit-maximizing behavior in a static sense by pushing up margin targets above what has been historically accomplished under the restriction that expected profits in each firm, in money terms, each period (quarter) do not diminish. We cannot, however, solve the system for maximum profits. It is important to note here that the "maintain or improve profit-margin principle (MIP)" that we apply gives rise to firm behavior that is often quite similar to, but also sometimes substantially different from, that of the maximizing firm.[8]

Price and wage expectations are fed into the individual firm production system, illustrated in Figure 2.3. Each firm is placed somewhere within its individual production frontier, that is a function of effective labor input $QFR(L)$.[9] Sales expectations determine the first step only. Each firm undertakes to search each quarter for a new labor input and output combination that satisfies its profit targets.

It would again take too long to describe in detail how this search goes on. Suffice it to say that there has been an effort to mimic the stepwise tradeoff that takes place between the sales, production, and the controller's departments in a firm before a short-term plan is reached, as described in an interview study of 60 firms that has stretched over more than 5 years (Eliasson, 1976a). One feature, that to my knowledge is very realistic and should be there is a "soft" upper capacity constraint (not shown in Figure 2.3). When under unusually tough market pressure, firms can "try harder" (within a limit) and raise productivity in order to maintain profit targets as described above. When the firm has found a satisfactory labor input-output combination based on expected prices and wages, it has a provisional recruitment plan and searches for additional labor in the labor market or it attempts to lay off labor (see below).

The production frontier $QFR(L)$ in turn shifts from quarter to quarter owing to new investment and depreciation of old output capacity. There is a volume and a quality aspect to investment. Simplifying somewhat, the volume effect moves $QTOP$ in the diagram upwards, while improved quality (higher performance) of in-

---

[7] See further in Eliasson (1976a, especially chapter 9 and supplement 6).

[8] See the discussion in Eliasson (1976a, pp. 236 ff. and pp. 258 ff.; and 1977).

[9] To see how $QFR(L)$ is determined, see the paragraph on the data base below.

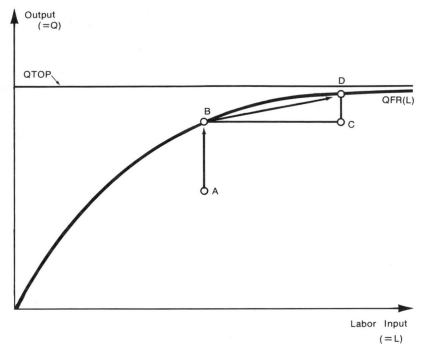

Figure 2.3. *Production system (one firm). The function describing the production system of one firm at one point in time is QFR = QTOP · (1 = e^{−γL}). How this function is estimated and how it shifts in time in response to investment is described in Eliasson (1976b, chapter 4) and in Albrecht (1978b).*

vestments bends the curve (makes it more convex). Improvement of the quality of equipment is determined by an increase in labor productivity of new investment over the productivity for the vintage investment of the period before. This rate of increase is entered exogenously by assumption and constitutes the technology constraint. New technology is entered through new investment and old equipment (measured as potential capacity in each firm, *QTOP* in Figure 2.3) depreciates at an exogenously determined rate. "Average technology" is a weighted average of past and new technology and determines the curvature of $QFR(L)$.[10] All this takes place in each firm in each quarter.

[10] Capacity to produce is expressed in terms of *QFR(L)* in Figure 2.3. Roughly speaking, new technology enters through an exogenous upgrading of λ (see Figure 2.3) by merging the old and the new (additional) *QFR(L)* through an harmonic average. We prefer to work with a production system with capacity expressed as potential output and no explicit aggregate measure of capital stock. The reason is that the estimation procedure is geared to direct use of individual-firm data on the format of each firm's own internal accounting and planning system. There one seldom or never meets with the concept of aggregate capital stock (see Eliasson, 1976a). The mere fact that *QFR(L)* shifts by investment of course means that one can define a measure of capital stock in terms of our system. If we do so, a somewhat generalized CES-type production function can be shown to appear (see Eliasson, 1978, pp. 63-65).

Investment is determined by a profit plow-back formula, complemented with a propensity to borrow that depends linearly on the difference between the nominal rate of return of the firm and the nominal interest rate. Total cash inflow so determined, net of mandatory claims on finance from dividends and current assets, defines the potential investment budget. Actual investment spending is adjusted downward from this upper limit depending on the degree of unused capacity. This is fairly straightforward and needs no further explanation here.[11] We are planning to formulate a more intricate long-term investment planning-financing model that is compatible with the present structure of the rest of the model but is more in keeping with the planning format of individual firms. Since this is not yet ready we do not describe it here.[12]

Markets

Once production search is terminated, the firm has a preliminary production and recruitment plan. It lays off people if the plan says so or enters the labor market in competition with all other firms (Figure 2.2, middle, bottom). Each firm can get what it needs or less, and the production plan has to be revised downward accordingly.

In the process, wages have been determined in the labor market. Firms search randomly within a more or less restricted market domain. If they find the pool of unemployed, they get what they need at their offering wage (a fraction of the expected wage increase). If they raid another firm, both compare offering wages and one of them has to adjust partially its wage level. A raiding firm offering a higher wage level gets what it demands up to a limit.

Wages feed into the household demand system and affect total product demand as described before.

In the middle of Figure 2.2, the production plan is transformed into a sales plan. Part of sales are channeled off to foreign markets, the fraction being dependent upon relative foreign/domestic price differentials.

After each firm has checked its final goods inventory situation to see to what extent it deviates from desired levels, it presents households (together with other firms in the market and import competition) with a price-volume offer of its products. Offering price in the first round again is based on the expected price.

Competitive imports flow in at a rate (of total supplies) that depends on the relative foreign/domestic price differential. Households respond by telling how much they want to buy at the offered price and trading goes on for a while. Households calculate their expenditure pattern at each offered relative price vector via the household demand system. Firms check against their individual profit targets to decide how much they will charge to supply these volumes. After a predetermined number of iterations prices are set, and firms adjust their volumes and inventories.

---

[11] It is based more or less directly on a generalized version of the Meyer and Kuh (1957) residual funds-accelerator theory as formulated and estimated in Eliasson (1969).

[12] This part is designed but not coded. See Eliasson (1976b, chapter 3).

Quarterly prices, profits, and sales flow back leftwards in the upper part of Figure 2.2 and wages flow in the lower part, all are then incorporated as historic data. A new quarterly round begins.

At each period, endogenous prices can be used as weights to compute an aggregate volume index. Similarly, in each period endogenously determined volumes can be used as weights to compute an aggregate price index.

Summing Up

It is impossible to explain all the algorithms of the model here[13]. To illustrate, let us define a subset $[\Theta]$ of endogenous variables (micro or macro) that we are interested in, say those macro variables that are studied in the tax experiments and listed vertically in tables 2.3 and 2.4 (*W, PDOM, M,...*).

Each of these variables chosen (and others as well) can be represented by a very general function.

$$\Theta = \Gamma(X).$$

This function is very complex and is not at all well behaved. It is generally not continuous and differentiable. Most of the theoretical and empirical work of this project consists of ascertaining the properties of Γ at various points in X space. This work is now going on and its empirical side will dominate the next phase of the project (see below). To get a feeling for the properties of Γ let us divide (X) into subsets of variables:

$X1$: hierarchial ordering of algorithms, illustrated diagrammatically in figures 2.1 and 2.2.

$X2$: structural (technical) parameters. Macro parameters and identities. Coefficients that are kept constant throughout simulation or are varied exogenously.

$X3$: time reaction parameters[14] (measuring how the individual firm transforms its price, wage, and sales information into expectations, how fast it changes its exports ratio in response to foreign-domestic price differentials, how it reacts when raiding or being raided in the labor market, how it determines its offering wages and prices, the number of searches it is allowed in labor and product markets, and so on in all 20 parameters).

$X4$: starting positional data matrix (micro and macro). Exogenous.

$X5$: historic input matrix. Exogenous until starting time.

---

[13] For this the reader is referred to Eliasson (1976b).

[14] A computer algorithm to estimate these parameters is defined in Eliasson and Olavi (1978). All the $X3$ parameters are listed and described there.

$X6$:   policy parameters (e.g., the nominal tax rates to be experimented with in this paper).

$X7$:   other exogenous input variables.

The $\Theta = \Gamma(X)$ structure of the model is graphically illustrated in Figure 2.4. If we look at one algorithm, at one particular point in time, we will find that most decisions in the model respond directly to classical expected price differentials (market disequilibrium) leading to an expected improvement in business profits in the short run as well as in the long run, that will be realized *ex post*, if not countered by aggregate market response. The general target of a business unit in the model is to maintain or improve its expected profit margin (MIP) position, and to stop responding when certain criteria are satisfied and/or when a certain amount of time has elapsed. These price-reaction functions are very simply expressed. But they are numerous, and when all interaction within a period (a quarter) is over most Θ will have become functions of most X and past Θ. This complexity is further increased when we move from period to period.

Hence the causal ordering of the entire system at the micro level ($X1$) is important to understand the entire model economy at work and the simulation results. The decision structure within the firm, as depicted in Figure 2.2, and the search order in the labor and product markets are most important. Profit targeting, for instance, has a strong impact on cyclical as well as long-run growth, properties of the entire system. Feeding back information from the employment or inventory parts of the system means less intensive enforcement of targets and results in very different behavior. Similarly, some simple experiments have shown that the way we loop together the sales planning, inventories, and product market blocks in Figure 2.2 can generate very different cyclical patterns. The core of the cyclical as well as growth processes of the model is defined by the links (over time and within Figure 2.2) between expectations and profit targeting on the one hand and wage setting in the labor market and investment determination on the other. Any change in the interlinking of these modules would strongly impact the behavior of the system. Perhaps the most illustrative example is when we close off labor market search between groups of firms or markets entirely. If relative product prices in foreign markets (exogenous) develop differently, a very uneven labor income distribution soon develops between closed-off sectors, and profit as well as total growth patterns changes significantly. This "theoretical" property alone emphasizes the importance of the market pricing process in the behavior of total economic systems and the need for more empirical research in this area. On the internal planning and decision structure of the firm the empirical specification is as well founded as it can be, owing to a 5-year interview study (Eliasson, 1976b) that preceded this project and that has strongly influenced the design of the firm model. On the market side the availability of relevant, systematized information is embarrassingly scanty. This means that an effort to become more knowledgeable about wage setting and mobility in the labor market at the micro level is planned and will be designed on the format of the model.

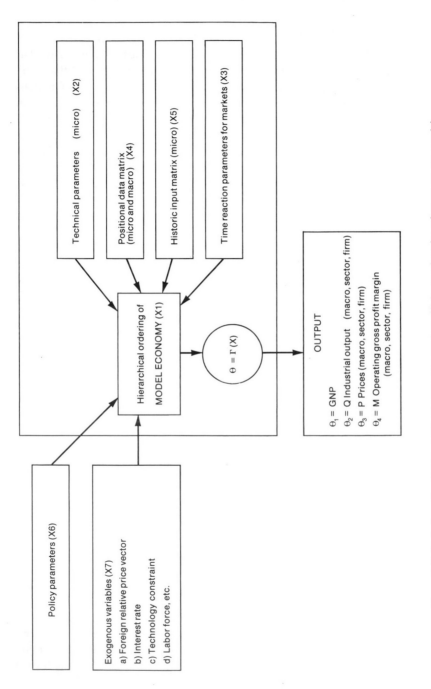

Figure 2.4. *Ordering of variables, policy parameters, and coefficients of entire micro to macro model.*

Technical parameters (micro) (X2)

Positional data matrix (micro and macro) (X4)

Historic input matrix (micro) (X5)

Time reaction parameters for markets (X3)

Hierarchical ordering of MODEL ECONOMY (X1)

$\Theta = \Gamma(X)$

Policy parameters (X6)

Exogenous variables (X7)
a) Foreign relative price vector
b) Interest rate
c) Technology constraint
d) Labor force, etc.

OUTPUT

Θ_1 = GNP
Θ_2 = Q Industrial output (macro, sector, firm)
Θ_3 = P Prices (macro, sector, firm)
Θ_4 = M Operating gross profit margin (macro, sector, firm)

The Tax System and the Public Sector

Figure 2.5 shows how the public sector interacts with the rest of the model via its taxes, transfers, spending, and borrowing (lending).

Firm profits are taxed at the individual firm level and we apply calculated effective tax rates to account for Swedish fiscal depreciation rules. Likewise the payroll tax (*WTAX*) is applied as wages are paid out. We here use the nominal rates on a properly specified tax base.

Similarly the value-added tax (*VATAX*) is applied at the going rate when the households purchase goods.

The problem of relevant specification refers mainly to the income tax (*ITAX*), and its progressiveness, as well as to transfer payments (*TRANS*). The model is equipped with a macro income tax function estimated by a simulation method in

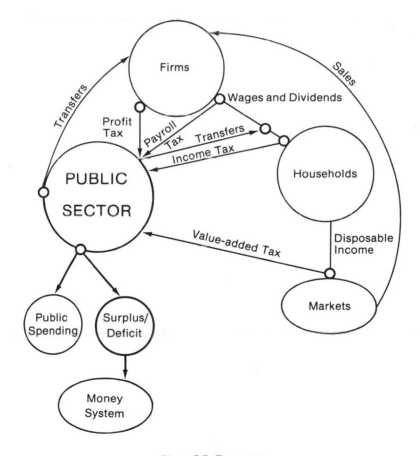

Figure 2.5. *Tax system.*

the highly disaggregated tax model developed by Jakobsson and Normann (1974). The tax rate function is of the following form:

$$TXI = \frac{ITAX}{L*W} = A \cdot W^{e-1},$$

where L is the number of taxpayers; W is average "total" income; A is a tax parameter (exogenous); and e is a tax elasticity representing the degree of progression.[15]

With these notations the average income tax paid will be $A \cdot W^e$. By entering A and e exogenously for each year, the fraction TXI of income paid as income tax will depend on how much income is endogenously generated in the model. Hence, varying the value-added or payroll tax or the $TRANS$ rates will exercise a feedback effect on total household income both through the whole economic system and through the $ITAX$ function above.[16]

Similarly $TRANS$ payments are entered exogenously as a fraction of total public expenditure. It should be noted here that in Sweden some transfer payments are subject to income taxation (e.g., pensions), and some are not. We disregard this and apply a uniform income tax rate on all taxable income each period. All transfer payments are treated as taxable income in the model to keep detail within limits. It should not affect the empirical results to be reported.

We should also remember that the public sector includes the large obligatory, supplementary pension scheme, which means that payments to and from the pension (ATP) fund are treated as payroll taxes and transfer payments respectively.

---

[15] e can be written $e = \frac{m}{t}$, where m = marginal tax rate and t = average tax rate.

[16] An inconsistent experimental design that we enacted by mistake illustrates some macro properties of the model system quite well. The scales of the Swedish income tax system are now indexed. During inflationary times like the 1970s absurd things occur if the scales are not frequently adjusted. This has been done several times since 1970. The inflation rate is endogenous. These corrections (in the model) have to be entered through e in the above TXI function. We forgot to enter such a correction after 1976 in a 20-year experiment that started in 1968. A gradual slowdown in total economic growth occurred; not extreme, but unexpected, and it led us to look for the reason. We found a rapidly decreasing current, after tax income inflow into the household sector, and a tremendous public budgetary surplus piling up and being deposited in the money system. (Public employment and expenditures were fixed in volume terms.) Household private consumption was still being maintained at high levels but at a diminishing growth rate. Why? Households were simply borrowing back the public surplus at the going interest rate to maintain their living standards. In the current version of the model the only hindrance to borrowing is the upward drift in the interest rate that occurs if total demand for funds grows faster than total supply of funds. Interest costs are fully tax deductible in the model as well as in Sweden. The slight slowdown in growth in private consumption was dictated by the permanent income or habit-formation part of the household expenditure system that determines how fast households reduce their addicted consumption levels, that are in turn determined by past consumption levels. This reduction was strongly dampened by the efficient inflation and income tax hedge that borrowing constitutes in the Swedish tax world, a hedge that is also effectively enjoyed by income earners possessing highly valued and mortgageable property. This property of the entire model system was never thought of in advance. With the right set of assumptions one should, however, expect to find it there.

TRANS also includes unemployment compensation, assumed to be 60% of the current average wage and available to all unemployed.

To give the reader an idea of the dimensions of the Swedish tax world, Table 2.1 presents the financial relations of two families with the public sector in 1969 and 1975. In both cases there are two children and only one income earner. We have chosen the average income of a skilled (male) worker and a well-paid salaried worker with a before-tax income about twice that of the worker.

Data Base

Even though fairly simple in outline, the model requires an enormous amount of data and numerical specifications by virtue of the number of micro agents. The

Table 2.1
Swedish Taxes (thousand Swedish Crowns[a])

	A		B		C	
					Taxes on Salaried Worker's Marginal Income above	
	Skilled Blue-Collar Worker		Well-Paid Salaried Worker		Skilled Blue-Collar Worker	
	1969	1975	1969	1975	1969	1975
Annual wage (salary), cost to firm	28.5	56	63	118	+34.5	+62
After deduction of payroll tax (WTAX)	25.5	45	57	100		
Income tax (ITAX)	7	14	24	52		
Transfer income (TRANS)	4	7	2	3		
DISPOSABLE INCOME	22	38	35	51	+13	+13
Disposable income as % of wage cost (1) above	77%	68%	56%	44%	38%	21%
Savings ratio[b] (macro), %	3%	10%	3%	10%	3%	10%
Value-added tax (VATAX), % on consumption expenditure	10%	15%	10%	15%	10%	15%
Returned to firms in the form of demand, in % of total amount paid out	67%	52%	49%	33%	35%	16%

Note: Column C gives the same information as in the preceding columns but tax rates, etc., are calculated on the extra income the salaried worker earned *above* the skilled blue-collar worker, or 118 - 56 = 62 thousand crowns in 1975.

[a] 1 Swedish Crown = $0.21 on January 24, 1978.

[b] The same average savings ratio for each year has been applied throughout columns A, B, and C. Savings data for different income groups or estimates on marginal savings ratios are not available.

full potential of the model in this respect (for instance "tailor-made" parameter specifications of individual firms) will not be utilized until far into the future.

All numerical specifications required by the model are more or less directly observable. All these needed data are not currently available. Since the start of the theoretical part of the project, however, a parallel data-base project has been going on that aims at gathering the necessary information eventually. The idea of this model has been to formulate it on the format of national accounts statistics at the macro level and internal accounting systems of the firm at the micro level. We believe that potential access to high-quality firm data bases and "technical" coefficients will compensate handsomely in the long run for our current estimating problems (see below). To run the model over historic time, however, we now lack large amounts of the required data, and substitute solutions have had to be resorted to. Also, some of the required data on expectations are currently not being collected. There is no good conventional method of estimating the parameters of the expectations functions, except by direct questioning of firms.

Parallel to the start of work on the model, a data-gathering process began. The annual planning survey of the Federation of Swedish Industries (Albrecht, 1978a) was designed on the format of the model in 1975 and in close contact with firms. We now have a 3-year time series on a large number of individual decision units with more than 200 employees in Swedish manufacturing.

The sample consists of approximately 250 units that are "measured" each of the three years. Among other things this survey collects data on the coordinates of points A, B, and D in Figure 2.3. This information allows us to approximate the production frontier $QFR(L)$ at initialization for each firm.[17] In a few years we should have enough time series data to estimate the relationships between investment and γ and $QTOP$ for individual firms as well.

A parallel project to collect a detailed data bank on the 40 largest Swedish corporations has been carried out at the Industrial Institute for Economic and Social Research (IUI). We will also be able to draw on two other IUI studies to handle the foreign operations of these firms. (Space does not allow for more detail on the micro data bases to be presented here.)

To be complete, we also need a matching and consistent macro data base to define the operating levels of the model in terms of Swedish national accounts statistics.

One thing that we have learned from work on this model is that a consistent demand and production measurement system is imperative for the proper functioning of a model with many linkages across firms and over time. It has been necessary to make substantial adjustments in the official Swedish statistics to obtain satisfactory consistency in this respect.[18] We have found that high quality in the measurement system becomes imperative especially when we introduce inter-firm markets and inventories with input-output coefficients entered exogenously.

---

[17] See Eliasson (1976b, p. 116) and Albrecht (1978b).
[18] See Ahlström (1978).

Such exogenous coefficients from official statistical sources have been found not to be consistent with the rest of the data base.

The macro data base has been prepared simultaneously with the model. This has not been possible for the micro data base. To be able to start experimenting with the model and to calibrate it against historic time series data, an interim synthetic firm data base has been put together. This data base currently consists of a very small number of real firms and split-up macro aggregates for each market. Whenever we have had the information on cross-sectional features, we have entered it. The experiments to be reported on below have been run on this mostly synthetic, micro data base that (for historic time) adds up to Swedish national accounts statistics supplemented with available cross-sectional information. On the estimation side, most of the parameters have been ascertained in the form of ratios from direct measurement. This goes for all the input-output coefficients. Each firm in one market has the same input-output structure on the purchasing side, even though the ratio of purchases to value added varies between firms.[19]

The household demand system is a modified version of a Stone-type expenditure system (1954). We rely on somewhat modified parameter estimates on such a system on Swedish macro data from Dahlman and Klevmarken (1971). These parameters are entered as *a priori* hypotheses. The system has a habit-formation feature for each consumption category which very much rests on the same idea as the permanent-income hypothesis. A simultaneous handling of saving and stocks of consumer durables has been added as a novelty. It should be recalled here that modeling short-period change at the micro level rids us of a number of coefficients that normally appear in macro models. They are replaced by sequential orderings and feedbacks. The estimation problem centers on the 20 time-reaction parameters called $X3$ and exemplified above. We will be able to estimate some of them for individual firms in the future by conventional econometric techniques.

For the time being, there is only one way to ascertain them—by trial and error experiments and checks against macro data (manually or by automated computer algorithms).[20] It sometimes (not often) happens that we find double or multiple parameter combinations that satisfy test criteria, and we cannot discriminate between them, except by *a priori* judgment. This is very time-consuming work. (It is also true that an element of subjectivity enters in a more manifest way than is apparent in conventional econometric work. I would like to add as a personal note, however, that in large-scale modeling of this kind, experience and judgment should take priority over mechanical, statistical procedure, whenever possible.) It is easy to understand how important it is to have a high-quality and consistent statistical base to work from, since this data base contains most of the numerical specification that determines the properties of the entire model economy.

I believe that this should give the flavor of the current empirical status of

---

[19] My experience is that firms do not have the kind of internal accounting system that makes direct questioning on their I/0 coefficients meaningful.

[20] See Eliasson and Olavi (1978).

model work. Much has been done, and the model, I believe, can give empirically valid answers to some questions. For the time being the model is capable of generating 5- to 20-year growth trends on real exogenous input data for a spectrum of macro variables with satisfactory accuracy as measured by closeness of fit (R^2s), and not badly for sectoral change. It traces price, wage, and profit cycles well[21] when run on real foreign price input for the various markets. We are currently somewhat uncertain about its capability of catching short-period (quarter-to-quarter and year-to-year) change well. We do not yet know whether unsatisfactory cyclical tracking depends on data-base inconsistencies at starting time (initialization), erroneous parameter specification, or lack of proper cyclical specification in some heavy exogenous input variables.[22] One satisfactory feature of the model, however, is that the 20 parameters can be grouped into some that operate only (or roughly so) on long-term trends, some that affect cycles only, and a residual group that affects both dimensions. One additional piece of observational evidence, which is comforting as regards realism on the cyclical side, is that exogenous step impulses (not large ones) in exogenous variables and policy parameters tend to spin off gradually dampened 4- to 6-year cycles in the entire economy. This property also has a bearing on the experiments to follow.

TAXES, BUSINESS-CYCLE POLICY AND INDUSTRIAL STRUCTURE: APPLICATIONS OF THE SWEDISH MICRO TO MACRO MODEL

Properties of the Model

We have chosen to present here a series of fiscal policy experiments on the entire model as described before, and more particularly those on the Swedish tax system. This should be of special interest for two reasons. First, the share of total resources taken out by the public sector (50% of GNP in 1976), which is partly used up and partly redistributed, is one of the highest in the world. This means that even minor modifications in the tax structure may have sizable effects upon the economy. Second, the very heaviness of the average tax burden raises particular problems of tax evasion and control. For that reason there has been an extensive discussion about modifying the tax system or even changing it drastically.

We will study the effects on growth, inflation, and industrial structure of a shift in emphasis from one tax type to another. To keep the number of pages down we will limit ourselves to two tax categories, the value-added tax (*VATAX*) and the payroll tax (*WTAX*).

---

[21] An illustration of this will appear in the next 1978 English edition of the IUI Current Research Project Report.

[22] For instance, public transfer payments to the household sector have been entered as the average fraction of total public spending 1965-1975 each year due to lack of consistently specified data. Hence there is no policy cycle in public transfer payments and the corresponding cyclical impact is absent.

We will also carry out a sensitivity analysis to study the relative importance of the two fiscal parameters. The simulation results will be compared with those of our current reference case, which tracks the growth paths of the variables studied 1968-1975 satisfactorily for this experimental purpose. The model has been loaded with the actual nominal tax parameters for the period 1968 through 1975, and all fiscal and other economic data have been correctly and consistently entered at the micro firm level and at the national accounts level at starting time. We should recall that numerical consistency throughout at starting time has been found to be a crucial prerequisite for the proper functioning of the model. We recall that the model forecasts historical, long-run growth trends of major macro variables well and prices, wages, and profits quite well both in the short and the long runs. We think that we can fairly safely say that the results indicate what would have happened to the Swedish economy over the 8-year period 1968 through 1975 if this or that fiscal measure had been enacted as described. We are, however, somewhat uncertain about the quarter-to-quarter effects and will not report such information except for illustrative purposes.

Recall again that the model, being a disequilibrium system, responds quite differently to policy measures or whatever exogenous disturbances it is subjected to, depending upon its positional description when this happens. This is a most desirable property. The problem is only to see to it that the data set that positions the model economy initially in 1969 and the exogenous inputs it runs on are consistently and relevantly specified. The year 1969 witnessed the recovery phase of a business cycle that peaked in 1970.

There are three important systems properties that we should mention before we proceed, since they explain some unexpected experimental results. First, under normal circumstances most firms hoard labor to some extent (see Figure 2.3). This means that firms experiencing a demand increase can increase supplies and productivity simultaneously for a while. This is a very typical cyclical phenomenon from reality. Only on the production frontier does productivity decrease as more labor is recruited to work with less productive machinery (above *B* in Figure 2.3). We have learned from model experiments that individual firms only seldom operate on that end of their production frontiers, and these experimental results seem to be supported by preliminary evidence from the planning survey of the Federation of Swedish Industries. Second, we have mentioned that an exogenous step impulse tends to spin off a 4- to 6-year cycle in the model system. This means that the system will behave according to the Le Chatelier principle at least in some time dimensions. The initial effect in one direction will reverse itself through an endogenous counter-response of the system. These properties are conventionally assumed away in the mainstream of economic modeling: in Keynesian models through the absence of supply feedbacks and in neoclassical models through assumed perfect foresight or a fixed rate of return. The property arises in this model through expectations, a disturbed market price signaling system, and the effects on the rate of return on investment and capacity growth. Third, one particularly important instance of this property is that sudden, unexpected inflationary shocks (not necessarily large ones) tend to have a long-lasting downward effect on economic growth after an initial positive effect.[23] It is difficult to test for this property directly. So far my own attempts to ascertain its relevance[24] have only turned out evidence in the affirmative. The property has been suggested by Professor Friedman in his 1976 Nobel lecture. Some econometric models report negative growth coefficients for the rate of change in the rate of inflation but this is too crude a test for the phenomenon we are discussing to be more than slightly helpful. Cagan's (1974) early report that common stock maintains its real value in the long run but that "stocks may take many years to catch up to an inflationary episode" (15 years is the median time in an international comparison) in fact refers more directly to the machinery in our model and hence is more supportive.

Throughout this empirical application we will be particularly interested in the effects of a fiscal parameter change on the absolute price level (inflation), total output, and the functional income distribution (profits and wages shares).[25]

We have defined most policy changes as a once-and-for-all step change throughout, and we allow the model economy to run for 7 years on that step input under the *ceteris paribus* assumption that firms are assumed to know about the duration of the policy when it has been enacted. For a short period like 2 or 3 years that is a reasonable assumption to make. However, over a longer time period, like 7 years, one may doubt the meaningfulness of the same assumption. For one thing, if bad effects are generated, a responsible government would enact new measures to counter them. This tends to make the *ceteris paribus* assumption somewhat strange for longer periods.

It is contrary to the logic of the model to reason in terms of a relative or absolute price change somewhere, assuming activity levels to be unchanged. A *ceteris paribus* experiment of this kind would break the core of the business decision system described in Figure 2.2 and would require the elimination of the labor and market processes. Such experiments simply cannot be run on this model, a specification that is strongly supported by reality. Period-to-period interaction between price and volume changes is not negligible, and, as mentioned, this very property tends to generate long-term systems results that are sometimes unfamiliar to persons drawing on their experience with more conventional macro models.

One problem that we have relates this dynamic feature to a persistent property of the model that appeared after the inter-industry market and inventory system was introduced into the model. Particular and temporary disequilibrium situations tended to develop here and there during simulation runs. Some of these disequilib-

---

[23] These systems properties have been extensively investigated on an earlier version of the model in Eliasson (1978).

[24] Together with Dr. H. Genberg, Institute Universitaire de Hautes Etudes Internationales in Geneva. Some results will soon be reported. Also, cf. some earlier research on the rate of foreign-domestic price transmission in Genberg (1974).

[25] In analyzing these experiments I have been very fortunate in being able to draw directly on a recent IUI study (Normann and Södersten, 1978) that includes a broad analysis of the Swedish tax system.

rium positions could be interpreted as being "real" phenomena during the test period 1965-1975. However, most of our tedious calibration work has consisted in removing the cause of those temporary disequilibrium situations in the model that could not be interpreted as real ones. Our experience is that most of the bugs have been in the data-base input rather than among the parameters.

The important aspect of this feature for our simulation experiments is that if we enact a policy change that pushes economic development in new directions, new temporary disequilibrium situations tend to show up at unexpected places, being dependent in turn on the structure of the initial data base. This has been especially so when parameter changes are large and sudden. Such situations in turn tend to spin off not only new 4- to 6-year cycles (as mentioned earlier) but cycles the amplitude of which cumulates for a while until the system settles back to normal owing to an endogenous readjustment of the economic structure (the data base). The 7-year period is not always sufficient to allow all this to happen, and our sensitivity analysis offers some examples of the importance of disequilibrium positions. We will furthermore see from the final, controlled experiments, when one tax system is gradually replaced by another and when effects tend to cancel from period to period, that the disequilibrium effects are much smaller. This time the long-term seven-year experiment also makes more sense.

The numerical analysis on the model economy carried out so far tells us that when fed with a steady state exogenous input, total output keeps oscillating around an emerging steady state growth path. Similarly, the cycles generated by various shocks tend to fade away in the long run. This convergence is, however, very slow, and it depends critically upon the time it takes for profit rates to steady themselves. So far, however, the properties of the model in this respect have not been fully investigated, and definite conclusions will have to await further analysis.

Sensitivity Analysis

In the first round we will analyze the response pattern of a *ceteris paribus* change in two fiscal parameters, one by one. These parameters are payroll tax rate (TXW); and value-added tax rate ($TXVA$).

The fiscal parameters above denote tax rates. Transfer payments in the model are to households in the form of various sorts of public benefits and total public expenditures for labor and purchases of goods and services. This is a macro variable. We do not distinguish between various categories of payments and the economic effects of changes in their composition.[26] Transfer payments and such expenditures are in principle entered exogenously in volume terms. They will, however, be determined partially endogenously, since both wages and prices are endogenous.

This section on sensitivity analysis serves two purposes. For one thing it responds to highly topical questions referring to the power of payroll and value-added

---

[26] This has been done in a recent study on a macro model of the Leontief-Keynesian type also developed at the IUI. See Dahlberg and Jakobsson (1977).

tax changes as countercyclical measures and to the absolute incidence of the parameter change. As regards the payroll tax in particular, this is a somewhat controversial issue. Second, this section serves a pedagogical purpose. We will tell what happens in the model step by step when we enact the parameter change. This way we will demonstrate, for instance, that the results are by no means apparent from one or two critical assumptions.

Value-Added Tax (TXVA)

We first raised and lowered the value-added tax rate in 1969 with ± 2.5 and 5 percentage points, respectively. Since the value-added tax rate was 10% on purchases of goods in 1969, the larger parameter change was a substantial one.

The effects of the increase in the value-added tax rate are quite straightforward. The experiment can be regarded as a case of restrictive fiscal policymaking. There is no corresponding feedback through increased public spending. There is a negative and not very large GNP effect that stabilizes at around 2% from the third year for parameter changes between +2.5 and 5 percentage points (Figure 2.6 and also Table 2.2). Industrial output is affected similarly. The initial first year (2nd and 3rd quarter) effects in Figure 2.6 depend on the habit-formation hypothesis embedded in the consumption system. The lowered purchasing power of households due to the increase in the value-added tax is buffered through less saving in the first round. It

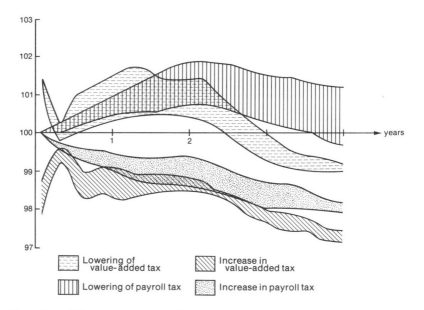

Figure 2.6. *GNP effects of value-added and payroll tax changes. Tax rate changes are up (and down) 2.5% and 5% respectively in the value-added tax case. The payroll tax has been increased and decreased so that the fiscal budget impact the first year is approximately the same as for the corresponding value-added tax change. Simulated results are shown as percentage of the corresponding values of the reference case.*

Table 2.2
Sensitivity Analysis with Value-added and Payroll Taxes

	GNP		Industrial Output (Q)		Industrial Employment (L)			CPI		Producer Prices (PDOM)		Wage Costs (W)		Profit Margins (M)	
	1969-1970	1969-1975	1969-1970	1969-1975	1969-1970	1969-1975	Year 7	1969-1970	1969-1975	1969-1970	1969-1975	1969-1970	1969-1975	1969-1970	1969-1975
VATAX															
+5[a]	98.5	97.5	98.4	97.6	98.1	97.8	100.1	104.6	104.4	105.3	106.0	100.1	94.4	100.6	109.3
−5	101.3	98.6	100.6	96.6	93.3	92.4	100.0	96.6	95.5	98.2	95.8	100.1	88.9	116.4	125.5
WTAX															
+5[a]	99.2	98.2	99.2	98.4	99.6	98.4	100.1	99.6	99.5	99.7	99.1	100.0	95.4	98.3	106.1
−5	101.0	101.2	101.0	100.9	100.3	100.7	100.0	100.3	100.3	100.5	100.8	100.0	99.6	102.1	102.0

Note:

W = Labor cost to firm (wages + all social charges incl. supplementary pension charge)

$PDOM$ = Domestic wholesale prices, industrial goods, incl. of $VATAX$

M = Operating gross profit margin

CPI = Consumer price index, incl. of $VATAX$

$PROD$ = Average labor productivity

Q = Industrial output

GNP = GNP

L = Labor input in industry; effective man-hours

$RSAVH$ = Household savings ratio out of disposable income

$INVFIX$ = Investment in industry in constant prices

$VATAX$ = Value-added tax (money terms)

$ITAX$ = Income tax, income earners (money terms)

$WTAX$ = Payroll tax including all social charges and ATP-charge (money terms)

$TXVA$

TXI = The corresponding nominal rates

TXW

If nothing else is said, all tables and figures are on index from where the endogenous variable reported (Q, $PROD$, etc.) is indexed with the reference run as the base. On a current basis: If $Q(1972) = 3.363$ in the reference run and $Q(1972) = 3.681$ in the experimental run, the index will say index = 3681/3363 × 100 = 109.5 (Diagrams). On an average basis: The indexes have been averaged from the beginning year 1969 to the year you read in the table.

[a] The payroll ($WTAX$) change has been graded so as to correspond to the corresponding value-added tax changes the first quarter.

73

is interesting to notice that the two parameter changes result in output effects of similar magnitude (see Figure 2.6). In both cases, the employment level is back to the initial level in year 7 (1975). The value-added tax rate increase (Table 2.2), furthermore, allows firms to push wage change (and temporarily employment) down, gradually realizing an improvement in the return to investment.

The surprise results come when we lower the value-added tax (expansive fiscal policy making). The first 2-year effect on industrial output and GNP is up. The GNP effect, however, extends for a somewhat longer period. Consumers spend more, and especially on goods from sectors 3 (durables) and 4, owing to a higher real disposable income. However, some of the increased purchasing power of households in the initial phase leaks into increased savings and some into more imports.

In the first round (2 years) exports are left fairly untouched (not shown). Since, however, firms do not lower their domestic prices (before value-added tax) by the full amount of the value-added tax rate change, they gain initially on the profit margin side. This is quite normal pricing behavior among firms. It is difficult to compensate for the tax by raising prices fast, and firms only reluctantly lower prices by the full amount of the reduction in the tax. This produces an assymmetrical profit response to value-added tax rate changes for the 7-year period of investigation that is supported by knowledge of firm pricing behavior. The higher price level (after tax) can be maintained for some time, and firms gain on selling more at home and relatively less in foreign markets. Export performance is coming down slowly from the third year and even though savings also decrease, the import effect persists. More import price competition hurts business profits, and firms begin to get tough on the wage side to satisfy their profit targets. The net impact is a worsened external balance, less domestic supplies in domestic markets (compared to the reference case) and a slowdown in industrial growth. Employment and real wages suffer in the medium term, but business profit margins are still maintained at a higher level at the end of the 7-year period, so the results correspond to quite rational responses on their part. We should note here that profit margins are on their way down strongly in 1975, probably to undershoot the reference case after a few years. This again underlines the new realistic and hence important feature of disequilibrium models of this kind. Depending upon initial conditions and the time period studied, the results may be very different. The possibility that the incidence and the allocation effects of changes in, for example, payroll tax rates may be very different depending on the cyclical situation is also emphasized in Normann and Södersten (1978, pp. 65 f). A deflationary spiral sets in from the fourth year that works counter to the initial fiscal measure. Firms come out all right with higher profit margins, but output suffers slightly. This deflationary cycle is just about to reverse itself at the end of the 7-year period. Note, also, that employment recovers faster than output, and the reason of course is a lowering of real wages.

The back side of this situation is a lower productivity growth than in the reference case. Quite in keeping with the dominant property of our model system, this dynamic reversal effect is stronger and faster the larger the initial parameter change. The reason is that the early overoptimism generated by the fiscal stimulant has created overexpansive output and recruitment plans. Since profit targets are based on excessive price and sales expectations, wage drift was allowed to occur without violating *ex ante* targets. Firms then experienced profit disappointments *ex post* and are consolidating their positions by releasing labor and pushing up profit margins at lower output levels. This is what normally happens in the early phases of a business recession, so in fact the initial boom created by the fiscal stimulus has generated its own "extra" slump after a few years, albeit a minor one.

These results may seem surprising to a reader more used to work with less dynamic macro models. The results reported on, however, only tell that growth is not the only way to maintain rates of return for firms, and when markets are not so competitive and when profits come easily, it may be better to slow down investment and growth. These results depend in part on the degree of competition in markets but also in part on the feedback, profit-targeting device (maintain or improve profits—MIP) in the firm model. As a result of improved profit performance, firms upgrade their targets and vice versa. This set of propositions is difficult to test owing to the long time dimension involved, but one has to remember at the same time that these unconventional results are conventionally assumed away in many econometric models. So there is no need to question the results except on empirical evidence to the contrary. A case in point here is Pratten's (1976) results from comparisons of matched Swedish and British firms. He found that while British firms were far below their Swedish counterparts in productivity and growth rates, they maintained systematically higher rates of return.

Again note (from Figure 2.6) the second quarter temporary reversal of the GNP effects. It depends partly on the fact that households do not adjust their consumption immediately to their lower or higher real purchasing power; they prefer to take part of the adjustment by way of their savings account.

Payroll Tax

We then raised and lowered the payroll tax[27] (*TXW*) by as many percentage points as needed to make the initial budget effect in the first quarter 1969 for the public sector equal to that in the value-added tax change above for each of the four cases in the table. This step change was then maintained as a percentage difference for the rest of the period, as in the earlier experiments.

This time the activity-level effects look more familiar. An increase in the payroll tax produces a negative output effect that tends to increase slowly over the experimental period. A lowering of the payroll tax produces a small but persistent plus effect on output. However, toward the end of the period, the process is begin-

----

[27]Note here that we have a very broad definition of the payroll tax. It includes all social charges together with the supplementary pension fee (the ATP charge) on total wages and salaries. The public sector is defined accordingly, making the supplementary pension system part of the government budget. However, to keep detail within limits we have allowed a misspecification to slip in. Public transfer payments to households are taxed as income, and this is not 100% correct. Since this is so in both the reference and the experimental runs, the difference is not more than marginally affected.

ning to reverse itself under the *ceteris paribus* assumption, and the gain is quite small in year 7.

Increasing the payroll tax without running up public expenditures simultaneously exercises a slight restraint on domestic prices, and the effect is the opposite when the tax is lowered. The initial effect on wage costs is nil in the sense that practically all the effect carries over to income earners in the form of lowered cash payments and very little carries forward to prices. Over the 7-year run wage costs are, however, further reduced relative to the reference case owing to a slowdown in economic growth but not in the inflation rate. These results may seem somewhat surprising considering earlier discussion of the incidence.

We should recall, however, that there is no assumption to guarantee this almost complete backward shifting of the payroll tax change to wages. The key assumption is that firms are keen on meeting their profit targets and do not bid up wage costs inclusive of payroll taxes to violate these targets. The uncertain element is to what extent profit target maintenance is enforced each period. We do not yet know. This is an empirical issue that relates to the specification of one of the crucial time reaction parameters ($X3$) mentioned in the model section. Available evidence (see below) suggests that a slight relaxation of the enforcement rate should be entered.

Business profit margins increase initially from a lowering of the payroll tax, owing to the positive output effect at no change in wage cost. Firms then strive to maintain these margins successfully. At the somewhat higher price level, and a slightly lowered output volume, real wages decrease over the 7-year period. Hence a lowering of the payroll tax seems capable of generating a very small growth effect through a slight increase in profit margins and investment.

On the other hand, raising the payroll tax seems to give rise to both faster and somewhat larger negative effects on output at no price increases, since the tax is shifted to wage earners quite fast again. The price level in fact comes down somewhat in the 7-year run. Even though business profits suffer initially, firms react strongly to counter this effect, and the long-term influence is higher rather than lower profit margins. This profit margin increase takes its time to generate more growth and employment through investment, and employment has just about recovered from the initial decrease in year 7. Again these results emerge under the assumption that the public sector does not use up its increased income by spending more. (See, however, below, when we move the payroll and value-added tax rate equally, but in opposing directions.)

The ways firms set and respond to their profit targets obviously are instrumental in producing the longer-term reversal of the initial effects that take place when policy creates a stimulus. In principle we believe that we have a very realistic specification of the operational functioning of profits in an economy. However, the profit-targeting device is also instrumental in producing the very fast carry-over (backwards) of payroll tax changes to wages and no carry-forward to prices at all. In the long run this is compatible with the results of Brittain (1972) and Vroman

(1974) but not with those of Leuthold (1975), who argues on the basis of U.S. data that the short-term incidence is *not* 100% on wage earners. Weitenberg (1969) finally reports (on the basis of a Dutch Central Planning Bureau model) that the medium-term incidence is all on wage earners but partly through backward shifting and partly through forward shifting to prices. We know from other empirical tests of the model that with the numerical specifications used here firms seem to be too fast and rational in pushing their profits up against their targets, so the incompatibility with the above-mentioned empirical results should rather be taken as a suggestion that further experimentation, checks, and fine-tuning of the model are needed on the short-term response before we can say that we know.

Finally note from Figure 2.6 that even though the average GNP effects over time are roughly the same, the quite different economic mechanisms at work generate different time profiles.

As a final check on the model we have rerun it with and without the temporary lowering of the value-added tax 2nd and 3rd quarters 1974 by 3 percentage points. Table 2.3 shows the effects on some macro variables. We note that the short-term GNP effect is of roughly the same magnitude as calculated elsewhere at the time of the real tax experiment. Even though the value-added tax is increased back again to the earlier level after 2 quarters, the output and employment effects do not cancel over the 2-year period. The price level effect in both directions is, however, almost simultaneous to the parameter change.

Substantial Modifications of the Swedish Tax System and Their Economic Effects

In the earlier sections we have analyzed the economic effects of differently sized countercyclical, fiscal parameter variations. In this section we are interested in the effects of a sizable modification of the tax system. Since the model runs on a market-price information-response system, where performance of the total economic system depends on the ability of agents (decision makers) to interpret these signals, we have to make major fiscal changes in a gradual way. Even so we should expect some economic effects of a negative nature to depend on disturbances in the infor-

Table 2.3
Effect of Temporary Lowering of Value-added Tax by 3 Percentage Points, 2nd and 3rd Quarters 1974

	After 2	4	8	12	quarters
GNP[a]	0	+0.3	+0.2	+0.3	Percentage points higher
Industrial employment	0	+0.4	+0.1	+0.2	Percentage points higher
Consumer price index (CPI) (incl. value-added tax)	−3	−0.1	−0.1	−0.1	Percentage points lower

[a] In *Industrikonjunkturen*, Spring 1974 (pp. 52-53), published *before* the temporary value-added tax change, the GNP effect of a 5-month reduction in the value-added tax was estimated at 0.2% on a 12-month basis.

mation system which demand a long time to learn and to correct for. This, no doubt, is a very relevant aspect of the problem we are about to study.[28]

Value-added and Payroll Taxes

We first have to look at a relatively minor shift in emphasis from a payroll to a value-added system (Table 2.4B) and vice versa (Table 2.4A). The experiment has been designed as a once-and-for-all change in 1969, graded so as to leave the total tax take of the public sector unchanged for the first period (= 1 quarter in 1969).

The relative speed of transmission of the incidence between the two tax types when moving from payroll toward more value-added taxes means that real purchasing power of the household—i.e., real wage costs to firms after payroll, income, and value-added tax—first increases and then decreases relative to the reference case. Over the entire period there is a slight increase in real (after all taxes) wages (103.8/ 102.7 $\approx$ 1.01) and vice versa moving in the opposite direction. It may be of interest to notice (Table 2.4A) that this time a somewhat different incidence pattern emerges compared to the earlier sensitivity analysis. There is now a net of *VATAX* producer price increase which in this case must be interpreted as a carry-forward incidence of the payroll tax. Also long-term wage costs increase. Just about the reverse happens when the tax change goes the opposite way (Table 2.4B), and these results are more in keeping with the empirical results referred to above.

Altogether the simulations so far suggest that there are no rules of thumb to tell beforehand to what extent the income earner carries the burden of or benefits from a tax change, when we allow for all interactions through markets in a total economic system like this model. (There is a fairly high probability that the simulations of reality are more complex.)

There is a slight upward drift in the general price level corrected for tax changes in final prices. However, the nominal wage cost level faced by firms comes down slightly and a small long-term improvement in profit margins occurs. Exports are left roughly unaffected in both the short and the long runs. There is very little long-run change in output and employment levels. Since household saving and business investment decrease, this obviously means an increased efficiency in the utilization of capital resources and an increase in rates of return.

As this is being written, the monetary system has not yet been integrated into the model. This means that the domestic rate of interest has been entered exoge-

---

[28] Individual decision makers (firms) in the model are equipped with a feedback learning mechanism for all their expectational signals that correct the interpretation of "new" signals asymptotically but quite fast. (See earlier description of micro part of model.) Very erratic disturbances that go on forever cannot be interpreted, however, and by definition the intelligibility of the market signaling system will then also be left forever in more or less disorder. However, if the change to a new system is smooth and means a steady and interpretable experience, the rules of interpretation can be relearned. We can then isolate the economic effects of the transition if we run the simulations long enough. We have not done that, because of time constraints and also because we then have to leave the domain of known historical experience (1969-1975) and interpret our results in a new, hypothetical economic environment. This is by no means easy.

Table 2.4
"Budget Neutral" Changes between Payroll and Value-added Tax Systems

	A Toward More Payroll Tax[a] (TWX up 0.05 and TXVA down 0.03 in 1969)		B Toward More Value-added Tax[a] (Vice versa)		C Value-added Tax Replaces Entire Payroll Tax, over 5-Year Period 1969-1974	
	Average 1969-70	Average 1969-75	Average 1969-70	Average 1969-75	Average 1969-70	Average 1969-75
W cost to firm	100.8	101.6	100.1	98.8	100.0	101.8
Take home W	95.7	96.5	105.1	103.8	104.2	115.5
PDOM	99.5	100.2	103.8	104.1	101.4	107.7
PDOM net of VATAX (to firm)	102.5	103.2	100.8	101.1	100.0	101.8
M	104.5	104.0	99.8	101.5	98.2	99.0
CPI	98.2	98.7	102.9	102.7	101.2	106.2
CPI net of VATAX	100.2	101.7	99.9	99.7	99.8	100.4
PROD	100.1	99.0	100.5	99.5	99.6	100.5
Q	100.3	100.3	98.8	99.6	100.2	99.9
GNP	100.9	101.0	98.8	98.7	100.0	100.1
L	100.0	101.3	98.4	100.0	100.6	99.4
RSAVH	126.7	109.5	68.3	91.3	143.3	119.0
INVFIX	110.0		106.9		100.5	94.1
EXPORTS	99.7	96.5	99.1	100.0	100.2	100.0
Sector Effects (Q)						
RAW (1)	99.8	100.0	99.1	101.0	99.9	100.6
IMED (2)	100.0	99.2	99.5	99.8	100.1	99.7
DUR (3)	99.9	98.1	99.0	99.8	100.4	100.6
NDUR (4)	101.1	103.2	97.0	98.0	100.0	98.9

Note: For explanation of the scaling see Table 2.2.
[a]Parameter change determined so that fiscal neutrality obtained first period (quarter) in A and B and approximately obtained for 5-year period in C. For all remaining periods, differences in the total public tax intake depend on changes in the various tax bases caused by the parameter changes.

nously with the same values in the experiment and in the reference case. The adjustment of the interest rate and the consequent financial flows due to lowered household saving and business investment spending has not been allowed to work itself properly through the entire economic system. One would expect monetary feedback here. It is at present impossible to say how large this feedback will be. We will have to leave this problem open, as most other students who have examined it have done. Since all cash flows associated with real transactions have been 100% booked, we know, in an accounting sense, that whatever is not invested accumulates as idle financial balances. What is gained in efficiency in the business sector idles away at no use elsewhere.

The case is just about reversed when we shift emphasis from the value-added tax toward the payroll tax (Table 2.4A). A slight lowering of real wages, a slight increase in volumes (Q, GNP, and L), more saving and more investment in business take place. Again, as in the reversed case, however, profit margins increase, and this time somewhat more. Note that both the price ($PDOM$) and profit-margin effects take place during the first two years and are then maintained.

The export effect is not symmetrical. Only in this case there is a slow, long-term decrease of expected direction. We noted earlier that feedback effects via foreign trade tended to affect domestic activity levels.

The extra expansion in output is less than what one would expect from the extra investment increase. Rather than piling up idle money balances, this time idle capacity increases in the business sector, and rates of return do not increase. Again this indicates that a money system should have had a chance to exercise a balancing effect here through interest rates. Compared to the United States, however, the Swedish credit market does not perform in any prominent way as a market when it comes to allocating resources (Teigen, 1976). So this result (as well as the opposite one above) should in no way be considered empirically wrong *a priori*.

When we now turn to a complete replacement of the payroll tax system with a value-added tax system over a five-year period, we are engineering a very smooth transition (Table 2.4C). The experiment is roughly controlled in the sense that the public budget and deficit (surplus) is only affected in a minor way throughout the 5-year transition period. Even though a substantial change occurs in the long run, one should recognize that each of the annual changes (steps) taken is smaller than the once-and-for-all changes in the earlier two experiments. Hence, the individual disturbances generated in markets are smaller this time. This is quite in keeping with a persistent property of our model. It tells us that rough policy treatment of the economy might generate adverse effects. It also suggests that the grading of a substantial institutional change may be important, since if it is done in a nice and smooth way, decision makers in the markets get a chance to learn how to reinterpret the signals.

The effects on price and wage levels are more pronounced, but the substantial institutional change generates no major economic disturbances. Activity levels, besides some small short-term turbulence (not shown), are left roughly unchanged over the 7-year period. This effect of course depends on the approximately unchanged budget position of the public sector. The reversed replacement (from value-added to payroll tax, not shown) yields perfectly symmetrical results almost throughout.

The only surprise is that compared to the small fiscal change in Table 2.4A and B, household saving this time responds in an opposite and expected way. The changeover to a value-added tax system, taking away the payroll tax, stimulates saving. And this is what we should expect, since household saving is now left un-taxed. We note again, however, that increased household saving does not generate more investment volume in industry. It is not needed, since output is left unchanged. Furthermore profit margins slide down a bit.

The increased household savings rate depends on the ambition of households to maintain real-transactions cash balances because of the higher inflation and wage rates. The increased savings accumulate in the monetary system for some use that we do not know in the present version of the model.

Structural Effects of General Fiscal Parameter Changes

We know intuitively that no general policy measure can be enacted in a struc-turally heterogenous economy leaving the structure unchanged. Conventional macro models of whatever type normally do not lend themselves easily to the analysis of such effects. To us a definition of structural change would be in terms of micro firm units and imply that the coefficients in a "corresponding" macro relationship, say a production or investment function, would not remain unchanged over time. Underneath this variability one would find a changing size distribution among firms or a shift in rate of return, investment, and growth relationships of such a na-ture that the aggregation assumptions that underlie the macro model would vary with the experimental design. In this context we will, however, have to limit our-selves to a few comments on and illustrations of the changes in relative sectoral sizes brought about by the above fiscal parameter changes via relative changes in price and rate of return among individual firms in the markets. Again we confine ourselves to a 7-year time span. To discern any sectoral effects we need fairly strong and, as it turns out, sudden parameter changes. We can of course discuss at length what is re-quired for a policy change to be general. We will find that there are no true measures. Every possible one is selective in one way or another. The value-added tax hits the households (we believe), and the payroll tax hits the firms, and so on. Such param-eter changes are, however, conventionally called "general" and we will do so as well.

This time we are interested in how the effects of one "general measure" are carried through the economic system, but not between various broadly defined macro aggregates (output, CPI, wages, profits, etc.). Rather we want to see how the whole carry-over (or through) process diversifies unevenly between firms and sub-production sectors. It should also be of interest to study and discuss how much of this selective impact between sectors depends on the degree of "selectivity" that af-fects the parameter change although this would take us too far in this context. One could easily imagine, for instance, that a change from a value-added tax to a payroll tax system is apt to hurt (or help) consumer goods producers more than other sectors. But no one knows for sure.

One thing is clear from Table 2.4. When we make a sudden, once-and-for-all change from a payroll tax system to a value-added tax system, it hits household demand. As a consequence, growth comes down in the consumption goods sector (4) and increases in the typical export sectors. This relative growth reallocation between sectors is, of course, reinforced by the fact that investment spending also decreases somewhat, and as a consequence total industrial output growth decreases as well.

When the tax system is changed in the other direction, the effects are also reversed. This time the differential impact "looks" somewhat bigger in the table, since the positive saving-investment growth effect combines with the direct consumption effect to favor growth in the consumer goods sector.

However, one should note that raised demand in domestic households as well as raised investment demand is partly at the expense of export deliveries. In the beginning, imports increase, as should be expected, and the foreign balance deteriorates (not shown). In the longer term both exports and imports balance off better in the downward direction compared to the reference case, but the long-term outcome is a worsened external balance.

Lower payroll taxes and a higher value-added tax as compensation, however, mean a long-term improvement in the external balance, even though both exports and imports decrease for the first few years.

Interestingly enough, however, when we allow for a smooth gradual replacement of the entire payroll tax system by a more dominant value-added tax system (Table 2.4 and Figure 2.7) we can study reactions of similar direction *during* the seven-year period. But the internal dynamics of the system this time are efficient enough to make relative prices and activity levels interact in such a way that the initial relative price structure is approximately restored toward the end of the simulation run and so is industrial structure, as measured by relative growth rates in output. Again, we should remember that if actors in the markets are allowed enough time to reinterpret the new signals, no adverse effects on total growth need occur. The long-term effect on the structure of the value-added and payroll tax switch seems to be fairly "neutral."[29]

When the direction of fiscal change is reversed (the payroll tax gradually replaces the value-added tax) the effects mentioned above are also reversed (see Figure 2.7). It is worth noting that the combined effect on household durable goods demand and business investment goods demand (both goods categories being supplied by sector 3 in Figure 2.7) is slightly positive on the average when going from payroll to a value-added tax system and vice versa. Furthermore, when the effect is negative, the cyclical swings generated in the durable goods producing sectors are much stronger. And, since the effect on total industrial production for the same

---

[29] We should note in this context that the foreign relative price spectrum is the same in all experiments, and the government and households do not change their demand patterns except through endogenous feedback by the fiscal parameter changes.

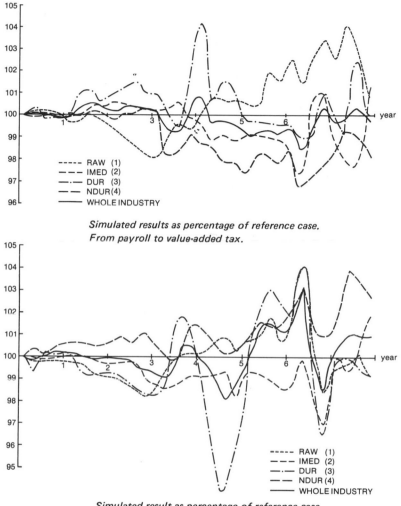

Simulated results as percentage of reference case.
From payroll to value-added tax.

Simulated result as percentage of reference case.
From value-added to payroll tax.

Figure 2.7. *Sector effects on industrial output of complete change of tax over 5-year period. (See Table 2.4.)*

period (the fiscal change going both ways) is approximately nil, part of the explanation lies in a reshuffling of investment spending patterns between firms and sectors. None of these results are *a priori* obvious but depend on the numerical specifications of the model.

We note that the changes in growth rates are quite small despite the large institutional change, and that initial sectoral balance is roughly restored by the end of the 7-year period. Furthermore, foreign trade plays an important role in the adjustment process, as witnessed by the opposite movements of the export sector 1 (raw materials) and the domestically oriented nondurable, consumer goods sector 4. The two effects roughly cancel over time, and movements are in opposing directions and depend upon the direction of the fiscal change.

Figure 2.8 finally, gives a micro illustration from a new experiment clarifying what takes place within the model. We have chosen to raise transfer payments to households and the payroll tax simultaneously in 1969 so that the initial (1969) public budgetary impact is approximately nil.[30] The expected change would be a shift in total consumption demand towards relatively more private consumption. Domestic producers of consumption goods would benefit, and typical export sectors would be hurt. How exactly business investment spending is affected cannot be foretold by simple reasoning. Since the fiscal parameter change is sudden, substantial, and of a one-shot type, we expect a negative total growth effect over the seven-year period owing to market disturbances. This conclusion is on the basis of our experience from interpreting tables 2.2 and 2.4. This would suggest less investment spending, but perhaps more household spending on durable goods. Increasing transfer payments while increasing the payroll tax, however, is very similar to lowering the value-added and increasing the payroll tax. Tables 2.3 and 2.4 would thus suggest slightly more investment and hence more growth in sector 3.

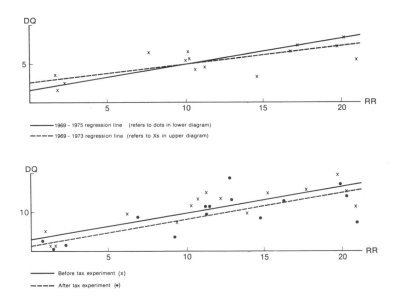

Figure 2.8. *Relationship between rates of return (RR) and growth in output (DQ) of individual firms in the market. The upper graph is a comparison between periods 1969-1973 and 1969-1975, 5- and 7-year averages respectively. The lower graph covers the period 1969-1975, before and after combined transfer payments (to households) and payroll tax change.*

[30] And so that each opposing parameter change roughly corresponds to a change in the value-added tax rate of 5 percentage points (see Table 2.2).

The outcome is not exactly as anticipated. Over the 7-year period both the raw materials sector and the investment and consumer goods sectors lose growth on the average, as a result of the fiscal change. For raw materials producers this would be considered normal as they export the bulk of their output. They do not benefit indirectly from the transfer payment to households, but are nevertheless affected by the payroll tax increase. For investment goods producers output decreases slightly, although earlier results suggest a slight demand benefit. For consumer goods the result is odd at first sight. The result is, however, due to the fact that firms respond fast to the payroll tax increase by reducing cash wage payments after payroll tax, so the net effect on disposable income (after tax and transfer payments), everything considered, is a reduction.

Figure 2.8 illustrates what has happened at the micro level for the investment goods sector. The upper scatter and dashed line in Figure 2.8 give the relationship between average rates of return and output growth rates for the 5-year period 1969-1973. There is a fairly strong relationship, as should be expected. When the same relationship is extended to 1975, the regression line (shown by the solid line in the upper and the dashed line in the lower part of the figure) pivots for two reasons. The high-performance (in terms of profitability) firms essentially stay with their relatively higher rates of return for the longer period. Since they reached that position in the inflationary period 1972-1973 and have plowed back profits in investment, and/or have borrowed more to invest because of the higher rate of return, the higher growth in capacity that occurs with a delay explains part of the pivoting. However, some of the firms in the low-performance end have suffered instead, owing to the wage drift induced by the generally higher inflation rate that they have to share. This reinforces the pivoting in the left-hand end of the diagram. The discriminating impact on firms in different performance brackets of sudden inflation bursts (1973 and 1974) followed by a sudden lowering of price increases (1975) is illustrated even better in Figure 2.9. The reason is that wage drift is governed by a margin of high-performance firms but spreads to all firms through the labor market. High-performance firms bid up wages to get more people to improve their profit position, so arrows above 10% rates of return in Figure 2.9 tend to go up and right. Low-performance firms have to take these wage increases in order not to lose people, and their rate-of-return position deteriorates. Arrows point upward and left in Figure 2.9.

When the fiscal change defined above is enacted, the effect is to shift down the whole cluster of (RR, DQ) points in Figure 2.8 (lower diagram) relative to what it would have been without the change. The same average rate of return for the 1969-1975 period is now associated with a lower average growth rate. The shift is in both dimensions, however, and the fiscal measure enacted both lowers the average growth rate for the sector and increases the rate of return. The reason is again indirectly clear from Figures 2.8 and 2.9. The two fiscal measures combined shift the composition of demand suddenly. Some firms are hurt and slow down their investment spending. Others benefit, but there is not time enough to catch up fully during the period, and total growth is lowered.

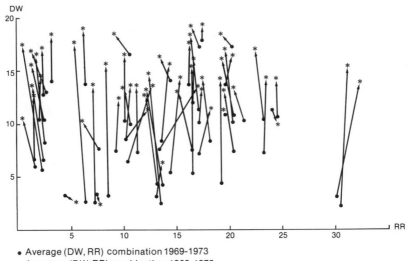

● Average (DW, RR) combination 1969-1973
∗ Average   (DW, RR) combination 1969-1975

Figure 2.9. *Rates of change in nominal wage costs to firms (DW) and real rates of return (RR) after inflationary period in investment goods sector. Arrows bind together individual firms and indicate directions of change.*

CONCLUSIONS AND PLANS FOR THE FUTURE

The analytical work performed so far on the total model system can be said to have produced an integrated picture of a total economy in operation that in some ways differs from what is conventionally believed. Among these effects are the seemingly different short-term and long-term responses of the entire model economy to a set of parameter changes. Other unusual effects are the responses of the system to disturbances in information signaling at the micro market level. Many of the effects mentioned have been suggested as empirically relevant in literature, but to my knowledge this spectrum of features has not been brought together in one explicit model system elsewhere. The core mechanisms that cause them to operate here are the explicit markets that integrate the micro (firm) and macro levels. Several of these properties have been illustrated in the tax experiments reported in this paper.

These results are of course highly conjectural. We have not yet been able to test and check the entire model to the extent that would make us willing to express ourselves with the confidence that is commonly displayed when results are reported from econometric models. The results that we have chosen to report, however, are such that we expect them to be able to weather quite well further testing by ourselves and others. In fact, further testing—or calibration—of the model system is the key word in our plans for the future.

The model system that we currently have consists of a series of more or less complete system versions. For the first 2½ years, the code of this model has been in a state of constant change. The most immediate plans call for calibrating the latest version with the monetary system and programming a long-term investment-financing system. No additional calibration will be needed, since this new module will be used only for some model firms with which we establish a direct interface between real firms and the model system. These firms will then supply their own data.

After this, it will be necessary to halt further mathematical development temporarily to allow the model to stabilize and us to understand its mathematical properties better.

The data base and the parameter sets still lack precision and quality in many important places (especially on the micro side), and the most important task after completion of the above model specification stages will be to improve and complete the data-base work.

Parallel with this we will start up a series of application experiments studying *inter alia* labor market mobility, wage setting, and economic growth; the effects on economic structure of relative price changes; the Keynesian-Monetarist controversy over growth and inflation; and the long-term effects on the Swedish economy of the massive subsidizing of firms in distress that is currently going on.

After this work has been done, we will decide to what extent it is worth while to improve further on the model's specifications.

DISCUSSION

Benjamin A. Okner

This paper by Professor Eliasson was somewhat surprising to me in a number of respects. Although I have spent a lot of time doing microsimulations in the past several years, I have always just assumed that the term "microsimulation" referred to microsimulation of the household sector. I think that both this paper and the conference in general are extremely useful because our attention has been directed to microsimulations involving other sectors of the economy—where, I am delighted to learn, there has been much progress in recent years.*

I would guess that it is only within the last five years or so that we have really started looking seriously at microdata simulations involving firms and other detail regarding the business sector. Yet, I think we have made substantial progress toward that future day when we will be able to generate our national income and product accounts on a microdata basis. Of course, when that occurs we will simply add up firm data to generate national income arising in the business sector; household data to generate that arising in the family household sector; and so forth. The great advantage of this latter approach is the possibility of disaggregating and combining information in different ways, each of which is most appropriate for specialized analyses.

It is clear from the papers that have been discussed at this conference that that day is not here yet. But I think we are going along the right path and more work and conferences of this type, where we can learn from one another, are clearly leading us in the right direction.

General Comments

I cannot deal in great depth with the technical aspects of the paper because I am unfamiliar with many of the institutional factors in Sweden and, of course,

*The author is grateful to Michael J. Kaufman for his extremely helpful comments, many of which are incorporated in this paper.

many of the relationships based on such factors are embedded in the Eliasson model. Nevertheless, it is quite clear from the paper that the main purpose of modeling the Swedish economy is to investigate changes in various policy parameters—inflation, growth, and various other things. It is also clear that "micro," as used in the title of the paper and in the model itself, refers to firms. The firms, of course, are embedded within industries—the major ones of which are the raw materials, intermediate goods, durable goods, and nondurable goods. Then the rest of the Swedish economy is dealt with primarily either exogenously or through the use of macro relationships. In a sense then, what we have in this model is a combination of both micro and macro relationships. It is hoped that when the model is solved and the various relationships aggregated, the results will add up to something resembling national totals for Sweden.

One thing that should be mentioned just as an aside is that while relationships are estimated on the basis of firm data, in the paper the author mentions that he hopes to add to national income and product figures. Of course, businesses do not keep their accounts on a national income and product accounts basis and therefore slight modifications will be needed if Professor Eliasson is to achieve this goal.

Eliasson's paper describes his efforts to use microdata to add to the stock of economic knowledge in an area that is surely one of the least developed and least satisfactory parts of modern macroeconomic theory: the branch dealing with the dynamic adjustment path of an economy in response to changes in monetary and fiscal policies. One of the main purposes of this model is to get an idea of the dynamic time path of variables such as unemployment and changes in the rate of inflation. I was genuinely interested in how Eliasson was planning to use macrodata to cast light on such issues. Unfortunately, my puzzlement was not abated after reading Eliasson's paper. In addition, one must also wonder how a model which includes a monetary sector only as an afterthought can explain inflation very well.

Specific Comments

The Model

The author states that, "Our concern is with understanding behavior at the macro level in the first place. We believe that more micro information is called for to explain macro behavior properly." An explanation of why Eliasson holds this position would be most desirable. On the same page he also states, "We expect a realistic micro-founded model to possess macro properties that are not exhibited by conventional macro models."

Unfortunately he does not spell out what he has in mind by his statements. Is it just the various kinds of over- and undershooting and the cyclical adjustment mechanism that comes out of his group's simulations? If so, these types of results can be easily derived from the familiar IS-LM framework with lags in the adjustment response. It is not clear whether this is what he is talking about or whether it is something else.

Further on, the author states, "At this time, financial flows do not yet exert a feedback effect on the real side through an endogenous interest determination and/or through financial 'quantity' constraints." Again, it is hard to understand how a model that neglects monetary policy, balance of payments adjustments, and so on, in this manner, can be very successful in predicting inflation in the long run.

The author also states that the model is a Keynesian-Leontief model. In the simplest version of such a model, the position of the economy is determined entirely by the behavior of aggregate demand. For example, if there is unemployment, the government can simply increase aggregate demand and get the economy back to full employment. However, such models generally have not been very successful in explaining inflation. Usually, some kind of supply-side constraint has to be added to introduce inflation into a Keynesian model. Yet, there is very little mention of any supply-side constraints whatever in the model—whether they be labor supply or capital supply.

It seems strange to have omitted supply-side constraints if the model is used to explain the dynamic path of the economy through time and the effects of fiscal policies on investment behavior.

Simulation Results

In the simulations reported in the paper, Eliasson considers the effect of various changes in the federal deficit on the aggregate behavior of the economy through time. Specifically, he considers an increase in the deficit caused by a decrease in payroll taxes and compares this with an equal increase caused by a decrease in consumption-type value-added taxes. He also examines the effect of increasing both taxes, which would reduce the federal deficit. A schematic representation of what these policies do to the time path of the economy is given in Figure 2.6. Quite interestingly, he finds that the GNP paths of the economy over time differ markedly when the changes are produced by different taxes, even though the effect on the deficit is the same.

If the simulations are accurate, these results are puzzling. Why should two tax policies that affect the deficit by the same amount have such different effects on the time path of the economy? This is not explained well in the text. Also in Figure 2.6, it appears as if lowering the payroll tax has a much longer-lasting effect; this raises the GNP level relative to what occurs when the value-added tax is lowered. This too is difficult to understand: If the long-run effect on the government deficit produced by the new tax policies is the same, the government will have to do an equal amount of borrowing in the capital market to finance its activities. With an identical amount of borrowing, there should be an identical amount of "crowding-out" of private investment in each case. On the other hand, if we are talking about substituting a value-added tax for a payroll tax in a full employment model, where the value-added tax is a consumption-type tax, it is possible that the "long-run" effect of this policy switch would be to increase the level of the GNP. This is because the switch to more reliance on consumption taxes would foster increased saving and hence capital formation and growth. But this is exactly the opposite of what Eliasson's simulations seem to indicate. Again, one is left wondering what in the structure of the model leads to the results that are reported.

The author indicates that, "As this is being written the monetary system has not yet been integrated into the model." This means that the domestic rate of interest has been entered exogenously with the same value in the experiment as in the reference case. The adjustment of the interest rate and consequent financial flows due to lower household saving and business spending has not been allowed to work itself through the entire economic system. Does this mean, in effect, that the monetary authorities are willing to supply any amount of money that is required to keep the nominal interest rate constant? If so, the consequent increases in the money supply should have a bearing on the amount of inflation caused by the policy changes. On the other hand, if the monetary authorities are not supplying sufficient amounts of money to keep interest rates pegged, one would expect interest-rate effects if the supply of saving is at all elastic. It is difficult to understand why the kind of disaggregation and micro work embodied in the Eliasson model is going to have much of a payoff in understanding the cyclical adjustment path of the economy if these supply effects are totally ignored in the model's basic structure.

I am further puzzled by the statement that, "The case is just about reversed when we shift emphasis from the value-added tax toward the payroll tax. A slight lowering of real wages, a slight increase in volumes, more saving and more investment in business take place." Apparently the value-added tax that Eliasson is talking about decreasing (relative to the payroll tax) is a value-added tax on consumption. Reducing the tax on consumption should lead to more consumption and less saving.

Eliasson should also elaborate on his comment that the Swedish credit market does not perform properly when it comes to allocating capital. I would have liked him to spell out for us what there is about the Swedish economy that causes this unusual effect.

Finally, the author states, "We note again, however, that increased household saving does not generate more investment volume in industry. It is not needed, since output is left unchanged." This result would seem to be possible, indeed, only if the credit market is not working properly and the rate of interest is not changing in such a way as to allow realized investment and realized saving to reach some equilibrium level. This result may also be related to the well-known deficiencies of some Keynesian models that concentrate only on aggregate demand.

Conclusion

In closing, it is important to note that Eliasson and his colleagues have constructed a model that attempts to deal with a very important problem—the behavior of the economy during its various cyclical phases. The model produces some rather interesting results (although they are not always explicable), and more work should be done to explain why these results are being produced. Also, the group's plans for future development of the model seem quite worth while. Eliasson is apparently thinking about how to incorporate financial effects directly into the model. This would be highly desirable. Apparently, he is also thinking about incorporating supply responses into his model, and this too would be an excellent extension.

DISCUSSION

Harold W. Watts

This model represents a still-early stage in the development of a very ambitious effort. The goal is to construct a model with micro elements that correspond to actual individual firms. The highly elaborated business sector is completed with macro components to form a full system that can simulate the entire Swedish economy on a quarterly basis. This approach contrasts and complements the models that place emphasis on detailed modeling of the household sector.

The model is not based on equilibrium principles for firm behavior. It depends instead on a recursive set of rules which aim at reaching targets that are similar to the "satisficing" behavior proposed by Simon (1959). By the process of "individualizing" each firm according to its actual behavior, current status, and self-described policies, there is the potential for a large amount of idiosyncratic behavior and corresponding points of model verification.

At present there is a limited amount of genuine individuality built into the firm structure, and the process of early validation and calibration has barely reached the point where the model can be regarded as a representation of the Swedish economy. The earliest simulations were called numerical exercises rather than serious experiments. The present application seems to be among the exercises which can both provide some evidence on the properties of the model and assert some tentative statements about how alternative policies will affect the Swedish economy.

The experiments involve variations of the payroll and value-added tax rates and evaluate the consequences over an eight-year time span covering 1968 through 1975. The sensitivity of the system to changes in the two tax rates is examined first, and then the consequences of substituting one for the other are examined. Finally, there is a simulation of a gradual but complete replacement of the payroll tax system by the value-added tax. It is useful to note that both taxes are important contributions to the overall high tax structure which characterizes the Swedish economy. Payroll taxes appear to range from 15-20% of wage costs (and are regressive with respect to wage levels) while the value-added tax amounted at 15% of household spending in 1975. Both rates were lower in 1968, but the two taxes are very important parts of the Swedish fiscal scheme.

It should be noted that the period 1968-1975 started in a recovery phase which reached a peak in 1970. This is only one of the "particularistic" features of the simulation that must be kept in mind when interpreting the results. As the author tells us, there are also some "bottlenecks" and similar sorts of imbalance that are produced when a major policy shift is abruptly introduced. While some of these may be reflections of what would have happened in that historical environment, they should not be associated with the policy for some other period—another history would produce its own particularistic set of imbalances.

I will not comment in detail on the results of the simulations because of my lack of familiarity with both the Swedish economy and the model's representation of it. It is interesting that tax reductions of either kind have a stimulating effect in the short run, but that in the longer run they lead to a less rapid rate of growth. Tax increases seem to depress growth both in the short and longer runs. Where one tax is substituted for the other, emphasis on value-added taxes tends to favor exports out of a reduced GNP and with increased profit margins. However, if the substitution takes place gradually, the effect on GNP disappears and there are slightly reduced profit margins. Price effects appear to be mostly due to the direct impact of the value-added tax.

It is difficult to know how much confidence to place in the findings without more information on the entire program of validation experiments. Before simulation results from the model will be widely persuasive, it is clear that the underlying assumptions behind the model need to be examined, the preliminary parameter estimates need to be scrutinized, and more policy experiments and attempts at forecasting or hindcasting outside the historical period used for "calibrating" the model need to be evaluated. Furthermore, the author readily admits the use of "a 100% synthetic firm micro data base" in the prototype model being reported on. Clearly, the model will become useful to policy analysts only after this data base has been replaced with actual data.

As mentioned previously, the emphasis of the model is on firm behavior, so comments will be limited to that phase of the work. It should be noted, however, that the firm microdata are imbedded in a full-blown macro model which includes household, government, and foreign trade sectors. The reliability of these other parts of the macro model contribute to the accuracy of the entire system, and consequently biases in these auxiliary parts of the model may offset or exacerbate biases in the producer sector.

The main assumption that drives the firm decision model is the "maintain or improve profit margin principle (MIP)" or, in other words, a particular type of satisficing behavior. Such behavior is not in general equivalent to profit maximization, and thus the usual neoclassical assumptions about wages, prices, and rents do not hold. An implicit assumption in the Eliasson MIP is the accounting period, which is not carefully specified. This period is crucial as real-life firms surely exhibit investment behavior in which short-term profits (or profit margins) are sacrificed for long-term returns.

The model is a vintage capital model in which all investment is assumed to be labor saving. The discussion seems to indicate that the rate of technical change is unique to the firm (which leads one to question its estimatability) and is exogenously specified. Furthermore an assumption of flexibility in terms of employee layoffs is assumed.

Finally, in a discussion of the robustness of the model, Eliasson points out that different assumptions and different parameter values can "generate very different cyclical patterns." Because the model allows so many parameters for each firm, it seems plausible to assume that estimates derived by any means (such as minimization of percentage error in aggregates such as GNP, employment, and so forth) will not be unique. If this is true, then the model results can only be evaluated on the basis of an *ex ante* judgment regarding the realizing of the assumptions and accuracy of the parameter values.

All in all, there appears to be a large amount of further improvement and testing on the agenda of the author, and I, for one, would be most interested in hearing about the progress in a few years. It is important to have a model with a highly disaggregated business sector, and this appears to be a promising approach to that objective.

3

CORPORATE AND PERSONAL TAX INTEGRATION IN THE UNITED STATES: SOME PRELIMINARY FINDINGS

Don Fullerton
A. Thomas King
John B. Shoven
John Whalley

INTRODUCTION

This paper analyzes four alternative plans for corporate and personal income tax integration in the United States.* A medium-scale, numerical, general equilibrium model of the U.S. economy and tax system is used to examine the combined distributional and efficiency impacts of these plans.[1] The results are considered provisional, however, since the model is rapidly evolving. This model integrates the U.S. tax system with consumer demand behavior by household and producer behavior by industry. The combined effects of alternative tax regimes on equilibrium prices and quantities are calculated using a variant of Scarf's algorithm.[2] Each of the integration plans considered is represented in model equivalent form prior to its incorporation. The analysis indicates that total integration of the personal and corporate income tax system would result in a static efficiency gain of around $6

*The previous version of this paper was presented at the Econometric Society Meetings in New York City, December 28, 1977. It is not for quotation without permission from the authors. The authors and this paper have greatly benefited from the comments and suggestions of Robert H. Haveman, Jon Kesselman, and Nicholas Kiefer.

[1] We gratefully acknowledge the financial support of the U.S. Treasury Department's Office of Tax Analysis in developing this model.

[2] The computational procedure is Merrill's algorithm (Merrill, 1972), similar to the well-documented Scarf technique (Scarf, 1973). Unlike Newton's or gradient methods, these algorithms are guaranteed to converge. An extremely large number of possible solutions are posited, and the algorithm provides rules which result in an efficient search through these possible answers. The present study builds on earlier applications of this methodology such as Shoven (1976).

billion (1973 dollars), and that partial integration would yield less. The plans differ in their distributional impacts.

We first discuss the objectives of corporate tax integration and describe the plans that we consider. Next we discuss the general equilibrium approach to the evaluation of corporate tax integration. We then set out the main characteristics of the current model and briefly list the major data sources. Finally we present the integration alternatives in model equivalent form and describe the preliminary results from our analyses.

OBJECTIVES OF TAX INTEGRATION AND THE GENERAL EQUILIBRIUM APPROACH

Objectives of Integration

Corporate and personal tax integration has been actively discussed in a number of countries for some years. Although several European countries now have integration plans in operation, this is not the case in the United States, where integration has been a major issue in recent tax reform discussion. Integration plans usually link individual income taxes to corporate profit taxes, but in the United States the integration concept has been widened to cover abolition and modification of corporate taxes with or without changes in personal income taxation.

Under the present personal income tax, stockholders pay taxes on dividends and on realized capital gains (at preferential rates) rather than on earnings per share. To the extent that retained earnings are capitalized into share values, a deferral and tax-rate advantage are given to stockholders. They receive an interest-free loan from the government of the amount of income tax liabilities on unrealized capital gains. The corporate income tax attempts to correct for these features through a separate tax on profits at the source, even though such a tax cannot wholly correct for these problems because the value of the advantages to each stockholder varies with his marginal income tax bracket and the holding period. This separate corporate tax leads to a number of problems. The first is "double" taxation of dividends; dividends are paid out of net of corporate tax profits and are further taxed under the personal income tax. This may reduce overall rates of return and adversely affect capital accumulation. The second problem is the impact on financing of investment. The efficiency of capital markets is impaired owing to the deferral and tax-rate advantage; firms can reinvest retained earnings in projects with a low yield and still earn a higher net of tax return than they would if their funds were distributed as dividends and reinvested elsewhere. Third, since only equity returns are subject to corporate taxes, there is a bias towards debt finance. Finally, the corporate tax introduces higher effective tax rates in some industries than others, owing to special provisions in corporate tax law and the varying degree to which industries are incorporated. These tax-rate differentials further disrupt an efficient allocation of capital. Integration plans seek to remove or mitigate these features.

General Equilibrium Analysis and Corporate Tax Integration

The objectives of plans to integrate corporate and personal income taxes are clear: to improve the efficiency of the economy through beneficial resource reallocation and to change the tax distribution in favor of certain groups. Actual effects may differ from intended effects of integration plans, however, and evaluation is made difficult by the interaction of the effects involved. Direct effects of corporate tax changes can be offset or reinforced by the induced changes in behavior.

Implementation of any corporate tax integration plan will result in a new set of effective tax rates on capital income by industry and on personal income by consumer group. While a new system may involve uniform tax rates and may be easy to evaluate in itself, the existing system is neither uniform nor easy to evaluate; thus all equilibrium prices and quantities can be expected to vary as a result of any tax change.

Because these effects are multiple, nonmarginal, and interlinking, general equilibrium analysis is a natural technique to use in evaluating the combination of these effects in terms of changes in distribution and efficiency. The general equilibrium model described in the next section combines a treatment of the U.S. tax system with competitive consumer and producer behavior. Equilibrium prices and quantities are determined, and the effects of alternative taxation regimes are evaluated.

The Plans Considered

Four alternatives for corporate tax integration are considered, each differing in the extent to which it removes the undesirable features of the present corporate income tax mentioned above.

Plan 1: Total Integration

Under this alternative the corporate income tax is eliminated and the personal income tax is modified to tax total shareholder earnings rather than just dividends. When capital gains are realized, the tax basis is set at the original purchase price plus the cumulated retained earnings during the holding period. This is the most comprehensive of the plans and contains the modifications to the income tax which, if they had originally been made, would have dispensed with the need for a separate corporate tax.

Plan 2: Dividend Deduction from Corporate Income Tax Base

An alternative way of removing double taxation of dividends is to allow a dividend deduction from taxable corporate income. Capital gains taxation of individuals is unaltered, and the corporate income tax is converted into a tax on retained earnings only. This plan differs from the first in that retained earnings are taxed at corporate tax rates rather than personal income tax rates.

Plan 3: Dividend Deduction from Personal Income Tax Base

A third way of removing double taxation of dividends is to allow a dividend deduction from the personal income tax rather than from the corporate income tax. Capital gains taxation is again unaltered. Under this plan, all corporate earnings are taxed at the corporate tax rate and none are taxed at the personal income tax rate. Despite the expectation that this policy would have a more regressive distributional impact than either Plan 1 or 2, it has frequently been suggested on efficiency grounds.

Plan 4: Dividend "Gross Up"

This is the plan most actively discussed in the tax reform debate during 1977. It seeks to reduce rather than remove the double taxation of dividends. Part of the income tax paid by corporations is given as an income tax credit to stockholders when dividends are distributed.[3] The credit is taxable, hence the description "gross up."

Corporate Financial Policies and Tax Integration

One important aspect of corporate tax integration which our model does not directly consider is the role of financial policies. In recent years a number of authors (Stiglitz, 1973, 1976; M. A. King, 1974) have emphasized a view of the corporate tax as a differential tax on the various financial instruments available for transferring capital income from firms to individuals. Under this view there are three different ways by which capital income of corporations can be "paid" to the owners of that capital: through interest payments, dividends, and retentions which are assumed to be "converted" into capital gains. Each of these instruments has tax and nontax advantages and disadvantages that govern their relative use by industry. When debt finance is used, interest is deductible from the corporate tax base. This tax advantage is counteracted by the disadvantage that a heavily debt-financed company has a higher probability of bankruptcy and/or takeover. Equity financing cannot avoid corporate taxation but may result in a large reduction in personal taxes if a retention policy is employed. Alternatively, though they have no tax advantage, dividends may be paid for a variety of other reasons.

For the purposes of the present paper, the important point is that with changes in tax law, firms can be expected to modify their financial policies. For example, if Plan 2 (dividend deduction from the corporate tax) encourages firms

---

[3] A 15% credit was often mentioned and is modeled here. A further possibility discussed was that differential credits might be given depending on the industry in which a company operates; this is not modeled.

to pay out all earnings in dividends, then Plan 1 (total integration) and Plan 2 are identical in their effects.[4]

With out parameters for financial elasticity, one procedure would be to assume several possible behavioral reactions and calculate the effects of the tax change given these assumptions. In evaluating each of the integration schemes, we consider plausible behavior and make calculations based on alternative extreme assumptions. Reasonable estimates should then fall within these bounds. We thus cannot claim a "true" general equilibrium model because within this sphere, adjustments are made to the dividend/retention ratio before other effects are allowed to be felt.[5]

A GENERAL EQUILIBRIUM MODEL OF THE U.S. ECONOMY AND TAX SYSTEM

In this section we describe the medium-size general equilibrium model used to analyze the four plans to integrate corporate and personal income tax. This model is parameterized with 1973 data. It possesses a capability for analyzing the general equilibrium impacts of many different tax proposals affecting not only corporate taxes, but also income, social security, sales, property, and other taxes. The model incorporates conventional consumer and producer behavior, savings and investment activity, foreign trade activity, and government purchase policies. The full range of taxes currently operating in the United States are incorporated into the model, and in general, these taxes affect the economic behavior of both producers and consumers. Even though savings behavior is endogenous in the model, only a single time period is considered, and the model is largely static in character. Dynamic extensions are currently being developed.

Nineteen producer good industries, 16 consumer goods, and 12 consumer types classified by income range are identified and shown in Table 3.1. These dimensions were governed by a tradeoff between model complexity, data availability, and computational expense. Capital and labor are the primary factor inputs, used by industry and owned by consumer groups in different proportions. These two factors are fixed in total supply but mobile between industries, and their use is dictated by the zero profit conditions of perfectly competitive markets.[6]

---

[4] There is some reliance on the assumptions of perfect markets and rationality when we say that Plan 1 (total integration) is equivalent to Plan 2 (dividend deduction) when all earnings are distributed. We implicitly ignore other effects, such as a possible change in the total savings of the economy due to consumers' lower propensities to save out of distributed earnings.

[5] There are, of course, other simplifications within the model where fixed adjustments are assumed.

[6] Future extensions of this approach should disaggregate labor into skill types, since these might have different rates of substitution for capital. Similarly, capital should eventually be broken down into land, equipment, and structures, or some other useful definitions. As described later, the present level of aggregation causes problems in measuring distributional effects.

Table 3.1

Classification of Industries, Consumer Goods, and Consumer Groups Used in Model

Industries	Consumer Goods	Consumer Groups (classified by thousands of dollars of gross income)
1. Agriculture, forestry, and fisheries	1. Food	1. 0-3
2. Mining	2. Alcoholic beverages	2. 3-4
3. Crude petroleum and gas	3. Tobacco	3. 4-5
4. Contract construction	4. Utilities	4. 5-6
5. Food and tobacco	5. Housing	5. 6-7
6. Textiles, apparel, leather products	6. Furnishings	6. 7-8
7. Paper and printing	7. Appliances	7. 8-10
8. Petroleum refining	8. Clothing and jewelry	8. 10-12
9. Chemicals and rubber	9. Transportation	9. 12-15
10. Lumber, furniture, stone	10. Motor vehicles, tires, and auto repair	10. 15-20
11. Metals, machinery, miscellaneous manufacturing	11. Services	11. 20-25
12. Transportation equipment	12. Financial services	12. 25+
13. Motor vehicles	13. Reading, recreation, misc.	
14. Transportation, communications, and utilities	14. Nondurable-nonfood household items	
15. Trade	15. Gasoline and other fuels	
16. Finance and insurance	16. Savings	
17. Real estate		
18. Services		
19. Government enterprises		

A major contribution of this model is the assembly of a recent and consistent microeconomic data set which shows the interaction of all U.S. taxation policies. Such a data set has never been constructed before, but it is essential for general equilibrium analysis of taxation policy. This data set provides information on factors used by each industry (and taxes paid for these), intermediate usage of products, outputs of both producer and consumer goods, purchases of consumer goods by household types, incomes by source and by household type, income taxes paid, and several other items, including business investment and foreign trade. Inconsistencies among the data sources and general equilibrium conditions are resolved using systematic adjustment procedures described in Fullerton et al. (1978). Carefully derived parameters and tax rates are used to calculate the benchmark equilibrium, replicating the consistent 1973 data base. Economic effects of a tax policy proposal are then estimated by changing the tax rates and recalculating a simulated equilibrium.[7]

Production

A schematic representation of our model can be seen in Figure 3.1. Each industry produces a single output, or a producer good, from a combination of capital services, labor services, and the outputs of other industries. Factor input decisions are assumed to be made on the basis of cost minimzation, and these decisions are affected by the tax system, since the relative producer prices of inputs are altered for each industry.

The use of primary factors by each industry is described by a separate Constant Elasticity of Substitution (CES) or Cobb-Douglas production function. The model embodies a capability for preselection of functional form in addition to selection of parameter values. The intermediate use of products by industries is described by a conventional fixed coefficient input-output matrix. This matrix is derived from published 1970 input-output data for the United States and updated to 1973. No substitution between primary factors and intermediate inputs is permitted.

A number of "legal" taxation instruments are treated as production taxes and directly affect the cost structures of the industries. The corporation income tax, corporate franchise tax, and the property tax are in combination treated as *ad valorem* taxes on the use of capital services.[8] The social security tax, unemployment insurance, and public workman's compensation are treated as *ad valorem* taxes on the use of labor services. It is debatable, of course, whether this treatment is appropriate. For example, some recent literature argues for treating the social

---

[7]This procedure assumes that the consistent 1973 data set represents a true equilibrium state of the economy even though there may have been some pure profits or other temporary influences in that year.

[8]The tax on capital services cannot be shifted in the short run, an assumption which is consistent with the perfectly competitive markets in this model. The purpose here is to evaluate the long-run incidence of the tax.

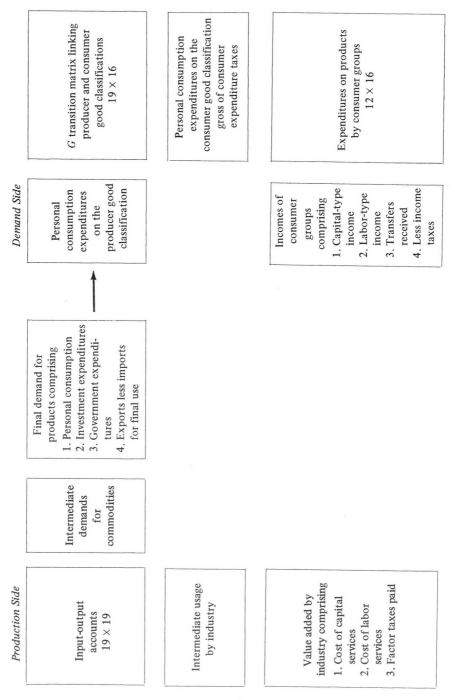

Figure 3.1. *Outline of the interrelation between data sets for the model.*

security tax as a benefit-related contribution and for treating the corporate income tax as a lump-sum tax or as a tax on the use of equity instruments. Our model abstracts from these controversies, but we are aware of them.

In addition to taxes on the use of primary factors, the model includes taxes on the intermediate use of producer goods by industry and taxes on outputs of producer goods. Intermediate input taxes include the registration fees paid on motor vehicles for business use; producer output taxes include the federal manufacturers' excise taxes, paid by purchasers for intermediate or final use. Table 3.2 describes the detailed treatment of all these taxes along with an outline of the entire U.S. tax system.

Consumption

Within the personal sector, twelve consumer groups are identified by their family gross of tax income as reported in the 1972-1973 Consumer Expenditure Survey of the Bureau of Labor Statistics. The number of groups is restricted in order to keep the model of manageable size, but other consumer groupings could be considered by the approach. Additional characteristics, such as family size, age, marital status of household heads, and regional location could be examined, as was done by Piggott and Whalley (1976) in their model of the tax system of the United Kingdom.

The income of each consumer group is determined by the ownership of labor and capital and receipt of transfer income, such as social security payments, from the government. Factor supplies are assumed fixed in this static model, though a labor/leisure choice is being developed. In the dynamic version, current savings will affect future capital stocks. Demands for consumer goods are assumed to be generated by utility maximization subject to the household budget constraint. Our computer programs allow the user to specify demand functions consistent with Cobb-Douglas, CES, or Stone-Geary utility functions.

Demands for the 19 producer goods are derived from the demands for the 16 consumer goods using a G transition matrix. An element g_{ij} of this matrix is the amount of producer good i needed to produce one unit of consumer good j. The distinction we made between producer and consumer goods enables us to simultaneously use national accounts data, defined for production goods, and the recently released 1971-1973 Consumer Expenditures Survey, defined for consumer goods. The G transition matrix solves the problem of distinguishing consumer demands for outputs of the trade and transportation industries from the demands for goods purchased at retail. Each consumer good requires some trade and transportation for its production. It also solves the problem of rare consumer purchases of goods such as "mining" output.

The 16th consumer good is savings, and the G matrix permits us to treat it like other goods. We assume that the demand for savings depends upon the rate of return, which is given by the current price of capital services relative to the pur-

Table 3.2
U.S. Taxes and Their Treatment in the Model

Tax	Treatment in the Model	Difficulties of Model Treatment
Corporate taxes (including state and local) and corporate franchise taxes	*Ad valorem* tax on use of capital services by industry.	Some argue for treatment as a lump-sum tax. model treatment ignores role of financial instruments.
Property taxes	*Ad valorem* tax on use of capital services by industry.	Differential rates across jurisdictions ignored.
Social security taxes, unemployment insurance, and workmen's compensation	*Ad valorem* tax on use of labor services by industry.	Benefit-related nature of contributions; arbitrary distinction between public and private insurance programs.
Motor vehicles' tax	*Ad valorem* tax on use of motor vehicles by producers.	In practice, a yearly registration fee and not a purchase tax; averaging over jurisdictions.
Retail sales taxes	*Ad valorem* taxes on purchases of consumer goods.	Averaging of rates over states.
Excise taxes	*Ad valorem* taxes on output of producer goods.	Taxes often expressed as charge per unit physical measure such as volume.
Other indirect business taxes and nontax payments to government	*Ad valorem* tax on output of producer goods.	Payments depend on output levels by industry to only limited extent; averaging of rates over states.
Personal income taxes (including state and local)	Linear function for each consumer where tax on capital affects industry allocation.	Detailed deductions and exemptions not specifically considered in model.

chase price of new capital goods.[9] Actual patterns of investment goods purchases are the basis for constructing the column of the transition matrix which converts the consumer's demand for savings into demands for producer goods. This treatment assumes an equality between savings and investment.

Excise taxes on selected items and general retail sales taxes are treated as *ad valorem* taxes on purchases of consumer goods. None of the tax rates considered in the model differ across households, so a single vector of tax rates is used.

Progressive personal income taxes are incorporated by a sequence of linear tax functions for each consumer. With an intercept that is usually negative and a marginal tax rate applied to all income, we can replicate observed payments and still subject changes in income to the proper marginal rate. Large changes, however, cannot push a consumer into the next bracket nor change his marginal rate. State and local income taxes are modeled as "piggyback" or percentage surcharge taxes applied to the federal levy.

Treatment of personal income taxes is complicated by the need to recognize the preferential treatment of certain capital income. Corporate retained earnings that are converted to capital gains have a lower present value tax liability than do earnings paid as dividends. Similarly, the extent to which capital earnings are sheltered by the unincorporated investment tax credit will differ by industry. Thus, the effective tax rate on personal income will differ by industry. Later we discuss the procedure used to introduce the preferential treatment of some personal capital income.

Government purchases are derived from a Cobb-Douglas demand function defined over producer goods. Government real expenditures are assumed to equal tax receipts less transfers, since the general equilibrium approach requires that the government budget be balanced. The foreign trade sector receives a simple treatment in order to close the model. By assuming that the net value of exports less imports for each producer good remains constant, we can calculate the net quantity transactions at any given vector of producer prices and transform domestic demands to market demands.

Data Sources and Procedures

The complete 1973 data set is derived from five major sources including the July 1976 *Survey of Current Business* (*SCB*) (U.S. Department of Commerce, 1976d), unpublished worksheets of the U.S. Commerce Department's National Income Division (NID), the Commerce Department's Bureau of Economic Analysis (BEA) input-output tables (1975), the U.S. Labor Department's 1972-1973 Consumer Expenditure Survey,[10] and the U.S. Treasury Department's Merged Tax File from the Office of Tax Analysis. Some of these data are not compiled in a suitable

[9] Current prices thus serve as expected future prices in the decisions of consumers to save for future consumption.

[10] The 1972-1973 Consumer Expenditure Survey of the Bureau of Labor Statistics is a body of data, mostly on computer tape, which became available in 1977.

form for this study, and adjustments have been made in order to obtain appropriate data that are mutually consistent. These adjustments are summarized below.

Labor Income and Tax

Our definition of labor return gross of tax is the sum of wages, salaries, employer contributions for social insurance programs, and the estimated return to labor of self-employed persons. This last category represents an unobservable fraction of the total return to the entrepreneur who invests his time and capital jointly, and it is estimated by the product of average employee compensation and the number of proprietors and partners for each industry. This component of the return to labor is substantial only for agriculture, construction, services, and trade. In some industries the estimated labor component of the self-employed exceeds the total unincorporated income. When this occurs, we have set the capital return at zero and assigned the total income to labor.

The tax on labor services consists of employer and employee contributions for social insurance. An industry breakdown of each employer payment was provided by NID, and the employee share of social security was derived from the employer share, since they are matching contributions. The total for self-employed contributions is given in the *SCB* and is allocated among industries by the proportion of self-employed labor income in each industry.

Capital Income and Tax

The return to capital net of tax includes corporate profits after tax, the estimated return to noncorporate capital, net interest paid, and net rents paid. The inventory valuation adjustment (IVA) and the capital consumption adjustment (CCA) are applied to these figures. Net realized capital gains are not included, as they refer to accrued gains of earlier years. Accrued gains on existing physical capital assets have not been included in our capital payments or income figures. This procedure is consistent with the assumption that such gains reflect only inflation, and it demands less data than alternative approaches. Financial capital gains of individuals, reflecting current retained earnings of corporations, are included.

The July 1976 *SCB* gives corporate profits after corporate taxes, property taxes, and other indirect business taxes for their classification of 59 industries, and we aggregate these figures to our 19 industries. The corporate IVA has been obtained in sufficient detail from NID and reduces the corporate profit figures.[11]

---

[11]Wherever negative returns result, we resort to an average of several years in order to avoid the implication that an industry "supplies" rather than uses capital. Two special adjustments are necessary. First, the national accounts for finance and insurance include the Federal Reserve Board earnings as corporate income and their payments to the Treasury as corporate tax. This government operation is exempt from the corporate income tax system, but its payments to the Treasury are included as a capital tax. Second, IRS corporate profits in extractive industries are understated by the combination of current expensing of exploration and allowances for depletion of reserves. We add to *SCB* income the portion of the percentage depletion deduction not included in Department of Commerce adjustments.

Unfortunately, the Commerce Department cannot provide the disaggregated CCA estimates necessary to measure income net of economic depreciation instead of tax depreciation. We use results from a study by Coen (1976) for the disaggregated manufacturing CCA. The noncorporate and real estate income figures in the national accounts include CCA adjustments; the remaining industries have no such adjustment owing to lack of data.

For noncorporate business, NID provides detailed income and IVA data. For each industry our earlier estimate of the labor return is subtracted from total income in order to obtain a residual estimate of the return to noncorporate capital.

Since we seek to measure all payments to capital used in each industry, we add the net rents originating in the paying industry to our capital use estimates. NID has provided net rents for farm realty, the imputed net rent from owner-occupied dwellings, and the net rent from the tenant-occupied dwellings. The first of these is placed in agriculture and the other two in real estate. Net rents paid by business are apportioned among the eighteen private industries on the basis of the data available on gross rents paid in the IRS *1973 Statistics of Income* (U.S. Department of the Treasury, 1977b). Royalties paid for natural resources, copyrights, and patents are counted as capital income in the industry where these assets are used. The use of natural resources by industry is approximated by the depletion deductions taken for tax purposes in 1973. These procedures are similar to those in Rosenberg (1969).

The final component of capital income is the net interest paid by each industry. This also may be thought of as payments for borrowed capital services used in the industry. NID industry worksheets showing interest flows for 1973 were used. The dollar payments of interest by industry, referred to as net "monetary" interest paid, are positive for all industries except finance and insurance (F&I), which has a large negative value for net monetary interest paid. Their receipt of net monetary interest is a return for the financial intermediation services that they provide. If, as for other industries, we add the (negative) net interest paid to profits, then the total return to capital in this industry will also be negative. We raise the F&I net interest paid to zero by "imputing" additional interest payments to other industries and to persons who then pay imputed finance charges to F&I. The Commerce Department NID has made some of these imputations but leaves a large negative value for F&I net interest paid. We allocate the remaining imputed interest in the same proportions as that already allocated by NID.

There are three components of tax on capital income: the corporate income tax, the corporate franchise tax, and property taxes. Information on the corporate income tax by industry is given in the *SCB*. The corporate franchise tax is treated as an indirect business tax in the national accounts, and data given in unpublished worksheets from NID are aggregated to eighteen industries. The same worksheets provide NID estimates of state and local property taxes paid by industry, but our movement of net rents paid out of real estate requires a further adjustment to these figures.

Intermediate Inputs and Production Taxes

The Bureau of Economic Analysis 1970 update of the 1967 input-output matrix is aggregated to our nineteen industries and adjusted to 1973 levels. We scale up each industry's intermediate use of producer goods by the ratio of 1973 to 1970 value added for that industry.

In the input-output table, the total value of each producer good equals the value of intermediate inputs, taxes on intermediate inputs, and value added. The value added includes labor services, labor tax, capital services, capital tax, and the taxes on output. Several of the indirect business taxes have been treated in the model as *ad valorem* taxes on the output of each industry at appropriate rates. For example, the public utilities taxes, severance taxes, and the business and occupation taxes apply to the outputs of particular industries. Other tax and nontax payments, although not legally defined as taxes on value of output, are so treated. Federal excise and customs duties are treated as *ad valorem* output taxes on producer goods. An adjustment is made to NID data to place retailers' excise taxes on corresponding producer goods instead of retail trade.

Registration fees on motor vehicles are treated as a tax on their intermediate use by industry. These data appear with other indirect business taxes in the worksheets provided by NID.

Government

A separate nineteenth industry represents the output of government enterprises including the post office, TVA, mass transit, local utilities, and other government-run business. Total employee compensation for these federal, state, and local operations is shown in the *SCB*, as are employer contributions for retirement programs, treated as a labor tax. Their use of capital services in 1973 is imputed using a weighted average of the gross-of-tax-capital/labor ratios for the private counterparts of these activities, including services, transportation, finance, and utilities. We treat the difference between our capital use estimates and the recorded government enterprise surplus as an output subsidy, while the effective rate of tax on the use of capital services is zero, since no corporate income or property taxes are paid by government. The intermediate input column for this industry is scaled up from 1970 to 1973 by the ratio of employee compensation between those years instead of value added, since the latter includes the "surplus" of government enterprises, often negative. The only indirect business tax paid by this industry is a federal nontax payment, modeled as an *ad valorem* output tax.

General government is modeled as a consumer, using its retained tax revenue to purchase capital and labor services and outputs of all nineteen industries. The 1970 input-output table of the BEA shows purchases by general government in the four categories of federal defense and nondefense, and state and local education and noneducation. Each of these is scaled to 1973 using totals from the *SCB*. Government purchases of capital services are estimated by imputing a rate of return to government capital stock data for 1973, available in Kendrick (1976). This procedure assumes that the government uses the private rate of return as its opportunity cost of capital.

Investment and Foreign Trade

Businesses invest in both capital formation and inventory accumulation. The input-output table's Gross Private Fixed Capital Formation column uses our nineteen producer goods, scaled from 1970 to 1973 with *SCB* totals. Similar scaling is done for the Net Inventory Change column, and the appropriate IVA is subtracted from each industry in order to measure only its purchases. Together these columns represent the manner in which savings are spent.

The export column of the 1970 input-output table is replaced with information for 1973 from U.S. foreign trade statistics, and similar information provides data for both final and intermediate use of imports.

Consumer Incomes and Expenditures

The capital and labor services used by producers and purchased by government are endowments of the consumer groups and government. These endowments, valued at equilibrium factor prices, determine factor incomes for each group. Information on factor endowments and transfer shares of each consumer group is available on the Treasury Department's Merged Tax File compiled from 1973 individual income tax returns. For each income group the capital endowment is indicated by the sum of interest and rent receipts, financial capital gains, dividends, and the income from unincorporated enterprises. Labor endowments are indicated by wage and salary income, while transfers from government include a number of items such as social security and welfare payments.

The Merged Tax File also furnishes average and marginal tax rates for each income group. All disposable incomes, after taxes and transfers, are spent by each consumer, since one of the purchased commodities is "savings." Information on consumers' expenditures for the other fifteen commodities is obtained from the 1972-1973 Consumer Expenditure Survey, which gives data for each income bracket used in the model.

Consistency and Parameterization

Since its sources are diverse, the data set does not meet the consistency requirements of a general equilibrium. The necessary adjustment procedures begin by accepting the "accuracy" of data on taxes and on capital and labor use by industry. Consumer income vectors are then scaled until the sum of each factor supply equals the sum of demand. Government expenditures are scaled to equal tax revenue, and similar adjustments ensure that supply equals demand for each good and that all consistency requirements are met. This approach and its justification are described in more detail by Piggott and Whalley (1977) and by Fullerton et al. (1978).

Once arranged in this consistent form, the basic data are used to generate parameters for the behavioral equations of the model. This involves a prior step of decomposing equilibrium observations on transactions in value terms into separate observations on equilibrium prices and quantities. For this purpose we follow Harberger (1959, 1962, 1966) by defining otherwise unobservable physical units of both factors and goods as those amounts which can be sold for $1 at the observed equilibrium. Thus, our benchmark equilibrium data set can be separated into price and quantity observations; all benchmark equilibrium market prices are unity, and all benchmark equilibrium quantities are those given by the data in value terms.

From the quantity and price observations and the assumption of agent optimization, it is possible to infer parameter values in the behavioral equations which are consistent with the equilibrium data set. For instance, if we assume a given industry has a Cobb-Douglas production function and cost minimizes, the factor employments observed in that industry are the direct outcome of solving the cost minimization problem at prices of unity. This uniquely determines the weighting parameters of the Cobb-Douglas functions. Similarly on the demand side, if a given consumer has a Cobb-Douglas utility function, his commodity purchases at equilibrium prices of unity imply unique values for the utility function exponents. Other equilibrium conditions are used to determine remaining parameters; for example, the zero profit conditions by industry are used to generate the normalization constant in each industry's production function. The data and equilibrium conditions thus determine all parameter values.

If more complex functional forms are used, additional parameter values must be provided before the same procedure can be used. In the CES case, an extraneous estimate of the elasticity of substitution is necessary for each industry or consumer. The source of the "best-guess" industrial factor substitution elasticities used in this paper is a recent article by Caddy (1976), which surveys most published estimates. For the Linear Expenditure System (LES) demand functions, we select an appropriate subsistence income, or total value of minimum requirements, and estimate the expenditure shares out of remaining income by ordinary least squares regressions.[12] Minimum requirement parameters are set by the model under replication requirements.

When parameters are selected in this manner, it is possible to use initial endowments, behavioral equations, and tax rates in the algorithm to calculate an equilibrium which replicates the benchmark consistent data set. This also allows for an important test of the solution procedure.

The complexity of the model makes it impossible to estimate without a large number of identifying restrictions on parameter values. It might seem natural to use extraneous econometric estimates of all parameters in the model rather than the replication procedure just described. However, the implementation of this procedure faces a basic methodological difficulty. If extraneous parameter values are adopted, there is no test of the overall performance of the model. It is quite

---

[12] These procedures are explained in A. T. King (1979).

possible, for instance, that the chosen or estimated combination of parameters will yield an equilibrium which bears little relation to the observed economy.[13]

REPRESENTING THE TAX INTEGRATION PLANS
IN MODEL EQUIVALENT FORM

Each of the tax integration plans we have described is represented in model equivalent form for the purposes of analyzing its impacts. For each plan we calculate a new set of appropriate effective tax rates and use these to compute a simulated equilibrium for comparison with the benchmark equilibrium.

In order to describe the discriminatory aspects of the personal and corporate tax systems in more detail, we first calculate each industry's capital income net of corporate income tax, corporate franchise tax, and property tax, and denote these by $K_i = 1, \ldots, 19$. The government's use of privately owned capital is represented by K_{20}. The sum of this capital income is received by the twelve consumer classes in the model, and

$$\sum_{i=1}^{20} K_i = \sum_{j=1}^{12} k_j, \tag{1}$$

where k_j is the capital income received by the jth consumer class.

For each of the twelve consumer classes we have data on their marginal tax rate from the Treasury Department's Merged Tax File. A weighted average marginal tax rate then can be calculated as

$$\tau = \sum_{j=1}^{12} k_j \tau_i \bigg/ \sum_{j=1}^{12} k_j \tag{2}$$

where τ_j is the marginal tax rate of the jth consumer group and the weights in the average are determined by relative capital ownership.

For each of the nineteen industries and government we define a fraction, f_i, which denotes the proportion of that sector's capital income which is subject to full personal income taxation. This fraction will differ across industries owing to a number of features. The primary reason is that industries vary in their dividend and retention policies. In addition to the corporate income tax, corporate franchise

---

[13] Our procedures also have a number of practical advantages. First, they enable direct use of national accounts data, avoiding the difficulty of providing definitions of units in physical form. Extraneous estimates are surprisingly sparse, often inconclusive, and usually presented for other classifications. We are able to use extraneous parameter estimates for unit-free elasticity parameters and avoid the problem of a conversion between units used in our model and extraneous estimation procedures.

tax, and property tax, we add another factor tax which is labeled the personal factor tax, t^p. For each industry the total personal factor taxes paid are given as

$$t_i^p = f_k k_i \tau, \quad i = 1,\ldots,20 \tag{3}$$

where the personal factor tax on K_i is $f_i \tau$.

The accounting for capital income for each industry is as follows:

total gross of tax capital income
(from benchmark equilibrium data set)

less: corporate income tax
corporate franchise tax
property tax
personal factor tax

equals: K_i^n = net capital income = $K_i(1 - f_i \tau)$.

The average fraction of K_i which is fully taxable by the personal income tax is given by

$$\bar{f} \quad \sum_{i=1}^{20} K_i f_i \Big/ \sum_{i=1}^{20} K_i. \tag{4}$$

The personal income tax applying to capital income at the consumer level is then given by

$$t_j^p = (\tau_j - \tau) k_j \bar{f}, \quad j = 1,\ldots,12. \tag{5}$$

These consumer taxes on capital income are both positive and negative and when aggregated over the twelve consumer classes yield no revenue. The modeled system operates exactly as a withholding system under which each industry pays tax on $f_i K_i$ at rate τ. The consumer income taxes in Expression (5) correct the tax rate for each consumer class (those with rates above τ pay more taxes, while those below get refunds). Since τ is chosen as the capital weighted average of marginal tax rates, the corrections sum to zero.

For each of our twelve consumer classifications, data are available on labor income (L_j), capital income (k_j), and hence total before-tax income. Data for total federal and state individual income taxes paid by each group (T_j^I) and their marginal tax rate (τ_j) are obtained from the Treasury Merged Tax File. This enables the tax on labor income to be determined and hence the intercept in the total tax function, shown as follows:

T_j^I = total income tax in 1973 of consumer class, j,

less: $\tau_j k_j \bar{f}$ = consumer j's share of total personal factor taxes on capital,

less: $\tau_j L_j$ = tax on labor income in 1973,

equals: C_j, constant in the income tax function for the jth consumer group.

The personal income tax then becomes

$$T_j^I = C_j + \tau_j L_j + \tau_j k_j \bar{f}. \tag{6}$$

To calculate the f_i, we make use of data on capital income types by industry, consisting of corporate profits (dividends and retained earnings), net interest payments (monetary and imputed), net rent payments (including the imputed net rent from owner-occupied homes), and the return to capital used in noncorporate business. These types of capital income are treated differently by the personal income tax, and each can be said to have a proportion g which is fully taxable by it. An industry's f_i is the weighted average of these g proportions, and each industry has different weights or amounts of these capital income types. Specifically,

$$f_i = \frac{DIV \cdot g_D + RE \cdot g_{RE} + INT \cdot g_I + RENT \cdot g_R + NCI - (NCITC/\tau)}{DIV + RE + INT + RENT + NCI}, \quad (7)$$

where DIV = dividends paid by ith industry (obtained from the July 1976 *SCB*); RE = retained earnings, obtained as the difference between dividends and corporate profits as corrected by the IVA, depletion, and capital consumption adjustment; INT = net monetary and imputed interest paid; $RENT$ = net rent paid; NCI = noncorporate capital income; $NCITC$ = noncorporate investment tax credit.

The g_D for dividends and g_{RE} for retained earnings are discussed below. g_I and g_R are taken to be 1, since interest and rents are entirely subject to the personal income tax. Because the noncorporate investment tax credit reduces the personal income tax liability, we include in the numerator the amount of income that would result in the reduced tax liability. It is the amount $NCI - (NCITC/\tau)$, which multiplied by τ yields tax collections $NCI \cdot \tau - NCITC$. For the housing industry, imputed net rents of owner-occupied homes are excluded from the numerator, since this imputed income is not taxable.

Use of capital by government enterprises is assigned an f_i of .75, roughly reflecting the portion of interest payments that are taxable by the personal income tax. Approximately one-fourth of government's interest payments are on nontaxable state and local bonds. General government use of private capital is assigned an f_i of 1.0, a simplification that aids in our computations, and can be justified by the largely federal nature of general government's capital stock.

In 1976 the government's revenue loss due to the $100 dividend exclusion from the personal income tax was estimated at $285 million (U.S. Congress, 1977a). We divide this by τ to get an estimate of nontaxable dividends of $1164 million. Since total dividends paid is $24,631 million, the proportion taxable is .9584 and this figure is used for g_D.

Bailey (1969) has shown that close to one-half of long-term capital gains are realized in a relatively short period, while the remainder is held for varying durations averaging perhaps 35 years or more. Weighing the advantages of deferral and these observations regarding holding periods has led us to the conclusion that a tax on $.25 of regular income would yield approximately the same personal income tax revenue as one dollar of retained earnings. That is, the g_{RE} for retained earnings is set at .25.

Estimates of noncorporate investment tax credit ($NCITC$) are intended to approximate the amounts which would have accrued by sector in 1973 had the present 1977 law been in effect and had there been no limitations on the use of the credits. The procedures used to derive these estimates are taken from the Treasury Department's Office of Tax Analysis.

The resulting values for all benchmark f_i are shown in Table 3.3, along with the effective tax rate on tax on capital (CTR) for each industry.[14] Each of the four integration plans implies different values for f_i and capital tax rates, also shown in Table 3.3. Because of its balanced budget, however, government must receive the same real tax revenue in the simulated equilibrium. Otherwise, the change in its pattern of expenditures or transfers would affect the outcome and prevent us from isolating the effect of the capital tax rate changes. For this reason, the column of capital tax rates for each plan is scaled during the computation, until the resulting equilibrium tax yield allows government to make the same real purchases and give the same real transfers to consumer groups, based on Laspeyres price indices.[15] In this way, we limit ourselves to considering the variations in interindustry discrimination of the capital tax rate system, without lowering those taxes generally.

Plan 1: Total Integration. This plan would remove the undesirable features of the corporate tax by merging the corporate income tax and personal income tax. The corporate tax would no longer operate and the personal income tax would be modified to tax earnings per share rather than dividends received. Corporate taxes are eliminated from the numerator of the new capital tax-rate calculations. The personal income tax is changed to tax earnings rather than dividends, implying changes in the f_i parameter values. The new f_i' values, where primes denote the revised values for the simulation, are calculated by Formula (7), where g_{RE} is set to 1. We have assumed the \$100 dividend exclusion is eliminated, and thus raise g_D to 1. The new f_i' values imply a new value for $\bar{f}$, represented as $\bar{f}'$. Since units of capital are defined as net of all taxes including personal factor taxes, new values of f_i' imply new values of K_i, written as K_i'. New units of capital net of all taxes equal $K_i'(1 - f_i'\tau)$, and these units are assumed fixed in total quantity.

Personal capital factor taxes paid are recalculated using the f_i', as

$$t_i^{P'} = f_i'K_i'\tau \tag{8}$$

and entered in the numerator of the new capital tax-rate calculations. New personal capital income tax functions are given by

$$t_j^{P'} = (\tau_j - \tau)k_j\bar{f}'. \tag{9}$$

---

[14] Note that a mostly noncorporate industry like agriculture has an f_i close to 1 and low CTR, since noncorporate income is fully taxed at the personal level, but not subject to the corporate income tax. The f_i values of industries differ according to the degree of incorporation, and the (1973) financial policies of corporate firms. CTR values differ according to the degree of incorporation, the use of depletion deductions, the number of firms making losses, and the intensity of their property, which is subject to the state and local property tax.

[15] Operation of the equal yield calculation is discussed in Shoven and Whalley (1977).

Table 3.3
f_i Proportion[a] and Tax Rate on Capital (CTR) for Each Tax Scheme

Industry	Benchmark Equilibrium		Plan 1 Total Integration		Plan 2 Dividend Deduction from Corporate Income Tax Base		Plan 3 Dividend Deduction from Personal Income Tax Base		Plan 4 Dividend Gross Up	
	f_i	CTR	f_i	CTR	f_i	CTR	f_i	CTR	f_i	CTR
Agriculture, forestry, fisheries	.93	.47	.94	.46	.93	.47	.93	.47	.93	.47
Mining	.58	.74	.97	.71	.58	.65	.36	.62	.60	.69
Crude petroleum & gas[b]	1.00	.80	.98	.71	1.00	.72	.24	.39	1.00	.78
Construction	.56	1.77	.72	.68	.56	1.45	.28	1.53	.61	1.45
Food & tobacco[b]	1.08	2.99	.99	.88	1.08	2.07	.45	2.19	1.06	2.26
Textiles, apparel, leather	.87	2.15	.99	.75	.87	1.74	.51	1.78	.88	1.71
Paper & printing	.57	1.34	.98	.63	.57	1.06	.27	1.13	.61	1.12
Petroleum refining	.30	.31	1.00	.44	.30	.31	.37	.33	.31	.28
Chemicals & rubber	.68	1.56	.99	.60	.68	1.03	.25	1.23	.71	1.27
Lumber, furniture, stone	.44	.71	.98	.52	.44	.62	.30	.63	.47	.63
Metals, machinery	.65	1.42	1.00	.67	.65	1.07	.37	1.21	.68	1.19
Transportation equipment[b]	2.37	20.84	.98	4.88	2.37	11.50	.68	8.19	1.91	9.77
Motor vehicles	.64	1.04	1.00	.47	.64	.61	.30	.83	.67	.89
Transportation, communication, utilities[b]	1.02	1.41	.88	.89	1.02	.99	.50	1.01	1.01	1.30
Trade	.60	1.54	.95	.83	.60	1.36	.33	1.33	.63	1.31
Finance & insurance	.42	1.67	.99	1.35	.42	1.37	.31	1.57	.47	1.47
Real estate[b]	.27	.58	.27	.56	.27	.57	.26	.57	.27	.58
Services	.89	.66	.95	.57	.89	.61	.84	.63	.89	.64
Government enterprises	.75	.26[c]	.75	.26	.75	.26	.75	.26	.75	.26
General government	1.00	.39[c]	1.00	.39	1.00	.39	1.00	.39	1.00	.39

[a]Proportion of sector's capital income that is subject to full personal income taxation.
[b]These industries had negative retained earnings in the national accounts data, which can result in f_i values greater than 1.
[c]These rates include only personal factor taxes.

Values of C_j in the personal income tax functions do not change, but all new capital income including the newly taxed earnings per share are subject to the marginal tax rate.

Plan 2: Dividend Deduction from Corporate Income Tax Base. This plan's corporate income tax base is undistributed profits of corporations. It is represented in model equivalent terms for each industry by removing a portion of the corporate tax paid from the 1973 capital taxation figures and recalculating the capital tax rate. The portion of corporate tax removed is given by the ratio of dividends to net of tax corporate profits by industry (U.S. Department of Commerce, 1976d). Neither the f_i nor the personal income tax function changes.

Plan 3: Dividend Deduction from Personal Income Tax Base. This plan removes the taxation of dividends from the redistributive power of the income tax system. In model equivalent terms, it is specified by considering the effect of dividend deductibility on the income tax functions of households. The value of the g_D proportion of dividends taxable by the personal income tax is set to zero and all new f_i' values are calculated using Formula (7). Other adjustments are analogous to the description of Plan 1.

Plan 4: Dividend "Gross Up." This scheme gives stockholders an income tax credit of a portion of the corporate taxes paid by their firm. It is most satisfactorily modeled as a reduction in corporate taxes of each industry by the amount of the credit. This amount is then treated as additional dividends in the calculation of new f_i' values. The new effective tax rates then include 85% of corporate income taxes and the new personal factor taxes. The higher dividends relative to retained earnings result in higher f_i' and $\bar{f}'$ values, so that consumers experience an increase in taxable capital income. The taxable nature of the credits is thus captured.

RESULTS

Our provisional results are presented in tables 3.4, 3.5, and 3.6, showing efficiency, distributional, and allocative effects, respectively. As a basis of comparison for the integration plans, we first discuss the economic effects of complete equalization of capital tax rates under the constraint that real government revenue is held constant.

In examples A, B, and C, the original capital tax rates on industries include the corporate income tax, property taxes, and personal factor taxes, while the original f_i values vary by industry. In order to eliminate any tax discrimination among industries, we must use a single tax rate for all industries, and equally tax all capital income at the personal income tax level. Thus, capital tax rates are set to a common rate providing government with enough revenue to make the same real purchases, and all f_i values are reset to $\bar{f}$, the overall fraction of capital income that is effectively fully taxed by the personal income tax system. Results in Table 3.4

Table 3.4
Welfare Gains[a] under Various Assumptions (billions of 1973 dollars)

Tax Replacement	Demand Functions	Production Function Elasticities	Paasche (Lower Bound)	Laspeyres (Upper Bound)	Geometric Mean
A. Equal capital tax rates on industry	Cobb-Douglas	CES Best Guess	7.58	9.92	8.67
B. Equal capital tax rates on industry	LES	CES Best Guess	7.72	9.77	8.68
C. Equal capital tax rates on industry	Cobb-Douglas	Cobb-Douglas	8.81	11.35	10.0
D. Integration plans					
1. Full integration	Cobb-Douglas	CES Best Guess	5.12	6.06	5.57
2. Dividend deduction from corporate income tax base	Cobb-Douglas	CES Best Guess	2.61	2.78	2.69
2a. With extreme behavior assumption	Cobb-Douglas	CES Best Guess	5.17	6.17	5.65
3. Dividend deduction from personal income tax base	Cobb-Douglas	CES Best Guess	2.41	2.52	2.46
3a. With extreme behavior assumption	Cobb-Douglas	CES Best Guess	2.49	2.65	2.57
4. Dividend gross up	Cobb-Douglas	CES Best Guess	2.24	2.32	2.28

[a]By welfare gain we mean a change in real national income per year.

indicate that the efficiency gain from this tax replacement is about $9 billion per year in 1973 dollars.

Example A is our standard of comparison for most of the other examples, B shows that the welfare gain does not differ significantly when LES demand functions are used in the calculations, and example C shows that estimates are sensitive to the elasticities of substitution in production. Most of the best-guess elasticities used here are less than one, some without information are set equal to one, while none are greater than one. The Cobb-Douglas case, with all elasticities equal to one, implies generally higher substitutability. A given tax distortion can then cause greater resource misallocation and a greater welfare gain from correction.

Table 3.4 also reveals an index number problem. However, Paasche and Laspeyres measures are fairly close together for most calculations. The geometric mean of the two indices provides a plausible point estimate.

In order to provide a measure of the distributional impact of the tax policy changes considered, the change in the real after-tax income of each of our twelve consumer classes is presented in Table 3.5. The new after-tax income for each

Table 3.5

Percentage Changes in Real Income after Income Taxes and Transfers by Consumer Group, for Each Tax Replacement

Consumer Group	Equal Capital Tax Rates on Industry			Plan 1 Full Integration	Plan 2 Dividend Deduction from Corporate Income Tax Base	Plan 2a With Extreme Behavior	Plan 3 Dividend Deduction from Personal Income Tax Base	Plan 3a With Extreme Behavior	Plan 4 Dividend Gross Up
	A	B	C						
$ 0- 3,000	0.65	0.72	0.81	1.37	0.20	1.27	-0.66	-0.96	0.25
3- 4,000	0.50	0.54	0.64	0.96	0.18	0.89	-0.38	-0.58	0.22
4- 5,000	0.43	0.43	0.54	0.68	0.17	0.63	-0.20	-0.34	0.19
5- 6,000	0.43	0.43	0.55	0.68	0.18	0.64	-0.14	-0.26	0.20
6- 7,000	0.49	0.49	0.60	0.68	0.22	0.64	-0.07	-0.17	0.22
7- 8,000	0.45	0.44	0.56	0.60	0.22	0.57	0.00	-0.07	0.21
8-10,000	0.37	0.34	0.46	0.48	0.20	0.46	0.07	0.02	0.20
10-12,000	0.44	0.41	0.53	0.53	0.24	0.52	0.14	0.11	0.22
12-15,000	0.48	0.45	0.57	0.49	0.25	0.49	0.18	0.17	0.22
15-20,000	0.52	0.48	0.60	0.48	0.25	0.48	0.25	0.27	0.22
20-25,000	0.75	0.74	0.86	0.54	0.30	0.55	0.34	0.38	0.25
25+	2.18	2.30	2.43	0.52	0.60	0.64	1.36	1.67	0.37

group, implied by each tax replacement, is divided by a price index based on the original purchases of that group in order to obtain the changes in real after-tax income. These price indices are steadily declining over the income groups for the equal capital tax-rate replacement, revealing that low-income groups tend to purchase commodities whose capital use is presently lightly taxed, like housing and petroleum, while high-income groups buy a greater proportion of manufacturing goods whose capital use is more heavily taxed. The industrial capital/labor ratios will also affect the new prices, since the net price of capital rises in the simulated equilibrium. The uses side of income thus has some regressive effects, but the total effects, as shown for the equal tax-rate replacements, are generally proportional.[16] In fact, the approximately $9 billion efficiency gain is distributed in such a way that every group experiences an increase in real income. In this sense, a Pareto improvement can be said to have been effected.[17]

In Table 3.6 we show percentage changes in price and in output by industry for each tax plan. Other information on new capital and labor usage, taxes, and all types of demands are available for each tax replacement.

Plan 1: Total Integration. This plan removes only part of industrial discrimination because property taxes remain within capital taxes by industry. It is an equal yield replacement as described earlier, such that capital tax rates are scaled up to meet previous tax revenues. Interindustry discrimination is still reduced enough to provide a $6 billion static welfare gain in each year, in 1973 dollars.

Equity effects appear to provide proportional or progressive gains to income brackets, as shown in Table 3.5, with every class again enjoying increased real income. Every consumer has reduced purchases of "housing" and "gas and other fuel," since these are the higher-priced consumer goods. These goods involve a large *G* matrix fixed-coefficient use of petroleum and real estate producer goods whose capital use was previously lightly taxed. Government and net export demands respond appropriately to price changes.

We do not need to consider changes in financial policies under this plan. With full integration, all forms of capital income are taxed identically. Since the tax does not depend on whether capital income is paid in interest, dividends, or retained, a change in either the debt/equity or dividend/retention ratio will not alter the new

---

[16] An important point must be made about the capital portfolios of individual consumers. We have summed all types of capital income in order to assign each consumer his endowment. The total endowment is then allocated among capital-using industries. The resulting implicit assumption is that each consumer has the same relative ownership among industries. Every individual's capital income is made up of the same fractions of dividends, interest, rent, capital gains, and the same fractions from each industry. In fact, of course, these fractions differ, and the difference can cause substantial changes in distributional impact. Capital of the low-income group is largely in housing; since tax integration with equal-yield adjustment raises the tax on real estate, it has a regressive impact.

[17] Although the simulated equilibrium is a Pareto improvement over the benchmark 1973 equilibrium, we have said nothing about the possible paths between the two. Short-run losses and transition costs should be considered before enacting such a change. Our model is essentially comparative static and does not measure these disequilibria or temporary influences.

Table 3.6
Percentage Changes in Relative Prices and Quantity Outputs by Industry, for Each Tax Replacement

Industry	Initial Capital/Labor Ratio	A Equal Capital Tax Rates on Industry		Plan 1 Full Integration		Plan 2 Dividend Deduction from Corporate Income Tax Base		Plan 3 Dividend Deduction from Personal Income Tax Base		Plan 4 Dividend Gross Up	
		Price	Quantity	Price	Quantity	Price	Quantity	Price	Quantity	Price	Quantity
Agriculture, forestry, fisheries	1.89	11.85	−0.99	5.05	0.29	2.15	−0.18	1.46	0.06	1.15	0.14
Mining	0.24	0.82	2.98	1.38	2.08	−0.11	0.86	−0.64	0.86	−0.01	0.58
Crude petroleum & gas	0.99	2.44	1.15	3.37	1.39	0.80	0.68	−6.11	−1.31	0.98	0.60
Construction	0.02	−1.13	2.98	−1.25	1.99	−0.37	0.70	−0.36	0.69	−0.38	0.53
Food & tobacco	0.11	1.91	−0.42	−0.58	0.80	0.01	−0.03	−0.27	0.19	−0.27	0.27
Textiles, apparel, leather	0.06	−3.23	2.76	−3.18	2.22	−0.64	0.40	−0.65	0.52	−0.79	0.58
Paper & printing	0.14	−2.53	1.69	−2.72	1.32	−0.79	0.49	−0.70	0.47	−0.71	0.40
Petroleum refining	2.92	13.59	−0.35	8.45	−0.07	1.49	0.13	−1.06	0.52	0.53	0.21
Chemicals & rubber	0.20	−3.26	2.29	−3.87	2.10	−2.01	0.79	−1.35	0.65	−0.99	0.56
Lumber, furniture, stone	0.24	1.38	2.73	−0.12	2.00	−0.02	0.65	−0.25	0.68	−0.31	0.57
Metals, machinery	0.12	−3.24	3.45	−3.00	2.49	−1.15	0.94	−0.68	0.84	−0.79	0.70
Transportation equipment	0.01	−9.27	8.14	−5.17	4.49	−2.27	1.85	−3.48	2.61	−2.92	2.14
Motor vehicles	0.32	−2.66	2.87	−4.90	2.77	−3.77	1.49	−1.47	0.90	−1.04	0.67
Transportation, communication, utilities	0.22	−2.79	1.93	−0.96	1.09	−1.80	0.88	−2.34	1.03	0.00	0.24
Trade	0.08	−2.20	1.52	−1.30	1.57	0.06	0.46	−0.31	0.55	−0.44	0.48
Finance & insurance	0.24	−7.30	5.75	1.38	−0.97	−0.82	0.58	0.58	−0.43	−0.70	0.50
Real estate	7.30	9.62	−5.47	6.35	−3.71	2.49	−1.54	1.95	−1.29	1.51	−0.92
Services	0.11	0.50	0.60	0.07	0.49	−0.11	0.32	−0.16	0.27	0.02	0.16
Government enterprises	0.52	8.52	0.91	1.76	0.35	.57	0.43	0.28	0.48	0.43	0.13
Labor	a	0.00	a	0.00	a	0.00	a	0.00	a	0.00	a
Capital	a	6.14	a	3.61	a	1.28	a	1.11	a	0.91	a

[a] Quantity changes are zero for capital and labor because of their fixed total supply in this version of the model. The authors are developing a model with labor/leisure choice and with a growing capital stock over time.

effective tax rates or the new f_i for the revised equilibrium calculation. The resulting solution would thus be the same even if the ratios changed.

Plan 2: Dividend Deduction from Corporate Income Tax Base. Here, dividends are treated like interest for tax purposes, though by assumption corporations continue to retain the same portion of income. The reduction of the corporate income tax causes some leveling of capital tax rates and a resulting $2.7 billion increase in yearly national income.

The distributional impact is essentially proportional. In none of the three plans that reduce taxes on dividends, however, do we observe the portfolio effects on the distribution of income. We only consider the effects of the price of capital on the distribution of capital income, whereas the distribution of dividend receipts is probably skewed more toward the upper income brackets. The result might be more regressive than indicated if the effects of the distribution of dividend-paying securities is taken into account.

With respect to financial policies, debt/equity is assumed constant. There does exist an incentive to replace retained earnings with now nontaxed dividends, however, so we consider the extreme case where all corporate earnings are distributed. The corporate income tax would thus be effectively eliminated and f_i calculations in Formula (7) would proceed on the assumption that all corporate earnings get multiplied by the higher g_D of .95. By increasing the dividend/retention ratio, corporations have removed income from the corporate income tax base but put more in the personal income tax base. The welfare gain from such a tax replacement is somewhere between the Paasche measure of $5.2 billion and the Laspeyres measure of $6.2 billion. The geometric mean is $5.6 billion per year. This welfare gain is substantially above the fixed-behavior estimate because corporate decision makers have reduced the effect of the corporate income tax with its differing effective capital tax rates. Distribution of all earnings would be unlikely, however, and the gain would probably be between the $2.7 billion and $5.6 billion estimates.

The Plan 2 extreme-behavior results also show more progressive gains among consumers. The relative price of capital rises more in the extreme case, and thus commodity prices vary more, though direction of commodity price changes are similar in the two cases.

Plan 3: Dividend Deduction from Personal Income Tax Base. The reduced tax on dividends again implies lower total tax rates on heavily incorporated industries and a leveling of all rates in general. This occurs through the lower f_i for dividend-paying industries. Welfare gains are $2.5 billion per year.

As might be expected, Table 3.5 shows that Plan 3 has more regressive effects than the second plan, since dividend income is all taxed at the corporate rates instead of being taxed at progressive personal tax rates.

When financial policy makers provide only the reduced tax dividends and no longer retain earnings, the welfare gain of this integration plan lies between $2.49 and $2.65 billion, with a geometric mean of $2.57 billion. The corporate tax remains the same, but new f_i from from Formula (7) include all corporate earnings as dividends with a g_D of zero. Less corporate income would then be subject to the personal income tax. The additional gain from the extreme-behavior assumption is small because the personal income tax deduction does less to eliminate interindustry discrimination than does the corporate income tax deduction of dividends.

Equity effects are still regressive for the extreme behavior case. All price and quantity changes are similar to those shown in Table 3.6 for the fixed-behavior case.

Plan 4: Dividend "Gross Up."   All plans that decrease the corporate income tax only on dividends can be termed partial integration plans. The fourth plan, because it reduces only part of the tax on dividends, might be called a partial-partial plan. The tax system is changed to a lesser degree, and welfare gain is smaller, at $2.3 billion per year.

Equity effects are generally proportional, though once more the price of capital rises. The relative prices of previously undertaxed products rise, and there is a relative fall in demands as seen in Table 3.6.

CONCLUSION

In this paper we have analyzed four alternative plans for corporate and personal income tax integration in the United States by using a recently constructed medium-scale general equilibrium model of the U.S. economy and tax system. The paper includes a brief discussion of the model and its use of data, in addition to outlining characteristics of the integration plans and their representation in model equivalent form. Because the model will soon include dynamic effects, a labor/leisure choice, and other new features, these results must be considered preliminary.

Total integration of personal and corporate income taxes are shown to yield static efficiency gains of $6 billion per year using 1973 data. Dividend deductibility from either the corporate income tax or the personal income tax results in an efficiency increase of slightly less than half of this. A 15% dividend gross-up scheme yields somewhat less than either dividend deduction plan. The distributional impacts vary between plans; full integration is shown to imply a slightly progressive change in the distribution of real income in such a way that every class is better off. Dividend deductibility from the corporate income tax and a dividend gross-up plan are shown to have close to proportional impacts, while dividend deductibility from the personal income tax is noticeably regressive.

DISCUSSION

Nicholas M. Kiefer

In the Fullerton et al. chapter general economic equilibrium methods are used to measure the efficiency gains from certain changes in U.S. tax policy. The changes considered are five plans for integration of corporate and personal income taxes. I will skirt the policy questions and focus my discussion on the model and technique. Below I outline and comment on some details of the elaborate structural model set up by the authors, then raise some questions about the technique and provide some suggestions for dealing with these questions.

The model consists of a production sector with nineteen single-good industries, each requiring labor, capital services, and producer goods as inputs; and a consumption sector involving twelve consumer groups classified by gross income. The nineteen producer goods are transformed into sixteen consumer goods, the demands for which are specified to be consistent with utility maximization. The use of intermediate inputs in production and the transformation of producer into consumer goods are both described by fixed-coefficient input-output matrices. Taxes are modeled in detail. This detailed model was constructed so as to be consistent with 1973 production, consumption, and taxation data from a number of different government agencies. Although a number of straightforward extensions can be suggested (straightforward to suggest, perhaps not to implement), e.g., the model should be dynamic to capture the effects of taxes on capital formation, or labor supply should be endogenous, the model as it stands is impressive in its detail. Realistically, the extension to a dynamic model is likely to be extremely difficult, and the static model should therefore be pushed as far as possible.

The relationship between the approach used in this paper, and in other papers at this conference, and the conventional structural-economic-modeling approach is worth examining. There are two points to be made. Consider the linear structural economic model

$$y_t\Gamma + x_t B = u_t, \tag{1}$$

where y_t is a $1 \times G$ vector of prices and quantities, x_t is a $1 \times K$ vector of K exogenous variables including tax rates, and u_t is a $1 \times G$ vector of errors, all in period t. Γ and B are the structural parameters. Given x_t and the structural parameters, the expected value of y_t is easy to calculate; in empirical work attention is focused on estimating B and Γ from observations on x and y for a number of periods. The first point can be made in the context of the ordinary regression model ($G = 1$). If only one observation is available, then only one element of B can be estimated, conditional on the value of the other elements. Obviously the "fit" will be the same no matter what the conditioning values of the preset elements of B are.

The Fullerton et al. model is highly nonlinear

$$\Psi(y_t, x_t, \Theta) = 0 \tag{2}$$

(where Θ is the vector of structural parameters) and difficult to solve for y_t, given x_t and Θ. Consequently, attention has been focused on specifying and solving $\Psi = 0$; however, the identification issue is still present. This issue is noted to some extent by·the authors, who use several different sets of restrictions on Θ in their experiments. The point is that the parameters are sufficiently restricted that one observation (1973) serves to identify the model. This point is sometimes lost in the terminology used in microsimulation studies: a model is "calibrated," not estimated, on the basis of a "benchmark," not an observation.

The prospects of assembling detailed, consistent data like that assembled for 1973 for additional years seem grim. Consequently, the question of whether there can be any verification of the model in terms of fit arises. Certainly one approach is to calculate the equilibrium prices and quantities for some year in which tax rates were different from those in 1973 and compare these predictions with the observed prices and quantities. I think something further can be done along these lines based on an approximate reduced form (2). The point here is that the structure is not needed for purposes of prediction. In the linear simultaneous equations, model predictions can be made on the basis of the reduced form alone,

$$\hat{y}_t = x_t \hat{\Pi},$$

although for purposes of calculating efficiency gains or losses, the structural parameters would be required. Corresponding to the structure (2) an approximation to the reduced form can be estimated by a regression of the y's on polynomials in x. Effects of tax changes on equilibrium prices and quantities could be predicted from this reduced form and compared with the predictions obtained by solving the hypothesized structure at the new taxes. This method requires accumulation of data for other years, however, the elaborate data on intermediate products, required to restrict the structure (2), is not needed. Indeed, a partial check could be made based on a part of the reduced form, depending on data availability.

The Fullerton et al. general equilibrium model is a remarkably detailed model which can be used for comparative statics experiments which would not be feasible without a numerical model and a powerful solution algorithm. The model establishes the "state of the art" in elaborate structural modeling involving full exploitation of the idea of equilibrium. The usefulness of this type of model and approach for tax analysis is clear. However, because the model has not yet been checked in terms of its fit or predictive ability (except that it reproduces the 1973 data as an equilibrium), the actual numerical predictions from the model, for example, dollars of efficiency gain, should be regarded as highly tentative.

DISCUSSION

Jonathan R. Kesselman

Any move to integrate the corporate and personal tax systems calls into question a complex web of input demands, product and factor prices, and consumption, savings, and investment behaviors. Major features of both tax systems require differentiation among intermediate products, among final products, and among income classes of households. It thus seems obvious that a disaggregated general equilibrium approach is needed to assess fully the net effects of any specified policy change. For this reason I am sure that everyone will welcome the first major effort to implement such a model, as undertaken by Fullerton, King, Shoven, and Whalley.[1] While the goal is clearly desirable, the *feasibility* of constructing a satisfactory model cannot be taken for granted. We must be careful to devise a set of standards by which their model and future elaborations can be judged. The primary goal of such models is to aid in the appraisal of tax policies, and this policy context dictates how any model is ultimately assessed.

A brief summary of the Fullerton et al. policy findings will serve as useful background for my discussion. They consider four plans for corporate tax integration, including total integration under the familiar "partnership" method. Two partial integration plans considered are deduction of dividends from the corporate income tax and from the personal income tax. The final plan would reduce but not remove the double taxation of dividends, the so-called dividend credit "gross up" method. Adjusting capital tax rates to yield unchanged revenues, they find that each integration method reduces the level of distortion in the economy. Their best-guess estimates of the annual welfare gains from U.S. corporate tax integration under the four plans range from $2.3 to $5.6 billion (1973 dollars). A capital taxation scheme that eliminates all interindustry distortions (except vis-à-vis

---

[1] This statement encompasses earlier work undertaken by these authors, individually and jointly. I also mean to distinguish their work from other microeconomic tax simulation models which do not allow for extensive changes in relative prices.

government enterprises) is found to improve welfare by up to $10 billion; yet, the requisite coordination of property and other business taxes is clearly infeasible. The authors next estimate the distributional impact of corporate tax integration, considering both household net incomes and the prices of consumer goods. Their most striking result is that all plans, except dividend deduction from the personal tax, raise net real incomes at all levels including the lowest income classes. Finally, they present estimates of each plan's effects on the prices and outputs of 19 broad industries.

In order to assess the relevance of the Fullerton et al. findings to practical policy, it is essential to examine the assumptions, structure, and techniques embedded in their model. I shall raise many questions of behavioral realism and institutional detail. At points I shall suggest the desirability of greater disaggregation than has been undertaken. These comments are meant to be constructive rather than critical. This ambitious project has tackled difficult modeling problems that had not been attempted previously. Indeed, my comments reinforce the view that a disaggregated general equilibrium approach is needed to assess prospective tax policies. I shall begin with several general comments about the methodology and assumptions of this model. Then I shall focus more closely on some channels by which an economist might expect the efficiency and distributional effects of corporate tax policy to be transmitted.

The authors have had to make a number of choices about modeling methods. Some of their choices were dictated by data availability and technical feasibility, but others were not so constrained. They have assumed full employment of the economy's resources, which seems appropriate given the interest in long-run outcomes. An integration plan may influence the economy's prospects of full employment and the effectiveness of stabilization policies. These issues, however, more properly fall in the domain of a macroeconometric model. In some cases the modeling of all nonpersonal taxes as *ad valorem* will obscure the effects on the marginal price of factors. As evidenced by Table 3.2, the authors are aware of these simplifications, and presumably refinements will prove feasible. The functional forms used for production and consumption decisions—Cobb-Douglas, Leontief, CES, and LES—are restrictive and exclude the complementarity of goods. Hopefully, the generalized functional forms developed in recent years might be applied in future models of this kind.[2] The method of model construction adopted by Fullerton et al. places a high premium on replicating the "benchmark equilibrium data set" as opposed to obtaining empirical estimates of behavioral responses. This approach elevates model consistency above the more proven methods of validating economic models. It would seem more important for policy appraisal that a model perform well in predicting induced changes than in fitting the initial values. This may be an unfair view, but unfortunately the authors give no clear rationale for their approach.

---

[2] For a review of these developments, see Blackorby et al. (1978), especially chapter 8. For an illustrative application, see Berndt et al. (1977).

Several market assumptions play important roles in the model and affect its policy application. All markets are assumed to be perfectly competitive. This rules out monopoly and oligopoly elements in product and labor markets—contradicting extensive evidence of concentrated industries dominated by a few corporations and unions. To model these features competently would require far more disaggregation and additional theoretical and empirical complexities. As usual the fate of the economist is to adopt the "as-if-competitive" behavioral assumption. Still, we must not forget that various theories of corporate tax shifting hinge upon the firm's price-setting behavior.

The model's other major set of market assumptions is that the aggregate capital and labor stocks are fixed, while these resources can move freely among industries. Moreover, savings behaivor is endogenous but is not allowed to influence the capital stock. These assumptions constitute an unusual twist on the shortrun versus long-run distinction. By implication, the corporate tax is at least partially borne by capital in the short run, but any induced long-run shifting is restricted by the fixity of the capital stock. A fair view of these matters is to observe that the authors are in the process of making their model dynamic. Their current model is to be taken as a halfway house in this respect. In spite of these potential extensions, I still have reservations about the ability of this kind of model to portray features of the industrial structure which may yield differential forward shifting. For example, public utilities can normally pass the tax forward as part of the rate-making process; the tax shifting of nonregulated industries is constrained to varying degrees by factors such as import competition.

I shall now examine more specifically several channels by which the corporate income tax might affect economic efficiency. If these are not captured in the model, then the estimates of gain from tax integration may be biased. In some cases one can hazard a guess as to the direction of bias for the Fullerton et al. model. The competition assumption implies only a normal return to capital in equilibrium and no pure economic profits. Since real-world oligopolistic markets generate pure profits subject to corporate tax, the model may exaggerate the welfare gains from integration. The bias is increased in the model because the rents to land are aggregated with the returns to reproducible capital. The latter aspect of the problem could be alleviated by disaggregating nonlabor inputs.

One would expect efficiency gains from integration to the extent that "the corporate way of doing business" is inherently efficient. This phrase connotes the scale economies of immense firms, which typically can be financed only in the corporate mode. However, the authors implicitly assume constant returns to scale at all levels of firm size and thus miss this effect entirely. Realistically, the profitability of firms varies within an industry, even among the incorporated firms. Corporate taxes are paid only by the profitable, and hence more efficient firms. To the extent that they shift the tax forward to consumers, the profitable corporations create a "price umbrella" protecting the inefficient firms.[3] Neither this

[3] The relation between "price umbrella" effects and corporate tax shifting has been discussed by Slitor (1966).

effect nor the gains that would accrue to reversing it under integration (or better, a value-added tax) is captured in the model. The requisite disaggregation within industries may be infeasible from both empirical and computational viewpoints.

The major efficiency concerns of the model are the differential tax rates paid by equity versus debt and dividends versus retentions. It is a commonplace that the bias toward retained earnings leads to the selection of low-return investment projects and hampers the overall efficiency of capital markets. Thus, tax integration policies which reduce the bias toward retentions should reap efficiency gains. Fullerton et al. consider alternative assumptions about the financial policies of corporations under dividend deduction from each of the two tax bases and obtain associated welfare estimates. As they note, the absence of empirical elasticity parameters for corporate financial policies means that theirs is not a "true" general equilibrium model. I do not regard this as a major shortcoming for the policy applications of their model. One might, however, question whether the inefficiencies of these biases are fully captured by the model, in part owing to the absence of *intra*industry disaggregation. One further efficiency concern of the model is the *inter*industry differentials in capital tax rates. Corporate taxes are only one of the taxes on capital income, so that full integration does not completely eliminate interindustry tax differentials.

A general equilibrium analysis allows the distributional impacts of tax policies to be assessed for both the sources and uses of household incomes. The authors have exploited this potential in their estimates. Their top income class is households with $25,000 or more gross income. A large portion of total capital incomes is received by this bracket, which spans marginal tax rates of about 28% to 70% (joint returns). It would be desirable to disaggregate the top income bracket, even if the consumption patterns cannot be more finely differentiated, for more accuracy in simulation and the interest of the distributional findings. The tabulated distributions reflect the altered net real capital incomes including retained earnings but do not capitalize any induced changes in share valuations. Horizontal equity effects of the integration plans—other than the relief from "double taxation" of dividends—are hidden in the results. We cannot tell how the gains or losses of any income bracket are distributed among its members nor how they might be related to characteristics such as age of head of household. But this is really a task for a *different* microsimulation model.

The channels for transmission of distributional effects plausibly include the initial factor endowments by income class, effects on gross factor prices, and effects on factor holdings or supplies. As noted earlier, the model has constrained aggregate capital and labor stocks to be unchanged. The distributions of both factor endowments or supplies are also assumed to be unaffected by changes in tax policy. It would be desirable for future models to disaggregate labor into several skill or occupational classes. To state this position more strongly, I place little credibility in the distributional estimates of a model which does not examine the labor market in greater detail. After all, labor endowments generate more than twice as much income as capital endowments. Since recent econometric studies find some kinds of labor complementary with capital, and other kinds to be sub-stitutable, corporate tax integration may potently affect distribution via differential labor demand.[4]

The Fullerton et al. modeling of capital endowments takes a fixed portfolio composition (by industries and by types of capital income) which does not respond to corporate tax policies. More worrisome than its exogeneity is the attribution of the *same* portfolio composition to the capital endowments of all income classes. Because of this, the estimated distributional effects of integration may be highly misleading. For example, the capital income of low-income groups is mostly net rent from owner-occupied housing (78% for the under-$3000 class), whereas this is not true for higher incomes (only 8% for the over-$25,000 class). Tax integration with the equal-yield adjustment raises the burden on the previously undertaxed housing industry, which has a regressive impact. The equality of portfolio composi-tions appears to be a more damaging assumption for policy purposes than their exogeneity. One can hope that this feature of the model will also prove easier to rectify.

I would now like to examine some less technical matters in assessing the model's findings for practical policy. To hold tax revenues constant under each integration plan, the model rescales a column of capital-tax rates as required. Because it bears both corporate and personal tax burdens, capital income is initially taxed more heavily than labor income. The equal-yield adjustment implies that, even under full integration, capital and labor income dollars are taxed differentially in the hands of households. A buck is not a buck. Practical implementation of total integration, however, may attempt to remove this discrimination as well. It would be interesting to know the distributional impacts implied by a buck-is-a-buck scaling adjustment for equal yield. As indicated earlier, I would remain skeptical of the distributional estimates within this model until the capital endowments and labor market structures are refined. Removing the differential tax burden on capital vis-à-vis labor may either augment or decrease the welfare gains of integration. As is well known in tax theory, efficiency is improved by concentrating taxes on factors or goods which are relatively unresponsive to price changes.

If we could believe the Fullerton et al. estimates, total integration would be preferred for its efficiency gains and Pareto-superior impact. However, the authors cite the partnership method of total integration, which appears to be both politically and administratively unacceptable. This method has four faults: (1) Corporations would face difficulties in allocating gross earnings across their various outstanding securities; (2) shareholders might face liquidity problems in paying taxes on retained earnings; (3) share gains in excess of cumulative retained earnings would still be taxed preferentially as capital gains; and (4) the inflation component of returns to capital would continue to bear tax. Total integration could avoid these faults under a "realization" method which would (1) eliminate the corporate tax; (2) tax dividends received at personal rates, as at present; and (3) tax inflation-

---

[4] See Berndt and Christensen (1974); and Kesselman et al. (1977).

adjusted capital gains upon realization at full personal rates and with a penalty factor for tax deferral based on the net-of-tax interest rate compounded over the holding period.[5] With this new visage, total integration might get a better reception in the policy arena. If relief from "double taxation" of dividends is granted under a partial plan, it would be politically inconceivable to adopt full personal taxation of retained earnings at some later time. For efficiency as well as equity, it may be essential to move directly to total integration rather than pursuing a piecemeal path. Unfortunately, no simulation model can help us in reaching policy insights of this nature.

What are the potentials and limitations of general equilibrium models of the Fullerton et al. genre for use in appraising tax policies? I really cannot give a credible forecast of their potential except to state that I have come away from this model more hopeful than when first encountering it. One barrier to assessing the model's reliability is that it has yet to be applied to predicting the effects of an actual discrete taxation change. Most of my suggestions for the model point toward greater disaggregation. Some of these items may be immediately feasible, while others will hinge upon improved data availability, behavioral estimates, and expanded computational facilities. My other concerns relate to the role of particular market assumptions in the modeling. I fear that microeconomists have tended to proceed with empirical modeling as if they knew the "correct" theory, whereas macroeconomists have long since realized the elusiveness of this notion.

A further analogy to the evolution of macroeconometric models seems apropos here. After many years in refining large-scale macromodels, economists still obtain divergent results and sometimes hopelessly inaccurate forecasts. Nevertheless, these models are widely judged to be a useful *component* in the appraisal of macro policies. We have to hope that this is not merely an expression of vested interests. Most economists are prepared to believe that the general equilibrium effects of tax policies can be as important as their direct effects in the market of impact. Since our minds are not up to the task of making general equilibrium computations, we need outside guidance. I expect that the Fullerton, King, Shoven, Whalley model will one day be seen as the first generation in a small family of general equilibrium models to simulate taxation policies. The role of these models will undoubtedly be to *aid* policy appraisal, not to *be* policy appraisal.

[5] For discussion of this problem outside the context of corporate taxes, see Brinner (1973).

MICRODATA MODELS WITH REGIONAL AND/OR SECTORAL IMPACTS

4

A MICROECONOMIC SIMULATION MODEL FOR ANALYZING THE REGIONAL AND DISTRIBUTIONAL EFFECTS OF TAX-TRANSFER POLICY: AN ANALYSIS OF THE PROGRAM FOR BETTER JOBS AND INCOME

Robert H. Haveman
Kevin Hollenbeck
David Betson
Martin Holmer

INTRODUCTION

Microdata simulation models are a phenomenon of the last decade. Their development can be traced to several factors, including frustration with the limited insights available from both analytical models and the empirical estimates yielded by more aggregative econometric models and the demands of policymakers for more detailed sectoral and distributional results. That the growth of these models has coincided with the growth in federal expenditures for transfer programs is no accident. These expenditures, more than exhaustive expenditures, have prompted questions about who wins and who loses and what the resulting behavioral responses will be.

Early studies of the distributional impacts of tax-transfer policies were limited to the estimation of the first-round (or direct) incidence effects of the programs considered. In effect, the methodology adopted in these first efforts involved mapping the rules of actual or proposed measures onto survey or published census-type data, and through the mapping, to estimate the allocation of total benefits paid to (or taxes collected from) various types of household units. While these analyses represented marked improvements over earlier empirical studies of tax-transfer programs, they stimulated still further efforts to develop reliable estimates of distributional and behavioral responses. With respect to the distributional analyses, it was recognized that the estimates of incidence assumed no shifting of benefit or burden owing to substitutions of leisure for work or consumption for saving. Moreover, the estimates did not account for the fact that the initial (or first-round) tax or transfer would stimulate a series of reactions which, in a highly interdependent economy, would lead to further distributional effects— effects which would either complement or offset the initial impact.

While concern with the "partial" analytical framework of the early studies led to more comprehensive and sytematic analysis, an additional factor has also en-couraged the search for more extensive models of analysis. This factor is the grow-ing availability of data. Until recent years, the data required for more systematic analysis involving the interrelationships of detailed sectors of national economies (individuals, regions, industries, occupations) have not been available. By and large, researchers have had to rely on survey data containing limited information on observations drawn from specially selected populations (and, hence, not reliable for estimating impacts on the nation as a whole). Moreoever, coefficients describing the interrelationships of various sectors of the economy (industry to industry, region to region, occupation to industry, and occupation or industry to income class) were either unavailable or very crude. The scarcity of such data served as a serious con-straint on more comprehensive and systematic analysis.

In recent years, this constraint has been significantly relaxed in the United States. Self-weighting national sample surveys with significant numbers of observa-tions have recently become available on computer tape: these include the Survey of Consumer Expenditures of the Bureau of Labor Statistics (20,000 households, 1972-1973), the Survey of Economic Opportunity of the Census Bureau (65,000 households, 1967), the Current Population Survey of the Census Bureau (50,000 households, now available for each year since 1967), the OEO-Michigan data from the Survey Research Center of the University of Michigan (5000 households, longi-tudinally observed since the late 1960s), and the Survey of Income and Education of the Census Bureau (151,700 households, 1976). While detailed national input-output models have been available for two decades, the first multiregional input-output model (involving input-out coefficients and interregional trade relationships for 79 industries in 44 regions) became available on computer tape only in the early 1970s. Similarly, data required to evaluate the relationship of changes in industrial output and the demand for labor of various detailed skills and occupa-tions have been gathered only recently. Such information is the material out of which more systematic and comprehensive analyses are built.

A third development relates to the behavioral responses that are induced by tax and transfer policies. While the existence of these responses (e.g., labor supply, migration, family structure) has long been recognized, the availability of reliable parameter estimates of these effects, which are specific to population subgroups, is a recent phenomenon. And, even now, such estimates are available only for labor supply, and these due mainly to the negative income tax experiments. Nevertheless, the availability of response estimates and their incorporation into impact models have permitted still richer analyses.

THE STRUCTURE OF THE SIMULATION MODEL

In this paper we describe one particular model that employs the recently available micro- and sectoral data sets and estimates of behavioral responses to yield more comprehensive and systematic analysis of the distributional effects of tax-transfer policies.[1] This model incorporates estimates of responses of both labor supply and consumption spending to changes in tax and transfer policies and seeks to trace the results of these responses through the economic system. The primary response that is exploited is the alteration in the level and composition of consumption spending due to a change in household disposable income. Such a response, however, is only the first step in a long chain of reallocations induced by the policy. As the composition of demands for goods and services changes—by industry and by region—various firms in various regions alter their production levels and call for a new constellation of indirect demands and employment patterns. After the economy has adjusted to this exogenous impact, some sectors—occupations, industries, regions, income classes—will gain and others will lose.

The simulation model has been designed to estimate these induced sectoral effects. This model is formed by the linkage of five separate modules. In the first module, the eligibility and benefit (tax) structure of the programs to be analyzed are used to simulate the net cost or benefit to each of the households on a nationally weighted microdata source. This first-round impact can be shown for various regions of the country and income classes. This data source is the Survey of Income and Education. In the first module, the labor supply responses of households to changes in tax and transfer policy are incorporated into the estimate of the net change in household income due to this policy.[2]

The second module simulates the changes in the level and pattern in consumption spending induced by the policy for each of the families. This consumption-demand simulation is obtained by applying the relevant expenditure sector coefficients to families distinguished by a variety of economic and demographic traits. The coefficients were estimated by fitting a 56-sector (equation) log-linear consumption expenditure system to the microdata of the 1972-1973 Survey of Consumer Expenditures. From this simulation, the change in consumption demand for 56 sectors in 23 regions is obtained.

The third module transforms these final demand changes by commodity into an estimate of changes in gross output required of all production sectors in various regions of the economy by incorporating the indirect demands placed by industries on each other. This is accomplished by means of a 79-industry, 23-region, multiregional input-output study. The changes in gross outputs required of each of 79 industries in each of 23 regions, caused by the policy change, are estimated in this module.

In the final two modules, the simulated changes in sectoral gross outputs are transformed, first, into estimates of the change in man-years of labor demand by occupation (module 4), and second, into dollars of induced earnings by earnings and income class (module 5). The estimates in the fourth module are derived by applying an industrial-occupation matrix containing labor-demand-per-dollar-of-

---

[1] A description of this model is found in Golladay and Haveman (1977).
[2] The paper by Betson et al., chapter 5 in Volume 1, describes this module in some detail.

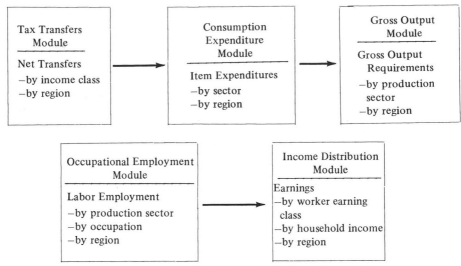

Figure 4.1. *A schematic flow chart of the simulation model.*

gross-output coefficients to the changes in gross output obtained in the previous module. The coefficients in the matrix were developed by the U.S. Department of Labor from Census data. In this simulation, 114 occupations in 23 regions of the country are distinguished. In the final module, the simulated estimates of occupational man-hour demands are combined with occupational earnings data to estimate changes in earned income for each occupation in each region.

As a final step, the estimates of regional-occupational earnings are mapped into incremental size distributions (consisting of 15 earnings and income classes) for each region and the nation as a whole. The coefficients for this last mapping are from special tabulations employing the 1-in-1000 data tapes of the 1970 Census.[3] The flow of this model is summarized in Figure 4.1. As shown there, the final output of the model displays the distribution of policy-induced earnings by 15 income classes in each of 23 regions and in the nation as a whole. A more formal statement of the model is found in Appendix A to this paper. There the component data sources of the model are also identified.

THE PROGRAM FOR BETTER JOBS AND INCOME—
THE BASIS FOR ANALYSIS

This sequential simulation model was applied to the welfare reform proposed by the Carter administration in 1977—The Program for Better Jobs and Income (PBJI). This program, which would replace the existing Aid to Families with Depen-

[3] Data tapes are available at the Center for Demography and Ecology, University of Wisconsin, Madison.

dent Children (AFDC), Food Stamps, and Supplemental Security Income (SSI) programs, has three components: (1) a program to create up to 1.4 million public service jobs for adult workers with children, (2) a cash assistance program consisting of a federal negative income tax and optional state supplements, and (3) tax reduction in the form of an expanded earned income tax credit (EITC). Appendix B of this paper details the state supplement features of the cash assistance component of the policy. Other details of this program and the module-1 simulation of its first-round distributional impacts are described in the paper by Betson et al., chapter 5 in Volume 1. Because of the state supplementation features of PBJI, net federal outlays for the program are simulated to be approximately $6.2 billion (1975 dollars) even though the transfers to households will be approximately $5.0 billion (1975 dollars). The residual $1.2 billion is "fiscal relief," and is assumed in this analysis to contribute to reducing the net deficit of government fiscal accounts, with no additional impacts on the economy. The federal income surtax simulated in this application of the model was designed to induce a 5.06% increase in the tax liability of every household liable for federal income taxes, hence raising the $6.2 billion (1975 dollars) required to finance the increased federal expenditures. Because of varying income levels and sources of income among regions, the implicit effective surtax rate among the 23 regions in the model varied substantially.

For any family (or group of families), the net change in disposable income attributable to the program is equal to (1) the benefit payment or earnings received from components of the plan minus (2) the changes in earnings induced by the plan through labor supply responses minus (3) the changes in earnings or benefits from programs modified or abolished by the program minus (4) increased federal taxes. In Table 4.1, the total change in disposable income of $5.1 billion (in 1975 dollars) induced by PBJI is distributed over the components of total

Table 4.1
Changes in Disposable Income from PBJI, by Income Source
(billions of 1975 dollars)

Source	Income Change
Private earned income	−1.1
Public service earned income	6.2
Income-conditioned cash or in-kind benefits	−1.7
Unemployment benefits	−0.7
Earned income tax credit	2.9
Federal income taxes	−0.1
Social security taxes	−0.3
State income taxes	−0.1
All sources	5.1

Source: Module 1 simulations by the Department of Health, Education, and Welfare, Office of the Assistant Secretary of Planning and Evaluation.

disposable income. The largest source of income change attributable to PBJI is for earnings from the public service employment component of the plan, which are simulated to be slightly over $6.2 billion. The only other changes in disposable income stem from the Earned Income Tax Credit (EITC). Net decreases in disposable income will occur in the form of losses in private earnings due to labor supply reductions or the switch to public employment, losses of income from transfer programs eliminated by PBJI, and increased payroll and income taxes.

Table 4.2 shows the distribution of this change in disposable income by income class. Of the class intervals shown there, the $6000-$12,000 class experiences the largest aggregate change in disposable income from PBJI, $1.5 billion. However, the increased tax liabilities for this class are virtually identical to the changes in disposable income from PBJI, so the result is a very small increase in disposable income per family of $.63. The group with less than $2000 of income experiences an increase in disposable income which is nearly as large as that of the $6000-$12,000 group. However, because this income class contains only 5.4% of the nation's families, and because it experiences only a minute increase in positive taxes, the increase in disposable income per family is $337.32. With the abolition of several transfer programs, the increased disposable income for the $2000-$3000 income group is low relative to the next lowest income class. It should be noted that because Table 4.2 summarizes average results within income classes, it disguises the fact that there is a distribution of effects within each class. Thus, even in the lowest income classes some families are adversely affected by the program, in particular current AFDC recipients in high-benefit states.[4]

Another dimension of the distributional impact of the change in disposable income, that by region, is shown in Table 4.3. Households in the South are the only census region group to experience a net increase in disposable income from the PBJI and federal income surtax—approximately $700 million. Households in the other three regions account for a combined decrease in disposable income of $1.9 billion. California and New York are the largest losers in terms of disposable income, with losses of $571.1 million and $402.4 million, respectively. These two states have relatively small income gains from PBJI because existing programs, which provide high benefit levels relative to other states, will be abolished. At the same time, these two states have the highest effective surtax rate. As might be expected, the regions that are relative gainers are all in the South: North Carolina, South Carolina, Georgia, Florida, Kentucky-Tennessee, Mississippi, and Texas. Because the federal income surtax is designed to cover both the transfer and public service employment costs of PBJI and fiscal relief to the states, the decrease in disposable income to the nation as a whole is $1.23 billion.

In response to these changes in disposable income, consumption demand changes, but these changes are not evenly distributed across commodities. Some of the expenditure changes increase demand for goods produced by local and regional industries, but others affect businesses far from the site of the increased expendi-

---

[4] HEW has estimated that 3.8 million current AFDC recipients and nearly 1 million current SSI recipients will be adversely affected by PBJI. See Haveman and Smolensky (1978).

Table 4.2

Distribution of Change in Disposable Income by Income Class

Current Family Disposable Income (1975 dollars)	Changes in Disposable Income from PBJI (millions of 1975 dollars)	Changes in Positive Federal Taxes (millions of 1975 dollars)	Net Changes in Disposable Income (millions of 1975 dollars)	Per Family, Change in Disposable Income
< $2,000	1,399.5	(1.3)	1,398.2	$337.32
2,000-3,000	517.3	(2.2)	515.1	97.51
3,000-4,000	578.2	(19.8)	558.4	107.39
4,000-5,000	544.9	(51.5)	493.4	91.27
5,000-6,000	482.9	(93.0)	389.3	68.99
6,000-12,000	1,480.7	(1,462.0)	18.7	.63
> 12,000	2.2	(4,609.9)	(4,607.7)	(209.38)
All families	5,005.2	(6,240.0)	(1,234.8)	(15.99)

Source: Module 1 simulations by the Department of Health, Education, and Welfare, Office of the Assistant Secretary of Planning and Evaluation.
Note: Columns do not add because of rounding.

ture. This is especially notable after the second, third, and nth order interindustry demands are accounted for.

Table 4.3 also presents measures of the distribution of induced gross output. For the nation, gross output increases by about $1.35 billion. The South experiences a substantial benefit from this increased production. In fact, its increase of $1.6 billion exceeds the national increase. The North Central region has a small net

Table 4.3
Change in Disposable Income and Gross Output from PBJI, by Region

	Change in Disposable Income			Change in Gross Output		
			(millions of 1975 dollars)			
Region	From PBJI	Increased Taxes	Net	From PBJI	Increased Taxes	Net
Northeast	*832.4*	*(1,537.0)*	*(704.6)*	*1,602.2*	*(1,670.5)*	*(68.3)*
1. CT, ME, MA, NH, RI, VT	283.2	(365.4)	(82.2)	531.8	(467.2)	64.6
2. NY	201.1	(603.5)	(402.4)	488.8	(609.9)	(121.0)
3. PA, NJ	348.1	(568.1)	(220.0)	581.6	(593.4)	(11.8)
North Central	*1,134.4*	*(1,688.2)*	*(553.8)*	*2,279.9*	*(2,169.8)*	*110.1*
4. OH, MI	482.7	(567.0)	(84.3)	718.6	(595.4)	123.5
5. IN, IL	287.6	(535.8)	(248.2)	523.4	(567.6)	(44.2)
6. WI, MN	119.0	(239.2)	(120.2)	354.2	(372.6)	(18.4)
7. IA, MO	131.0	(207.3)	(76.3)	355.3	(344.6)	10.8
8. KA, NB, ND, SD	114.1	(138.9)	(24.8)	328.4	(289.6)	38.8
South	*2,429.2*	*(1,721.4)*	*707.8*	*5,028.8*	*(3,424.6)*	*1,604.2*
9. DE, DC, MD	76.3	(212.1)	(135.9)	339.5	(365.8)	(26.3)
10. VA, WV	199.1	(190.4)	8.7	435.3	(330.7)	104.6
11. NC	214.3	(121.4)	92.9	438.8	(279.6)	159.2
12. SC	141.4	(54.7)	86.8	358.6	(224.8)	133.8
13. GA	202.7	(114.8)	87.9	392.0	(241.8)	150.2
14. FL	308.2	(213.4)	94.8	505.2	(326.0)	179.1
15. KY, TN	284.2	(158.3)	125.9	506.6	(301.8)	204.8
16. AL	140.2	(75.4)	64.8	356.8	(234.4)	122.3
17. MS	134.5	(42.6)	91.9	335.6	(196.3)	139.2
18. AR, OK	168.1	(112.2)	55.9	383.2	(263.8)	119.4
19. LA	132.6	(83.8)	48.8	341.3	(233.7)	107.6
20. TX	427.6	(342.3)	85.3	635.9	(425.9)	210.0
West	*609.2*	*(1,293.4)*	*(684.2)*	*1,290.2*	*(1,589.1)*	*(298.9)*
21. AZ, CO, ID, NM, UT, NV, WY, MT, AK	264.3	(302.8)	(38.6)	473.2	(428.5)	44.8
22. WA, OR, HI	136.0	(210.5)	(74.5)	358.8	(395.0)	(36.2)
23. CA	208.9	(780.1)	(571.1)	458.2	(765.6)	(307.4)
Entire U. S.	5,005.2	(6,240.0)	(1,234.8)	10,201.5	(8,854.0)	1,347.3

Source: Modules 1-3 simulation of PBJI and federal income surtax by the Department of Health, Education, and Welfare, Office of the Assistant Secretary of Planning and Evaluation.
Note: Columns do not add because of rounding.

increase, while the Northeast and West have net decreases of $68.3 million and $298.9 million, respectively. It is interesting to note that gross output is estimated to increase by $1.35 billion even though disposable income experiences a reduction of $1.23 billion. This result occurs because the recipients of the transfers have larger propensities to consume than those bearing the increased taxes. In this situa-

Table 4.4

Ratios of Gross Output to Changes in Disposable Income and Induced Manpower Demand from PBJI, by Region

Region	Ratio of Gross Output to Disposable Income Changes		Changes in Induced Manpower Demand (*thousands of man-years*)		
	From PBJI	From Increased Taxes	From PBJI	From Increased Taxes	Net
Northeast	*1.92*	*1.09*	*70.1*	*(81.6)*	*(11.5)*
1.　CT, ME, MA, NH, RI, VT	1.88	1.28	23.6	(22.6)	1.0
2.　NY	2.43	1.01	19.8	(28.4)	(8.6)
3.　PA, NJ	1.67	1.04	26.7	(30.6)	(3.9)
North Central	*2.01*	*1.29*	*96.5*	*(101.9)*	*(5.4)*
4.　OH, MI	1.49	1.05	31.7	(28.3)	3.3
5.　IN, IL	1.82	1.06	21.9	(27.2)	(5.3)
6.　WI, MN	2.98	1.56	13.9	(16.9)	(3.0)
7.　IA, MO	2.71	1.66	15.4	(16.1)	(.7)
8.　KA, NB, ND, SD	2.88	2.08	13.6	(13.4)	.2
South	*2.07*	*1.99*	*240.2*	*(164.0)*	*76.2*
9.　DE, DC, MD	4.45	1.72	12.0	(15.9)	(3.9)
10.　VA, WV	2.19	1.74	20.0	(16.1)	3.9
11.　NC	2.05	2.30	21.6	(13.3)	8.3
12.　SC	2.54	4.11	18.3	(11.1)	7.2
13.　GA	1.93	2.11	15.5	(9.2)	6.3
14.　FL	1.64	1.53	26.3	(17.0)	9.3
15.　KY, TN	1.78	1.91	24.6	(13.9)	10.7
16.　AL	2.54	3.11	16.1	(10.4)	5.8
17.　MS	2.50	4.61	20.1	(11.8)	8.3
18.　AR, OK	2.28	2.35	18.4	(12.9)	5.5
19.　LA	2.57	2.79	15.8	(10.6)	5.2
20.　TX	1.49	1.24	31.5	(21.8)	9.7
West	*2.12*	*1.23*	*53.6*	*(71.7)*	*(18.1)*
21.　AZ, CO, ID, NM, UT, NV, WY, MT, AK	1.79	1.42	22.5	(21.2)	1.3
22.　WA, OR, HI	2.64	1.88	13.8	(16.0)	(2.2)
23.　CA	2.19	.98	17.3	(34.5)	(17.2)
Entire U. S.	2.04	1.42	460.6	(419.4)	41.2

Source: Modules 1-5 simulation of PBJI and federal income surtax by the Department of Health, Education, and Welfare, Office of the Assistant Secretary of Planning and Evaluation.
Note: Columns do not add because of rounding.

tion, financial markets would be affected, as there would be substantial dissaving among the low-income population and decreases in saving among the high-income population. The model does not capture these impacts.

Table 4.4 shows the ratio of induced gross output to the change in disposable income from PBJI and the associated increase in taxes for each of the regions and the United States. For the entire nation, the ratio associated with the disposable income changes from PBJI is 2.04, indicating that for each dollar of transfers, an *additional* $1.04 of gross sales revenue is generated. On the tax side, the ratio is only 1.42, indicating that each dollar of taxes reduces gross industrial sales by an *additional* $.42. Among the regions, the ratios vary significantly. For example, while the ratio from PBJI for the region comprising Delaware, the District of Columbia, and Maryland is 4.45, the ratio for Texas is 1.49. Although it is not shown in the tables, the distribution of gross output by region is less unequal than the distribution of changes in disposable income from the PBJI surtax policy. Hence, as the induced expenditure demands stimulated by the policy are reflected in gross output patterns, the regional disparities in the distribution of net transfers become evened out, and the induced output tends to reflect the general geographic location of productive capacity.

Table 4.5 presents another set of sectoral impacts, in this case by production sector. While the model yields estimates of the induced change in gross output by 23 regions and 79 production sectors, Table 4.5 presents the production sector impacts only for the nation as a whole and aggregated to 15 production sectors. The primary output impacts are in the manufacturing sector, which accounts for almost 39% of gross output increases. The second column of Table 4.5 displays an industrial impact indicator that reflects the size of the net induced impact on a sector relative to a measure of the total size of the sector.[5] Over all production sectors, the size of this indicator is .74 for the PBJI/surtax policy. The major sectors with high indicators are the motor vehicle, mining, and medical and educational services sectors, with indicators of 5.51, 2.27, and 1.66, respectively. Because of the net impacts of PBJI and increased taxes, the structure of national output will tend to be shifted toward these industries, and away from those with low impact indicators.

Of interest is the fairly large negative indicator for the finance and insurance sector. This industry will be a substantial loser under the program. This result stems from the difference in marginal consumption patterns among income classes, in combination with the net income distributional impact of the PBJI/surtax policy change. As Table 4.2 indicated, families in the lowest income class (less than $2000) gained $1.4 billion of disposable income, while families in the highest income class (more than $12,000) lost $4.6 billion of disposable income. The former group has

---

[5] This indicator is defined as

$$I_i^G = \frac{G_i}{.001(O_i)}$$

where I_i^G is the industrial impact indicator for industry i, G_i is the program-induced net change in gross output in industry i, and O_i is the 1970 gross output in industry i (expressed in 1973 dollars).

Table 4.5
Net Change in Gross Output from PBJI and Federal Income Surtax, by Production Sector

Production Sector	Change in Gross Output (*millions of 1975 dollars*)	Industrial Impact Indicator
Agriculture, forestry, and fisheries	54.9	.57
Mining	70.2	2.27
Construction	17.3	.11
Manufacturing	*519.4*	*.70*
Nondurables	*132.1*	*.36*
Food and kindred products	128.5	1.12
Other	3.6	.01
Durables	*387.3*	*1.02*
Primary iron and steel	1.6	.04
Motor vehicles	309.8	5.51
Other	75.9	.28
Transportation and warehousing	49.5	.78
Wholesaling and retail trade	257.1	1.28
Services	*379.1*	*.70*
Electricity, gas, water, and sanitation	60.2	1.25
Finance and insurance	(306.1)	−4.96
Real estate and rental	320.8	1.27
Medical and educational services, nonprofit organizations	103.7	1.66
Other	200.5	.99
Entire U. S.	1,347.3	.74

Source: Modules 1-5 simulation of PBJI and federal income surtax by the Department of Health, Education, and Welfare, Office of the Assistant Secretary of Planning and Evaluation.

a very small estimated marginal expenditure response for finance and insurance services; the latter group has a rather high propensity to reduce spending on the services of this industry when income falls. The combination of these effects results in a fairly negative impact of the program on this industry.

A final set of induced effects of the program is summarized in Table 4.6. There the labor demands estimated by the model for 114 occupations in 23 regions are aggregated across regions and occupations to yield detailed estimates for 16 occupational groups in the United States. Again, an impact indicator is presented to enable comparison of the pattern of program-induced demands with a measure of the preprogram occupational composition of the labor force.[6]

---

[6] The occupational impact indicator is defined as

$$I_o^e = \frac{M_o}{.001(L_o)}$$

where I_o is the occupational impact indicator for occupation o, M_o is the program-induced change in labor demand in occupation o, and L_o is the total employment in occupation o in 1970.

Table 4.6
Net Change in Induced Manpower Demand from PBJI and Federal Income Surtax, by Occupation

Occupation	Change in Labor Demand (*thousands of man-years*)	Occupational Impact Indicator
Professional, technical, and kindred	10.2	.78
Managers, officials, and proprietors	2.5	.28
Sales workers	2.3	.39
Clerical and kindred	*−.5*	*−.03*
Stenographers, typists, and secretaries	−.2	−.05
Bookkeepers and accounting clerks	−.3	−.22
Others	*a*	*a*
Craftsmen, foremen, and kindred	*7.4*	*.65*
Construction craftsmen	1.9	.40
Metalworking craftsmen	.9	.76
Printing-trade craftsmen	−.4	−1.31
Transportation, public utility, mechanics and repairmen	3.9	1.59
Other craftsmen	1.1	.78
Operatives and kindred	4.7	.32
Laborers except farm	2.3	.61
Service workers	*9.9*	*.75*
Food service workers	3.2	1.20
Others	6.7	.64
Farmers	1.7	.50
Entire U. S.	40.5	.45

Source: Modules 1-5 simulation of PBJI and federal income surtax by the Department of Health, Education, and Welfare, Office of the Assistant Secretary of Planning and Evaluation.
[a] Less than .05.

Of the 40,000 man-years of employment generated by the program, over one-fourth are concentrated in the category of professional and technical workers. The next largest categories are service workers (24%) and craftsmen and foremen (18%). In terms of impact indicators, the major occupational groups of professional and technical workers, craftsmen, and service workers are favored, while clerical workers, operatives, and managers all have impact indicators below .45, the indicator for the United States as a whole.

In Table 4.7, the effect of the program on the distribution of earned income is shown for 23 detailed regions, four census regions, and for the entire United States. A complex pattern emerges.[7] For 12 of the 15 regions with net manpower increases, the lowest-skill/lowest-earnings class (less than $4000) has the *lowest* impact indicator. These tend to be the states and regions in the South, where the bulk of disposable income changes from the policy are concentrated. For these

[7] The table entries denoted by an (*a*) are the minimum for that region and those denoted by a (*b*) are the maximum.

Table 4.7
Earnings Class Net Impact Indicators from PBJI and Federal Income Surtax, by Region

Region	Impact Indicators by Earnings Class				Regional Impact Indicator
	Less than $4,000	$4,000-10,000	$10,000-20,000	More than $20,000	
Northeast	$-.42^b$	$-.50$	$-.54$	$-.90^a$	$-.49$
1. CT, MA, ME, NH, RI, VT	.16	$.15^a$	$.24^b$	.17	.17
2. NY	$-.78^b$	-1.01	-1.06	-1.45^a	$-.94$
3. PA, NJ	$-.73$	$-.42^b$	$-.45$	$-.89^a$	$-.44$
North Central	$-.23$	$-.20$	$-.15^b$	$-.43^a$	$-.21$
4. OH, MI	.37	$.34^a$	.45	$.47^b$	.37
5. IN, IL	$-.71$	$-.66^b$	$-.68$	-1.30^a	$-.70$
6. WI, MN	$-.77$	$-.74^b$	$-.85$	-1.14^a	$-.78$
7. IA, MO	$-.26$	$-.19$	$-.06^b$	$-.40^a$	$-.21$
8. KA, NB, ND, SD	$-.00^a$	.10	$.28^b$	.26	.07
South	2.71^a	2.82	3.36	3.70^b	2.86
9. DE, DC, MD	-1.67	-1.57	-1.47^b	-2.82^a	-1.71
10. VA, WV	1.48^a	1.54	1.75	1.76^b	1.55
11. NC	3.22^a	3.41	5.34	7.68^b	3.51
12. SC	4.84^a	6.46	9.35	15.21^b	5.84
13. GA	2.82^a	2.99	4.48	5.15^b	3.10
14. FL	3.01^a	3.48	3.80	4.57^b	3.32
15. KY, TN	3.26^a	3.38	5.21	6.59^b	3.54
16. AL	3.69^a	4.30	5.38	5.64^b	4.11
17. MS	8.36	11.01	15.65^b	8.03^a	9.73
18. AR, OK	2.60^a	2.87	3.91	5.07^b	2.85
19. LA	3.44^a	3.98	4.56	5.58^b	3.81
20. TX	1.88^a	1.96	2.29	2.80^b	1.99
West	-1.05^b	-1.24	-1.29	-1.84^a	-1.19
21. AZ, CO, ID, NM, UT, NV, WY, MT, AK	$.27^a$	.36	.46	$.50^b$	.33
22. WA, OR, HI	$-.72$	-1.26^a	$-.70^b$	$-.78$	$-.87$
23. CA	-1.84^b	-1.88	-1.96	-2.76^a	-1.91
Entire U. S.	$.55^b$	.42	.26	$.15^a$	.45

Source: Modules 1-5 simulation of PBJI and federal income surtax by the Department of Health, Education, and Welfare, Office of the Assistant Secretary of Planning and Evaluation.
[a]Minimum for region.
[b]Maximum for region.

states then, the induced output changes tend to concentrate their employment demands on relatively high-skill/high-earnings workers, offsetting some of the pro-poor first-round distributional impact of the program. However, in seven of the eight regions with predicted manpower declines, the highest-skill/highest-earnings class (more than $20,000) has the most negative impact indicator. These are largely higher-income regions with a substantial surtax burden. The implication is that the expenditure reductions in these regions are concentrated on sectors employing relatively high-skill/high-earnings workers. This is consistent with the production sector and occupational results noted earlier, which suggest low or negative impacts on the finance and insurance sector and managerial and clerical workers. This latter pattern seems to have a stronger overall effect, as the impact indicator for the nation is highest in the less than $4000 class and lowest in the more than $20,000 class.

These comparisons indicate that the full redistributional impact of PBJI alone is weaker than that indicated by the high concentration of changes in disposable income in the lowest income classes. However, when PBJI is combined with a federal income surtax, the induced effects on income redistribution, while weaker than the initial redistribution, also tend to favor the lower earnings groups.

Among regions, however, this net income redistributional impact has an interesting twist. The southern states, which experience net increases in disposable income, net increases in output, and substantial first-round net benefits to the poor population, find the net pattern of changed manpower demands favoring high-skill/high-earnings workers. On the other hand, the northern and western states, which experience net decreases in disposable income, net decreases in output, and substantial income losses to the high-income population, find the net pattern of manpower demands adversely affecting high-skill/high-earnings workers. In the South, both poor welfare recipients and higher-income workers gain; in the North and West, the poor gain a relatively modest amount, while high-skill/high-earnings workers are adversely affected.

SOME POLICY IMPLICATIONS

The purpose of the simulation model is to enable analysis of both the direct and the induced effects of tax and transfer policies. The induced effects stem from the consumption expenditures of those who experience a change in disposable income because of the policy. The income changes result from both changes in the pattern of tax and transfer flows, and the changes in earned income resulting from labor supply responses to the incentive implicit in the policy.

We have applied the model to the welfare reform proposal of the Carter administration—The Program for Better Jobs and Income (PBJI) and a simultaneous federal income surtax. The analysis indicates that there is extreme regional variation in the final impacts of the plan. Full evaluation of proposed policy changes in the tax or transfer fields requires the analysis of total effects, direct as well as induced, if informed decisions are to be made. For example, on the basis of first-round effects, the PBJI would appear to benefit low-income families in the southern region of the country by more than is suggested by the results of the full analysis. The induced production tends to be concentrated on relatively high-wage/high-skill earners in the South. Hence, the indirect output and employment effects of PBJI tend to offset its primary distributional impact in that region. And, as we have indicated, in the North, the policy change leaves low-income families slightly better off, but it imposes both tax increases and employment reductions on higher-income groups.

The policy implications of the analysis are twofold—one specific to PBJI and the other more general. PBJI achieves many of the objectives of welfare reform. Horizontal inequities, marginal tax rates, and the poverty gap are all reduced. The cash transfer system has been integrated with the provision of public jobs for low-wage workers, and cash has been substituted for some in-kind transfers. However, while about $9 billion will be spent providing public service jobs and increased subsidies to low-wage/low-skill workers, the induced effects of the welfare-reform program appear to shift the distribution of private-sector jobs only slightly toward low-wage workers. The beneficial impacts of PBJI must be tempered by the information provided by these estimates of induced effects in order to yield a full evaluation of the program.

The more general implication follows directly from this. Any change in tax or transfer policy will have substantial effects on resource allocation and income distribution. Some will be consistent with the objectives of the policy; others may not be. Only by a more complete evaluation of these impacts, in particular an evaluation of the induced effects hidden from view by the complex spending, production, and employment decisions buried within the economic system, can the full efficiency and equity implications of the policy be understood. Such evaluations represent the contribution of microdata simulation models.

CAVEATS AND FUTURE DIRECTIONS OF RESEARCH

The reliability of the simulation estimates presented in this paper depends jointly on the accuracy of the underlying data and behavioral specifications. Limitations on both accounts exist for this model, although it is virtually impossible to gauge empirically the magnitude of any resulting biases.

Data limitations can be categorized into problems of timeliness and accuracy. For survey data, the major contributors to inaccuracy are sampling variability and misreporting by respondents. For example, the cash transfers portion of the policy that has been simulated will overestimate the costs of the program if income is underreported on the underlying survey. Similarly the estimated marginal commodity expenditure patterns depend on the accuracy of the data reported in the Survey of Consumer Expenditures. The most severe data timeliness limitation comes from using mid-1960s technology and interregional trade matrices in the regional input-output calculations. The recent pattern of industrial growth in the South and West must certainly blunt the simulated regional first-round impacts that have been reported.

In interpreting the simulation results, it must be noted that the model is not a full general equilibrium model in that numerous important economic relationships are omitted. First of all, other behavioral responses to income-transfer policy, such as migration or changes in the composition of households, are suppressed. Household financial adjustments are not adequately modeled. While saving (or dissaving) is included in the model, no asset adjustments in the form of financial assets, consumer durables, or housing investments are modeled. In estimating output and employment responses to expenditure changes, Leontief production functions, implying homogeneity, linearity, nonsubstitutability, and constant market prices are employed. Finally the only sources of income that are assumed to change are earnings and some transfers, but certainly property-type income (e.g., rent, interest, dividends) and some employment-conditioned transfers (e.g., pensions) would change with a major shock to the economy.

A key area of future development of the model is in the specification of the induced impact on employment. The assumptions of linearity and nonsubstitutability are very strict and probably unrealistic. If the labor supply effects of the transfer program cause low-skill wages to rise relative to the prices of other inputs, then employers may substitute capital and higher-skill labor for low-skill labor. This would accentuate the shift in demand for new employees away from low-skill, low-wage workers. Conversely, if short-run substitutability of low-wage labor for other factors is high, then there may be a short-run shift in demand toward those employees. A second area of development is in estimating Keynesian multiplier effects. Because the model is not run recursively, adjustments induced by second, third, and nth rounds of income and consumption increases are not estimated. It is conceivable that the structure of these multiplier effects could offset or exacerbate the first-round results presented in this paper.

All in all, the measures of program impact that are reported are the most comprehensive to date, but the results should be regarded as indicative of orders of magnitude and directions of change only. Nevertheless, the applicability of the current simulation model has been demonstrated, and the general regional, output, employment, and income distributional impacts estimated by the model stand.

APPENDICES

APPENDIX A: THE DETAILED STRUCTURE OF THE MICROECONOMIC SIMULATION MODEL FOR ANALYZING THE REGIONAL AND DISTRIBUTIONAL EFFECTS OF TAX-TRANSFER POLICY

The simulation model is composed of five submodels (referred to here as "modules,") which portray economic processes from the incidence of the initial transfer to the ultimate impact on the distribution of earnings. These processes are (1) the direct tax and transfer allocation process; (2) the consumption expenditure process; (3) the sectoral gross output process; (4) the factor demand process; and (5) the regional earnings distribution process.

The *tax-transfer module* simulates the incidence of changes in tax and transfer policies. The eligibility rules and benefit (tax) schedules implied by the policy are applied to a national sample of households, containing detailed information on demographic characteristics, earnings, and nonearned income.[1] From this simulation, estimates of the first-round benefits and tax liabilities generated by the policy are obtained for households classified by race, region, family size, education of the household head, and preprogram income level. These estimates incorporate the effect of the program on labor supply,[2] but presume no migration or family structure responses to the program.

Assume y_s is a vector, each element of which is the 1975 income level of a household included in the Survey of Income and Education (SIE).[3] Each house-

---

[1] Data from the Survey of Income and Education (SIE) were employed in this module. The survey contains 1975 income information on 151,900 family units. A detailed statement of the information contained in the survey and its use in this module is found in Betson et al., chapter 5 in Volume 1.

[2] See Betson et al., chapter 5 in Volume 1, for a discussion of the labor supply analysis incorporated into this module.

[3] Uppercase Greek letters represent matrices and lowercase italic letters represent column vectors.

hold is indexed by family size, place of residence, marital status, and all other socio-demographic characteristics that determine the eligibility and benefits of the transfer and taxation programs to be simulated. Assume Φ is a diagonal matrix portraying the eligibility rules and benefit (tax) schedules of the program in the form of taxation and/or benefit rates corresponding to each element of y_s; Φ_{ii} (the ith element along the diagonal) is the taxation (and/or benefit) rate corresponding to the ith element of y_s. By premultiplying y_s by Φ, an estimate of the program-induced change in income is obtained for each family in the sample. Call this vector t_s.

$$t_s = \Phi \cdot y_s \tag{1}$$

Let Ω be a diagonal matrix of weights, which when applied to t_s yields national estimates of program-induced income changes.

$$t_n = \Omega \cdot t_s \tag{2}$$

The summation of all the elements of t_n yields the total national transfer cost (or tax yield), t_n^o, of the program.

These estimates of policy-induced changes in the disposable incomes of families imply alterations in the level and composition of their expenditures for consumption. Such expenditure responses are estimated in the *consumption expenditure module* through the application of savings propensities and marginal budget shares defined on current income to the estimated changes in family income.[4]

In estimating the change in total household expenditures resulting from the policy, all households in the SIE file are aggregated into six preprogram income classes, and marginal expenditure propensities specific to each class are applied to the policy-induced change in household disposable income.[5] The resulting change

---

[4] By employing estimates of changes in current income, this approach implicitly assumes that changes in current income rather than in normal or permanent income motivate consumption behavior. However, if the policy change represents a permanent alteration in the income generation process, the evaluation of normal income will be affected. As a result, families not eligible for benefits in any given year may well experience increments in their normal income because of the policy and, in response, alter their consumption behavior. Moreover, because of transitory shifts in income, the change in normal income may well be quite different from the change in current income for families eligible for benefits in any given year. Simulation estimates of consumption responses to changes in normal income have been developed and, while not presented here, are available from the authors on request. The primary empirical results from this normal-income approach are not, in substance, different from those presented here.

[5] The marginal propensities are based on analysis of the 1960-1961 Survey of Consumer Expenditures reported by Friend and Jones (1966). They represent current expenditure out of current income. In the lowest income class where approximately a third of the households have higher permanent incomes, the marginal propensities are in excess of unity. Marginal propensities were adjusted for price-level changes between 1960-1961 and 1973. For the six preprogram income classes (in 1960-1961 dollars), the marginal propensities are as follows: less than $2500, 1.09; $2500-$3500, 1.01; $3500-$4500, .89; $4500-$6250, .84; $6250-$8750, .70; $8750 or more, .57.

in household expenditure is allocated among individual categories of commodities by multiplying the expenditure change by a vector of marginal budget shares specific to the income class of the household.[6] From this calculation, induced changes in expenditures by detailed commodity categories are obtained for each household. By aggregating these vectors over all the family units in a region, a vector of policy-induced changes in expenditures within a region for each of 79 commodities is obtained.

　　More formally, let M be a diagonal matrix in which the ith element along the diagonal is the estimated marginal propensity to consume from current income for the ith household. The elements of M can assume one of six values depending on the pretransfer income class to which the corresponding household belongs. By premultiplying t_n from the transfer module by M, the household consumption expenditure induced by the tax-transfer program is estimated for each weighted observation. This vector is represented by c.

$$c = M \cdot t_n \tag{3}$$

Summing the elements of c yields c^o, an estimate of total national expenditure for personal consumption induced by the program.

　　The estimated changes in aggregate household expenditure by region are allocated among individual commodity categories by multiplying the estimated change in total expenditure for each of the income groups in a region by a vector of estimated marginal budget shares for the 79 commodity categories for that income class. First, the vector c, which is indexed by region and income, is aggregated over households to form a new vector $\hat{c}$ of aggregate expenditures by region and income class. This is accomplished by premultiplying c by an operator matrix Σ.

$$\hat{c} = \Sigma \cdot c \tag{4}$$

　　The marginal budget shares estimated from empirical data are used to construct a block diagonal matrix B. Each block along the diagonal is a submatrix of marginal budget shares for a region. The ith row of a submatrix is the vector of budget shares for the ith income class for that region. By premultiplying $\hat{c}$ by B we obtain e, the vector of commodity-specific expenditures of each region.

$$e = B \cdot \hat{c} \tag{5}$$

[6]The marginal budget share vectors are obtained from a piecewise loglinear regression analysis in which household expenditures on each of 56 commodities were regressed against family income, family size, education of head of household, and urban-rural location. The regression model was chosen to accommodate nonlinearities observed in previous studies and was patterned after that developed in Moeller (1970). The analysis employed household data from the 1972-1973 Survey of Consumer Expenditures file.

where:

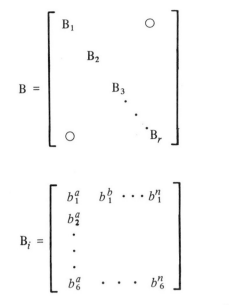

$$B_i = \begin{bmatrix} b_1^a & b_1^b & \cdots & b_1^n \\ b_2^a & & & \\ \cdot & & & \\ \cdot & & & \\ \cdot & & & \\ b_6^a & \cdots & & b_6^n \end{bmatrix} \qquad (6)$$

and in which b_g^h is the marginal budget share for commodity h and income class g. The marginal budget shares for each income class are normalized by the marginal propensities to spend and hence sum to unity. It is assumed that $B_1 = B_2 = \ldots = B_r$.

Policy-induced changes in the commodity and regional composition of consumption expenditures affect the demand for outputs of individual firms and result in a revised pattern of production throughout the economy. The ultimate impact of these changes on the structure of production is obscured by the complexity of interindustry and interregional dependencies. In the *regional gross output module*, the indirect responses of regional and industrial production to changes in commodity expenditures are estimated.

The empirical module is adapted from the Multi-Regional Input-Output Model (MRIO).[7] This model relies on a Leontief production technology—implying linearity, additivity, and nonsubstitutability—for each of 79 sectors in each of 44 regions.[8] The input-output requirements for the several sectors of this model were estimated individually for each region.[9] Trading patterns were estimated by dividing shipments from each region to each region by total uses in the receiving region; the column sum of the coefficients is therefore unity.[10] The product of a

---

[7] This model is described in Polenske (1975).

[8] In order to ensure conformability between the regional breakdown in the prior modules and this module, it was necessary to reduce the number of regions from 44 to 23. Aggregation was in transactions and shipments form.

[9] The regional technical coefficients are based upon the 1963 input-output study for the United States and upon sector studies for agriculture, mining, and construction. (See Polenske, 1974.)

[10] The interregional trade flows are from a study conducted by John Rodgers of Jack Fawcett Associates and are based upon sources for the standard public modes of transportation. (See Rodgers, 1973.)

block diagonal matrix of input-output coefficients with a matrix of trade coefficients estimates the input by commodity and the origin per unit of output by sector. Solution of the Leontief equation then reveals the gross output by region and sector required to satisfy the increment to final demand.

In the previous module, policy-induced consumption demands were estimated for each of 79 production sectors in each of 23 regions and summarized in an 1817-element vector e in Equation (5). Let Γ be a square matrix of dimension 1817×1817 composed of 79×79 diagonal submatrices. Each element (Γ_i^{gh}) describes the fraction of total uses of commodity i in region h that is imported from region g. Further define $\hat{A}$ to be a block diagonal matrix (1817×1817) with 23 square submatrices (79×79) of input-output coefficients along the diagonal describing the structure of production in each region.

$$\hat{A} = \begin{bmatrix} A^1 & & & O \\ & A^2 & & \\ & & \ddots & \\ O & & & A^{23} \end{bmatrix}$$
$$1817 \times 1817$$

$$A^r = \begin{bmatrix} a^r_{1,1} & \cdots & a^r_{1,79} \\ \vdots & \ddots & \vdots \\ a^r_{79,1} & \cdots & a^r_{79,79} \end{bmatrix} \tag{7}$$
$$79 \times 79$$

$$\Gamma = \begin{bmatrix} \hat{\Gamma}^{1,1} & \hat{\Gamma}^{1,2} & \cdots & \hat{\Gamma}^{1,23} \\ \hat{\Gamma}^{2,1} & \hat{\Gamma}^{2,2} & \cdots & \hat{\Gamma}^{2,23} \\ \vdots & \vdots & & \vdots \\ \hat{\Gamma}^{22,1} & \hat{\Gamma}^{22,2} & \cdots & \hat{\Gamma}^{22,23} \\ \hat{\Gamma}^{23,1} & \hat{\Gamma}^{23,2} & \cdots & \hat{\Gamma}^{23,23} \end{bmatrix}$$
$$1817 \times 1817$$

$$\hat{\Gamma}^{gh} = \begin{bmatrix} \Gamma_1^{gh} & & & O \\ & \Gamma_2^{gh} & & \\ & & \ddots & \\ O & & & \Gamma_{79}^{gh} \end{bmatrix} \tag{8}$$
$$79 \times 79$$

Multiplying e by the matrix of trade coefficients (Γ), the allocation of final demands by industry among the regions is obtained. The resulting vector is multiplied by the inverse of an identity matrix minus the block diagonal matrix of input-output coefficients, which has been premultiplied by (Γ). This calculation yields an 1817-element vector of gross output (x).

$$x = (I - \Gamma \hat{A})^{-1} \Gamma e \tag{9}$$

Equation (9) yields an estimate of the change in gross output in each of 79 industries in each of 23 regions resulting from the policy change. (In the empirical calculation, power series expansion, rather than general solution by inversion, was employed in estimating indirect requirements.)

The final two modules trace policy-induced demands back to the household sector—first by developing estimates of the pattern of induced labor demands by occupation and then by deriving the implications of this pattern for the distribution of earned income. The *occupational employment module* provides estimates of the occupational distribution of new job opportunities and, hence, of the effect of the program on the employment prospects of workers of various skill levels. As suggested above, these indirect effects may either reinforce or offset the primary antipoverty objective of the program.

Employment effects are estimated in two steps. First, the total change in regional and sectoral employment is obtained by multiplying unit labor requirements[11] by the detailed incremental gross outputs from the previous module. Second, the estimates of total sectoral employment are distributed over 114 occupational categories by applying a matrix of the percentage distribution of employment by occupation for each industry[12] to the sectoral employment estimates.[13]

Following the above notation, total employment requirements by industry and region (n) are obtained by multiplying the 1817-element gross output vector (x) by the matrix of employment-output coefficients (Λ) (composed of 23 block diagonal 79 × 79 matrices).

$$n = \Lambda \cdot x \tag{10}$$

The occupational composition of the employment is determined by multiplying the vector of incremental employment by sector and region n by the matrix of occupational composition ratios (Θ). The matrix (Θ) is block diagonal with submatrices (Θ') of dimension 114 × 79, giving the occupational composition of employment by sector and region. In this study, it is assumed that $(\Theta^1) = (\Theta^2) = \ldots = (\Theta^{23})$. The increment to the demand for labor in each of the 114 occupations in each of the 23 regions is given by the vector w.

$$w = \Theta \cdot n \tag{11}$$

---

[11] The employment-output coefficients are based upon employment by sector and region reported in the MRIO project. (See Rodgers, 1972.) Annual compound productivity growth rates computed for each sector for the 1947-1963 period are employed in aging 1963 coefficients to 1973.

[12] The estimates of occupational composition by sector are from a BLS study based on the 1970 Census of Population. For a description of the methodology employed, see U.S. Department of Labor (1969). It is assumed that the occupational employment patterns in any sector are constant across regions.

[13] While this is obviously a highly simplified model of the labor market, its use in a short-run, intraequilibrium framework is justified. Adjustments to relative wages are likely to be modest within a one-year period, and the nonlinearities in the derived demands for managerial and professional workers are in part offset by their lower supply elasticity.

Finally, the implications of this induced pattern of occupational demands on the marginal size distribution of labor income is ascertained in the module that provides the regional distribution of earnings: the *income distribution module*. It is assumed that any earned income attributable to incremental employment in an occupation and region is distributed by earnings class as existing earned income is distributed over those currently employed in an occupation and region.[14] The incremental labor demand in each occupation and region (estimated in the previous module) is multiplied by the relative frequency distribution of all employed members of the labor force by earnings class in the corresponding region and occupation.[15] By aggregating these distributions over occupations within a region (or the nation), the induced employment by earnings class for the region (or the nation) is obtained. The structure of these marginal distributions may then be compared to the preexisting earnings distributions to determine the effect of the policy on high-skill/high-wage relative to low-skill/low-wage workers. Through such comparisons the impact of the indirect demands of the policy change in reinforcing or offsetting the primary incidence of the program can be ascertained.

This final module can be stated formally as

$$f = \Psi \cdot w, \tag{12}$$

where Ψ is a block diagonal matrix constructed from the 23 regional relative frequency distributions[16] and f is a vector of the distribution of jobs induced by the transfer policy by earnings class.

APPENDIX B: SIMULATED STATE SUPPLEMENTATION UNDER THE PROGRAM FOR BETTER JOBS AND INCOME

The Carter administration's welfare reform proposal the Program for Better Jobs and Income—contains a nationally uniform, federal cash assistance program. In addition, the proposal provides substantial financial incentives for the adoption of state supplementation programs that use the same eligibility rules (filing unit definition, income definition, accounting period, assets test, etc.) as the basic federal program. A state with a congruent supplement program will be eligible for partial federal subsidization of the cost of supplemental benefits up to certain levels, and these congruent supplements will be administered (free to the state) along with the basic federal program. Or, if the state elects to retain the intake and eligibility determination functions, it will be reimbursed by the federal government for 90%

---

[14] This implicitly assumes that the preexisting distribution of earned income reflects the distribution of skill, ability, and work effort of the pool of workers available in an occupation in a region.

[15] The regional relative frequency distributions are from a special tabulation using 1-in-100 tapes of the 1970 U.S. Census of Population. A total of 114 occupational categories and 23 regions are employed. Fifteen earnings classes are distinguished.

[16] Each block of Ψ is a 15×114 matrix representing a regional distribution.

to 110% of its administrative costs, depending on the level of its administrative error rate.

On the other hand, a state that adopts a supplementation program that is not congruent with the basic federal program will have to administer it, and that state will be ineligible for federal subsidy of benefit payments and administrative costs. While not encouraged, noncongruent supplements are definitely permitted. Indeed, through the maintenance-of-effort and hold-harmless provisions of the proposal, states are encouraged to adopt one type of noncongruent supplements—those that "grandfather" existing SSI and AFDC recipients during a transition period following the implementation of the program.

If a state adopts a congruent supplement program, it can change only two elements of the federal cash assistance program. One is the guaranteed income payable to an eligible filing unit with no other income, and the other is the benefit reduction rate applicable to earned income. The amount of the increase in a unit's guaranteed income is determined by its supplementation ratio. This ratio equals a filing unit's guaranteed income, including the supplement, divided by its guaranteed income in the basic federal program. For example, if a state adopts a supplementation ratio for not-expected-to-work families of 1.10, then the annual guaranteed income of a mother and her two young children would be $3960, or $360 more than their $3600 guaranteed income in the federal program. A state can choose different supplementation ratios and benefit reduction rates for different filing units, but the ratio and rate must be the same for all units within each of several demographic categories to be specified by regulations. For each category a state may select any supplementation ratio that is 1.00 or larger and any benefit reduction rate that is between the federal program's 50% and 70% for not-expected-to-work categories or 52% for expected-to-work categories, so long as the quotient obtained by dividing the supplementation ratio by the benefit reduction rate is no less than two. This final restriction ensures that the break-even earnings level under state supplementation is no less than the break-even level in the basic federal program.

Once a state has selected a ratio and rate for each demographic category, a filing unit's actual benefit is computed exactly as is its federal benefit with no state supplementation. The benefit is calculated using the same computation procedure, except that the unit's guaranteed income is equal to its supplementation ratio multiplied by its guaranteed income in the federal program. In addition, the unit's benefit reduction rate and its earned income exclusion may be different from those in the federal program. In the federal program filing units eligible for an earned income exclusion receive an annual exclusion of $3800. If a state chooses to supplement, the new exclusion is $1900 multiplied by the supplementation ratio divided by the new benefit reduction rate. For example, if a state adopts a ratio of 1.10 and a rate of 52% for expected-to-work families with children, then the annual earned income exclusion for all families in this category is $1900 times 1.10 divided by 0.52, or approximately $4019. The annual benefit for a filing unit in a state with a congruent supplement program is simply the benefit calculated using the new guaranteed income, the new earned income exclusion, and the new benefit reduction rate. The unit's supplement benefit is simply the difference between this actual benefit and its federal benefit, which is computed with a ratio of 1.00 and a rate of 50%.

A filing unit's supplement benefit is eligible for federal subsidy. In order to calculate the federal share of a supplement benefit, it is necessary to define the concept of the maximum benefit eligible for subsidy. In every state a not-expected-to-work filing unit's maximum benefit eligible for subsidy is calculated using a supplementation ratio of 1.512, a 70% benefit reduction rate, and an earned income exclusion of $4104. And an expected-to-work unit's maximum benefit eligible for subsidy is computed using 1.1232, 52%, and $4104, respectively. (In Alaska and Hawaii these 1.512 and 1.1232 supplementation ratios are multiplied by the ratio of the state's poverty-line income to the poverty-line income for the continental United States.) The federal share of a filing unit's actual supplement benefit is the sum of three-fourths of the 75% portion of the supplement benefit and one-fourth of the 25% portion. The 75% portion of the unit's supplement benefit equals the smaller of two numbers, one of which is the unit's supplement benefit, the other of which is the product obtained by multiplying the unit's federal benefit by 0.1232, or by zero in the case of a filing unit that consists of an aged, blind, or disabled individual or couple. The 25% portion also equals the smaller of two numbers, one of which is the filing unit's supplement benefit minus its 75% portion, and the other of which is the unit's maximum supplement eligible for subsidy minus its 75% portion.

The effect of these rules is that the federal government will not subsidize any portion of a supplement benefit paid to a filing unit whose earnings net of the child-care expense deduction exceed 108% of the break-even earnings level in the basic federal program. The rules also imply that the federal government will end its subsidy beyond certain guaranteed income levels. For not-expected-to-work families the limit of federal subsidy (1.512 times the federal guaranteed income) is approximately equal to the poverty-line income, while for expected-to-work families the limit (1.1232 times the federal guaranteed income) is roughly three-fourths of the poverty-line income.

The proposal's state supplementation provisions present the states with financial incentives that differ considerably from those inherent in existing welfare programs. In particular, the federal matching rate structure is significantly different from those in present programs. Also, it is unclear how states would choose to spend the budget savings, or fiscal relief, that the implementation of the proposal would generate. It is difficult, therefore, to predict exactly what supplementation ratios and benefit reduction rates a state will select for different demographic categories. Rather than attempting to predict exactly each state's behavioral response to the fiscal relief and altered matching rates, the simulation simply assumes that each state follows these rules in designing its state supplementation program:

1. For the category of not-expected-to-work families with children, the basic ratio equals the annual guaranteed income resulting from the combination of the state's AFDC Program and the federal Food Stamp Program for a four-person family during 1975, divided by $4200 deflated to calendar year 1975 (that is,

about $3584). The supplementation ratio for this category equals this basic ratio or 1.512, whichever is smaller. The benefit reduction rate on earned income is one-half of the supplementation ratio if the ratio is less than 1.40, and 70% otherwise.

2. For the category of expected-to-work families with children, the supplementation ratio equals the supplementation ratio for the category of not-expected-to-work families with children if this latter ratio is less than 1.04. If the not-expected-to-work ratio is between 1.04 and 1.40, the expected-to-work ratio equals 1.04. Finally, if the not-expected-to-work ratio is between 1.40 and 1.512, then the expected-to-work supplementation ratio equals the product of (0.52/0.70) and the not-expected-to-work ratio. The benefit reduction rate on earned income for this category is 52% unless this category has a supplementation ratio that is less than 1.04. In this low supplementation case, the benefit reduction rate equals one-half of the supplementation ratio.

3. For the category of aged, blind, or disabled individuals, the supplementation ratio equals the annual guaranteed income resulting from the combination of the federal SSI Program, the state's optional SSI supplement program, and the federal Food Stamp Program (except in California and Massachusetts, where SSI recipients are ineligible for food stamps) during 1975, divided by $2500 deflated to calendar year 1975 (that is, about $2133). The benefit reduction rate equals one-half of the supplementation ratio unless the ratio exceeds 1.40. If the ratio is greater than 1.40, the rate is 70%.

4. For the category of aged, blind, or disabled couples, the supplementation ratio equals the annual guaranteed income resulting from the combination of the federal SSI Program, the state's optional SSI supplement program, and (except for California and Massachusetts) the federal Food Stamp Program during 1975, divided by $3750 deflated to calendar year 1975 (that is, about $3200). The benefit reduction rate on earned income equals the smaller of two numbers, one-half of the supplementation ratio and 70%.

5. Neither the category of single individuals who are not aged, blind, or disabled, nor the category of childless couples, no more than one of whom is aged, blind, or disabled, receive state supplement benefits except in six states. In California, Illinois, Massachusetts, Michigan, New York, and Pennsylvania, both categories have a supplementation ratio of 1.1232 and a benefit reduction rate of 52%.

DISCUSSION

Anne P. Carter

The microeconomic simulation model discussed in the Haveman et al. paper consists of a sequence of "modules," or linked submodels, for assessing the detailed income implications of any specified tax-transfer program, or any other policy change inducing change in the bill of final demands imposed on the economy. The core of the sequence is the U.S. Multi-Regional Input-Output (MRIO) System (Polenske, 1975), partially aggregated from the original 50 state and 79 sector detail to 23 regions and 79 sectors. As far as I know, this is the only instance where the MRIO model has been used by an independent research group for multiregional work. The research strategy is commendable.

The authors concentrated their efforts on building models to generate values of exogenous variables required by the multiregional input-output model and to trace the income implications of the regional output estimates generated by that multiregional system. Thus, module 1 is a model to generate regional income and payment implications of a given government distributive program, and module 2 translates those regional payments into industry-specific consumption demands. Together, the first two modules translate a government program into changes in regional final demands, specified for the multiregional input-output system (module 3). Module 4 takes as data the regional gross output vectors generated by the multiregional model and generates estimates of their occupational consequences. Finally, module 5 applies standard earnings distributions to the occupational employment estimates computed in module 4. It generates estimates of the effects of the initially given government program on the regional size distributions of earnings. Module 1 is discussed in another paper for this conference (Betson et al., chapter 5 in Volume 1).

By taking advantage of the earlier work of the MRIO model builders, the authors were able to produce a very elaborate instrument for policy analysis on the basis of a manageable effort. In economics, where the reward structure stresses originality at the expense of cumulative development, this precedent is very welcome. Since the simulation model incorporates the multiregional input-output system, however, it shares this system's problems as well as its strengths. The remainder of this discussion raises four general questions about the structural specifications of the model. At least three of these are commonly raised in critical appraisals of regional input-output systems, and there may be some impulse to dismiss them as standard caveats. I raise them nevertheless, because they may determine whether or not a model is applicable for policymaking. In addition, I hope that thoughtful attention to these questions will strengthen rather than discredit the work that has already been done.

1.   Should the model be "closed" with respect to households?

The function of the input-output system in the model is to compute total (direct plus indirect) requirements of sectoral outputs in each region, based on the specified increases in consumption spelled out by modules 1 and 2. While open input-output systems incorporate these interindustry multipliers, they do not take account of the Keynesian multiplier effects associated with household spending of additional income generated by an initial stimulus. The omission of the Keynesian multipliers has some consequences that may be important for policy analysis:

> Since Keynesian multiplier effects are not taken into account, the simulation results tend to understate the total impacts of programs.

> Individual products differ in their relative importance to final, as compared with intermediate, consumers. Thus, the omission of consumption multipliers affects output estimates for some sectors more than for others. Apparel, food, automobiles, and retail margins are sold primarily to final demand. Without consumption multipliers there is very little "indirect" consumption of these items generated by the model. Steel and electric power, on the other hand, are primarily intermediate goods. A fair proportion of their computed output levels is already "indirect" in the present model, that is, it is generated by interindustry multipliers. The introduction of consumption multipliers would tend to increase the relative importance of consumer as compared with intermediate goods in the computed output vector.

> In an interregional system, an initial spending program affects regions differentially, since regional interdependence differs from sector to sector. Therefore, the omission of consumption multipliers does not understate all regional incomes to the same extent.

It is not easy to sort out the effects of omitting consumption multipliers on the simulation results reported in this paper. Closing the model with respect to consumption would increase the relative volume of low-earnings employment generated, because it would trigger relatively more local services and retail trade. On the other hand, some of the responding would reinforce the high initial spending in the motor-vehicle sector. It seems likely that the emphasis, in the simulations, on highly paid operatives and on regions with large transportation-equipment sectors would be softened by the introduction of consumption multipliers.

Some experimentation with partial closure of the multiregional input-output model should be well worth while. Since household consumption functions (in module 2) are now specified on a per-family and not a per-earner basis, the present model cannot be closed without some additional information on the pooling of individual earnings into family income. Models of income pooling (see, e.g., Carter and Everett, 1974) can readily be adapted for this work. In addition, a method for converting earned to disposable income would have to be developed for module 2.

2.   Should transactions on capital account be ignored?

In conventional input-output accounting, coefficients represent input require-ments on current account only. Capital requirements are treated as an exogenous final demand component. Thus, the output consequences of a change in, say, con-sumption or exports, computed with the standard static model, take no account of change in replacement requirements nor of induced investment for the expansion of capacity.

This standard convention is carried into the model, and its presence provides some explanation of the composition of the vector of changes in gross outputs com-puted for the Program for Better Jobs and Income. Since automobile purchases are considered current account items, their purchases are induced by the expenditure programs of this model. Increased housing expenditures result in increased sales by the real estate and rental sector. However, since only a very small amount of con-struction (i.e., maintenance), is included in the current account matrix, induced construction activity is necessarily minimal. Along the same lines, induced pur-chases of durables are dominated by consumer durables, whose accounting treat-ment is like that of automobiles. Producer durables cannot be affected by any welfare program in this model. The exclusion of capital goods from the vector of induced outputs, in turn, has important bearing on the regional and occupational composition of the simulation results. Indirect effects of the program are con-centrated in the regions that contribute relatively large shares of automobile pro-duction but employment in sectors producing capital goods is understated.

While it is easy to recognize the bias imposed by omitting the capital account items, it is difficult to model capital formation adequately in a model of this detail, and, indeed, in any model. Adding explicit investment equations would greatly compound the modeling effort, and economists' success in predicting investment is not impressive. If the results are to be taken seriously for policy purposes, however, it would certainly be worth while to scan the incremental output estimates now generated in relation to the implicit capital requirements. Depending on the state of capacity utilization, it might be appropriate to estimate additions to the gross capital formation vector. If such an *ad hoc* approach seems too cumbersome and too crude, then it may be worth while to consider the addition of capital replace-ment coefficients to the current account matrix. While the latter would tend, in general, to understate capital demands, it would understate them less than the present model. In any case, recognition that changes in capital items are omitted is essential in the interpretation of simulations using the present model.

3.   Should the trade structure of the multiregional input-output model be revised?

Since the MRIO system is based on 1963 input-output and interregional trade data, its validity for current simulations should certainly be questioned. Given that there is no more recent version of this system available, what are the prospects for at least a partial updating effort?

Needless to say, this question cannot be answered within the scope of a short discussion. The present "column coefficient" model requires data on shipments of each traded commodity between all pairs of regions. These data are very difficult to obtain and this difficulty, in turn, explains the time and expense required to produce a more up-to-date version of the system. I know of no systematic attempt to evaluate the stability of these interregional trade coefficients, nor to compare the results of simulations using alternative trade structures. Certainly multiregional models based on market shares, or on trade "pools," are easier to implement and hence to update. At this point, however, we don't even know whether the present more detailed specification would be preferable in the absence of data constraints. If policy decisions are to be based on multiregional models, these questions must be addressed.

4.   How is the size distribution of earnings related to sectoral output levels?

Changes in the size distribution of earnings for each region are based on modules 4 and 5. The former relates output to employment and then subdivides employment into 114 occupational categories, assigning a vector of occupational proportions to each sector. In the current model it is assumed that the matrix of occupational proportions by sector is the same for all regions. Module 5 assigns a distinct size distribution of earnings to each occupational group in each region and sums earnings across occupations for each size category.

The authors do not say whether the estimation of a distribution of employment by occupation was itself a goal of the model, or whether the distribution of occupations is seen merely as a link in the chain from sectoral output to the earnings distribution. If the distribution of earnings is the prime research objective, it is not at all clear that occupational detail need be introduced. The simpler route would be to attach size distributions of earnings directly to sectors in each region, thus collapsing modules 4 and 5 into a single earnings-generating module.

Unfortunately, the research that would help us to choose the better earnings model remains to be undertaken. Right now we know that wages vary among occupations and among sectors. Were occupation a reliable index of labor quality, one might argue that (under competitive conditions) each occupation should be associated with a single wage. Under such circumstances, interindustry wage differentials should be explained by differences in occupational mix. To my knowledge, this linkage has not been explored. In any case, the present treatment assigns an empirically based earnings distribution to each occupational category, thereby denying the assumption that a unique wage is associated with each occupation. We are left, then, without an explicit economic rationale for the earnings-generation module.

DISCUSSION

Benjamin Chinitz

This model traces the induced effects on employment and earnings of a proposed tax and transfer program, such as the PBJI. The first step is to calculate the direct effect of the program on disposable income in each income class in each region. These net changes in disposable income are fed into consumption functions which generate net changes in consumer demand by income class by region for a classification of goods. These in turn are fed into a multiregional input-output model which calculates the incremental change in gross output for each sector in each region. The gross output estimates are translated into net demands for man-hours of labor by sector, by region, and by occupation. Finally, these labor demands are translated into earnings increments by occupation and in turn by earnings classes.

The authors find that for the expenditures generated by PBJI (ignoring the taxes used to finance the program) the induced effects on income distribution run counter to the direct effects, thus detracting from the redistributive power of the program. The lowest earnings class (<$4000) gets less than its share of the extra earnings, and the highest earnings class (>$20,000) does best, confirming the cynical observation of the mid-1960s that antipoverty programs are good business for the upper classes.

This is literally true in this model. What fundamentally makes the results come out the way they do is the simple fact that the lower-income families experiencing the increased income tend to spend their income increments on goods and services produced by relatively high-earnings groups. The authors seem surprised. Data on the impacts of only PBJI spending (not reported in the paper) indicate that the service worker category accounts for but 11% of the incremental labor demands from the transfers and public service wages. Since when do the poor hire each other to shine their shoes, do their laundry, or clean their apartments?

In their brief section on policy implications, the authors offer the following observations: "The beneficial impacts of PBJI must be tempered by the information provided by these estimates of induced effects in order to yield a full evaluation of the program. . . Only by a more complete evaluation of these impacts . . . can the full efficiency and equity implications of the policy be understood." Agreed! But a lot more is needed to put these exercises in proper perspective. Let me try to be helpful on that score.

Although I was reared on input-output in graduate school some 25 years ago, I have conducted a personal vendetta in the regional field against models that are driven exclusively by demand linkages and that implicitly assume complete elasticity of supply (i.e., wherever the buck appears in space, resources will rise up to devour it).

As the dollars flow through this model to generate demands for labor and implicitly for other resources within regions, industries, and occupations, supply responds exactly as dictated by the technical "requirements." Among their caveats the authors include the conventional concerns about the vintage of the technology and interregional trade matrices and the validity of the fundamental assumption of fixed coefficients. But all of that relates to the correct specification of labor demands. The increment of man-years demanded in occupation i, in industry j, in region k is always supplied.

Paradoxically my main concern here is not with the regional dimension of the supply assumption but with the national dimension. The model generates a net national increase in labor demand which is met by an equivalent increase in labor supplied in the national economy as a whole. In other words, PBJI is being evaluated not only as a redistributive device but implicitly also as a device for stimulating employment and earnings in a period of labor surplus. The model generates an estimate of the first-round multiplier—a by-product of considerable interest to some of us—which, I suppose, could be compared with first-round multipliers associated with other kinds of stimuli: tax cuts, public works, pure public employment programs, and other forms of public expenditure that can be worked through this kind of a model.

I feel very uncomfortable about all this. It's true that we're weighing the merits of PBJI right now, and right now there is plenty of slack in the economy so that the assumption of pervasive perfect elasticity of supply is probably realistic. But I would have thought that the redistributive efficacy of PBJI or any kind of welfare reform ought ideally to be evaluated in the context of full employment, which this model can't do.

But what really intrigues me are the policy implications of this kind of exercise at full employment. You define the first-round changes in disposable income by income class. These are strongly positive for the lower classes and strongly negative for the upper classes. You run them through the model and you discover that the required distribution of employment by occupation (and region) is changed from the existing one.

What kinds of changes would please us most? The tone of the paper suggests that what would please the authors most would be to find that the induced effects favored the low-skill/low-earnings occupations. In their framework, that would give the proposed program an even higher score in terms of redistributive power. Such secondary impacts could be viewed as favorable because they would improve the earnings of the poor by putting pressure on wage rates, reducing unemployment, and increasing labor force participation.

This, then, is a scenario for greater equality. But, do we want to achieve greater equality by so manipulating the bill of goods that the derived demand for labor by occupation favors the low-skill/low-earnings occupations? Are we really committed to a demand theory of poverty?

An alternative view, with which I am more sympathetic, is that ultimately we achieve greater equality by increasing the supply of workers to the so-called high-skill/high-earnings occupation and decreasing the supply of workers to the so-called low-skill/low-earnings occupations, thereby narrowing the earnings differentials. That trend is encouraged by the direct labor supply effects of PBJI, a caveat to their paper which the authors view with skepticism because "then employers may substitute capital and higher-skill labor for low-skill labor." It is also encouraged by expenditures out of increased disposable income, which are more like investments in human capital than pure consumption (e.g., health and education). But these expenditures are precisely the kind which, from a demand standpoint, will initially favor the high-skill/high-earnings occupations.

In summary: the macro setting in which the authors run their very useful model is the current one, and I certainly applaud them on that score for an unusual degree of relevance. To maximize the redistributive power of PBJI in the current situation, the recipients ought to eat more hamburgers at McDonalds and make fewer visits to the doctor. But in anything like a full employment economy, and in the longer run, I am likely to be more pleased with their results than they seem to be.

5

REHABILITATING CENTRAL-CITY HOUSING: SIMULATIONS WITH THE URBAN INSTITUTE HOUSING MODEL

Larry Ozanne
Jean E. Vanski

INTRODUCTION

This paper presents a model of urban housing markets and then uses that model to simulate the effects of federal policies to rehabilitate central-city housing.* The policies are chosen because they are being considered for expanded roles in the administration's plans to revitalize central cities. The specific policies examined are an expansion of the Section 312 Rehabilitation Loan Program and the Section 8 Housing Program.[1]

The scale of the programs simulated in this paper are a good deal larger than is currently being implemented for any city. However, the purpose of these simulations is to make apparent the types of effects that are present but not easily observable when the programs are small. The questions addressed include, Does rehabilitation improve the stock of central-city housing over the long run? Does it cause

---

*The research reported in this paper was conducted at the Urban Institute under Contract H-2821, Task Order 6 with the Department of Housing and Urban Development, Office of Policy Development and Research. The original idea for this paper came from Raymond J. Struyk. Several others offered useful advice as the idea was being implemented: James Follain, Neil Mayer, and John Weicher. Dennis Manning provided information on the Section 312 Rehabilitation Loan Program; and Ronnie Alburger performed numerical analyses. John L. Goodman, Jr., Morton Isler, and Raymond J. Struyk reviewed the draft of the paper and offered helpful suggestions. Marilyn Whipple prepared the manuscript within a very short time deadline.

[1] The Section 312 program provides low-interest, long-term loans for upgrading dwellings with code violations. The Section 8 program provides assistance payments for households to help defray the cost of adequate housing. Section 8 has components for new, existing, and rehabilitated housing. (Descriptions of the programs can be found in *Housing and Development Reporter Reference File*, 1977. For the Section 312 program, see section 14, p. 17. For the Section 8 program, see section 30, pp. 55ff.)

housing elsewhere to decay by an offsetting amount? Are the poor forced to move to other neighborhoods? What are the effects of subsidies enabling the central-city poor to occupy the rehabilitated housing?

The answers to these questions will depend on conditions within urban housing markets; for example, whether the demands for low- or moderate-quality housing are growing or declining. Thus even though the questions are about national housing and urban policy, they must be analyzed in terms of local housing markets.

An urban housing market is a series of related submarkets; changes in one of these submarkets set off rippling effects in others. But even large changes in one urban area are unlikely to affect another as close as one hundred miles away. The main reasons for this are the two characteristics of housing that differentiate it from other goods, such as bread or automobiles. The characteristics are durability and immobility, and they give this housing market model its unique cast.

The durability of housing means more than that a dwelling lasts a long time; it means that many of the detailed characteristics of a dwelling unit—the type of structure it is in, its lot size and other features—are very difficult to alter once it is built. Furthermore, in any one year the stock of existing housing represents most of the available supply.

The immobility of housing means that neighborhood effects are necessarily a part of the decisions to produce and to consume housing services. Neighborhood effects include more than those from the surrounding dwellings. They include all of the neighborhood characteristics—public amenities, social status, personal safety, ethnicity and race, and so on—which households consider in deciding where to live.

The remainder of the paper is divided into three sections. The next section describes the structure of the Urban Institute Housing Model, first verbally and then mathematically, and concludes with a discussion of the model's limitations and current developments. The data bases used in the model to date are then described. The last section describes in detail the policies to be simulated, reports the results of these simulations, and draws implications for federal policy.

THE MODEL

Model Structure

The Urban Institute Housing Model[2] deals with ten-year changes in housing quality and household location within a metropolitan area. This capsule description of the model contains four key phrases: "ten-year changes," "housing quality," "household location," and "within a metropolitan area." Each of them serves to distinguish the model from other models or studies—for example, from short-run

[2] For a complete description of the model, see de Leeuw and Struyk (1975). The discussion in this section is taken in large part from pp. 12-22 of that book.

explanations of housing market dynamics, from location-free theories of the filtering process, or from macroeconomic analyses with a national focus. The model emphasizes two characteristics that distinguish housing from most other goods: the durability of housing and the inescapable link between housing and neighborhood.

The model represents a metropolitan housing market by a few dozen "model" households, a few dozen "model" dwellings, a building industry, and possibilities for a variety of government restrictions or programs. The four "actors" in the model are thus households seeking a place to live, owners of existing dwellings offering housing services at various prices, a building industry meeting demands at an acceptable rate of return, and governments able to regulate the housing-location process at many different points. The model searches for a "solution"—a situation in which no one can improve his position according to the rules of behavior and constraints he obeys—through a matching of households with new or existing dwellings. The brief description in this section takes up each of the four actors in turn and describes the solution process. Then limitations of the model and current developmental work are discussed. The final subsection presents the behavioral rules and constraints in mathematical terms.

Model Households

Each model household represents several hundred or thousand actual households, the exact number depending on the size of the metropolitan area to which the model is being applied. A household belongs to one of several household types and is characterized by two measures of its income. The household types with which we have worked in the model so far include white nonelderly families, white elderly/ single-person households, black nonelderly families, black elderly/single-person households, and, in the case of Austin, chicano nonelderly families, and chicano elderly/single-person households. Some of the parameters of the model—as we shall see in a later section—differ by household type.

Model households are further characterized by two income measures: (a) an actual-income figure—the mean actual end-of-decade gross income of the households it represents; and (b) a version of permanent income—called "model income"— which is a weighted average of the actual income of a model household and the median end-of-decade income for its household type. An actual-income figure is necessary because some of the programs that the model is intended to analyze—for example, income subsidies—operate on actual income rather than any transformed version of income. The income elasticity embedded in the utility function of the model, however, is inappropriate to actual single-year incomes; the model's utility function requires a second, smoothed version of income.[3] The model thus uses

[3] Pioneering studies of the income concept appropriate to housing demand are those of Muth (1960) and Reid (1962). The proposition that a single year is much too short a time horizon for measuring the effect of income on housing demand, strongly supported by these two studies, is now generally accepted, even though controversy about other aspects of housing demand continues.

actual income as the variable directly affected by certain housing, tax, or transfer programs and uses smoothed or "model" income in determining the choice of location and quality that each household makes. A change in actual income—due to a cash subsidy, for example—is of course translated into a change in model income, but the latter change is smaller than the former change.

The behavior of households in the model consists of deciding which of all possible dwellings to occupy. "All possible dwellings" includes a new dwelling of any desired level of services (subject to any government-imposed minimum standards for new construction) or any of the existing dwellings in the model. The household makes its decision on the basis of the quantity of housing services that each dwelling offers, the price per unit of housing service at which it offers those services, the household's model income, and three characteristics of the zone in which each dwelling is located.

The three zone characteristics to which households pay attention are (a) average travel time to and from work, (b) average net rent per dwelling, and (c) the proportion of zone residents which belong to the same racial group as the household making the choice. The first of these, travel time, is simply fed into the model as a piece of exogenous information about a zone. The other two, average net rent and racial composition, are determined by the model itself, so that there is a two-way interaction between household choice and these zone characteristics.

All of these variables influencing household choices are combined into a utility function which the household is attempting to maximize. The utility function has four parameters whose values decisively influence what the model predicts about the effects of housing policies. One of the principal goals of the application of the model to specific metropolitan areas is to obtain estimates of these parameters.

Model Dwellings

Each model dwelling, like each model household, represents several hundred or thousand actual cases—in fact, the number of actual cases per model unit should be the same for dwellings as it is for households. Each model dwelling belongs to one of several zones (5-6 zones are being used so far) differing in accessibility, initial wealth, and/or initial racial composition.

Each model dwelling is also characterized by the quantity of housing services which it is supplying at the beginning of the ten-year interval being examined. The level of housing services of a dwelling, one of the basic concepts of the model, refers to an index of all the things of value that a physical structure provides—space, shelter, privacy, pleasing design, and a host of others. It does not refer to the neighborhood characteristics associated with each dwelling; these are measured by the various attributes of the zone in which a dwelling is located. The measure of housing services is obtained from an index relating dwelling characteristics to rent or value.

The behavior of the owners of existing dwellings consists in making price-quantity offers with the goal of maximizing expected profits. Each price-quantity offer consists of a quantity of housing services to be provided at the end of the decade to which the model refers and a price at which that quantity will be provided. The offers thus resemble rental advertisements appearing in newspapers. The price-quantity offers for each dwelling must lie along a supply curve whose position depends on (a) the initial quantity of housing services offered by the dwelling, and (b) two parameters of the model, one related to a depreciation rate and the other related to an elasticity of supply with respect to price.

The basic model does not separate owner-occupants from renters; owner-occupants are in effect viewed as landlords renting to themselves. Some work, however, on modifying the basic model to incorporate tenure choice has been done and is reported elsewhere.[4]

The owner of each existing dwelling seeks to locate as high up along his supply curve as he can, for his expected profits are an increasing function of his position along the supply curve. Competition among the owners of actual dwellings composing each model dwelling is assumed sufficient to keep landlords from making offers *above* their supply curves.

The model includes a minimum price per unit of service, defined as that price which is just sufficient to cover the cost of operating a dwelling. If the owner of a dwelling is unable to find an occupant at any price above the minimum price, then his dwelling is withdrawn from the stock of housing. The model does not distinguish among abandonment, conversion to nonresidential use, long-term vacancy, or other forms of withdrawing a unit from the stock. Dwellings are assumed not to influence the amenity of their zone once they are withdrawn.

Builders

The third actor in the model, the building industry, plays a more passive role than model households and model dwellings. The building industry is characterized by a horizontal supply curve. That is, it is prepared to offer new dwellings at a monthly total cost which is proportional to the level of services that the dwelling provides. The price per unit of service at which new dwellings are available is taken as given for each housing market. Empirically it is measured on the basis of data from the Federal Housing Administration (FHA) for each metropolitan area separately.

This exogenous price tends to set a ceiling for the price structure of the existing stock, although existing dwellings with especially favorable zone characteristics can command prices moderately above the new-construction price. Newly constructed dwellings are assumed to be concentrated in a single "zone of new construction" in most applications of the model, including the one reported later in this paper.[5]

Governments

The final actor of the model, "government," can influence the housing-location process at many different points. Tax changes, subsidy payments with or

---

[4] de Leeuw and Struyk (1975, pp. 151-174); Andreassi and MacRae (1978).
[5] For an example in which the location of new construction is endogenously determined, see de Leeuw and Struyk (1975, pp. 175-190).

without earmarking for housing, minimum new construction requirements, and minimum quantities of housing services in a particular zone are among the ways in which governments can affect housing markets in the model.

An income tax can be represented by replacing a household's actual income by income less the tax (and by making a smaller reduction in its model income) before it enters the housing market. The tax rate and other parameters of the tax formula—for example, an exemption level—can be set separately for each household type, or even for each model household. A transfer payment is represented using the same procedure as an income tax. A transfer earmarked for housing, as in the Section 8 Housing Program, can be represented by requiring an eligible household to consume at least some minimum level of housing services while not spending over some maximum amount on housing in order to receive the transfer; the household then determines its utility-maximizing choice without the transfer, its choice with the transfer and its requirements, and chooses the larger of these two maxima. A restrictive zoning ordinance can be represented by setting a minimum quantity of housing services for all of the dwellings in a zone. The results of a government rehabilitation program can be represented by increases in the initial quantity of services provided by the rehabilitated model dwellings.

The Solution Process

The solution of the model, as mentioned earlier, is a situation in which none of the four actors has any incentive to change his position. Each household is the unique occupant of one dwelling, the one which maximizes its satisfaction given its model income and all the price-quantity offers facing it. The owner of each existing dwelling is as high up along his supply curve as he can be without finding his dwelling vacant. (If a dwelling is vacant even at the lowest point on its supply curve, it is withdrawn from the stock.) The building industry is supplying the number of new dwellings which households are willing to purchase. Government regulations are strictly enforced.

The computer program to solve the model searches for a solution with these properties through a process of trial and error. Departures from solution conditions in one trial govern the way in which the solution is modified for the next trial. The steps in the search process have no theoretical or empirical significance; a housing market may search for a solution in a different way from the computer program. It is only the final solution of a problem which is of interest. Once the program finds a solution, the results are tabulated in a variety of ways: prices, quantities, and locations are shown by household, by dwelling, by zone, by household type, and in the case of certain subsidy programs, by eligible households.[6]

To summarize the description so far, the model can be said to represent the

[6]The computer program to solve the model is written in the Fortran programming language and has been used on both the Control Data 6600 and the IBM 360 computers. The program generally takes between 50 and 150 seconds to execute, depending on the number of model households, the similarity in their demands, and the similarity of dwellings supplying services.

housing market as a set of demand and supply functions for closely related sub-markets. Prices per unit of housing service in all these submarkets need not be the same because one submarket is not a perfect substitute (in demand or supply) for another. Prices in various submarkets cannot differ too much, however, because substitution is strong enough to cause vacancies or overoccupancy if the price in any submarket is out of line with prices in closely related submarkets.

Main Mathematical Functions of the Model

This subsection specifies in mathematical terms the utility function of house-holds and the supply function of the owners of existing dwellings. It includes only brief explanations of functional forms.[7]

Household Utility Functions

Each household evaluates each dwelling by means of a utility function. The utility of the dwelling j to household i, U_{ij}, can be represented as

$$U_{ij} = HXZ_1Z_2Z_3.$$ (1)

H, the term representing the utility of housing services, is defined as follows:

$$H = (Q_j - \alpha_i \gamma_1 Y_i^m / P_n)^{\alpha_i},$$ (2)

in which Q_j is the quantity of housing services offered by dwelling j, a_i is a para-meter expressing the strength of housing preferences (versus preference for other goods) of households of the type of household i, γ_1 is a parameter expressing the degree to which households will alter their housing choice in response to a price discount, Y_i^m is household i's model income after adjustment for specifically im-posed taxes and transfers, and P_n is the price per unit of service of newly con-structed dwellings.

X, the term representing the utility of nonhousing goods, is specified in a manner analogous to H. The budget constraint facing the consumer is used to define nonhousing goods as $Y_i^m - P_j Q_j$, where Y_i^m is the household's model income and P_j and Q_j are the price and quantity of services of dwelling j. The term defining X is as follows:

$$X = \left[(Y_i - P_j Q_j) - (1 - \alpha_i) \gamma_1 Y_i^m \right]^{1 - \alpha_i}.$$ (3)

The terms in this expression are defined following Equation (2) above.

The three zone characteristics, Z_1 through Z_3, relate to accessibility, wealth, and racial composition. Z_1, the term representing accessibility, is defined as follows:

$$Z_1 = (200 - T_j)^{.5 + \alpha_i - \alpha_1},$$ (4)

where T_j is the average travel time (in hours per month) of the zone in which dwelling j is located, α_i is a parameter expressing the strength of housing prefer-

[7]A more complete discussion appears in de Leeuw and Struyk (1975, pp. 22-31).

ences of households of the type of household i, and α_1 is the value of α_i for white nonelderly families. The term in parentheses, $200 - T_j$, is an approximation of monthly hours of leisure time available to an average worker in the zone in which dwelling j is located. The exponent of this term is based on studies of the value households place on travel time and on analysis of how we might expect this value to vary with strength of housing demand.

The second zonal characteristic is defined as follows:

$$Z_2 = \left[\frac{(P_j' - P_o') Q_j'}{(P_j' - P_o') Q_j''} \right]^{.01\gamma_2},\tag{5}$$

where P_j is price per unit of housing services, P_o is minimum operating costs per unit of housing services, Q_j is quantity of housing services, and γ_2 is a parameter expressing the strength of preferences for a wealthy zone. The variables with single primes refer to a zonal average (the zone in which dwelling j is located), while the variables with double primes refer to a Standard Metropolitan Statistical Area (SMSA) average. This term represents the average net rent (gross rent less operating costs) of a zone relative to the average net rent in an SMSA and serves as an indicator of zonal wealth.

The third and final zonal characteristic is defined as follows:

$$Z_3 = R_{ij} + [1000/(100\gamma_3 + 1)],\tag{6}$$

where R_{ij} is the proportion of households in the zone of dwelling j belonging to the same racial group as household i, and γ_3 is a parameter expressing the strength of preferences for racial homogeneity. The larger the parameter γ_3, the more sensitive Z_3 (and hence U_{ij}) is to variations in R_{ij}. With γ_3 equal to zero, Z_3 can vary only between 1000 and 1001, a range of one-tenth of a percent. With γ_3 equal to one, Z_3 can vary between approximately 10 and approximately 11, a range of 10 percent.

Existing Dwelling Supply Functions

The supply curve for existing dwelling j is specified as follows:

$$Q_j = \left\{ \beta_1 + \beta_2 (2/3) [P_j - P_o] / P_c] \right\} Q_o,\tag{7}$$

in which Q_j is the level of housing services currently provided by dwelling j, Q_o is the level of housing services provided by dwelling j ten years ago, P_j is the price per unit of service offered by dwelling j, P_o is operating costs per unit of service, and P_c is capital costs per unit of service for a new dwelling. β_1 and β_2 are parameters to be determined empirically. Prices are all on a flow basis—that is, they are costs per unit of service per month, not costs per unit of capital stock.

Equation (7) is derived from assumption of maximization of expected profits, an expression for expected profits, a production function for housing services, and values for the 1960s of interest rates and expected rent changes.[8]

[8] The derivation is sketched out in de Leeuw and Struyk (1975, pp. 26-28).

Limitations and Current Model Development

Before concluding this brief account of the model, it may be useful to mention some of the things which the model does not do. The model does not attempt to capture any of the short-run dynamics of the housing market; it restricts its attention to ten-year changes. The model does not analyze the markets for inputs into housing services such as construction materials, labor, or financing; it simply takes costs of these inputs as given. The model does not take account of the feedback from housing quantities and prices to incomes; the distribution of incomes is held fixed regardless of rent levels or landlord profits.

At present the basic model does not separate renters from owner-occupants, and it deals in only a restricted way with the market for urban land. It takes no account of nonresidential uses of land, and it takes the shortcut of locating all new dwellings in a single zone rather than attempting to explain the geographic location of new construction in detail. Modifications of the basic model, however, do allow for tenure choice and for differential land prices and new construction by zone.

The model lacks a comprehensive benefit/cost measure for comparing the economic efficiency of alternative simulated policies. Consequently, simulated policies are evaluated in terms of their impact on housing market outcomes—changes in housing consumption, prices, or new construction—to name a few. The components of a benefit/cost measure are present in the model, but they are yet to be combined in a satisfactory fashion.[9]

Model development is occurring on several fronts: validation of the basic model, development of new solution procedures, and a combined incorporation of homeownership and the income tax system. The basic model, as described in this section, is being used to predict the outcomes of the Housing Allowance Supply Experiment (Rand, 1978). Results from the experiment, when available, can be used to validate the model and to suggest features that need improvement. Of particular importance will be experimental information on landlord supply functions, market price structure curves, and household responses to the housing allowance offer.

Two separate efforts are under way to develop a new solution procedure which could be incorporated into the model. One restricts model households to choice along their demand functions rather than the entire utility space.[10] This reduction in choice reduces the computational time spent searching for a solution by a factor of about 8. Restricting the choices of households may not result in any reduction in the accuracy with which the model can reproduce existing market outcomes. The reason is that the time saved per solution can be spent to search a wider range of potential parameters. In the five metropolitan areas fit with both solution procedures, the restricted choice procedure has found parameters producing as small or smaller errors four out of five times in 1960 and two out of five times in 1970. Which procedure provides the more accurate predictions is yet to be tested.

[9] Ozanne (1977).
[10] A full discussion of this procedure is in MacRae (1978).

A separate effort to develop a new solution procedure retains the full range of choice permitted households in the present procedure.[11] It increases efficiency of the solution procedure by solving analytically for several of the solution conditions rather than using the present trial-and-error method. Application of this procedure to the case of a fixed housing stock with no neighborhood externalities has produced solutions using less time than the current algorithm. Extension of this procedure to include new construction is currently under way.

A final area of model development is explicit representation of homeowner-ship and the income tax system in the model.[12] Homeowners and the income tax system are implicitly included in the basic version of the model; homeowners being represented as part tenant and part landlord while the income tax shows up as expenditure for goods other than housing. These two characteristics have been explicitly represented in a version of the model to simulate the effects of changing the tax treatment of homeowners. This version exogenously determines whether households are owners or renters. Work to make tenure choice endogenous was dis-continued because of the computational burden it would impose on the present solution procedure, however.

DATA BASES UNDERLYING THE MODEL

As the previous section described, the simulation model presented in this paper is one of urban housing markets. Thus the data underlying the model are inputs specific to an urban area. The model can be calibrated to any Standard Metropolitan Statistical Area (SMSA) for which census SMSA statistics are available at the beginning and end of the decade. There are over 175 such SMSAs in the 1960-1970 decade and there will be over 240 for the 1970-1980 decade. The model has been applied to 8 SMSAs over the 1960-1970 decade, representing a wide range of U.S. urban conditions.[13] The model can also be used with hypothetical "cities," whose inputs are aggregated from data for all SMSAs to form representations of the nation's urban areas. These prototypical cities are the ones that have been used for most simulations of national housing and welfare policies. This section describes the data underlying these prototypical cities and describes simulations of basic market conditions in these cities.

The Prototypical Cities

For simulations of national housing and welfare programs, four hypothetical metropolitan areas are used rather than the actual SMSAs to which the model has

[11] A description of the initial steps in developing this algorithm can be found in Muth (1978).

[12] For a description of this work see Andreassi and MacRae (1978).

[13] The 8 SMSAs to which the model has been calibrated are Austin, Chicago, Durham, Green Bay, Pittsburgh, Portland (Oregon), South Bend, and Washington, D.C. A description of the calibration process is in de Leeuw and Struyk (1975, pp. 57-114).

been fit.[14] There are three reasons for this choice. First, the hypothetical cities could be designed so that between them they are representative of the entire U.S. metropolitan population, whereas the eight actual areas, although they exhibit a wide range of metropolitan characteristics, are in no sense a representative sample. Second, the hypothetical cities were designed in such a way that the differences between them are small in number and precisely identifiable, making it possible to generalize about how initial conditions influence the effects of housing policies. Each actual city, in contrast, differs from each other city in a multitude of complex ways, with the consequence that it is hard to know what might account for differences in policy results among actual cities. Finally, the four hypothetical cities could be designed so that they yielded model solutions relatively easily and efficiently, whereas solutions proved somewhat difficult and expensive to obtain for two of the actual cities.

The four hypothetical areas vary in racial composition and in the growth rate of low- and moderate-income households. These two dimensions have important influences on housing policy outcomes. Racial composition is important because segregation, besides being a market characteristic of direct interest in itself, may prevent an efficient matching of households and dwellings. The growth rate of low- and moderate-income households is important because of its bearing on the price structure and the emergence of excess supplies of or demands for low-quality housing. Therefore, four cities were designed: (1) a high-minority rapid-growth area, labeled City HR; (2) a high-minority slow-growth area, City HS; (3) a low-minority rapid-growth area, City LR; and (4) a low-minority slow-growth area, City LS. Some characteristics of the four cities appear in Table 5.1.

The design of the four cities began with the construction of a joint distribution, for a random sample of SMSAs weighted by population, of (a) minority proportions and (b) growth rates of low-to-moderate-income households (defined as 1970 households with incomes of $10,000 or less compared to 1960 households with incomes of $7000 or less). Each city represents one quarter of this joint distribution and hence the four cities are representative of the nation's entire SMSA population.

The model households for each of the four cities were based on census data on the distribution of incomes in all U.S. metropolitan areas. These yielded separate income distributions for (a) white nonelderly families, (b) white elderly households and single individuals, (c) nonwhite nonelderly families, (d) nonwhite elderly households and single individuals. By specifying the number of actual households per model household for each of the four household types, a relatively small number (30-45) of model households were then created with income distributions resembling those of actual households.

The number of actual households per model household was varied among household types in order to obtain cities with the desired combination of growth rate and minority proportion. For the high-minority cities a smaller number of

---

[14] The description of the prototypical cities is taken in large part from de Leeuw and Struyk (1975, pp. 121-127).

Table 5.1
Characteristics of Four Hypothetical Metropolitan Areas

Name[a]	Minority Households as a % of Total, 1970	1960-1970 Growth of Low-to-Moderate-Income Households	1960-1970 Growth of All Households
City HR	20%	+12%	+25%
City HS	21	− 3	+ 7
City LR	5	+22	+39
City LS	6	− 3	+13

[a] H = high minority; L = low minority; R = rapid growth; S = slow growth.

actual households per model household were used for the two nonwhite household types than for the two white household types, while for the low-minority cities the reverse was done. For the high-growth-rate cities a smaller ratio of actual to model households was used for all household types than was used for the low-growth cities. The high-growth cities thus have more model households than the low-growth cities; and since the number of existing dwellings is the same in all four cities, there is more pressure to utilize the existing stock fully and to build new dwellings in the high- than in the low-growth cities. In 1970 there are the following number of households: 33 for City HS, 35 for City LS, 40 for City HR, and 43 for City LR.

Since the model households for each prototypical city are derived from distributions for all metropolitan areas, characteristics of model households can be aggregated to give metropolitan totals. For this purpose, the households of each city represent one-fourth of the households in Standard Metropolitan Areas as of 1970—about 11 million households.[15] The number of model households per city differs so that the number of actual households represented by one model household also differs by city. The range is from 225,000 actual households per model household in City LR to 332,000 in City HS.

In all respects other than household characteristics, the four cities are identical. They have identical initial-year model dwellings, based on an average for all U.S. metropolitan areas in 1960. Specifically, there are 31 existing dwellings in 1960 for each of the four cities. It would be possible, of course, to vary initial stock among cities just as we have varied household characteristics. Since market outcomes depend essentially on household demands relative to the initial stock, however, varying household characteristics accomplishes much the same purposes as varying the initial stock.

The existing housing stock in each city is divided into four zones, similar to those defined in the model applications. Zone 1 is a zone of relatively low housing quality and high minority proportion in the initial year; it represents the central-

[15] There were 43,858,775 households in SMSAs as of 1970, accounting for about two-thirds of the 63,446,192 households in the United States at that time (U.S. Department of Commerce, 1972c, tables A7 and B7).

city core of a typical metropolitan area. Zone 2 is the area of higher housing quality within the central city. Zones 3 and 4 are suburban zones, with Zone 3 containing a relatively high proportion of moderate-quality stock and Zone 4 containing a high proportion of high-quality stock. The numbers of model dwellings in zones 1 through 4 are 7, 6, 9, and 9, with average levels of initial housing services (expressed in dollars per month at average initial-year housing prices) of 89, 94, 99, and 106 respectively. The fifth zone is the zone of new construction, the location of all of the new dwellings built during the 10-year span to which the model refers.[16]

The four cities are also identical in travel times associated with each zone and in the price of new construction. Our estimates of travel times were based on information for six of the SMSAs to which the model has been calibrated. In the hypothetical cities it takes approximately 25% more time to travel to work from the suburban zones than it does from the city zones. Based on the adjusted FHA data for all SMSAs, the average price of new construction per unit of housing services during the decade was put at $1.24, or 24% higher than the average price per unit of services of the housing stock in the initial year. This $1.24 new construction price has two components—operating costs and capital costs, which are set at 50 cents and 74 cents, respectively. Finally, the minimum quantity of services required in a newly constructed dwelling was based on our estimates for six sample SMSAs and was put at 65 units of housing services. This level is also used to represent housing codes for existing dwellings.

Two Sets of Parameters

Simulations for each of the four model cities are run under two sets of supply function parameters, one implying relatively inelastic supply and the other a relatively elastic supply of housing services from the existing stock. The parameters chosen for variation are parameters which clearly can and as the simulation results below demonstrate, in fact do—have major effects on the results of subsidy programs. These two parameter sets are utilized to overcome a wide variance in our estimates of the true supply parameters. The two sets give results in a band that is wide enough to be certain that they include the actual behavior of producers of housing services from the existing stock.

The inelastic supply assumptions consist of values of 0.7 for β_1 and 0.5 for β_2, the two model parameters describing the behavior of the existing stock. These are approximately the values found in the Green Bay, South Bend, Chicago, Durham, and Pittsburgh applications and are felt to be a realistic lower bound to the true values. At prices close to the new construction price, they imply an elasticity of supply of about 0.5. The elastic set of supply parameters consists of values of 0.3 for β_1 and 1.3 for β_2. These imply an elasticity at the new construction price of about 1.2. This is a greater response of supply to price than was found in any of the

---

[16] The basic model household and dwelling distributions are listed in de Leeuw and Struyk (1975, pp. 124-125).

sample SMSAs, but it is believed to be a realistic upper bound. Washington, Portland, and Austin all had an estimated β_2 of .9 with values of β_1 ranging from .4 to .6.[17]

The No-Policy Simulation

Simulations performed for the prototypical cities give market characteristics for those cities in 1970, the end-of-decade year.[18] When no new programs are specified in the model, the simulations predict what the 1970 housing market would be like as a result of the basic market forces of the decade and existing government policies. When a new or expanded program is specified, the results reflect both the existing conditions and the policy change. The effects of the policy change can be isolated only by comparing a simulation with the policy change to one with no change. This section describes the outcomes of the no-policy-change simulations which will be used in the next section to isolate the effects of expanded programs of housing rehabilitation and household subsidy.

Table 5.2 presents no-policy outcomes for all eight cases. Comparison of the various columns in the table indicates differences in several characteristics associated with growth rates and supply elasticity assumptions. For example, prices are higher in rapidly growing cities and under elastic supply assumptions. Prices are higher in rapidly growing areas because the demand for additional housing keeps the price up near the new construction price throughout the market. In slowly growing areas the price remains near the new construction price for higher-quality housing but falls at the lower-quality levels. In the higher-quality sector of the market the price stays high because the demand for additional housing stimulated by population growth is complemented by rising incomes and depreciation of the existing stock. However, in the low-quality sector of the market the price falls because demand for such housing created by population growth is offset by rising incomes. At the same time, depreciation of the existing stock provides an expanding supply.

The association of higher prices with higher supply elasticities does not follow from the preceding discussion but is not difficult to understand. "Adaptability" is one way to describe the housing stock under elastic, as contrasted to inelastic, supply conditions. Adaptable existing dwellings are capable of providing a wider range of housing services over the same range of price changes and can furnish households with the levels of services they want; thus they are more likely to command high prices. Adaptability also lies behind the higher average quantity of housing services purchased, in spite of higher prices, under elastic than inelastic supply assumptions.

Levels of new construction and dwelling withdrawals are also associated

[17]Estimates of the seven household utility functions parameters showed little variance across actual markets, hence the average for each parameter is used here. Those values for α_1 through α_4 are .18, .26, .19, and .27. The γ_1 through γ_3 values are .8, .4, and .7.

[18]The discussion in this section is taken in part from de Leeuw and Struyk (1975, pp. 128-130).

Table 5.2
No-Policy Simulation Results, Eight Cases, 1960-1970

	High-Minority Areas				Low-Minority Areas			
	High-Growth City HR		Low-Growth City HS		High-Growth City LR		Low-Growth City LS	
Housing Characteristics	Inelastic Supply	Elastic Supply	Inelastic Supply	Elastic Supply	Inelastic Supply	Elastic Supply	Inelastic Supply	Elastic Supply
Average quantities, prices, incomes								
Quantity of services per household	124.2	125.0	124.4	127.9	128.7	129.4	129.4	131.7
Price per unit of service (*dollars*)	1.179	1.222	1.129	1.208	1.179	1.250	1.160	1.222
Income per household (*dollars per month*)	826.7	826.7	826.0	826.0	865.5	865.5	872.0	872.0
New dwellings and withdrawals								
New model dwellings	12	9	8	5	15	12	10	7
Withdrawals from existing housing stock (zones 1-4)	3	0	6	3	3	0	6	3
Withdrawals from existing housing stock (Zone 1)	1	0	2	1	1	0	2	1
Location of minority households								
Number of black model households								
Zone 1	6	5	4	4	1	2	2	1
Zones 2-5	2	3	3	3	1	0	0	1
Entire area (zones 1-5)	8	8	7	7	2	2	2	2
Ratio, black to total households								
Zone 1	1.00	.71	.80	.67	.17	.29	.40	.17
Zones 2-5	.06	.09	.11	.11	.03	0	0	.03
Entire area	.20	.20	.21	.21	.05	.05	.06	.06
Segregation measure (Zone 1 ÷ entire area)	5.0	3.6	3.8	3.2	3.4	5.8	6.7	2.8

Source: de Leeuw and Struyk (1975, p. 129) by permission of The Urban Institute.

with growth rates and supply assumptions. The number of dwellings built is larger and the number withdrawn smaller in the rapidly growing cities, as would be expected. New construction and withdrawals are also greater under the inelastic supply assumptions. This is because an existing dwelling is less adaptable to current demands and therefore more likely to be replaced by a new one when it has an inelastic supply response.

With respect to segregation, Table 5.2 indicates that in three of the four cities segregation—measured as the ratio of black to total households in Zone 1 relative to this ratio in the entire area—is somewhat greater under the inelastic supply assumptions than under the elastic supply assumptions. This difference is more obvious in the figures on ratios of black to total households than in figures on numbers of black model households. The ratios show more pronounced differences because they take account of the fact that under inelastic supply assumptions there are typically fewer end-of-decade total dwellings in Zone 1 than under elastic supply assumptions. A given number of black households in Zone 1 therefore represents a greater concentration in the inelastic-supply than in the elastic-supply simulation.

These racial differences characterize only three of the four hypothetical cities. In the low-minority, rapid-growth area—LR—there is more racial segregation under the elastic supply assumption than under the inelastic assumption. In view of this exception, caution is advisable with respect to any conclusion about the association between segregation and supply elasticity in the model. Caution is also advisable with respect to segregation results throughout this paper for another reason; namely, that the solution procedure of the model works so as to minimize changes in racial composition.[19]

SIMULATING REHABILITATION PROGRAMS

This section begins with a discussion of the simulated policies and then reports their results. The policy simulations focus on the effects of rehabilitation subsidies and of rehabilitation subsidies coupled with direct cash assistance for low-income families. The rehabilitation subsidies are intended to represent an expansion of the Section 312 Rehabilitation Loan Program, while the direct cash assistance reflects elements of the Section 8 Housing Program.

The Policies Simulated

The Department of Housing and Urban Development (HUD) is attempting to focus its programs more sharply on central cities in distress. This includes an increased concern for the decaying parts of central cities and the low-income inhabitants of those areas. One objective is to revitalize the physical environment of decaying central-city neighborhoods through improvements to the housing stock. A closely related goal is to improve the housing of the low-income residents in these areas.

[19] For an explanation of this see de Leeuw and Struyk (1975, pp. 35-36).

The policy simulations of the model attempt to assess the success of potential HUD activities to achieve these goals. First, the effects of a large-scale rehabilitation of central-city housing are simulated. Then a program with direct cash assistance to households is added to the rehabilitation subsidies to permit the lowest-income households to remain in the improved housing.

Rehabilitation Subsidies

The Section 312 program makes loans in urban renewal areas, code enforcement areas, and other approved program areas, largely for the purpose of bringing substandard dwellings up to code. The approved areas are predominantly in close-in central-city neighborhoods. The loans are made from a federal reserve of funds, carry only a 3% interest rate with a 20-year repayment, and have a $27,000 maximum value. They are mostly used by low-income homeowners, but a current administration proposal would expand the program among low-quality rental dwellings.

In the simulations, rehabilitation is assumed to take place in 1960, at the outset of the decade simulated. The average dwelling rehabilitation costs $10,500 in 1960 (equivalent to $25,000 in 1977). This brings the dwelling slightly above code and represents an average 70% increase in services provided beyond the pre-rehabilitation level of output. Only the lowest-quality dwellings in the central-city core (Zone 1 of the model) are rehabilitated, but they amount to almost 30% of the entire core-area dwellings and just over 6% of the entire stock in existence in 1960.[20] Table 5.3 provides more details on the changes in the 1960 stock brought about by the assumed rehabilitation.

To get an idea of the magnitude of such a program, consider an urban area of about a million people. There would be close to 310,000 dwellings in such an area. The central-core area identified in the model would contain about 70,000 dwellings, roughly 20,000 of which would be rehabilitated under a program like the one simulated. With an average expense of $10,500 per rehabilitated dwelling, the total cost comes to $210 million. Assuming a private mortgage interest rate for similar loans of 6% to 8% annually, the subsidy cost to the government comes to from $50 million to $70 million in 1960 dollars ($117 million to $164 million in 1977 dollars).[21]

---

[20] The figures on changes in output and costs of rehabilitation are derived from the production function for housing services in the model (averaging for elastic and inelastic supply assumptions) and Department of Commerce indexes of new housing costs. Housing codes are represented by a minimum quantity of services; 65 units have been used in this and in most other policy simulations with the model.

For a general description of the derivation of the cost index, see *Revised Deflators* (1974), where the index used for 1960-1962 is given in Table 1. The index for 1963-1978 is described in U.S. Department of Commerce (1973). The indices in the two sources differ in their treatment of the value of the site, but this does not materially affect the trend.

[21] The subsidy cost component is calculated assuming the true opportunity cost of the government's loan fund and the risk of mortgage default are accurately reflected by a private mortgage rate of 6% or 8% instead of the 3% interest charged under the Section 312 program. Total cost reflects a 20-year repayment period.

Table 5.3
Assumed Rehabilitation in 1960

Changes in Housing Stock	Central-City Core Zone 1	Market-wide Zones 1-4
No. of model dwellings in prototypical cities	7	31
No. in rehabilitation program	2	2
% rehabilitated	28.6	6.5
Average quantity of housing service[a] per dwelling	88.7	99.8
Average quantity of housing services[a] initially per rehabilitated dwelling	40.5	40.5
Average increase in services from rehabilitation[b]	28.5	28.5
% increase in service by rehabilitated dwellings	70.4	70.4
% increase in services by area	9.2	1.8

[a]The quantity of housing service per dwelling is a weighted average of the major individual services provided by a dwelling—space, shelter, sanitary facilities, etc. The weights reflect the contributions of individual services to rents or values. Thus dwellings with more rooms or better thermal controls provide more services and generally command higher rents or values. The average quantity of service here refers to the simple average among a number of dwellings in one area.

[b]In the simulations of this paper the two smallest of the seven model dwellings in Zone 1 are brought from 31 to 68 and from 50 to 70 units of service in 1960. The full distribution of 1960 dwelling outputs is given in de Leeuw and Struyk (1975, p. 124).

In practice, the Section 312 program has been much smaller than the scale of the above example. The entire program's loan fund is only $80 million currently, and a request for an expansion to $275 million is pending. The purpose of simulating a larger program is to explore the full effects of an expansion of current programs to meet stated objectives and to make visible the type of effects accompanying the present, smaller-scale program.

The rehabilitation program is implemented in all four prototypical cities. As we have explained, all four of these cities have identical 1960 housing stocks and differ only in the rate of growth and racial composition of their populations. Since there are two sets of supply parameters associated with each prototypical city, there are a total of eight rehabilitation simulations.

How might rehabilitation affect the housing market? In the central-city core essentially all low-quality dwellings would be upgraded, and the supply of moderate-quality dwellings greatly expanded. Some of the lowest-income households may spend more to occupy the upgraded housing, but most would probably be outbid by households with higher incomes. These increases in housing quality and household income could create spillover effects leading to a general upgrading of all dwellings in the core.

While rehabilitation may lead to upgrading of the central-city neighborhood, there could be offsetting changes elsewhere. Low-income households may simply move to similarly low-quality housing in other neighborhoods, and the relocation of moderate-income households to the central city could be at the expense of new construction or private upgrading that would have happened elsewhere. Thus rehabilitation could lead to a general improvement in housing quality, or it could reflect a reshuffling of people without significantly improving market-wide housing quality.

The extent of the above shifts market-wide and neighborhood-specific can be amplified or muted by the particular characteristics of the market in which they occur. In a slowly growing market with an excess supply of low-quality housing, the rehabilitation might reduce abandonments and attract moderate-income households to the central city without raising prices or greatly reducing the choice of low-income households. In a rapidly growing market the reduced supply could significantly raise prices for the poor and cause greater locational changes for them.

Differences in the racial composition of metropolitan areas could alter households' willingness to move between neighborhoods relative to their willingness to adjust to changes in the housing available in their original neighborhood. Metropolitan areas with large concentrations of black households in the central city probably would find low-income blacks less willing to move to low-quality housing in white neighborhoods and more willing to occupy the more expensive, rehabilitated, central-city housing. Likewise moderate-income whites could be expected to be less willing to take advantage of lower-priced moderate-quality housing in a largely black central-city area.[22]

Subsidies to Households

One direct result of rehabilitation identified in the preceding discussion is that the lowest-income households, who would have occupied the dwellings in their unimproved condition, probably will no longer be able to afford them when they are upgraded. These "displaced" households would have to compete for housing elsewhere and could well be worse off than they would have been without the program.[23]

Rehabilitation could be made to work directly for occupants of the designated dwellings rather than displacing them. One way to do this is to provide them with rent subsidies for occupying the dwellings once they are upgraded. A policy making this possible would be a combined Section 312 and Section 8 Rehabilita-

---

[22] Conceivably the rehabilitation could make central-city housing so attractive to whites and so expensive for low-income blacks that integration might increase. This could be very unstable, though, leading to an all-white central city and one mostly black zone elsewhere. This outcome is unlikely to occur in the simulations because, as we noted, the model solution procedure is based on an assumption that the racial composition of neighborhoods is very resistant to change.

[23] "Displaced" households refers to those who occupy the designated dwelling in the no-policy simulations in 1970. These are the ones who would have occupied the run-down dwellings had they not been rehabilitated. The original occupants of the dwellings in 1960 prior to rehabilitation are not considered, as they cannot be identified in the model.

tion Program. The Section 8 Rehabilitation Program provides long-term commitments to dwellings undergoing substantial rehabilitation. The commitments are to supplement the rents of low-income occupants up to the fair market rent.[24] In combining Section 8 with Section 312, modifications would have to be made to ensure that the displaced households were the ones offered the rehabilitated housing.

A combined household-assistance and dwelling-rehabilitation program is implemented in the model by adding a restricted household subsidy to the same rehabilitation subsidy described above. Households who occupy the dwellings targeted for improvement by the program in the no-policy simulations are assigned the same dwellings in the combined assistance and rehabilitation simulations. If the targeted dwellings are unoccupied in the no-policy simulations, other very low income households are assigned to occupy them when they are rehabilitated.

Since program-improved dwellings are not competing for occupants over the decade they, and their assigned occupants, are removed from the market simulations. The results of the market simulations are used to determine a 1970 price and level of output for the removed dwellings. Since the dwellings are under long-term commitments to the program, it has been assumed that the dwellings will remain above code, as identified in the model, and will receive an average price across the private markets of the cities simulated.[25] Once the rents of the housing are determined, the occupying households are assumed to receive subsidies in accordance with Section 8 program regulations. The regulations provide for payment of the difference between market rent and 25% of the household's adjusted gross income.

The combined household-assistance and dwelling-rehabilitation program is simulated for the two high-minority prototypical cities under both supply assumptions. This makes a total of four simulations.

Simulation Results

The simulation results of the pure rehabilitation program are presented first. These results cover all four prototypical cities under both supply assumptions. Findings from simulations of the combined household-assistance and dwelling-rehabilitation program follow for the two prototypical cities with large minority populations. For both programs, the simulation results are presented as changes from the no-policy simulations described earlier. Thus they indicate how conditions differ in 1970 from what they would have been in the absence of the programs. The following discussion highlights the main changes caused by the programs while the accompanying tables provide more details.

---

[24] Fair market rents are set by HUD with the intention that program recipients can find standard housing at or below these rents. They are set by SMSA or county, depending on the area.

[25] Specifically, the price per unit of service is set at $1.06 and the rehabilitated model dwellings provide 65 and 67 units of service, 65 units being the code minimum. The price level is an average for dwellings with similar output in the combination-program simulations. Outputs for the rehabilitated dwellings are determined by their supply functions and the price.

Dwelling Rehabilitation Simulations

The ten-year impact of the rehabilitation program can be described in terms of its effect both on the stock of housing and on the households occupying that stock. With regard to the housing stock, results are presented separately for the dwellings rehabilitated; the rest of the dwellings in the central-city core; existing dwellings in other parts of the urban area; and new construction. Among these categories, the largest changes occur for the rehabilitated dwellings. As Table 5.4 shows, both model dwellings rehabilitated in 1960 remain in service a decade later in all cities under both supply assumptions. In the absence of the program one of them, on average, would be withdrawn by the end of the decade. The one (on average) other dwelling that would remain in service without the program provides an average of 36% to 85% more housing services because of the program, and is attracting households with higher incomes than in the no-policy simulations. Ten years after being improved, these rehabilitated dwellings retain significant portions of their original improvements.

Effects in the rest of the market are typically smaller and tend to offset changes for the rehabilitated dwellings. These trends, nonetheless, lead to some surprising patterns.

Unsubsidized dwellings in the central-city core experience slight declines in the quantity of services they provide and the prices they command, presumably because of the increased supply of moderate-quality housing there. The rehabilitation program does not force any of these dwellings to withdraw from the market, although one model dwelling now produces fewer services than either rehabilitated dwelling. These other dwellings in the central-city core show no signs of benefiting from the improvements to their neighborhood. Their prices decline about the same, or slightly more than those for existing dwellings in other zones. Likewise, the incomes of their occupants show little change relative to incomes in other zones or to what they would have been in the absence of the rehabilitation program.

Taken together, the Zone 1 dwellings present an unexpected picture of the effects of rehabilitation on the central-city core. The Zone 1 averages on Table 5.4 show in six of eight cases that the dwelling which represents the average provides less housing and the household which represents the typical one is poorer under rehabilitation than without it. This is surprising because one normally imagines that rehabilitation which increases the quality of some dwellings will raise the average quality of a neighborhood and, probably, also raise the average income.

The reason for the declines in the averages here is that rehabilitation increases the number of moderate, but below-average-quality dwellings. How this affects the averages can be illustrated by a simple example. Suppose a block in Zone 1 in 1960 has one high-quality dwelling on it and one very low quality dwelling. By 1970, in the absence of rehabilitation the low-quality dwelling has been abandoned and demolished; average housing quality on the block is then that of the high-quality unit. Alternatively, when the very low quality unit is rehabilitated it becomes attractive to modest-income households and remains in service in 1970. In this case the block has both high- and modest-quality dwellings and the average is somewhere in between. Thus, the effect of rehabilitation in the example, as well as

Table 5.4

Percentage Changes in Housing Services from the Stock under a Rehabilitation Program

Market Area[a]	High-Minority Areas				Low-Minority Areas			
	High-Growth City HR		Low-Growth City HS		High-Growth City LR		Low-Growth City LS	
	Inelastic Supply	Elastic Supply	Inelastic Supply	Elastic Supply	Inelastic Supply	Elastic Supply	Inelastic Supply	Elastic Supply
Center-City Core (Zone 1)								
Rehabilitated Dwellings								
No. of dwellings in service[b]	1	0	2	1	1	0	2	1
Quantity[c]	44	85	n.a.	36	65	59	n.a.	45
Price[c]	10	9	n.a.	− 8	39	− 6	n.a.	4
Occupant income[c]	82	182	n.a.	73	150	80	n.a.	159
Other Dwellings								
No. of dwellings in service[b]	0	0	0	0	0	0	0	0
Quantity	− 1	− 1	− 2	− 1	− 2	− 2	− 1	− 1
Price	− 3	− 2	− 6	− 2	− 4	− 2	− 4	− 2
Occupant income	1	0	− 1	− 5	1	− 1	− 2	− 2
Average								
No. of dwellings in service[b]	1	0	2	1	1	0	2	1
Quantity	− 4	10	− 16	− 4	− 3	7	− 15	− 3
Price	− 6	1	− 16	− 5	− 1	− 3	− 13	− 1
Occupant income	− 5	14	− 20	− 10	− 2	6	− 18	0

Suburban, other central city (zones 2, 3, 4)								
Dwellings in service[b]	−1	0	−1	−1	0	−2	0	−2
Quantity	2	−2	3	2	1	6	2	6
Price	−3	−2	−1	3	1	3	1	3
Occupant income	2	−3	9	2	1	8	2	8
New Construction (Zone 5)								
No. of dwellings built[b]	0	0	−1	0	0	−1	0	−2
Quantity	0	0	4	0	0	1	0	2
Price[d]	0	0	0	0	0	0	0	0
Occupant income	0	0	5	0	0	2	0	4
Market-wide								
No. of dwellings in service	0	0	0	0	0	0	0	0
Quantity	0.1	0.4	−2.3	−0.4	0.3	0.2	0.0	0.7
Price	−2.5	−0.8	−4.4	−3.3	−1.7	−1.6	−0.9	−0.8

Note: n.a. = not applicable.

[a] All numbers are percentage changes in rehabilitation simulations relative to no-policy simulations for 1970, except where otherwise noted. The entries for quantity, price, and occupant income refer to percentage changes in average values, which differ from total values when the number of cases change.

[b] The entries for the number of dwellings in service or built report the change in the number of model dwellings in service between the rehabilitation and no-policy simulations; they are not percentages.

[c] For rehabilitated dwellings, the changes in quantity, price, and income apply to those in service in the rehabilitation and the no-policy cases.

[d] The price of new construction is exogenously held constant.

in the simulations reported on Table 5.4, is to lower average quality at the same time it improves the quality of specific dwellings. The same example applies to the incomes of the occupants, which also decline in Zone 1 because of rehabilitation.[26]

In the remainder of the central city (Zone 2), and in the suburbs (zones 3 and 4), additional dwellings are withdrawn from use under the rehabilitation program. Table 5.4 shows that the increased withdrawals in these zones just offset the reduction in withdrawals in Zone 1. (The exact offset occurs because rehabilitation is assumed not to affect the 1970 population.) In addition to these withdrawals, some other dwellings decline in quality though they remain in use. (More will be said about this shortly.) Table 5.4, however, reports an increase in average quality and income for these outlying areas. This unexpected trend is the exact counterpart of the declining average quality and income in the central-city core. The removal of low-quality housing in the suburbs raises average quality and incomes there just as expansion of below-average-quality housing in the inner city lowers average quality and incomes there. Thus rehabilitation can have the unexpected effect of accentuating already existing disparities in housing quality and incomes between central cities and their suburbs.

New construction is essentially unaffected by the rehabilitation program. Only in the case of the high-minority, slow-growth city with inelastic supply assumptions does the rehabilitation of existing dwellings in 1960 reduce the number of new dwellings built over the next decade. In the other cases the quality of newly constructed dwellings is too high for the rehabilitated ones to act as alternatives.

Market-wide it can be seen that after a decade the total change in services is very small. Of course, the amount of upgrading in 1960 is small (as shown on Table 5.4), but the 1970 change is even smaller. Also, housing prices are slightly lower because of the rehabilitation.

The effect of the rehabilitation in 1960 on the output of housing services a decade later is examined in more detail in Table 5.5. It shows the absolute—not the percentage—change in housing services for each zone and for the market as a whole.

---

[26] An actual case from the simulations showing how average income in Zone 1 can decline in spite of rehabilitation attracting higher-income households is provided by the rapid-growth, high-minority city. Zone 1 contains seven model dwellings, two of which are upgraded under the rehabilitation program. In the no-policy simulation one of these target dwellings is occupied by a model household with a monthly income of $207.63; the other one is unoccupied. Monthly occupant incomes in the other five model dwellings are $1287.50, $847.04, $674.75, $530.54, and $183.42. The average income for all six households is $620.31.

In the rehabilitation simulation, the new household in the previously occupied target dwelling has an income of $378.67, 82% above that of the occupant in the no-policy simulation. The previously unoccupied target dwelling is occupied by a household with a $183.42 income. Occupant incomes in the five other model dwellings are $1287.50, $847.04, $674.75, $530.54, and $207.63. The average for these seven households is $585.79, 5.5% lower than in the no-policy simulations.

Average housing expenditure behaves similarly in Zone 1. Both average incomes and housing expenditures behave precisely the reverse in zones 2, 3, and 4, accounting for their increases in spite of specific dwelling declines.

Table 5.5

Absolute Changes in Housing Services from the Stock under a Rehabilitation Program

Market Area[a]	High-Minority Areas				Low-Minority Areas			
	High-Growth City HR		Low-Growth City HS		High-Growth City LR		Low-Growth City LS	
	Inelastic Supply	Elastic Supply	Inelastic Supply	Elastic Supply	Inelastic Supply	Elastic Supply	Inelastic Supply	Elastic Supply
Zone 1, 1970								
Rehabilitated dwellings								
Withdrawn in no-policy case	57	0	105	62	62	0	112	74
In use in no-policy case	20	71	0	20	26	57	0	24
Non-Rehabilitated dwellings	− 7	− 6	− 10	− 5	− 9	− 7	− 6	− 5
Zone 1, Total	*70*	*65*	*95*	*77*	*79*	*50*	*106*	*93*
Zone 2, 3, 4, 1970								
Withdrawn in rehabilitated case	−39	0	− 53	−51	−32	0	− 97	−48
Continuing in rehabilitated case	−22	−48	− 12	−45	−33	−37	− 10	−38
Zones Total	*−61*	*−48*	*− 65*	*−96*	*−65*	*−37*	*−107*	*−86*
Zone 5, 1970								
% change in no. of units built[b]	0	0	− 12.5	0	0	0	0	0
Change in services	0	5	−124	0	0	0	0	26
Market-wide change in service, 1970[c]	9	22	− 95	−20	14	12	0	34
Change in services from rehabilitation, 1960	57	57	57	57	57	57	57	57

[a]All entries give the difference in the output of housing services between the rehabilitation and no-policy simulations, except where noted otherwise.

[b]Entries in this row are in percentage changes in number of new dwellings built.

[c]Entries may differ from sums of zones 1 to 5 because of rounding errors.

The bottom two lines on the table show that after a decade, the net change in output is much less than the original rehabilitation. In only one city is output in 1970 increased by as much as half of the 1960 improvements. The median increase is less than a fifth and one city actually experiences a decline in output.

Interestingly, the rehabilitated dwellings, identified on the top rows of the table, retain or add to their improvements over the decade. The largest increases generally come from retaining a dwelling in the stock that otherwise would have been removed. Even though the housing services provided by nonrehabilitated dwellings in Zone 1 decline slightly, Zone 1 as a whole shows larger increases in output from the program in 1970 than occurred in 1960 when the units were rehabilitated.

Offsetting the increases in Zone 1 are decreases in the rest of the stock in other parts of the urban area. In all simulations, zones 2, 3, and 4 experience declines in output both from increased withdrawals and from declines in output by those dwellings remaining in service.

In sum, the rehabilitation in these simulations has generally shifted more of the supply of below-average, modest-quality housing to the central-city core. This shift lowers average incomes and housing quality there while raising them in the rest of the urban area. Net of these redistributions, total output of housing services is increased by only a fraction of the amount of rehabilitation undertaken a decade earlier.

The effect of the rehabilitation differs considerably by market type and elasticity assumption. For example, the two rapidly growing cities under the elastic supply assumptions do not experience the unanticipated results found in the other simulations. In these two cases, average income and quality increase in Zone 1, and fall in the other zones. The two slowly growing cities under the inelastic supply assumptions are at the other extreme. For them, average output and income in Zone 1 decline more than in other cases and in the remaining zones rise more than elsewhere.[27] Neither extreme, however, is successful at retaining much of the increased output a decade after rehabilitation takes place.

The 1960 rehabilitation of low-quality central-city housing affects the 1970 residents of the cities as well as the stock of housing. Table 5.6 presents the changes for households. The table identifies households displaced by rehabilitation, those moving into the upgraded units, all low-income households, and all others. Recall that displaced households are not the original occupants of the dwellings in 1960, when rehabilitation is assumed to occur; rather they are the households who would have occupied these dwellings in the absence of the program—that is, in the no-policy simulations. Low-income households are defined as the bottom 20% to 25%

---

[27] The differences between the two sets of simulations arise because of differences in the withdrawal of Zone 1 dwellings in the absence of the 1960 program. Neither dwellings are withdrawn in the rapid growth, elastic supply cases, while both are in the slow growth, inelastic supply cases.

of the income distribution—a group eligible for most current housing programs. All other households are classified as high-income households.[28]

Every occupant of a program-designated dwelling in the no-policy simulations is displaced in the rehabilitation simulations. The number involved varies from case to case depending on how many of the program-rehabilitated dwellings would otherwise have been unoccupied in 1970 (see Table 5.6). In most cases, the displaced households locate outside the central-city core. In spite of having to choose other dwellings, all households maintain their level of housing consumption, or improve it, and all pay a lower price per unit of service, except in one case. In this case, where the displaced households pay higher prices, and in another case, where housing expenditures rise even though the per unit price falls, the displaced households are made worse off by the program. This is measured using the utility function assigned to the households in the model.[29] In all other cases the displaced households are better off according to their utility functions. Thus, in six of the eight market conditions represented on Table 5.6, rehabilitation which increases the supply of modest-quality housing spreads housing improvements and lower prices to the displaced households. However, since the net increase in housing by 1970 is small, the indirect benefits to the displaced households are also small.

In most of the simulations more households move into the rehabilitated dwellings than are displaced. This is possible because some of the dwellings would be unoccupied if they were not rehabilitated. Those moving in have higher incomes than those who would otherwise have been there, but they are almost all still low-income households. About two-thirds come from outside Zone 1, averaging across all simulations.

Households become occupants of the rehabilitated dwellings through a competitive bidding process. Hence these low-income occupants share the benefits of rehabilitation with all similarly situated households. Looking, therefore, at all low-income households, Table 5.6 shows an increase in housing consumption, a decrease in price, and, in most cases, a slight increase in utility. Generally, the magnitude of these changes is smaller than for the displaced households. Wherever rehabilitation leads to an increase in the number of occupied dwellings in Zone 1, the number of low-income households living there is increased. This accounts for the decrease in average zonal income, noted earlier, that occurs even though incomes are lower for those displaced than for those moving in.

Racially, the effect of the rehabilitation program is to reduce or leave unchanged the proportion of black households in Zone 1. That occurs because the

---

[28] High income is simply a convenient label; many households in this category have incomes below the area average.

[29] It can be recalled that the components of the utility function are housing, nonhousing goods and services, and three neighborhood characteristics. There is no weight given to remaining in one's old neighborhood; in fact, past locations cannot be determined in the model. See the section on the description of the model.

Table 5.6

Changes for Households under a Rehabilitation Program

| | High-Minority Area | | | | Low-Minority Area | | | |
| | Rapid-Growth City HR | | Slow-Growth City HS | | Rapid-Growth City LR | | Slow-Growth City LS | |
Households	Inelastic Supply	Elastic Supply	Inelastic Supply	Elastic Supply	Inelastic Supply	Elastic Supply	Inelastic Supply	Elastic Supply
Households "displaced" from rehabilitated dwellings[a]								
Number[b]	1	2	0	1	1	2	0	1
Income[c]	$208	$151	n.a.	$227	$162	$201	n.a.	$176
Race[d]	B	W,B	n.a.	B	W	W,W	n.a.	W
Zone of relocation	1	3	n.a.	1	3	3,2	n.a.	4
Housing consumption[e]	18	0	n.a.	11	0	6	n.a.	11
Housing price[e]	−15	−4	n.a.	−11	−12	−4	n.a.	8
Household utility[f]	+	−	n.a.	+	+	−	n.a.	−
Households moving into rehabilitated dwellings								
Number[b]	2	2	2	2	2	2	2	2
Income[c]	$281	$426	$199	$304	$333	$362	$258	$388
Race[d]	B,B	B,W	B,W	B,W	W,W	B,W	W,W	W,W
Zone under no policy	1,4	4,3	3,4	3,1	1,3	1,3	1,3	3,4

Low-Income Households[g]								
Zone 1 occupancy[h]	1	−1	1	1	1	−1	2	2
Housing consumption[e]	2	5	−9	−3	4	4	0	3
Housing price[e]	−12	−5	−18	−10	−11	−6	0	5
Household utility[f]	+	+	+	+	+	+	0	—
High-Income Households[g]								
Zone 1 occupancy[h]	0	1	1	0	0	1	0	−1
Housing consumption[e]	0	0	−1	0	0	0	0	0
Housing price[e]	0	0	−2	0	0	0	−1	0
% change in fraction of Zone 1 occupied by black households	0	0	−29	−15	−18	0	−28	−100

Note: n.a. = not applicable.

[a] "Displaced" households are those who occupy the program-rehabilitated dwellings in the no-policy, but not the rehabilitation simulations. No occupants of these dwellings in the no-policy simulations remain in them in the rehabilitation simulations. In this sense, all the original occupants are displaced.

[b] Entries indicate number of model households.

[c] Incomes are in 1970 dollars per month.

[d] Race is B if model household is headed by a black, W otherwise, B corresponds to household types 2 and 4 in the model, W to types 1 and 3.

[e] Percentage change in item between rehabilitation and no-policy simulations.

[f] Only direction of change is given for average utility change. Utility is calculated in the model from each household's utility function.

[g] Low-income households are those whose incomes are insufficient to afford adequate housing without spending more than 25% of their income for it. In the prototypical cities this includes 20% to 25% of the model households. All other households are classified as high income.

[h] Change in the number of Zone 1 model households belonging to indicated income class

additional housing in Zone 1 is occupied in part by white households. Thus, the program tends to increase racial integration among zones.

In the two high-minority cities, the households displaced by the program are mostly black, and they generally choose to relocate elsewhere in Zone 1, where other blacks live. In the two low-minority cities the displaced households are not black, and none of them choose to remain in the center-city core.

Dwelling Rehabilitation and Household Assistance Simulations

The second set of simulations includes the same rehabilitation program in 1960 combined with a subsidy in 1970 which enables the would-be displaced households to occupy their dwellings after rehabilitation. In cases where no household would have occupied a dwelling in 1970, low-income and primarily Zone-1 households are assigned to the rehabilitated dwellings. The simulations are done for the two high-minority cities only.

Tables 5.7 and 5.8 present the results of these simulations for the housing stock and the household population, respectively. Turning first to the stock of housing, the bottom of Table 5.7 shows that most of the increased output from the units rehabilitated in 1960 remains as a net increase market-wide in 1970. This contrasts with the pure rehabilitation simulations, where most of the 1960 improvement was offset by other declines in 1970. The greater output under the combination program does not come from the rehabilitated dwellings. Comparing the top rows of tables 5.7 and 5.4 reveals that the rehabilitated dwellings show less improvement with the household subsidy than without it.[30] Rather, the increased output occurs among the other existing dwellings throughout the urban area. These other dwellings maintain or slightly increase their housing services under the combined assistance-rehabilitation housing program, whereas their service level declined under the pure rehabilitation program. The difference between the two policies is caused by the household subsidies. These subsidies provide an increase in demand for housing which is able to sustain the increased supply provided by the rehabilitation program. This increased demand is felt throughout the market even though the subsidies are restricted to the rehabilitated dwellings.

Table 5.8 shows the effect of the combined assistance-rehabilitation program on households. The primary change, in contrast to the pure rehabilitation program, is that most of the benefits are focused on the low-income occupants of the rehabilitated housing. They show the largest increases in housing consumption and utility. The other low-income households experience much smaller increases in housing consumption and insignificant or negative changes in utility. Even though total housing improvement and benefits are smaller under the pure rehabilitation program, they are more evenly spread among the low-income households.[31]

---

[30] The quantity of housing services provided from the rehabilitated dwellings is set exogenously to the model, as are their price and their occupants in the combined subsidy simulations.

[31] Other comparisons can be made between the combination and pure rehabilitation programs, although they are not discussed here. However, it should be remembered that in the combined assistance-rehabilitation housing program occupants are exogenously assigned to the rehabilitated units, and the prices and quantity levels of these units are set outside the model.

Table 5.7

Change in Housing Services from the Stock under a Combined Household-Assistance and Rehabilitation Program

| | High-Minority Areas | | | |
| | Rapid-Growth City HR | | Slow-Growth City HL | |
Market Area	Inelastic Supply	Elastic Supply	Inelastic Supply	Elastic Supply
Center-city core (Zone 1)				
Rehabilitated dwellings				
No. dwellings in service[a]	1	0	2	1
Quantity[b]	49	61	n.a.	20
Price[b]	14	−2	n.a.	−12
Occupant income[b]	0	0	n.a.	0
Other dwellings				
No. dwellings in service[a]	0	0	0	0
Quantity	0	1	0	− 1
Price	−1	1	− 3	− 1
Occupant income	2	0	− 1	0
Average				
No. dwellings in service[a]	1	0	2	1
Quantity	−1	8	−11	− 5
Price	0	0	− 3	− 4
Occupant income				
Suburban, other central city (Zones 2, 3, 4)				
No. dwellings in service[a]	−1	0	− 2	− 2
Quantity	2	1	7	7
Price	−1	2	1	1
Occupant income	3	0	10	8
New construction (Zone 5)				
No. dwellings built[a]	0	0	0	1
Quantity	0	0	0	−11
Price[c]	0	0	0	0
Occupant income	0	0	0	−14
Market-wide				
No. dwellings in service[a]	0	0	0	0
Quantity	0.8	1.7	0.9	1.4
Price	−1	+ 2	+ 2	− 2
Quantity change 1970 (absolute)	38	83	40	57
Quantity change by rehabilitation 1960 (absolute)	57	57	57	57

Note: All numbers are percentage changes in combination simulations relative to no-policy simulations for 1970, except where otherwise noted. The entries for quantity, price, and occupant income refer to percentage changes in average values, which differ from total values when the number of cases change. n.a. = not applicable.

[a]The entries for number of dwellings in service or built reports the change in the number of model dwellings in service between the rehabilitation and no-policy simulations; it is not a percentage.

[b]For rehabilitated dwellings the changes in quantity, price, and income apply to those in service in both the combination simulations and the no-policy simulations. Furthermore, the values for these variables in the combination simulations are determined outside the model.

[c]The price of new construction is exogenously held constant.

Table 5.8

Changes for Households under a Combined Housing-Assistance and Rehabilitation Program

| | High-Minority Area | | | |
| | Rapid-Growth City HR | | Slow-Growth City HS | |
Households	Inelastic Supply	Elastic Supply	Inelastic Supply	Elastic Supply
Assisted households in rehabilitated dwellings				
Number[a]	2	2	2	2
Income[b]	$200	$151	$178	$178
Race[c]	B,B	B,W	B,W	B,W
Housing consumption[d,e]	47	61	29	22
Housing price[d,e]	14	− 2	45	− 15
Household utility[f]	+	+	+	+
Other low-income households[g]				
Number[a]	8	8	6	6
Income[b]	$280	$291	$284	$284
Housing consumption[d]	2	6	0	8
Housing price[d]	− 5	6	− 4	5
Household utility[f]	0	−	0	0
All low-income households[g]				
Zone-1 occupancy[h]	1	0	2	1
Housing consumption[d]	7	14	6	11
Housing price[d]	− 2	4	7	0
High-income households[g]				
Zone-1 occupancy[h]	0	0	0	0
Housing consumption[d]	0	0	0	0
Housing price[d]	0	0	1	0
Fraction of Zone 1 occupied by black households[d]	− 14	+ 6	− 10	− 16

[a]Entry indicates number of low-income households.

[b]Incomes are in 1970 dollars per month.

[c]Race is B if model household is headed by black, W otherwise.

[d]Entry is percentage change between combined policy simulation and no-policy simulation.

[e]For assisted households in rehabilitated dwellings, housing consumption and price are determined exogenously.

[f]Only the direction of change is given for utility change. Utility is calculated in the model from each household's utility function.

[g]Low-income households are those whose incomes are insufficient to afford adequate housing without spending more than 25% of their income for it. In the prototypical cities this includes 20% to 25% of the model households. All other households are classified as high income.

[h]Change in the number of Zone 1 model households belonging to indicated income category.

SUMMARY, CONCLUSIONS, AND IMPLICATIONS

The main finding of the simulations is that rehabilitation of the existing stock results in relatively small *net* gains over time unless there is a corresponding *net* increase in demand for that housing. The 1960 rehabilitation of central-city dwellings succeeded in raising output and preventing withdrawal among these units in 1970. But this effect is largely offset by decreases in output and increases in withdrawals in other areas. Thus, the lasting effect of rehabilitation, by itself, is to alter which dwellings get withdrawn from use and where households locate.

Surprisingly, the shift in household locations and dwelling withdrawals under both policies leads to a decline in the average dwelling size and income in the central-city core and an increase in these averages throughout the rest of the urban area. In spite of these zonal shifts, or possibly because of them, there do not appear to be significant neighborhood effects on other households and dwellings arising from the program. Existing dwellings in the central city experienced about the same changes in price and output as their counterparts in other zones.

Households occupying dwellings designated for rehabilitation in the no-policy simulations are much better off under the combined assistance-rehabilitation program, since the subsidy that they receive allows them to occupy their upgraded dwellings. Interestingly, these households also experience some improvement under the pure rehabilitation program, even though they are forced to leave the rehabilitated dwellings. The benefits are lower, but all low-income households benefit about equally under the pure rehabilitation program.

The moderate-quality rehabilitation in these simulations turns out to be insufficient to attract households away from new construction in almost all cases.

Two implications for further work emerge from these simulations. The first is to investigate combinations of supply-side and demand-side programs for revitalizing central cities. A combination program appears to be necessary to accomplish lasting improvements in the central city without detrimental effects to the rest of the urban area. A second is to investigate the effects of rehabilitation which converts low-quality dwellings into luxury housing. The displacement and welfare effects of this type of rehabilitation are likely to differ from those in the present simulations, and they are of great policy interest.

DISCUSSION

Bruce Hamilton

The Urban Institute Housing Simulation Model forms the basis of the housing policy simulations reported by Ozanne and Vanski. I shall direct my initial remarks to the model itself, and will turn later to some technical aspects of the specific simulations carried out here.

The model essentially comes in two parts, a "nonspatial" market for housing and an explicit mechanism for allocating people over space. The nonspatial part of the model is straightforward—so straightforward, in fact, that it could probably be specified without the aid of simulation techniques. In the initial period there is an exogenous population with an exogenous size distribution of income, and on the supply side there is a standing stock of housing with a given quality distribution. The stock is auctioned off with the highest-quality house going to the highest-income bidder, and so on down the line. If at any point in the quality distribution housing sells at a price above construction cost, new housing is built. The results that come essentially from this nonspatial part of the model are plausible and convincing, as I will discuss below.

The second feature of the model is the allocation of households to five zones in the city. This is done by endowing households with preference rankings for some features of the city which vary spatially, such as the racial composition of the zone, proximity to work places, and a variable which is called a proxy for neighborhood wealth. The parameters of the utility function are essentially estimated, by searching for those values which optimize the model's fit to the various cities used for calibration.[1] Equilibrium is achieved when no household could increase its utility by moving.

---

[1] The problem with estimating parameters by finding the best fit of a simulation model is that confidence intervals or t-statistics are generally not reported. But there is no reason why estimated t-statistics could not be calculated. Optimizing the fit involves minimizing some sum of squares, and the change in the sum of squares as a parameter is varied gives the information necessary to calculate a t-statistic.

The spatial preference and location equilibrium portion of the model is at the same time its strength and weakness. Spatial interactions are precisely the complicated kind of general-equilibrium problems which are almost impossible to analyze without a simulation model. My problem with the spatial part of the model comes from my belief that our understanding of the determinants of consumer location preferences and decisions is so primitive that it is premature to build a simulation model upon such a shaky analytical foundation. It seems to me that our research effort in this field would be better spent trying to get a better understanding of the basic forces to which consumers respond when making location decisions. Once we have more faith in the structural components, we will have a great deal more with which to build a simulation model.

I will describe two simple but important cases of our ignorance on spatial questions. The nature of race prejudice and preferences for racial characteristics of neighborhoods is very poorly understood, with serious research just beginning. Bailey's (1959) racial-boundary model suggests that price gradients between the interior and the boundary of racially homogeneous neighborhoods will reveal, for instance, whether blacks prefer to live near blacks or whites. But this interpretation of such a gradient requires that all blacks (or whites, if you analyze the other side of the boundary) have the same preferences. If blacks disagree as to the attractiveness of whites, they will sort themselves out with the white-likers living on the boundary. In this case the interpretation of the boundary is blurred. In any case, there have been few serious attempts to estimate such gradients. Work by Kain and Quigley (1975) and A. T. King and Mieszkowski (1973) represents an excellent start, however.

There are a whole host of other unanswered questions surrounding the question of race and location, the foremost (at least emotionally) being integration of public schools. Two comments are in order here. First, we know even less about the effects of school integration upon location than the effects of race preference *per se*. Second, the Urban Institute model lacks a public sector, so this interaction between race and location is not modeled.

A second question about location choice is that of neighborhood effects. With the work of Crecine et al. (1967), and numerous refinements of that work, a consensus seems to be building that many of the land uses which neighborhood associations complain about (such as apartment buildings and mom-and-pop stores) have no significant effect upon residential property values. This raises the possibility that many so-called neighborhood effects are unimportant or at least sufficiently localized that private bargaining handles the problem. But here again, there is another plausible explanation, consistent with the empirical findings, which has been offered by Thornton (1978). For example, land use that generates noise may make a neighborhood unattractive to some of its occupants. But if these people can sell their homes, say, to deaf people, then there is no reason to expect a price effect. Again, the conclusion at this point seems to be that we do not know very much. Of importance for this model, we do not know whether taste differences are sufficiently important to have an important bearing on geographic mobility and the nature of the ultimate spatial equilibrium.

To repeat, I have trouble believing that this degree of understanding is sufficient to serve as the core of a large simulation model. It is particularly serious because it is almost impossible for the reader to see the relationship between the results and particular assumptions and parameter values. The model is necessarily too complicated to permit this, so the reader who has doubts about a particular assumption would have difficulty judging the direction or importance of the biases which might be caused.

There is one other problem with the spatial nature of the model, and indeed with the spatial nature of reality. The indivisibilities inherent in space and spatial decisions introduce a large measure of nonconvexity, which among other things destroys our faith in the uniqueness of equilibrium. Different equilibria can be achieved by different adjustment paths. (An excellent discussion of this appears in a somewhat different context in Eaton and Lipsey, 1976.) Spatial reality undoubtedly has this non-uniqueness property, and the model apparently reflects this feature of reality. It is hardly fair to criticize a simulation model for reproducing reality, and I do not intend to do so. But it does raise a troubling question: When we use the model to simulate a policy change, particularly a major policy change, how do we know that the model converges to the same new equilibrium as does reality? We can only know this if we believe that the adjustment path of the model accurately reflects the adjustment path of reality. The model has no dynamic adjustment path *per se*; rather, it has a solution algorithm. The algorithm is described in the paper as "...a process of trial and error...(which has) no theoretical or empirical significance; a housing market may search for a solution in a different way from the computer program." While the solution algorithm may yield results that mimic the market adjustment process, the fear that the model arrives at the "wrong" solution would be greatly diminished if the solution algorithm were explicitly modeled after that adjustment process.

The claim that the spatial features of the results are suspect is dramatized in the policy simulations which are presented. Ozanne and Vanski consider two policy changes: (1) subsidized upgrading of all the substandard housing in the core of a central city, and (2) a subsidy as in (1) plus rent subsidies to occupants of the formerly substandard dwellings sufficient to permit them to remain in their homes without suffering financial losses. Nonspatially, the authors find that the supply experiment (1) has little long-term effect upon the quality distribution of the stock of housing, but that when the demand subsidy (2) is added, most of the initial upgrading effects remain after ten years. These are plausible results.

The spatial results can be summarized by stating that (in general) both policy simulations tend to reduce the concentration of blacks in the core of the central city and to increase the concentration of low-income people in the core. In both cases the changes are offset by changes in the outer portions of the city and in the suburbs. Hence, the core supply-side subsidy increases the number of blacks locating in the outer parts of the city. The sequence seems to be as follows: (a) A disproportionate number of blacks are displaced from the core substandard housing when it is upgraded, and they are unable to afford the housing after the improvement and rent increase; (b) the upgraded housing is occupied by below-average-income people most of whom are white and who come from the outer rings of the city; the displaced blacks move mostly into core housing, but a few move into the housing vacated by the new occupants of the upgraded housing. The reduced blackness of the core is caused largely by the influx of fairly low-income whites, and to a lesser degree by the exodus of a few blacks.

Poverty becomes somewhat more concentrated in the central city because the core housing which is upgraded causes the abandonment of fairly low-income housing in the remainder of the city, leaving the noncore housing stock higher-quality and the population richer. This raises the question, Why don't the displaced poor simply take the houses vacated by the new core dwellers? In this case the outer portions of the city would become somewhat poorer and the core somewhat richer. Also, I believe that such a move would give the displaced poor somewhat higher-quality housing than they find by largely restricting their search to the core. The answer is that the displaced households fail to take the best-quality available housing because of their strong desire for neighborhood characteristics, and their limited willingness to trade off neighborhood traits for housing quality. The racial-preference argument seems to be playing the most important role, quantitatively. Thus black preference for black neighborhoods is sufficient to overcome the low price and relatively high quality of the vacated noncore housing. Blacks could improve their housing quality by decentralizing, but they would have to move into white neighborhoods.

Would we really expect fairly low-income whites to move into renovated housing in the largely black core, and would we really expect blacks not to move into adequate-quality vacated housing further out? If race preferences are misspecified, or if neighborhood preferences in general are highly restricted geographically, or if race preference is heavily influenced by public-school considerations, or if blacks are subjected to nonmarket restrictions on residential location, the results would be quite different from a market where each racial group has a simple preference for living among its own. If neighborhood preferences are more localized than the 5-zone analysis suggests, blacks would be less inhibited about leaving the core, since it would be fairly easy to establish small pockets of black residence in the suburbs. If public schools are important, blacks might try harder to suburbanize (and whites might try harder to stop them). If blacks face a price markup in white neighborhoods, they would have less of a tendency to suburbanize. All of these conjectures are plausible and potentially crucial to the spatial results. But there is little reliable evidence one way or another, on the qualitative importance of these considerations.

DISCUSSION

Edgar O. Olsen

Larry Ozanne and Jean Vanski use the Urban Institute Housing Model to analyze the effects of a supply-side subsidy, namely rehabilitation loans at below-market interest rates, and a combination of this supply subsidy with a demand-side subsidy. The model has previously been used to estimate some effects of a housing allowance scheme, public housing, and interest rate subsidies for new construction.

At the outset, I would like to express the opinion that this is a very good and useful paper. I think that the basic structure of the model is quite satisfactory.[1] It contains households who are assumed to have indifference maps and to maximize their well-being subject to certain constraints. It contains profit-maximizing firms with production functions. It contains a government able to change the constraints facing households and firms. The equilibrium solution is the situation in which none of the actors has any incentive to change his or her behavior.

In my opinion, this paper and other applications of the model are highly policy relevant. The model is able to provide estimates of many important effects of almost any proposed housing program. Policymakers in the housing field have too often been preoccupied with the immediate effects of their programs on the dwelling units and households directly affected. Ozanne and Vanski address these traditional concerns, but their paper is not limited to such concerns. I think that their analysis will help policymakers to see the broader implications of several proposed housing programs.

Let me briefly describe how the model is used to predict the effects of a housing program. Then I will summarize Ozanne and Vanski's findings and comment in more detail on the relevance and reliability of these results for public policy decisions.

---

[1] I also think that there is enormous room for improvement in the details of model specification.

Their analysis is conducted separately for four prototypical cities that differ with respect to the rate of population growth and the proportion of households that are black, in the belief that the impact of a government housing program depends to a large extent on these factors. Within each city the analysis is conducted under two alternative assumptions concerning the elasticity of supply of housing services from the existing stock. Since I do not think that these matters are important for understanding how the model is used, I will not discuss them further.

In the model, a city contains 30 to 45 households and dwelling units. The households are intended to be representative of the entire population with respect to income, race, and age of the household head. The dwellings are intended to be representative with respect to location within the city and rent. The data are from the 1960 and 1970 Census of Population and Housing.

After obtaining estimates of the parameters of the indifference maps of households and supply functions of firms producing housing services from the existing stock, the equilibrium matching of households and dwellings in 1960 is calculated. These estimates of the state of the economy in 1960, the estimated indifference maps and supply functions, the numbers and incomes of households, and the cost of new construction in 1970 are fed into the computer, and out come predictions of (1) which units that were in the stock in 1960 will be withdrawn from residential use by 1970, (2) which will be upgraded and which allowed to deteriorate and how much, (3) how many new units will be constructed between 1960 and 1970 and how much housing service will they provide, (4) which families will occupy which units, and (5) what will be the rent and the price per unit of housing service for each dwelling. In brief, this is how Ozanne and Vanski predict the state of the economy in the absence of new government programs in 1970.

To estimate the effect of a new government housing program, the constraints facing households and firms are changed and a new equilibrium state of the economy in 1970 is calculated. The difference between these two predicted states of the economy is the estimated effect of the new program.

Ozanne and Vanski first analyze a rehabilitation loan program which increases the quantity of housing services provided by the lowest-quality housing in the central-city core in 1960 up to a level roughly corresponding to the minimal requirements of occupancy codes. That is, in this year firms are induced to upgrade their substandard units to a certain level, and there is no further government involvement. Estimates of the effects of this program after ten years are as follows: The program prevents some rehabilitated units from being withdrawn from the stock, and other rehabilitated units are of much higher quality than they would have been in the absence of the program. The program also affects the quality of housing elsewhere in the central-city core and who lives there. The net effect is to slightly reduce average housing quality and income in the central-city core, because units that would have been removed from the stock are upgraded to quality levels below the central-city average. In other parts of the city, both housing quality and income are higher. The program has no perceptible effect on new construction. What it does is to change the location of the dwelling units that are withdrawn from the stock. Over time, the effect of the program on total consumption of housing services vanishes. Much to their credit, Ozanne and Vanski also examine the effects of the program on different types of households. Under most assumptions, the program results in small gains to low-income households. Strangely, the direction of change in well-being for high-income households is not reported.

Ozanne and Vanski then analyze the effect of this same rehabilitation program combined with a direct subsidy to the families who would have occupied the upgraded units in the absence of the program. To receive the subsidy the households must live in the rehabilitated units, and these units must be maintained to code standards. The owners are paid market rents for their units, and the subsidy is more than adequate to induce households to participate. This is quite similar to the way that the Section 8 Housing Rehabilitation Program works. Ozanne and Vanski estimate that almost all of the increased output from the units rehabilitated in 1960 remains as a net increase market-wide ten years later. The demand-side subsidy provides an increase in demand for housing which is able to sustain the increased supply provided directly under the rehabilitation program. The other main difference in the effect of the two programs is that the combination program confers benefits almost exclusively on the low-income households who are assisted, while the rehabilitation program alone spreads very small benefits over the entire low-income population.

Now, I would like to make a few comments about the relevance and reliability of these results for public policy decisions.

A draft of the Carter administration's urban policy statement says that one objective of national urban policy will be "to revitalize the physical environment of decaying central-city neighborhoods through improvements to the housing stock." It is for this reason that Ozanne and Vanski estimate the effect of the programs on the quality of housing in the core of the central city. I think that this objective involves a confusion between ends and means. I believe that the primary ends of government housing policy are to have low-income households occupy better housing than they would choose were they given equally costly unrestricted cash grants and to reduce racial segregation in housing. In the process of achieving these goals while minimizing cost, certain dwellings would be improved, others would be allowed to deteriorate, some would be withdrawn from residential use, and some new units would be constructed. Whether this policy results in better or worse housing in a particular area is irrelevant. It is the effect on the housing of low-income families and racial segregation that matters. I see no reason to be concerned about which dwelling units are upgraded and which downgraded except as this affects the cost of achieving these goals.

It is typical of analyses of government housing programs to focus on their effects on housing prices and ignore effects on the prices of other goods. The Urban Institute Housing Model assumes that housing programs have no effect on nonhousing prices. Indeed, it assumes that changes in taste or government programs which increase the demand for housing and decrease the demand for other goods raise the overall price level because they result in higher housing prices and no change in the price of other goods. In a satisfactory two-good general equilibrium model, these changes would lead to higher housing prices and lower nonhousing prices. The neglect of the effect of housing programs on nonhousing prices has often led to the fallacious conclusion that nonparticipants are hurt more with respect to their own consumption of goods by a government program that exerts a larger upward effect on housing prices than by an equally costly program that has a smaller upward effect. This conclusion is true for households with the strongest taste for housing but is false for households with the strongest preference for other goods. The assumption of constant nonhousing prices is a fundamental defect of the Urban Institute Housing Model, which reinforces mistaken policy analysis.

Ozanne and Vanski find that a one-shot supply-side program has a smaller effect on housing consumption ten years later than would a combination of this program with a permanent demand-side subsidy. Since it costs more, however, it does not follow that the combination is to be preferred. A comparison of the alternatives would be facilitated if they were designed to have the same cost to taxpayers.

The authors conclude from their empirical findings that "a combination program appears to be necessary to accomplish lasting improvements in the central city without detrimental effects to the rest of the urban area." This may have been a slip of the pencil. What they found is that a supply-side subsidy alone will have no lasting effects. Since they did not analyze a demand-side subsidy alone, their conclusion does not follow from their empirical results.

One important effect of a rehabilitation loan program that they fail to estimate is its effect on the efficiency with which housing services are produced. This program subsidizes only one method of production, namely, rehabilitation of existing housing financed with borrowed money. Therefore, it will lead to inefficient production of housing services because this method will be used too extensively relative to other methods such as new construction and ordinary maintenance.

Let me close with a few words about the reliability of Ozanne and Vanski's results compared with the hunches of housing policymakers and the results obtained using another model.

I certainly expect the results generated by the Urban Institute Housing Model, even in its present form, to be more reliable than the hunches of a housing policymaker selected at random. In my experience, the majority of these people believe, for example, that if a dwelling unit is built under the auspices of a HUD program, the net effect of the program is to add one unit to the housing stock, and if the program does not directly involve new construction, no new building will be induced.

I have already said that the Urban Institute Housing Model can be used to provide estimates of many important effects of almost any proposed housing program. There are some important questions that the model in its present form is not well suited to answer. For example, it does not appear well suited to predict the effects of a housing program that has only enough funding to serve a small fraction of eligible households and serves them essentially on a first-come first-serve basis. This is characteristic of all existing programs of housing subsidies to low-income families in the United States. For this type of housing program, the problem is to predict who will participate. Since the model does not account for differences in the cost of participation, I doubt that it could accurately predict participation. Furthermore, the number of model households would have to be expanded greatly in order to analyze housing programs of the size in existence because at present a single model household represents many more people than are served by any of these programs. In general, I would say that studies using large bodies of data on individual households and their dwellings and assuming no effect on market prices provide better estimates than the Urban Institute Housing Model of the effects of existing housing programs.[2] Furthermore, evidence from the Experimental Housing Allowance Program suggests that even massive housing programs for low-income families such as a comprehensive housing allowance plan would not have large effects on market prices, partly because they do not increase aggregate demand for housing very much and partly because households do not adjust their housing consumption immediately to changes in their circumstances.[3] This suggests that studies based on large bodies of microdata and the assumption of constant market prices will provide better answers to some questions (e.g., concerning the distribution of well-being) than the Urban Institute's model.

The forte of the Urban Institute Housing Model relative to empirical models previously used to analyze housing programs is that it takes account of intraurban differences in housing prices and the effects of housing programs on these differences. The model is also useful for analyzing the effect of housing programs on household location. However, the number of model households will have to be increased substantially before the Urban Institute model will yield even moderately reliable estimates concerning racial segregation.

To sum up this point, the Urban Institute's model can provide answers to many important questions. Other approaches can provide better answers to some of these questions. However, the Urban Institute's model can provide answers more cheaply and quickly. Given the time frame within which policy decisions are often made, this is an enormous advantage.

---

[2] See, for example, Olsen (1972); DeSalvo (1975); and Murray (1975).

[3] See Rand Corporation (1978). A massive housing allowance program for low-income families would have a small effect on aggregate demand for housing services because participating households account for a small fraction of total demand prior to the program and other households reduce their demand in response to the taxes collected to support it.

6

IDIOM: A DISAGGREGATED POLICY-IMPACT MODEL OF THE U.S. ECONOMY

Stephen P. Dresch
Daniel A. Updegrove

INTRODUCTION

This paper describes IDIOM (Income Determination Input Output Model), a model designed for the assessment of the multifaceted economic effects of large-scale changes in fiscal structure (tax, transfer, and expenditure policy) and of other exogenous economic developments.* The central objective of this research has been the adaptation and development of techniques of analysis capable of identifying these effects at a relatively high degree of disaggregation (e.g., by region, industry, and occupation). The substantive character of the model is illustrated by its application to the assessment of the domestic economic effects of a reduction in military exports.

Clearly, this type of analysis cannot be undertaken within the confines of the easy *ceteris paribus* assumptions of partial equilibrium analysis. "All else" does not

*Financial support for the development of IDIOM has been provided by the Ford Foundation, by the United Nations Department of Economic and Social Affairs, by grants to the National Bureau of Economic Research (NBER) from the Office of Economic Research of the Economic Development Administration, U.S. Department of Commerce (in association with the Office of Minerals Policy and Research Analysis, U.S. Department of the Interior, and the Office of Competitive Assessment and Business Policy, U.S. Department of Commerce), and by unrestricted funds of the NBER. Since early 1976, further development of IDIOM has been continued by the Institute for Demographic and Economic Studies with the support of the Economic Development Administration (Grant Number OER-575-G-77-20 [99-7-13382]) and of the Federal Preparedness Agency (Contract Number FPA-76-11).

We are indebted to our current and former colleagues Carl Lagoze, Ruth Schultz, Robert D. Goldberg, An-loh Lin, Elisa Nash, and Wu-lang Lee, and to Allan Olson of the Economic Development Administration, John Kaler of the Office of Competitive Assessment, Edward Zabrowski and Paul Krueger of the Federal Preparedness Agency, and Douglas Samuelson of the Office of Minerals Policy. During the NBER phase of the effort, John R. Meyer and Edward K. Smith provided continuing interest and support.

remain constant when major changes in areas such as tax, transfer, or expenditure policy are undertaken. Thus, the identification and meaningful evaluation of the full consequences of such changes require an approach that permits the explicit recognition of interacting responses in various sectors of the economy to changes in policy and other "exogenous" variables. The present modeling effort has been directed toward the incremental, and, we hope, cumulative, implementation of this approach.

Drawing upon the previous work of Leontief et al. (1965), a prototype version of IDIOM was developed in 1972 and applied to the assessment of the domestic economic effects of a contraction in U.S. military expenditure (general or strategic) under alternative compensatory policies (United Nations, 1972; Dresch, 1972). The first fully articulated version of IDIOM (Dresch and Goldberg, 1973) represented a generalization of that prototype. In late 1973 and early 1974 the model was modified to permit the assessment of various policy responses to the petroleum embargo (Zabrowski, 1974; Zabrowski and Krueger, 1974), and the capacity to impose a selective excise tax (on a single commodity) was added. Over the ensuing year the policy substitutions component of the model was extended to incorporate changes in personal tax rates. Finally, over the last two years the structural formulation and empirical basis of the model were substantially altered by (1) the conversion from a total to a domestic base input-output system, (2) a major extension of the Regional Model to incorporate differential regional growth rates by sector, (3) the generalization of the selective excise tax capabilities to consider a full spectrum of general excise or consumption taxes, (4) provision for the virtually automatic linkage of IDIOM to various macroeconomic forecasting models, and (5) the incorporation of provisional unemployment/labor-force-participation relationships at the regional level. The model is currently being extended to incorporate regional unemployment, labor force participation, and migration relationships, and the development of a fully articulated household model is in the design stage.

In summary, IDIOM is a two-stage model, consisting of a primary National Model and a secondary Regional Model. The National Model is driven by a set of exogenous or predetermined final demands (exogenous or predetermined components of GDP [gross domestic product] , specifically including gross investment, government purchases of goods and services, gross exports, and transferred imports). The production required to fulfill these exogenous final demands generates labor and nonlabor income. These incomes then serve to determine endogenous consumption final demands via consumption functions.

Thus, the income determination component of the National Model is in essence a rather simple Keynesian multiplier model. Exogenous components of GNP operate via the multiplier (that is, the consumption functions) to determine the level of income and output. The departure from the simple Keynesian model resides in the specification of the exogenous final demands; rather than as scalar magnitudes (e.g., investment or government expenditures), these appear as vectors of final purchases from individual producing sectors (industries). In addition, these producing sectors are represented via an input-output model as making intermediate purchases from other sectors, with each sector exhibiting unique labor and nonlabor input (and income generation) coefficients. A change in either the level or the sectoral composition of exogenous demands induces changes in the level and/or composition of income. Thus, the value of the implicit multiplier depends on the nonlabor- and labor-income consumption functions, and in addition on the sectoral distribution of exogenous and endogenous demands that determine the labor/nonlabor distribution of income. The outputs of the National Model are indicated in Table 6.1.

Public policy enters the National Model either through the government components of exogenous final demands, through tax leakages from the income stream, or through consumption by recipients of transfer payments. Thus, in principle, the model can assess the effects of any policy substitution which can be represented by a change in taxes, expenditures, or transfers.

The Regional Model represents a variant of the balanced regional growth model first suggested by Leontief and Isard (Leontief et al., 1953) and begins with

Table 6.1
National Model Outputs

Variable	Variable (*continued*)
Total output by industry (vector)	Tax revenues, gross (exclusive of special excise taxes)
Gross domestic product (GDP)	Indirect business taxes
Depreciation	Corporate profits taxes
Consumption	Nonlabor personal taxes
Consumption out of labor income	Labor personal taxes
Consumption out of nonlabor income	Transfers (government)
Consumption out of transfer income	Net tax revenues
Aggregate demand by other final demand component (investment, state and local government, federal nondefense, exports, transferred imports)	Employment, total
	Employment by industry (vector)
	Employment by occupation (vector)
	Raw materials consumption (vector)
Net nonlabor income	Effluent production
Labor income	Capital requirements, total
Nonlabor net savings	Capital requirements by capital goods producer industry (vector)
Labor savings	Capital requirements by capital goods user industry (vector)
Transfer savings	

Note: Except for those specified as vectors, all model outputs are scalar magnitudes.

the solution of the National Model. One product of the National Model is a vector of sectoral (industry) outputs. For a subset of these sectors—designated "national industries" on the basis of high degrees of interregional trade and the presumption of the existence of "national" markets for their outputs—total outputs from the National Model are distributed over regions according to predetermined distribution matrices indicating the share of each region in the total output or output change of each national industry. The underlying distribution matrices are exogenously specified, but marginal shares of output expansions/contractions may differ from average shares.

The critical assumption of the Regional Model is that any demands within a region for the outputs of "local industries" (all nonnational industries, primarily services) must be supplied from within the region.[1] For national industries there are no barriers to interregional trade, and the regional distribution of output can be made exogenously. In the case of local industries, however, there is by assumption no interregional trade, and as a result, the regional distribution of outputs of local industries is endogenous, determined by the prior distribution of other activities.

Each of the exogenous final demands on local industries is distributed over regions according to industry-region matrices describing the base and marginal change distributions. Thus, the regional distributions of military and of fixed investment purchases from the construction sector (a local industry) may differ, reflecting the underlying differences in the regional distributions of military relative to investment activities.

The only significant departure of the Regional from the National Model is in the treatment of nonlabor income. In the National Model nonlabor income is endogenous. However, once determined at the national level, nonlabor income is distributed over regions according to the more basic distribution of wealth. Thus, nonlabor income generated in a region need not be received in that region. The distribution of nonlabor income then determines the consumption demands of recipients of this income by region.

Given the distribution of outputs of national industries across regions, the consumption final demands of employees of national industries have also, simultaneously, been regionally distributed. Thus, the only endogenous component of final demand at the regional level is the consumption of employees of local industries. Simultaneous solution of the implied set of intraregional equations results in a configuration of outputs of regional (local) industries consistent with the technical structure of local industry production and with the assumed distributions of national industry outputs, of nonlabor income, and of employee consumption demands of national and local industry.

---

[1] A somewhat more complex, multitiered hierarchical version of this model, distinguishing between "local," "regional," and "national" industries, has been suggested by Leontief et al. (1965). A hybrid alternative, in which a variable fraction of requirements from any industry is allocated to the region of use on the basis of its share of national output, with the residual distributed as in the case of national industry outputs, has been employed by Haveman and Krutilla (1968).

To summarize, local industry outputs in a region must be sufficient to meet demands on local industries emanating from (a) the predetermined outputs of national industries within the region (intermediate purchases by national from local industries), (b) the predetermined regional shares of exogenous final demands (including consumption final demands of recipients of nonlabor income) from local industries, (c) the consumption demands on local industries by local employees of national industries, and (d) the consumption demands on local industries by employees of local industries themselves. The outputs of the Regional Model are summarized in Table 6.2.

The strength of this formulation resides in the independence of the National from the Regional Model solution. However, this strength is also the most serious weakness of the model. It is achieved only on the basis of the assumption that sectoral technologies (input-output relationships) are invariant across regions. Thus, the National Model solution is also invariant with respect to the spatial distribution of economic activity. Because data characterizing the technical structure of production are more reliable at the national than at the regional level (when indeed these data are available at all below the national level), the confidence which can be placed in the National Model is substantially greater than that which can be placed in the Regional Model. But, the greater reliability of the National Model is purchased at the price of lesser reliability at the regional level, since it is necessary to ignore evidence that is available concerning apparent interregional differences in sectoral technologies, differences which are especially notable in the agricultural sectors (differences in crops and in technology related to soil and climate) but can be observed in other sectors as well, such as utilities (differences in relative reliance on the different primary energy sources in the production of electric power) and manufacturing (differences in factor proportions and in the vintage of the capital stock). It might be noted that this difficulty to a degree reflects and is compounded by interregional differences in sectoral product mix, which are ignored in aggregating to the 86-sector level.

The regional distortions resulting from the assumption of common sectoral technologies across regions are exacerbated by the failure to take into account patterns of interregional trade: by the fact that, while "multiregional," the model is not "interregional." The advantage of the present formulation in this regard is that it requires no information concerning interregional trade—information which is only fragmentary, quite difficult to construct, and as a result often quite out of date. Given evidence that even over the intermediate term (five to ten years) sectoral trade patterns change significantly (Riefler, 1973), it is notable that the most fully articulated interregional model, MRIO (Polenske, 1972), is still dependent on interregional trade coefficients estimated for 1962. However, notwithstanding the unreliability and obsolescence of interregional trade data, the alternative of ignoring interregional trade, assuming either that any requirements must be met within the region of origin (implicitly assuming infinite transportation costs) or that the requisite production is nationally diffused independently of the spatial distribution of demand (implicitly assuming zero transportation costs), is clearly unrealistic and implies inevitable distortions, especially for purposes of short-run analysis.

Table 6.2
Regional Model Outputs

Variable	Variable (*continued*)
Total output	Savings
Local industries (matrix)	Labor
National industries (matrix)	Nonlabor
Gross regional product	Transfer
Local industries	Net tax revenues (exclusive of
National industries	special excise taxes)
Depreciation	Indirect business taxes
Local industries	Local
National industries	National
Consumption purchases from	Corporate profits taxes
local industries	Local
Labor	National
Local industry employees	Personal taxes
National industry employees	Labor
Nonlabor	Nonlabor
Transfer	Transfers
Total consumption	Employment
Labor	Total
Local industry employees	Local industry
National industry employees	National industry
Nonlabor	By industry (matrix)
Transfer	By occupation (matrix)
Aggregate local industry final demands	Raw materials consumption
of other final demand components	(matrix)
Net nonlabor income generated	Effluent production
Local industries	Capital requirements
National industries	Total
Net nonlabor income received	By capital goods
Labor income	producer industry
Employees of local	(matrix)
industries	By capital goods user
Employees of national	industry (matrix)
industries	

Note: All outputs are vectors over regions, except those designated as matrices.

In short, the power of the model is seriously eroded by the many stringent and unrealistic assumptions underlying it. While this is especially true with regard to the regional dimension, even at the national level the assumptions of fixed sectoral input coefficients, of consumption behavior conforming to an extremely simple

Keynesian multiplier model, and generally of equality between average and marginal relationships represent at best serious oversimplifications. Finally, the model is fundamentally static, identifying only those equilibrium states consistent with its behavioral assumptions rather than the dynamic paths by which national and regional economies would adapt to policy change. Thus, the model can be viewed only as providing comparative static assessments of the consequences of any policy, with the quantitative estimates of various variables serving primarily as indicators of directions of change and of relative impact. However, in light of the paucity of information available concerning the relative effects of alternative policies, even qualitative and tentative estimates represent potentially valuable inputs into informed choice.

IMPLEMENTING THE MODEL

Originally representing the U.S. economy in 1970, the National Model has been updated and calibrated to represent the economy in 1973. The current model is based upon the Bureau of Economic Analysis (BEA) 1970 interim summary table, an updated version of the 1967 benchmark input-output table expressed in 1970 prices (U.S. Department of Commerce, 1975). This system was converted from a total to a domestic output basis and restated in 1973 prices.

The 1970 interim summary table, expressed on a total output basis, incorporates both transferred and directly allocated imports in intermediate transactions. Roughly speaking, the distinction between these classes of imports rests on their substitutability for domestic outputs: Transferred imports are substitutes for domestic output, while directly allocated imports are not. Thus, in a total-output-base direct requirements matrix, transferred imports are represented as constant proportions of total sectoral outputs.

In the conversion from a total to a domestic output basis, transferred imports (expressed in foreign port prices), and their associated trade, transportation, and insurance margins, are removed from intermediate transactions and incorporated as a (negative) final demand vector. Thus, the model incorporates gross export and transferred import final demand vectors. The algebraic sum of these vectors, less directly allocated imports (determined as a function of domestic outputs) gives net exports. With this formulation domestic outputs are permitted to respond to increases or decreases in the availability of transferred imports.

Given the domestic base variant of the 1970 interim summary table, the direct requirements matrix was computed and then revalued in 1973 prices. In this process it was assumed that technical requirements per unit of output, a_{ij}, were unchanged between 1970 and 1973. Thus, 1973 value added per unit of output measured in 1970 prices, v_j^*, is simply

$$v_j^* = p_j^* - \sum_i p_i^* a_{ij} \tag{1}$$

Table 6.3
1973 IDIOM National Income Accounts Calibration Procedures

Variable	Target Value	Final IDIOM Value
	(millions of dollars)	
Gross domestic product	1,286,500	1,289,042
Personal consumption	799,626	799,578
Labor	n.a.	565,736
Capital	n.a.	120,865
Transfer	112,977	112,976
Private fixed investment	194,000	194,002
Net inventory change	15,369	15,369
Depreciation	110,818	110,849
Government expenditure	276,378	276,383
Federal	106,558	106,562
Defense	74,398	74,400
Nondefense	32,160	32,162
State-local	169,820	169,821
Exports	100,400	99,793
Imports	96,400	96,074
Directly allocated	n.a.	26,043
Transferred	n.a.	70,031
Taxes	411,500	411,407
Indirect business taxes	119,200	119,176
Corporate profits taxes	49,800	49,811
Personal taxes	242,500	242,420
Labor	n.a.	205,141
Capital	n.a.	37,279
Labor income	786,000	785,982
Federal government	52,816	52,816
Defense	36,874	36,874
Nondefense	15,942	15,942
State-local government	95,592	95,592
	(thousands)	
National total employment	82,008	81,983
Federal government	4,305	4,300
Defense	n.a.	3,226
Nondefense	n.a.	1,074
State-local government	10,978	10,964

Note: Control totals not available (n.a.) in national income accounts. Source of control totals, *Survey of Current Business* (July 1974).

where p_i^* is an index of 1973 relative to 1970 prices for sector i.

Then, 1973 value added per unit of output measured in 1973 prices, v_j^{**}, is simply

$$v_j^{**} = v_j^*/p_j^* = 1 - \sum_i (p_i^*/p_j^*)a_{ij} \qquad (2)$$

or

$$v_j^{**} = 1 - \sum_i a_{ij}^{**} \qquad (3)$$

where a_{ij}^{**} represents intermediate requirements from sector i per unit of sector j output, with outputs of both i and j valued in 1973 prices.

The above process provided direct estimates of the direct requirements coefficient matrix, A, and the value-added coefficient vector, V, for 1973. Unfortunately, sufficiently detailed information concerning, for example, the composition of value-added or total employment were unavailable by input-output sector, requiring that 1970 coefficients be calibrated to conform to the model's aggregates to the 1973 national income accounts and related aggregate data. The results of this calibration are summarized in Table 6.3.

Other coefficients (e.g., capital requirements, effluents, and materials), were simply adjusted from 1970 to 1973 prices whenever necessary, with no attempt to update individual sectoral coefficients or to calibrate the model to independent national estimates.

The sources of these various parameters and coefficients are summarized in Table 6.4. Table 6.5 indicates the dimensionality of the various vectors and matrices.

DIRECTIONS OF SUBSTANTIVE MODEL DEVELOPMENT

From the outset this modeling effort has had dual objectives: first, to develop a closed-system capability, if at the outset only an "accounting framework," within which the initial impacts of changes in policy and other variables could be identified in multidimensional and highly disaggregated terms, and second, to incorporate, in an incremental, evolutionary manner, important behavioral-economic responses to these changes. Clearly, if alternative policies are to be meaningfully evaluated, the responses of individuals, households, and firms must be adequately taken into account. However, even partial equilibrium characterizations of the determinants of important aspects of behavior are complex and, in a number of dimensions, for example, migration, labor force participation, and fertility, rudimentary and seriously incomplete. Thus, to require that the full range of significant behavioral responses to policy change be incorporated at the outset would effectively paralyze the undertaking. Recognizing that a complete, fully specified model was not a feasible immediate objective, and committed to a developmental strategy which would permit the application of even emerging analytical capabilities to the explication of contemporary policy options, we have devoted our initial efforts to those important "first round" policy consequences to which later behavior would respond.

Model development is currently continuing at two levels. First, the various data bases are being improved and updated, and second, the model is being redesigned to incorporate greater behavioral content. At the first level, work is under way to completely update the model to represent the U.S. economy circa 1977. The 1972 benchmark input-output table should be released shortly. A conversion will again be made to a domestic input-output base, and all coefficients will be revalued in 1977 prices. In addition to final demands, virtually all other coefficient vectors and matrices will be reestimated.

Table 6.4
IDIOM Parameter and Data Documentation

Parameter/Input Data	Source
A matrix of direct I-O coefficients, domestic base in 1973 prices, and V vector of value-added coefficients.	BEA (1970) summary table converted to domestic base and adjusted to 1973 prices, with scaling of directly allocated import row and rebalancing of table to conform to total 1973 imports.
Value-added component vectors T^B, K^D, S^L, T^C.	Unpublished data provided by Milton L. Godfrey, Cybermatics, Inc., Englewood Cliffs, N. J., scaled to conform to 1973 control totals.
Personal tax and savings rates t_l, t_k, s_l, s_k, s_n.	Estimated judgmentally and scaled to conform to 1973 control totals for personal taxes and consumption expenditure.
Final demand vectors Y^i.	Unpublished data provided by Federal Preparedness Agency, converted to 1973 prices and scaled to conform to 1973 control totals.
E vector of employment coefficients.	Unpublished 1970 data provided by Bureau of Labor Statistics, adjusted to 1973 prices and scaled to conform to national employment control total, with direct estimation of 1973 government employment coefficients.
O matrix of occupational distributions by sector.	Unpublished 1970 data provided by Bureau of Labor Statistics, unadjusted.
K matrix of 1970 capital requirements by user and producer industry.	Fisher and Chilton (1971), adjusted to 1973 prices.
M matrix of raw materials requirements coefficients by sector.	Leontief and Petri (1971), adjusted to 1973 prices.
U matrix of effluent coefficients by sector.	International Research and Technology Corporation (1970), adjusted to 1973 prices.
D^N national industry distribution matrix by sector and state, c. 1970.	Various output (sales, shipment, etc.) by state and industry from censuses of manufacturing and agriculture, Mineral Yearbook, etc.
D^2 capital income distribution vector, by state, 1970.	Property and proprietors income by state, *Statistical Abstract of the United States* (1972).
D^3 transfer payment distribution vector, by state, 1970.	Transfer payments by state, *Statistical Abstract of the United States* (1972).
D^{iL} exogenous final demand distribution matrices, by state and type of exogenous final demand, c. 1970.	Construction contracts, government payrolls, etc., from various sources.

Major effort is currently being devoted to reestimation of the various regional distribution matrices. Available evidence clearly indicates that regions do not share in sectoral expansions and contractions in proportion to their shares of activity at any point in time, and further that growing regions not only share disproportionately in expansions but contract less than proportionately in contractions. When the estimation of the positive and negative net change distributions is completed, the model will reflect these differential patterns of regional growth by sector.

Table 6.5
IDIOM Dimensionality

Symbol	Designation	Dimension
nn	Producing sectors	86
n	National industries	60
l	Local industries	26
m	Final demands	10
	Labor consumption	
	Capitalist consumption	
	Transfer consumption	
	Private fixed investment	
	Net inventory change	
	Gross exports	
	Federal government defense	
	Federal government nondefense	
	State-local government	
	Transferred imports	
r	Regions	51
o	Occupations	25
q	Raw materials	11
u	Effluents	14
	Air pollutants	5
	Water pollutants	8
	Solid waste	1

Efforts to increase the behavioral content of the model are currently focused in two related domains. First, the model is being extended to incorporate labor force participation and unemployment effects of policy or other exogenous change. Second, a relatively highly articulated household model is in the design stage and is expected to be implemented within the next year.

An albeit crude capability for assessing the consequences of exogenous developments on unemployment and labor force participation has recently been added to the model. In its current rudimentary form, the base solution at the regional level is augmented by vectors of base period unemployment and labor force participation rates. When the various regional distribution matrices are reestimated and updated, these rates should be reasonably compatible with the regional distribution of employment as predicted by the model, that is, the implied labor-force-age population should closely correspond to the actual regional population between the ages of 16 and 64.

The household sector currently enters IDIOM only implicitly, through the determination of disposable income and of induced consumption expenditure. Three components of income are identified: labor income, net nonlabor income (defined as gross nonlabor income less depreciation and corporate profits taxes), and government transfer payments to individuals. Personal tax and savings rates unique to each of these components of income are specified, determining aggregate personal consumption expenditure as a function of the level and composition of income. Aggregate transfer payments are incorporated as a governmental policy variable, while labor and nonlabor factor incomes are determined by the level and sectoral composition of output. The composition of consumption expenditure (market basket of goods and services) is assumed to be invariant with respect to the source of income: a marginal dollar of consumption expenditure is assumed to have the same sectoral composition (automobiles, food, health services . . .) regardless of the type of income (labor or nonlabor income, transfer payments) giving rise to it. While the model does identify employment by industry, occupation, and region, this has no operational significance; it does not influence the disposition of income (the level or composition of consumption). Similarly, because transfer payments are specified as an aggregate policy variable, changes in the level of employment and income do not serve to alter transfer receipts.

Thus, in the household dimension the model rests upon a number of extreme and unrealistic assumptions that can be relaxed only if a reasonably rich household sector is incorporated.

AN APPLICATION TO MILITARY EXPORT POLICY AND COMPENSATORY ALTERNATIVES

Early in 1977 the Carter administration initiated a major reassessment of U.S. military export policy. As part of an interagency study of the implications (domestic and international) of a potential reduction in foreign military sales, participants from the Departments of Commerce and Treasury utilized IDIOM to assess the domestic economic effects of a reduction of $4.77 billion in military exports (valued at 1973 prices). The results of the interagency analysis are included in a subsequent report to the U.S. Senate (U.S. Congress, 1977b).

To demonstrate how IDIOM can be applied to a concrete policy issue, the military export reduction assumed in the administration's analysis is examined here in conjunction with two alternative compensatory policies: first, a public works (construction) program specifically designed to minimize regional employment effects, and second, a reduction in personal tax rates on labor income (e.g., a reduction in payroll taxes). In both cases the scale of the compensatory program is automatically determined by the model so as to maintain a constant level of national employment in the face of the military export contraction.

Table 6.6
Arms Export Reduction by Industry

IDIOM Industry Number	Industry	Arms Export Reduction *(millions of 1973 dollars)*
10	Ordnance	1135
41	Construction, mining & oil field machines	231
47	Office, computing & accounting machines	368
52	Radio, television & communication equipment	279
55	Motors, vehicles & equipment	548
56	Aircraft & parts	1871
57	Other transportation equipment	338
Total:		4770

Source: Jonathan Menes, Office of International Economic Research, U. S. Department of Commerce, 1977.

The sectoral composition of the assumed change in military export final demand is indicated in Table 6.6. Ignoring induced consumption (multiplier) effects, that is, assessing the implications of this reduction in exports in conventional input-output terms, the national economic implications of the contraction are indicated in the first column of Table 6.7.

Because $52 million in directly allocated imports are required directly or indirectly to fulfill the indicated military export demands, these exports account for $4.713 billion (0.4%) of gross domestic product and generate total employment of 244,000 persons (0.3% of national employment). Although exhibiting less than average labor intensity in terms of man-years, compared to the economy as a whole, the military export sectors and their suppliers are, on average, exceptionally high-wage industries, with average employee compensation of almost $14,300, in contrast to a national average of $9600. Thus, these arms exports account for 0.4% of aggregate labor income but only 0.2% of aggregate nonlabor income (defined here net of depreciation and corporate profits taxes).

Selected industrial, occupational, and primary material inputs into these military exports are indicated in the first column of Table 6.8. The aircraft and ordnance industries are the sectors most heavily involved, although military exports also draw significantly on the sectors of office and computing machinery, general industrial machinery, construction machinery, and communications equipment. Occupationally, over 1.5% of engineers and of metal craftsmen are estimated to be engaged, directly or indirectly, in this military export production. Of the primary materials, bauxite, copper, and molybdenum enter importantly into military export production.

As indicated in Table 6.9, the regional distribution of arms-export-related employment is surprisingly uniform, ranging from 0.5% of total employment in southern New England to 0.2% in the Southeast and Mountain regions, with effec-

Table 6.7
National Income and Product Impacts for Four Scenarios of Arms Export Reduction (millions of 1973 dollars)

Impacts	Plan 1[a]		Plan 2[b]		Plan 3[c]		Plan 4[d]	
	Amount	% Change	Amount	% Change	Amount	% Change	Amount	% Change
GDP	-4713	-.4	-9856	-.8	42	.0	-662	-.1
Depreciation	-401	-.4	-911	-.8	-11	.0	1	.0
Indirect business tax	-236	-.2	-822	-.7	235	.2	226	.2
National income	-4076	-.4	-8124	-.8	-172	.0	-889	-.1
Profits tax	-233	-.5	-460	-.9	-78	-.2	-54	-.1
Transfers	0	.0	0	.0	0	.0	0	.0
Labor tax	-909	-.4	-1612	-.8	-89	.0	-5312	-2.6
Capital tax	-60	0.2	-248	-.7	41	.1	87	.2
Labor savings	n.a.		-119	-.8	-7	.0	103	.7
Capital savings	n.a.		-433	-.7	71	.1	152	.2
Transfer savings	n.a.		0	.0	0	n.a.	0	n.a.
Consumption	n.a.		-5251	-.7	-112	.0	4314	.5
Labor income	-3481	-.4	-6178	-.8	-339	.0	-1357	-.2
Capital income	-363	-.2	-1485	-.7	243	.1	522	.2
Aggregate tax	-1438	-.3	-3142	-.8	109	.0	-5053	-1.3
Net tax	-1438	-.5	-3142	-1.1	109	.0	-5053	-1.7
Govt. expenditures	0	.0	0	.0	4914	1.8	0	.0
Govt. surplus	-1438	-6.5	-3142	-14.3	-4805	-21.8	-5053	-22.9

Employment (thousands of jobs)	-244	-.3	-555	-.7	0	.0	0	.0
Unemployment (change in unemployment rate)	n.a.	0.3	5.9^e	0	.0	0	5.6^e	5.6^e
Directly allocated imports	-57	-.2	-165	-.6	-19	.0	27	.0
Total imports	-57	-.1	-165	-.2	-19	.0	27	.0
Trade balance	-4713	-126.7	-4606	-123.8	-4751	-127.7	-4797	-129.0
Labor PCE	n.a.		-4447	-.8	-244	.0	-3852	.7
Capital PCE	n.a.		-804	-.7	132	.1	283	.2
Exports	-4770	-4.8	-4770	-4.8	-4770	-4.8	-4770	-4.8
Nondefense	0	.0	0	.0	4914	15.3	0	.0

Note: n.a. = not applicable.

[a] Considering only direct and indirect effects.

[b] Considering direct, indirect, and induced consumption effects.

[c] Compensated by public works program targeted to states in proportion to partial employment loss (from Plan 1).

[d] Compensated by reduction in tax rate on labor income.

[e] Ex post unemployment rate.

Table 6.8
Selected Effects of Arms Export Reduction on National Industry, Occupation, and Primary Materials (percentage change)

	Plan 1[a]	Plan 2[b]	Plan 3[c]	Plan 4[d]
Industry output				
Forestry products	− 0.5	− 1.9	1.9	0.6
Ferrous mining	− 1.3	− 1.7	− 0.4	− 1.0
Ordnance	−15.4	−15.5	−15.4	−15.4
Stone & clay products	− 0.2	− 0.4	2.1	− 0.1
Struct. metal products	− 0.2	− 0.3	2.2	− 0.2
Construct. machinery	− 2.7	− 2.7	− 2.5	− 2.6
Industrial machinery, gen.	− 2.4	− 2.7	− 2.0	− 2.2
Office, computing machinery	− 2.5	− 2.6	− 2.5	− 2.5
Communications equipment	− 2.0	− 2.3	− 1.9	− 1.7
Aircraft	−14.1	−14.2	−14.1	−14.1
Occupational employment				
Engineers	− 1.5	− 1.8	− 1.0	− 1.2
Metal crafts	− 1.6	− 1.8	− 1.0	− 1.3
Construction	− 0.3	− 0.5	1.7	− 0.2
Primary materials				
Bauxite	− 1.2	− 1.4	− 0.1	− 1.0
Copper	− 1.1	− 1.4	− 0.1	− 0.9
Molybdenum	− 1.1	− 1.4	− 0.6	− 0.9

[a]Considering only direct and indirect effects.

[b]Considering direct, indirect and induced consumption effects.

[c]Compensated by public works program targeted to states in proportion to partial employment loss (from Plan 1).

[d]Compensated by reduction in tax rate on labor income.

tively no military export employment in Alaska and Hawaii. However, several states exhibit particularly high concentrations of employment dependent on military export: Connecticut (0.9% of total employment), Washington (0.6%), and California (0.4%).

Effects taking into account only production directly and indirectly required to fulfill military export demands clearly represent only a fraction of the total economic impact of an uncompensated reduction in military exports. Thus, the second columns of tables 6.7, 6.8, and 6.9 extend the analysis to include induced (multiplier) effects of changes in labor and nonlabor income. The decline in GDP generated by the $4.77 billion export reduction is then estimated to be $9.86 billion (0.8%), implying a military export multiplier of 2.07. Personal consumption declines by $5.25 billion or by 0.7%. Total employment is also reduced by 0.7%, or by 555,000 jobs, with the loss of 311,000 jobs accounted for by multiplier effects. The aggregate unemployment rate rises by 0.3 percentage points, from 5.6% (1973) to 5.9%.

In contrast to mean compensation of displaced arms-export employees of $14,300, mean compensation of employees displaced by the consumption contrac-

Table 6.9

Regional and State Employment Impacts of Four Scenarios of Arms Export Reduction

Region and State	Plan 1[a] Jobs (thousands)	Plan 1[a] % Change	Plan 2[b] Jobs (thousands)	Plan 2[b] % Change	Plan 3[c] Jobs (thousands)	Plan 3[c] % Change	Plan 4[d] Jobs (thousands)	Plan 4[d] % Change
Regions								
New Eng N	− 2.2	−.3	− 5.3	−.7	0.4	.1	0.5	.1
New Eng S	−19.5	−.5	−38.5	−1.0	− 5.3	−.1	−11.6	− .3
Mid East N	−43.5	−.3	−102.0	−.7	0.4	.0	5.2	.0
Mid East S	− 5.6	−.2	−12.1	−.5	− 1.2	−.1	1.2	.1
Great Lakes	−62.6	−.4	−138.4	−.8	1.4	.0	− 7.3	.0
Plains	−17.7	−.3	−43.7	−.7	− 2.0	.0	2.4	.0
SE Atlantic	−13.6	−.2	−41.9	−.5	3.9	.0	19.5	.2
SE Gulf	− 5.5	−.2	−17.2	−.5	5.1	.1	8.4	.2
SE Central	− 6.6	−.2	−18.2	−.6	2.3	.1	5.3	.2
South West	−16.2	−.3	−36.5	−.6	0.6	.0	0.7	.0
Mountains	− 4.1	−.2	−10.0	−.5	1.8	.1	1.8	.1
West	−47.0	−.4	−90.2	−.8	− 8.0	−.1	−27.5	−.3
Noncoterminous	− 0.2	.0	− 1.0	−.2	0.5	.1	1.5	.3
U.S. Total	−244	−.3	−555	− .7	.0	.0	.0	.0
Selected states								
Oregon	− 1.5	−.2	− 3.8	−.5	3.6	.4	1.2	.2
Pennsylvania	−14.7	−.3	−33.3	−.7	2.7	.1	− .3	.0
Illinois	−13.4	−.3	−31.7	−.6	2.1	.1	3.1	.1
N. Carolina	− 2.6	−.1	−10.9	−.5	1.7	.1	7.2	.3
Washington	− 9.4	−.6	−16.6	−1.1	− 0.7	−.1	− 8.5	− .6
New York	−20.0	−.3	−47.3	−.6	− 2.7	.0	3.8	.1
Connecticut	−12.6	−.9	−21.8	−1.6	− 5.3	−.4	−12.9	−1.0
California	−35.9	−.4	−69.4	−.8	−11.1	−.1	−20.6	− .2

[a]Considering only direct and indirect effects.
[b]Considering direct, indirect and induced consumption effects.
[c]Compensated by public works program targeted to states in proportion to partial employment loss (from Plan 1).
[d]Compensated by reduction in tax rate on labor income.

229

tion is only $8700, or significantly below the $9600 national average. Thus, the disproportionate negative impact on labor income, when the export contraction is examined in isolation, is greatly reduced when multiplier effects are considered.

The regional impacts of the induced decline in consumption are almost as diffuse as those associated with the military export contraction in isolation, with the additional employment declines ranging between 0.2% and 0.5%. Southern New England, with high concentrations of both military-export and consumption-related employment, however, is particularly hard-hit, suffering a 1% decline in total employment. Because of the high local component of consumption-related employment, overall declines are found to be even more severe in Connecticut (1.6%), Washington (1.1%), and California (0.8%). Furthermore, these state-level contractions are still concentrated in a few occupations, especially engineering and metal crafts.

Clearly, an examination of the contractionary economic consequences of the military export reduction is of only limited value, since alternative uses of the freed resources presumably exist, and federal economic policy would be expected to respond to the depressive impact of the export reduction. One possible compensatory policy is provided by a public works (construction) program of the type enacted for countercyclical purposes in 1976. It is assumed that the regional distribution of public works would mirror the regional distribution of military-export-related employment, ignoring induced consumption effects.

To restore national employment to its original level, the third column of Table 6.7 indicates that public works expenditure of $4.914 billion would be required. Although mean employee compensation in the construction industry and its direct and indirect suppliers, $12,750, is above the national average, it is below that of military exports; as a result, labor income would decline marginally. In contrast, net nonlabor income would rise by 0.1%.

As indicated by Table 6.8, in general, the public works program would not compensate at the sectoral level for the military export contraction. However, outputs in forestry, stone and clay, and structural metals would rise significantly. Occupationally, public works would compensate somewhat for the decline in employment in the metal crafts and engineering, although differences in the distribution of demand for various specialties might negate much of the beneficial effect, especially in the latter case. Not surprisingly, construction employment would rise significantly. Because of the intensive use of aluminum and copper in construction, demands for these materials would be virtually unaltered. Only molybdenum requirements would fall significantly.

Regionally, utilization of employment that had been absorbed directly or indirectly by military exports as the basis for the distribution of public works would compensate remarkably well for geographic differences in the effects of the military export contraction. Across regions employment would change by less than ±0.1%. However, a state such as Oregon, with a concentration of forestry and related construction-materials activity, would experience a 0.4% increase in employment. Conversely, Connecticut, without significant construction-supply activity, would experience a corresponding decline in employment. Thus, the unemployment rate in Connecticut would rise from 5.7% to 5.9%, while the unemployment rate in Oregon would decline from 5.3% to 5.1%.

The interest in public works arises because of the possibility of substantial political pressure for enactment of geographically targeted programs to compensate for the military export contraction. Should such pressure be encountered, an appropriately targeted public works program, ignoring induced consumption effects in determining the distribution of awards, can be demonstrated to be highly effective in offsetting the regional disparities implied by the military export contraction.

However, the social value of additional public works, compared to, for example, increased personal consumption, might well be questioned. Also, the $4.9 billion of required public works expenditure is 5.6 times larger than actual 1977 public works expenditure (valued in constant 1973 dollars), suggesting the potentially low political feasibility and valuation of a public works program of this magnitude. Thus, as an alternative to public works, IDIOM has been utilized to determine the labor tax rate reduction which would be required to compensate in terms of total employment for the military export decline.

A 0.6 percentage point cut in the labor tax rate, from 26.1% to 25.5%, is estimated to be required to generate additional consumption expenditure sufficient to compensate for the military export contraction. After this menu of policy change, labor income would decline by 0.2%, owing to the relatively low-wage employment generated by consumption relative to military exports. In effect, 244,000 workers in jobs based on military export, with mean compensation of $14,300, would be replaced by an equal number of employees in consumption-related industries, with mean compensation of $8700. Nonlabor income, however, would rise by the same relative amount. Total consumption would rise by 0.5%, labor consumption by 0.7%. The government deficit would rise by almost $5.1 billion, in contrast to $4.8 billion under the public works alternative, indicating the lower implicit multipliers associated with tax reductions than with expenditure increases.

At the more disaggregated level (Table 6.8), the only marked difference between the compensatory tax reduction and public works alternatives is in the demand for primary materials. Requirements for these materials, which would decline significantly as a result of the military export contraction, would be only marginally restored by the consumption increase.

Regionally, the labor tax reduction exhibits substantial variability, with employment rising by 0.3% in Alaska and Hawaii and declining by 0.3% in the West and in southern New England. Employment in Connecticut would decline by 1%, raising its unemployment rate from 5.7% to 6.1%. Aggregate consumption would rise in all states other than Connecticut and Washington.

The foregoing example of the application of IDIOM is only suggestive of the broad range of possible uses of the model. To some extent this example understates the power and usefulness of the model, since the basic program examined, a selective military export contraction, is rather small and its regional impacts, direct and indirect, quite diffuse. On the other hand, this application does point up very clearly the need to employ a model such as IDIOM to assess policy options of this type. For example, if the regional distribution of activity of only those industries appearing in the military export final demand vector (e.g., aircraft and ordnance), had been utilized to assess the differential regional effects of an arms export cut, then the degree of regional concentration of the impact would have been greatly overestimated. IDIOM, however, traces direct and indirect flows into exported military material, permitting recognition of the much broader geographic impacts of this potential policy action.

Moreover, the example points up the multiple possible uses of the model. In this case the model first examined the direct and indirect effects of an arms export contraction in isolation, identifying the types and quantities of different types of resources (industry capacity, employment by occupation, primary materials) absorbed by military exports. Next, the model assessed the full economic consequences (including regional economic consequences) of an uncompensated cut in military exports. Both of these applications were restricted, in themselves, to *policy assessment*. However, the first also provided a critical input (the geographic distribution of employment contractions implied by a military export cut) into *policy design*. The third and fourth applications (introducing the compensatory public works and labor income tax changes) then can be seen as *tentative determinations of specific compensatory policies*. Finally, these latter applications provide the type of substantive comparative information necessary (although certainly not sufficient) for concrete *policy choice* (whether or not to actively pursue a contraction in military exports, and if so, in conjunction with what compensatory policy).

APPENDIX: A MATHEMATICAL DESCRIPTION OF IDIOM

The National Model Base Solution

As in its earlier prototype form (Dresch and Goldberg, 1973), the current version of IDIOM conjoins a Keynesian income determination model and a conventional input-output model, resulting in a variant of a closed input-output model. This section develops the National Model in mathematical detail.

In the algebraic presentation, italic capital letters denote vectors and matrices, with dimensions specified in parentheses. In some cases it will be necessary to express previously defined vectors as diagonal matrices, in which case a bar will appear over the letter, for example, if the vector V ($n \times 1$) is expressed $\bar{V}$ it will be understood that $\bar{V}$ ($n \times n$) contains the elements of V on the diagonal, all other elements of $\bar{V}$ being zero. A bar beneath a vector designation (e.g., $\underline{C}$), indicates a square matrix formed by repeating the vector; thus if C ($n \times 1$), then $\underline{C}$ ($n \times n$) = $(C, C, \ldots, C)$.

Lowercase italic letters indicate scalar magnitudes (e.g., GDP and nonvector tax rates). The symbol i will denote a vector, all of the elements of which are unity.

The Basic National Model

The primary variables and parameters entering the National Model are identified in Table 6.10. Employing this notation, the model solves for the vector of total outputs, X, and the vectors of consumption by labor and nonlabor income recipients, Y^1 and Y^2, as functions of the exogenous final demands, Y^3 through Y^m.

The fundamental input-output identity, that final demand equals total output minus intermediate requirements, can be stated as

$$(Y^1 + Y^2 + \cdots + Y^m) = X - AX = (I - A)X \tag{4a}$$

or as

$$X = (i - A)^{-1}(Y^1 + \cdots + Y^m). \tag{4b}$$

If all of the final demands were known, the model would be solved. However, endogenous labor and nonlabor consumption demands are functions of their respective disposable incomes. Thus, it is necessary to express labor and nonlabor incomes and consumption demands as functions of total outputs.

Gross domestic product (GDP) is given by

$$GDP = X'V \tag{5}$$

where V is a vector of sectoral value-added coefficients. To obtain disposable labor and net capital incomes, it is necessary to deduct the following:

$$\text{Indirect Business Taxes} = X'\bar{V}T^B \tag{6}$$

$$\text{Depreciation} = X'\bar{V}(I - \bar{T}^B)K^D \tag{7}$$

where T^B and K^D are vectors of sectoral indirect business tax and depreciation rates, respectively. Disposable labor income, z_l, is then

$$z_l = (1 - t_l)X'\bar{V}(I - \bar{T}^B)(I - \bar{K}^D)s^L, \tag{8}$$

in which t_l is the tax rate on labor income and S^L is a vector of labor income coefficients. From the residual, gross nonlabor income, and deducting

$$\text{Corporate profits taxes} = X'\bar{V}(I - \bar{T}^B)(I - \bar{K}^D)(I - \bar{S}^L)T^C, \tag{9}$$

disposable nonlabor income is

$$z_k = (1 - t_k)X'\bar{V}(I - \bar{T}^B)(I - \bar{K}^D)(I - \bar{S}^L)(I - T^C) \tag{10}$$

where t_k is the personal tax rate on net nonlabor income.

Proportions s_l and s_k of labor and nonlabor disposable incomes are assumed to be saved, giving consumption demands, c_l and c_k, of

$$c_l = (1 - s_l)z_l \tag{11}$$

$$c_k = (1 - s_k)z_k. \tag{12}$$

Table 6.10
Base National Model Variables and Parameters

Symbol	Explanation
n	The number of producing sectors.
m	The number of separate final demand components, the last $m - 2$ of which are exogenous.
X $(n \times 1)$	Total output vector.[a]
Y^i $(n \times 1), i = 3, m$	Exogenous final demand vectors.
Y^1 $(n \times 1)$	Endogenous labor consumption vector.[a]
Y^2 $(n \times 1)$	Endogenous consumption from nonlabor income.[a]
C $(n \times 1)$	Consumption distribution vector, the elements of which sum to unity, indicating the sectoral distribution of consumption final demands.
A $(n \times n)$	Matrix of interindustry direct input requirements coefficients, per unit of output.
V $(n \times 1)$	Vector of value added coefficients.
T^B $(n \times 1)$	Vector of indirect business taxes, as a proportion of value added.
K^D $(n \times 1)$	Vector of capital depreciation rates, proportion of value added net of indirect business tax.
S^L $(n \times 1)$	Vector of labor shares of value added net of indirect business tax and depreciation.
T^C $(n \times 1)$	Vector of corporate profits tax rates, proportion of capital's residual share of value added (net of labor, indirect business tax, and depreciation).
t_l	Tax rate on labor income.
t_k	Tax rate on nonlabor income (net of corporate tax and depreciation).
s_l	Labor savings rate (out of disposable income).
s_k	Nonlabor savings rate (out of disposable income).
t_n	Aggregate government personal transfer payments.
s_n	Savings rate out of transfer income.

[a] Except for the items X, Y^1, and Y^2, all are inputs into the model.

Table 6.10 *(continued)*

Symbol	Explanation
E ($n \times 1$)	Employment coefficients vector (employment/output).
O ($o \times n$)	Occupation distribution matrix, o = number of occupations (distribution of employment by industry over occupations).
M ($q \times n$)	Raw material coefficient matrix, q = number of materials (materials requirements/output).
U ($u \times n$)	Effluent coefficients matrix, u = number of effluents (effluents/output).
K ($n \times n$)	Capital coefficients matrix, capital requirements per unit of output by producer (row) and user (column) industry.
T^X ($n \times 1$)	Vector of special excise taxes per unit of output (endogenous when T^{XR} excise tax rates, or P^*, target prices, are specified).
T^{XR} ($n \times 1$)	Vector of special excise tax rates (endogenous when T^X, excise taxes per unit of output, or P^*, target prices, are specified).
P^* ($n \times 1$)	Price vector inclusive of taxes when special excise taxes are specified ($P^* = i$ if $T^X = T^{XR} =$); P^* can be set exogenously, determining T^X and T^{XR}).
P ($n \times 1$)	Price vector exclusive of special excise taxes when special excise taxes are specified.
T^{XC} ($n \times 1$)	Vector of consumption type value-added or retail sales tax rates (apply only to final consumption purchases).
P^{C*} ($n \times 1$)	Consumer price vector inclusive of taxes when consumption taxes are specified.
P	Consumer price index.
C^* ($n \times 1$)	Effective consumption distribution vector ($C^* = C$ if special excise or consumption taxes are not specified).

These consumption aggregates are then converted to final demand vectors via an effective consumption distribution vector, C^*, that is,

$$Y^1 = c_l C^*, \tag{13}$$

the labor income consumption vector, and

$$Y^2 = c_k C^*, \tag{14}$$

the nonlabor income consumption vector.   In general, the elements of C^* will sum to unity. However, as discussed below, for certain applications the elements of C^* may sum to less than unity.

Finally, it is necessary to express consumption demands from transfer income, Y^3, as a function of total transfers, t_n, the transfer savings rate, s_n, and the effective consumption distribution vectors:

$$Y^3 = (1 - s_n) t_n C^*. \tag{15}$$

At this point the model consists of $3n$ unknowns, X, Y^1, and Y^2, and $3n$ equations,

$$X = (I - A)^{-1} (Y^1 + Y^2 + \ldots + Y^m) \tag{16a}$$

$$Y^1 = (1 - s_l)(1 - t_l) X' \bar{V} (I - \bar{T}^B)(I - \bar{K}^D) s^L \tag{16b}$$

$$Y^2 = (1 - s_k)(1 - t_k) X' \bar{V}(I - \bar{T}^B)(I - \bar{K}^D)(I - \bar{S}^L)(i - T^C) \tag{16c}$$

The solution of this system is, simply,

$$X = (I - (I - A)^{-1} M)^{-1} (I - A)^{-1} (Y^3 + \ldots + Y^m) \tag{17}$$

where

$$M = (1 - s_l)(1 - t_l)\underline{C}^* \bar{S}^L (I - \bar{K}^D)(I - \bar{T}^B)\bar{V} + (1 - s_k)(1 - t_k)\underline{C}^*(I - \bar{S}^L)$$
$$(I - \bar{T}^C)(I - \bar{K}^D)(I - \bar{T}^B)\bar{V}.$$

Given the solution of Equation (17) for X, Y^1 and Y^2 can be determined, as can the full panoply of other National Model results.

The Regional Model

The conceptual foundation of the Regional Model is provided by the admittedly arbitrary and unrealistic distinction between *national* and *local* industries. This distinction is based upon the degree of interregional trade in the output of any industry. Those industries, primarily services, the outputs of which are necessarily almost entirely supplied from within the using region, with little or no opportunity for regional imports or exports, are designated local. Thus, for local industries, supplies and demands are required to balance within each region. National industries, conversely, are assumed to produce outputs which move freely in interregional trade. For national industries it is only necessary that total national outputs equal total national requirements, with no requirement that supplies and demands balance *within* regions. Regional outputs of national industries are assumed to be determined independently of the regional distributions of demand, and any regional (positive or negative) excess demands are implicitly assumed to be met through interregional trade.

In the present version of the model, national industry outputs, as determined in the National Model, are assumed to be distributed across regions according to the distribution of activity in the base period (1970). Similarly, exogenous final demands for outputs of local industries are also allocated to regions on the basis of historical distributions of final demands. The function of the Regional Model is, then, to determine endogenously the levels of regional outputs of local industries.

Certain modifications of the National Model notation are required for the algebraic description of the Regional Model. Overall, the National Model consisted of n industries; in the Regional Model this designation is altered to nn, that is, $n_{\text{(National Model)}} = nn_{\text{(Regional Model)}}$. Of these nn industries, the first n are identified as national industries, the last l as local industries, with $nn = n + l$.

All of the basic variables entering the National Model are employed in the Regional Model, with several notational changes or elaborations (see Table 6.11). First, all input vectors, for example, the value-added coefficient vector $V(nn \times 1)$, can be decomposed into two subvectors: V^N $(n \times 1)$ and V^L $(l \times 1)$, the first referring to national industries and the second to local industries. Thus,

$$V = \begin{bmatrix} V^N \\ V^L \end{bmatrix}$$

and similarly for all other parameter vectors.

With this national-local industry ordering, the direct requirements coefficient matrix can be represented by

$$A = \begin{bmatrix} A^{NN} & A^{NL} \\ A^{LN} & A^{LL} \end{bmatrix}$$

where A^{NN} represents inputs of national industries into national industries, A^{NL} national industry inputs into local industries, A^{LN} local industry inputs into national industries, and A^{LL} local industry to local industry inputs.

Table 6.11
Regional Model Variables and Parameters

Symbol	Explanation
$nn (= n + l)$	Number of producing sectors (designated n in National Model).
n	Number of "national industries."
l	Number of "local industries."
r	Number of regions.
$X(nn \times 1) = \begin{bmatrix} X^N(n \times 1) \\ X^L(l \times 1) \end{bmatrix}$	Total output vector, partitioned into national and local vectors.[a]
$Y^i(nn \times 1) = \begin{bmatrix} Y^{iN}(n \times 1) \\ Y^{iL}(l \times 1) \end{bmatrix}, i = 2,m$	Partitioned exogenous (including capitalist consumption) final demand vectors.[a]
$X^{NR}(n \times r)$	Matrix of national industry output by region.
$D^N(n \times r)$	National industry output distribution matrix.
$X^{LNR}(l \times r)$	Matrix of input requirements by national from local industries, by region.
$X^{LR}(l \times r)$	Matrix of local industry total outputs by region.[b]
$Y^{iLR}(l \times r), i = 2,m$	Matrix of "exogenous" final demands from local industries by region.
$D^2(1 \times r)$	Regional capital ownership distribution vector (D^{2L} matrix obtained by repeating D^2 vector l times).
$D^3(1 \times r)$	Regional transfer payment distribution vector (D^{3L} matrix obtained by repeating D^3 vector l times).
$D^{iL}(l \times r), i = 4,m$	Exogenous final demand regional distribution matrices.
$Y^{iN, LR}(l \times r)$	Local industry consumption demands of national industry employees, by region.
$Y^{1L, LR}(l \times r)$	Local industry consumption demands of employees of local industries, by region.[b]
$C^*(nn \times 1) = \begin{bmatrix} C^{N*}(n \times 1) \\ C^{L*}(l \times 1) \end{bmatrix}$	Partitioned consumption distribution vector.[a]
$\underline{C}_n^{L*}(l \times n)$	Matrix formed by repeating local consumption distribution vector, C^L, n times.
$\underline{C}_l^{L*}(l \times l)$	Matrix formed by repeating local consumption distribution vector, C^L, l times.
$A(nn \times nn) = \begin{bmatrix} A^{NN}(n \times n) & A^{NL}(n \times l) \\ A^{LN}(l \times n) & A^{LL}(l \times l) \end{bmatrix}$	Partitioned direct input requirements matrix.[a]

[a]Identical to National Model.
[b]Endogenous to Regional Model.

Table 6.11 *(continued)*

Symbol	Explanation
$V(nn \times 1) = \begin{bmatrix} V^N_{(n \times 1)} \\ V^L_{(l \times 1)} \end{bmatrix}$	Partitioned value-added coefficients vector.[a]
$T^B(nn \times 1) = \begin{bmatrix} T^{BN}_{(n \times 1)} \\ T^{BL}_{(l \times 1)} \end{bmatrix}$	Partitioned indirect business tax rate vector.[a]
$K^D(nn \times 1) = \begin{bmatrix} K^{DN}_{(n \times 1)} \\ K^{DL}_{(l \times 1)} \end{bmatrix}$	Partitioned depreciation vector.[a]
$S^L(nn \times 1) = \begin{bmatrix} S^{LN}_{(n \times 1)} \\ S^{LL}_{(l \times 1)} \end{bmatrix}$	Partitioned labor share vector.[a]
$T^C(nn \times 1) = \begin{bmatrix} T^{CN}_{(n \times 1)} \\ T^{CL}_{(l \times 1)} \end{bmatrix}$	Partitioned corporate profits tax rate vector.[a]
t_l	Tax rate on labor income.[a]
t_k	Tax rate on nonlabor income (net of corporate tax and depreciation).[a]
s_l	Labor savings rate (out of disposable income).[a]
s_k	Nonlabor savings rate (out of disposable income).[a]
t_n	Aggregate government personal transfer payments.[a]
s_n	Savings rate out of transfer income.[a]
$E(nn \times 1) = \begin{bmatrix} E^N_{(n \times 1)} \\ E^L_{(l \times 1)} \end{bmatrix}$	Partitioned employment coefficients vector (employment/output).[a]
$O(o \times nn) = \begin{bmatrix} O^N_{(o \times n)} \\ O^L_{(o \times l)} \end{bmatrix}$	Partitioned occupation distribution matrix, o = number of occupations (distribution of employment by industry over occupations).[a]
$M(q \times nn) = \begin{bmatrix} M^N_{(q \times n)} \\ M^L_{(q \times l)} \end{bmatrix}$	Partitioned raw materials coefficient matrix, q = number of materials (materials requirements/output).[a]
$U(u \times nn) = \begin{bmatrix} U^N_{(u \times n)} \\ U^L_{(u \times l)} \end{bmatrix}$	Partitioned effluent coefficients matrix, u = number of effluents (effluents/output).[a]
$K(nn \times nn) = \begin{bmatrix} K^{NN}_{(n \times n)} & K^{NL}_{(n \times l)} \\ K^{LN}_{(l \times n)} & K^{LL}_{(l \times l)} \end{bmatrix}$	Partitioned capital coefficients matrix, capital requirements per unit of output by producer (row) and user (column) industry.[a]
$Z^{LR}_{(r \times 1)}$	Local industry labor income by region.[b]
$Z^{NR}_{(r \times 1)}$	National industry labor income by region.
z_k	National nonlabor net income.[a]

The economy is divided into r regions. In the Regional Model base solution total outputs of national industries, previously determined in the base solution of the National Model, are allocated to regions on the basis of an exogenous (or, more generally, predetermined) national industry distribution matrix, $D^N(n \times r)$, each cell of which specifies the share of a given region (column) in the total output of a national industry (row). The matrix $X^{NR}(n \times r)$, obtained by

$$X^{NR} = \bar{X}^N D^N \qquad (18)$$

then specifies the output of each national industry in each region.

When national industry outputs have been distributed to regions, it is possible to determine the outputs of local industries in each region required to service these regional levels of national industry production. Specifically, the rectangular matrix A^{LN} contains coefficients representing input requirements from local industries, per unit of output of national industries. Thus, total local industry requirements of national industries are

$$X^{LNR} = A^{LN} X^{NR}. \qquad (19)$$

These national industry requirements from local industries are equivalent at the regional level to final demands, since required intermediate local industry purchases from national industries have already been taken into account in determining the national industry outputs which have been regionally distributed via Equation (18).

Similarly, exogenous local industry final demands are distributed to regions on the basis of distribution matrices unique to each type of exogenous final demand, for example, private fixed investment or defense, each cell of which specifies the share of a given region (column) in the particular exogenous final demand on a given local industry (row). Thus,

$$Y^{iLR} = \bar{Y}^{iL} D^{iL}, \quad i = 3, \ldots, m \qquad (20)$$

where $Y^{iLR}(l \times r)$ is a matrix of the ith final demand by local industry and region, and $D^{iL}(l \times r)$ is the ith final demand distribution matrix, the rows of which distribute local final demands by industry over regions.

Although net nonlabor income and consumption nationally are determined endogenously, a procedure which could be perpetuated at the regional level by assuming that nonlabor income generated in a region is also received in the region, it is assumed instead that national nonlabor income is distributed independently of the regional sources of that income. Specifically, a region's share of nonlabor income is assumed to be proportionate to its wealth ownership and hence is independent of levels of activity and of profits within the region.

Thus, given Y^{2L}, national consumption demands on local industries generated by nonlabor income, if the distribution of wealth over regions is represented by the row vector $D^2(1 \times r)$, then the distribution over regions of nonlabor consumption demands on local industries will be represented by $D^{2L}(l \times r)$, which simply repeats the vector D^2 to create the l rows. Thus,

$$Y^{2LR} = \bar{Y}^{2L}{}_E{}^{2L}, \tag{21}$$

nonlabor consumption demands by local industry and region.

Finally, the distribution of local industry consumption demands by employees of national industries is determined by the distribution of national industry outputs. Incomes of employees of national industries by region, $z^{NR}(r \times 1)$, are simply

$$z^{NR'} = S^{LN'}(I - \bar{K}^{DN})(I - \bar{T}^{BN})\bar{V}^N X^{NR}$$

from which consumption demands on local industries, by region, can be determined, that is,

$$Y^{1N,LR} = (1-s)(1-t)C^L_{-n}\overset{*}{S}{}^{LN}(I - \bar{K}^{DN})(I - \bar{T}^{BN})\bar{V}^N X^{NR}. \tag{22}$$

Only local industry consumption demands of local employees of local industries remain to be determined. These are determined in a manner identical to those of national industry employees:

$$Y^{1L,LR} = (1-s_l)(1-t_l)C^L_{-l}\overset{*}{S}{}^{LL}(I - \bar{K}^{DL})(I - \bar{T}^{BL})\bar{V}^L X^{LR}. \tag{23}$$

However, unlike X^{NR}, regional outputs of national industries, regional outputs of local industries, X^{LR}, are not known.

Thus, the Regional Model equation system consists of $2 \cdot l \cdot r$ equations, Equation (22), and the following:

$$X^{LR} = (I - A)^{-1}(Y^{1L,LR} + Y^{1N,LR} + Y^{2LR} + Y^{3LR} + \cdots + Y^{mLR} + X^{LNR}) \tag{24}$$

and $2 \cdot l \cdot r$ unknowns, X^{LR} and $Y^{1L,LR}$. As in the National Model, the solution of this system results in a set of output equations, in this case equations for regional outputs of local industries:

$$X^{LR} = (I - (I - A^{LL})^{-1} MM)^{-1}(I - A^{LL})^{-1}$$

$$\times (Y^{1N,LR} + Y^{2LR} + Y^{3LR} + \cdots + Y^{mLR} + X^{LNR}). \tag{25}$$

where $MM = (1 - s_l)(1 - t_l)\underline{C}_l^L \bar{S}^{LL}(I - \bar{K}^{DL})(I - \bar{T}^{BL})\bar{V}^L$.

Given the solution for total outputs of local industries in each region, local industry consumption by local industry employees can be determined via Equation (23).

DISCUSSION

Steven B. Caldwell

Like other input-output models, IDIOM pursues the important insight that consumption decisions touch off systematic chain reactions of interindustry flows which benefit some industries more than others, some categories of labor more than others, and some regions more than others. Hence, consumption decisions have powerful distributional consequences.

Standard criticisms of input-output models focus on flows in representing the behavior of industries. Fixed input-output coefficients are assumed in IDIOM, though Dresch and Updegrove plan to make the coefficients sensitive to price. The absence of supply factors and market adjustments leaves the model quite one-sided. Outcomes are deterministic; they do not come equipped with estimates of uncertainty. Finally, the fact that neither outcomes nor processes are embedded in time hinders validation efforts.

IDIOM has two distinctive features. First, final demands generated by labor and capital income are not set exogenously, but rather are determined endogenously by a Keynesian consumption multiplier. This feature has the advantage of closing one loop, but the loop's validity rests on implicit labor supply and consumption over simplifications. Second, given a national equilibrium solution, the second stage allocates national outcomes among regions. This regionalization multiplies the usefulness of the model only insofar as the allocation process is realistic. In IDIOM, all industries are assumed to be either national or local. For the sixty national industries, total outputs are allocated among regions according to pre-set ratios. For the twenty-six local industries all regional demands for their outputs must be supplied by the portion of the local industry within the region.

The regional solution assumes that the input-output coefficients are constant across regions. IDIOM's authors defend this assumption on the grounds that it reduces the need for region-specific input data and makes the model computationally more tractable. Such defenses are bound to make the reader uneasy. The fact that reliable region-specific data are hard to find suggests that credible regionalizations are also hard to find. Furthermore, if additional complexity chokes off an analytic solution, then perhaps a less restrictive solution is required, rather than a simplification of the model. Above all, the regional outcomes suffer from the lack of market adjustments. In making locational choices, people and firms respond in complex, time-lagged ways to economic and social forces. Without region-specific evidence on these market adjustments, IDIOM is unable to generate credible regionalized outcomes.

IDIOM is well documented, is accessible through a remote-access, time-net system, and is inexpensive to run. Because these admirable qualities are not widely shared by large microanalytic models, many such models have been slow to achieve the wider use they need and deserve.

Any policy which can be translated into a change in taxes, expenditures, or transfers can be cranked into IDIOM. Dresch and Updegrove rightly argue that policy analyses with IDIOM should examine differences across different final demand scenarios, rather than simply reporting one unconditional scenario in isolation. A most likely set of taxes, transfers, and expenditures will serve as benchmark, with alternative policy scenarios represented as deviations from the benchmark. Differences among outcomes are then attributable to differences among policies. This conditional forecasting mode is the desirable strategy for all policy exploration via microanalytic models, though it is not always easy to so convince users who start out wanting a single unconditional forecast rather than a set of sensitivity tests.

A fault IDIOM shares with many other microanalytic models is a shortage of information about important qualitative features of its response surface. Modelers are in the position of betting that the whole will turn out greater than the sum of its parts, but they too seldom probe that assumption. A complete mapping of outcomes is impossible, but analysts should do more prowling through their complex response surfaces, looking for important twists and folds worth reporting. Such qualitative features provide benchmarks for validating the model against comparable qualitative features of the real world and also give users greater familiarity with the model.

Dresch and Updegrove are well aware of the lack of individual, household, and firm behavioral responses in the current IDIOM and report plans for broadening the model in supply directions. As an initial strategy for incorporating labor supply, IDIOM now generates region-specific employment changes which in turn generate updated aggregate labor force participation and unemployment rates for the region. In theory, migration flows could be generated in a similar manner so that population and employment would flow explicitly among regions. However, IDIOM's static framework is not suited to representing time-dependent behavioral responses such as migration. Nor will incorporating aggregate responses address genuine distributional issues.

If addressing distributional issues and including household transfer payments are goals, one strategy would link IDIOM—itself a comparative statics model—to a static household model such as MATH (Micro Analysis of Transfers to Households) or TRIM (Transfer Income Model). Region-specific and industry-specific employment outcomes from IDIOM could determine employment aggregates in the household model. Once employment was adjusted, earnings, taxes, and transfers might respond within the household model. However, the credibility of the linkage would depend on the accuracy with which aggregate employment changes from IDIOM were given distributional translations in the household model. For example, if employment declines in a particular industry, would blacks, females, or younger workers in the industry be disproportionately affected? Which groups would be hired first by an expanding industry? Though IDIOM does not address these questions, they are central in estimating distributional impacts. Once households responded to employment changes induced by IDIOM, detailed consumption functions at the household level could be activated to generate new final demands. In turn, IDIOM could then respond to the updated demands and hence generate new employment patterns. It would be interesting to discover whether such a marriage between IDIOM and a static household model would iterate toward a solution.

A static model like IDIOM is unfortunately not suited for pairing up with a dynamic household model like DYNASIM (the Urban Institute Dynamic Simulation of Income Model). Yet the advantages of a truly dynamic and microanalytic treatment of supply and demand would be enormous. Both jobs and people would be explicitly represented. Like people, jobs would be born, develop, move, and die. Persons would make human capital investments in response to the job market. Vacancies and people would connect in markets. Firms would make offers, hire and fire; people would accept or reject offers and quit jobs. Distributional outcomes would be affected by both the movement of jobs and the process by which people were matched to jobs. Through their purchasing decisions, consumers would affect the birth and death rates for various categories of jobs, and the jobs in turn would determine employment opportunities available to people. The full promise, and the enormous difficulties, of the microanalytic paradigm would be faced if such a strategy were adopted. In the meantime, we can hope that IDIOM's creators will carry out their plans to link supply-side processes and distributional outcomes to their input-output framework, so as to better assess the possibilities of static input-output models as components in a fully microanalytic strategy.

DISCUSSION

James R. Hosek

IDIOM is a balanced regional input-output model that has been coupled to a Keynesian-style multiplier model of income determination. In this paper, it is applied to investigate the effects of a proposed reduction in U.S. military exports. For purposes of policy evaluation the reduction, by industrial sector, has been defined in terms of export sales rather than export quantities. Using this information IDIOM computes the implied changes in GDP, employment, labor income, capital income, and other variables that would apparently result from the decline in arms exports. These changes are also reported at a regional level.

To IDIOM, the arms-reduction policy is represented as an exogenous change in the vector of final demands. This causes changes in production and, as a consequence, changes in the incomes of suppliers of labor and capital services. The changes in income bring forth changes in consumption, which then induce changes in production, and so on. Thus the initial as well as induced effects are taken into consideration in determining the consequences of a policy change. Given a vector of reductions totaling $4.7 billion in foreign military sales, IDIOM finds an additional induced decline in GDP of $5.2 billion. The overall decline in GDP comes to $9.9 billion, more than twice the initial effect. Similarly, there is an initial loss in employment of 244,000 persons and an induced loss of 311,000 for a sum of 555,000 fewer employed.

Dresch and Updegrove consider two alternative compensatory policies to mitigate the contractionary effects of the arms sales limitation policy. The compensatory policies were designed to keep total employment unchanged. The first compensatory program involves an expansion of public construction activities, and the second includes a reduction in taxes on earned income.

A compensatory program of public works, distributed across regions in the same proportions as military employment, would have to be slightly larger than the reduction in arms sales—$4.9 billion versus $4.7 billion—to maintain national employment at its original level, and would entail small employment changes within any region—less than ± 0.1%. The reduction in the tax rate on labor income would entail a foregone tax "expenditure" of $5.1 billion to hold national employment constant, and would bring about greater net regional employment changes and a larger decline in labor income than predicted under the public works alternative. The decline in labor income occurring under either compensatory policy is caused by a shift in demand from the defense sector, where average income among workers is high, to other sectors having lower average remuneration.

My basic reaction to the IDIOM analysis is that the researchers have let their interpretation of the results be governed by the highly restrictive assumptions of the simulation model. The adoption of a broader viewpoint, one not tied to fixed coefficients technology or to a world without a market adjustment mechanism, would bring greater perspective and understanding to the numbers generated by the simulation model. Also, IDIOM itself could be used to probe the effects of relaxing certain assumptions built into its method of policy analysis.

The arms export reduction policy is presented to IDIOM as a new vector of final demands. There is no sense of whether this policy change is anticipated or unanticipated by arms exporters. Nor is there a sense of the form and timing of implementation of the policy. A fully anticipated and gradually implemented policy is likely to entail far lower adjustment costs than a policy without these attributes. For example, many policy changes are implemented gradually simply by stipulating that only transactions after a certain date are affected by the new policy. This procedure focuses the effect of the policy on the flow of new business rather than the stock of current business, and I believe this was the procedure discussed in regard to the limitation of military exports. Second, IDIOM offers no information on the time path of adjustment to the policy change, regardless of whether the policy is seen to be anticipated or not. Rather, IDIOM computes the final, equilibrium values of income, employment, and so forth, implied by the policy change. With this approach it is difficult to understand how IDIOM would differentiate its treatment of a permanent policy shift, such as embodied by the arms-sales reduction, or a transient reduction which nevertheless could entail significant reallocations of resources.

Looking at the problem from a different angle, recall that a novel feature of IDIOM is the inclusion of induced, or multiplier, effects. Many time series studies of consumption have shown that multiplier effects do not occur instantaneously but operate with a lagged effect. The same has been found for production responses. Since IDIOM could display the initial, input-output effects separately from subsequent input-output effects and the induced effects, the initial effects could be interpreted as rough estimates of the short-run response, and these plus the subsequent effects would represent the economy after full adjustment. Under this interpretation the time subscript to attach to the equilibrium values would depend on the rate of implementation of the policy change, the rate of input-output adjustment, and the speed of the consumption multiplier. Still, this attempt to modify the interpretation of IDIOM results is not entirely satisfying because, over time, factor and product markets will adjust to the shifts in demand and supply caused by the policy change. The input-output model takes no account of these adjustments, and as a result, the equilibrium values of IDIOM could be far from the truth.

So far I have said that IDIOM is deficient as a dynamic model because it offers no insight into paths of adjustment and how these paths might change under alternative procedures for implementing policy. I have also said, in effect, that IDIOM—like any other input-output model—is unreliable as a comparative static model because IDIOM has no way of including information about market adjustments. This does not mean that IDIOM should not be used, but again that caution and imagination should be brought to bear on judging the validity of its results. In the present case, Dresch and Updegrove might review studies of the past responsiveness of the arms export industry to increases or decreases in demand. Have reductions in output been met by an accumulation of inventories; by shifts into domestic product lines or into unrestricted export lines; by a reduction in hours per man, or an increase in layoffs or in permanent separations? The reduction in arms sales totals $4.7 billion, and dollar amounts of the reduction are specified for each sector. What fraction of annual sales is this, and does it lie beyond the band of usual sales fluctuations? How many of the potentially unemployed workers are eligible for transfer income such as unemployment insurance benefits, AFDC, or AFDC-Unemployed Fathers, and to what extent would these benefits mitigate the reduction in labor income?

Apart from using existing research to provide a context for the interpretation of IDIOM results, Dresch and Updegrove could also run a series of experiments on IDIOM to examine various forms of the policy change. I grant that the final demand vector of the arms export limitation policy is given exogenously. But for the sake of speculation, suppose some fraction of the reduction could be accommodated by each sector without causing any significant decline in value added or employment. The fraction could vary from industry to industry and would presumably be larger the longer the time frame chosen for analysis, the smaller the fraction of total sales affected, the greater the number of substitute products produced by firms within the industry, and the more elastic the remaining (i.e., unrestricted) demand for these substitutes. Without detailed knowledge, the fraction could be assumed the same across sectors, and new IDIOM results could be generated as the fraction varied from one level to another. This would help reveal how income and employment reductions vary with the effective, not nominal, policy change. Further, IDIOM could be used to calculate marginal changes in income and employment when the policy vector is perturbed in a given direction (i.e., for a given industry), other things constant. This would offer information on which dimensions of a policy have the greatest potential for increasing or reducing income or employment, and provided judgment were used, the results could be useful in policy design. A variant of this approach would be to program IDIOM to determine, say, a $4.7

billion arms export reduction in a given set of industries such that the policy minimized the effect on some target variable (e.g., income).

There are two other experiments I would suggest. The first is a sensitivity analysis whereby a policy is analyzed under alternative values of the marginal propensity to consume, that is, under alternative multiplier effects. The range of variation to be examined could be defined from standard errors of estimates of the consumption function. The same idea is applicable to input-output coefficients, but to my knowledge these coefficients are derived from accounting relationships rather than regressions, and consequently there are no estimates of the precision of the reported coefficients. The second experiment is to use IDIOM to simulate a past policy, the results of which are available to serve as a basis for comparison to the simulated results. The objective here would be not so much to make a strict quantitative comparison as to gain greater awareness of where and how the actual results differ from those computed under the assumptions of IDIOM.

Next, the compensatory policies: the comments already made about the anticipation, form, and rate of implementation of a policy are also applicable to the analysis of compensatory policies. For example, Dresch and Updegrove propose a compensatory policy of public works, yet existing research shows a variable time lag, averaging perhaps a year, from the availability of funds to the start of public works construction. Further, the notion of a compensatory policy deserves more motivation than it receives in the paper. There are a few instances in which the federal government is willing, under current law, to compensate interested parties for the adverse effects of a policy change. Two examples are shipbuilding and shoe manufacturing. But historically the government has changed policy—and thereby bestowed or confiscated virtual property rights to streams of income—without assuming liability for taxing away the benefits or for remunerating the losers. There is no policy for compensating the aircraft industry because the government decided not to buy the B-1 bomber, or for compensating taxpayers because of a change in the taxation of personal income.

Dresch and Updegrove offer no analysis of the effects of the form of financing the compensatory policies. Also, the design of the compensatory programs does not take account of income support automatically provided by existing transfer programs. Finally, although IDIOM can display net regional changes in income, employment, and other variables, there is no sense of how these changes are distributed across and within demographic groups (e.g., by income class or by occupation or skill levels). However, IDIOM's capability is being expanded in that regard. The expansion is welcome because it is probably more efficient and politically adept to focus compensatory policies on the groups chiefly affected by a policy change.

AN APPRAISAL OF MICRODATA
SIMULATION MODELS

7

MICRODATA SIMULATION:
CURRENT STATUS, PROBLEMS, PROSPECTS

Kenneth J. Arrow

The purpose of this conference, which is reflected in all of the papers, is to present and discuss efforts to get information at a much finer level of detail than can be obtained from macroeconomic models. Within this basic unity of purpose, two very different approaches are represented. One is to take the standard idea of complete, preferably dynamic systems and carry the disaggregation much further than has been customary. The other, quite different, approach is to construct synthetic samples of data. I know much more about the first than the second, but I will endeavor to make a contribution to the discussion of each. Before I do so, however, I would like to note that both approaches have a common core which is in line with one of the main traditions in economics—emphasis on the individual decision maker as the unit of analysis.

In the classical, textbook view, the economy is a universe composed of decision-making units. The household and the firm are the typical entities, together with the government. Each unit makes its decisions subject to outside pressures—prices and incomes—which are not completely under its control. It has certain decisions to make within a framework that is limited by these opportunities, and it makes choices which, in turn, have repercussions on the rest of the system. We factor the economic world into these decision-making units plus certain links between them, the markets, about which we have less to say.

I notice in the microsimulation research an emphasis on getting back to the individual unit; each individual unit is examined in terms of what it can do, the decisions it is free to make and not free to make, and the conditions under which it makes those decisions. We are so accustomed to this procedure that it almost seems self-evident; we tend to think that there is no other way to proceed.[1] This is not

---

[1] This approach is sometimes known as "methodological individualism." Many who place particular emphasis on the methodological aspect also have strong libertarian beliefs, especially the followers of the Austrian school, though, in fact, virtually all economists tend in the same direction.

logically correct. One can imagine models in which the individual does not appear in the statement of social laws. One sociologist, George Mead (1934), used to argue that there are no individuals as such; that what we call an individual is merely the intersection of the various roles he or she plays in different social groups. And one can, for example, reinterpret Keynesian models as social laws at an aggregate level. We usually think of them as representing individual behavior, but they are stated in aggregate terms.

With all the novelty in the papers presented here, however, no model has been based on principles stated in purely social terms. Rather, in many ways even more stress than is common has been placed on the individual behavior unit, models of the whole economic system being built up from behavior at the level of the individual. The individual decision-making unit appears in the conference papers both as the mover and doer and also as the entity whose behavior we are interested in studying and in predicting from the point of view of, say, welfare implications.

Disaggregation of Complete Systems

The first approach represented in the conference papers, then, is to try to work down to much finer levels of disaggregation than national income aggregates.

Most macroeconometric models try to get down to thinking, analytically at least, about decision-making units. The major equations—those for investment demand, consumption functions, and the like—sound like behavioral equations, although writ large. But you will always be able to find additional equations that can't be rationalized in terms of individual behavior. They seem to have no other function than to complete the system. In fact, it is hard to go through these models any more, they are so large and complex. The microdata models presented here are more coherent in that respect.

In terms of empirically implementing models of the entire economy, one conceivable line, which is represented in the conference papers, is to take the good old-fashioned general competitive equilibrium theory seriously. It certainly has all the features of emphasizing the decision-making unit. It yields, in principle, all the numbers that are involved as a basis for policy judgment. In fact, if it is carried out completely, it gives you the welfare itself because it has utility functions written in to begin with (one need no longer worry about approximations like consumer surplus).

There have been several empirical applications of general equilibrium theory in recent years. To the best of my knowledge, the first appeared in attempts to work with developing countries. These were still highly aggregated; they were general equilibrium models wherein the word "individual" was not to be taken very literally. I am thinking of such models as those of Adelman and Robinson (1977), and, somewhat earlier, Raduchel (1971). Part of the problem in handling general equilibrium models, of course, is solving simultaneously large numbers of equations—especially accompanied by inequalities, which good general equilibrium theorists tend to emphasize. Recent breakthroughs in computer technology are making this progressively easier. Herbert Scarf (1973) developed the first successful algorithm, and we have seen today a rich illustration of its possibilities (see Fullerton et al., chapter 3 in this volume).

To digress slightly, I might mention that there have been countrywide planing models using linear programming which could be regarded as general equilibrium models, although they are somewhat degenerate in that there is effectively only one consumer. I remember particularly the large model that Eckaus and Parikh (1968) fitted in India. The time span was five years. The temporal disaggregation was quite fine, to quarters, and there were some thirty sectors. The computation was regarded at the time as reaching the limit of feasible computational complexity. No doubt there has been a tremendous change in that respect in the last decade. A model like that could probably now be taken with equanimity.

The objections to this form of general equilibrium micromodel are, of course, the standard objections to the competitive theory. The question is not, Does the specific model represent the general theory well? It does, and in a reasonably disaggregated form. However, it does not permit testing the validity of competitive theory. (It is somewhat hard, for example, to explain unemployment in a fully competitive model.)

General equilibrium models so far have tended to be static in nature. Dynamic elements can be introduced in theory through developing a sequence of static models in which each step leads into the next. This approach will probably be implemented empirically in due course. When technological advances enable the general equilibrium solution to be computed in ten seconds, for instance, the problems of dynamizing the models are not going to look so formidable.

In dynamic models, since all relations include present and past variables the simultaneous nature of the problem, in a sense, becomes less important. It still exists though, because there are usually a number of contemporaneous variables—except in the limiting case of a dynamic model, where each equation has only one contemporaneous variable. Such a system is completely recursive: When I consider what to consume today, I may take yesterday's income as my budget constraint. The shorter the time spans involved, presumably, the more reasonable this approach becomes. From the viewpoint of appropriate statistical methodology, Herman Wold (1959) was arguing long ago for completely recursive systems in his polemics with the Cowles Commission on simultaneous equations methods. I don't think we need take a dogmatic stand on that question. But we can say that nonsimultaneous models become much more reasonable when very short time periods are considered.

Two of the models presented at the conference (Bennett and Bergmann's model of the U.S. economy and Eliasson's, of the Swedish, chapters 1 and 2 of this volume) represent, in effect, models of the complete economy, highly disaggregated in both sector and time and carried to the limit of essentially one contemporaneous variable per equation. The difficulties of simultaneous solution become trivial in these cases. They are replaced by other complications, however—a large number of variables to handle and a large number of computations to be made at each stage.

Several of the models presented at the conference are sector models, with everything outside the sector treated exogenously. Methodologically, they are complete models, though not necessarily equilibrium models, of course, in that there may be little or no simultaneity. The model of the health care sector, by Yett et al. (chapter 7 of Volume 1), and Ozanne and Vanski's housing model (chapter 5 in this volume) fall into this category. Here again the basis is disaggregation into individual decision-making units, with market links of some kind.

All the models I have discussed so far form an emerging family of models, contiguous with but more highly developed than the macroeconometric models with which we are more familiar.

Synthetic Sampling

Let me talk, more briefly, of my understanding of synthetic sampling. As I understand the matter, it is really a question of estimating certain properties of multivariate distributions by observing joint distributions of subsets of variables. To use the simplest case, let us take three variables: Suppose there are some observations in which variables 1 and 2 are measured; there are other observations on variables 2 and 3, and still others on 1 and 3. There are few or no observations on all three variables simultaneously, but nevertheless it is desired to estimate their joint distribution. If the variables have a joint normal distribution, then this information is adequate since the joint distribution is determined by the means and covariances. Instead of actual observations on all three pairs of variables, some other information may be used to complete the description of the joint distribution.

This procedure has been used, for example, in the studies on inequality by Christopher Jencks et al. (1972); they were fitting regression equations, but they never had a sample in which all the variables they wanted to work with appeared. They sought, among other things, to predict income from schooling, parental status, intelligence, and other factors. But they never had all these observations in the same study. Instead, they estimated the sample covariances between income and the independent variables and among the independent variables by using different pieces from different studies.

Among the papers at this conference, Minarik's MERGE file (chapter 1 of Volume 1) is the easiest one for me to understand. A tax law is a mapping from a vector whose elements are the income characteristics of the individual (wage income, dividends, capital gains, and all the other items in the income tax form) to tax liabilities. It is supposed to be a well-defined function; no economic analysis is needed. (Perhaps, realistically, the variables should be extended to include the ability of the taxpayer's attorney.) In fact, to use this information one wants to know the distribution of the burden by some classification of lower dimensionality than that used in the tax law. To go one step further in the simplification, let us suppose that tax liability was completely determined by capital gains and income other than capital gains. Then, the tax law would be a mapping from those two variables to tax liabilities. But if what we really want are tax liabilities by income class, what we need is the conditional distribution of capital gains for any given income. For a given income, tax liability is a function of capital gains; hence, average tax liability can be computed for each income level.

One of the most powerful applications of this technique was estimation of underreporting; that is, with some kinds of information, it is possible to correct the data. Presumably, hypothetically there is a joint distribution of true income and reported income, and therefore a conditional distribution of true income given reported income; the logic of this correction is the same as that just given. The results are a bit discouraging for those who fit regressions to published data—as in the very large volume of empirical work done on the basis of looking up a few columns in the *Statistical Abstract*. After listening to Minarik's story, one feels very inhibited, for at least a few months!

The joint distributions are not only contemporaneous, they can also be between variables at different points of time. Much emphasis has been placed, in fact, on the dynamic aspects of the simulation where individuals have characteristics that evolve over time according to some stochastic process. Myself today and myself tomorrow are two individuals whose characteristics differ, though their values are related. Some changes are simple; my age next year will be one greater than my age this year, although even that simple proposition has to be adjusted for the probability of survival. More meaningful and complex correlations among characteristics at different times will usually need to be estimated. For example, income transformations over time may be estimatable, from one set of data, such as the Michigan Panel Study of Income Dynamics. One might then estimate an auto-regressive relationship or some other Markov process representation of income changes. Estimates of geographic mobility come from yet a different source. Although the context is now dynamic, the problem of putting together a number of separately estimated joint marginal distributions to find a joint distribution is logically the same as in the static context.

To return to our example of the tax law situation, synthetic sampling can be used to derive tax liabilities as a function of income. But, in fact, nobody is really satisfied to stop with such a relation. Everybody knows some economics; the economists have their professional pride at stake; so they all say, "The tax law is going to change things." The next step is to consider the rather old-fashioned concept of the incidence of the burden. The analyst starts to estimate the shifting of the taxes; and then—particularly if the taxes being shifted are considered significant—somebody brings up the question of implicit taxes: "After all, you've got to predict changes in municipal bond returns; they are going to adjust because of the corporate income tax (because otherwise there would be disequilibrium in the market)."[2]

Once the model builder starts considering the incidence of the initial, legal relation, he or she is moving toward a general equilibrium model, or at least toward

---

[2]On that particular point, it should be noted that among the alternative incidence assumptions in Pechman and Okner (1974) was the so-called "new view," where the corporate income tax falls on all property. This assumption automatically takes care of the implicit-tax argument.

a complete model if disequilibrium is admitted. The synthetic sample yields one relation—a very complicated relation, in general—but still one that, of itself, becomes an input into the kind of model I discussed in my first section. It is in this sense that the two topics of this conference are complementary. The MATH model (see Beebout, chapter 2 in Volume 1) illustates the first step in going from a technical relation derived from a synthetic sample to the most immediately adjacent behavioral and feedback relations. Sometimes, especially when talking about an impulse starting in a relatively small sector, it may be perfectly reasonable to say that certain feedback relations are negligible. This principle applies to relatively specialized income maintenance programs, for example. The number of individuals on a particular income maintenance roll who will be employed as a result of the purchasing power generated by an increase in the scale or generosity of the program and therefore removed from the roll may reasonably be neglected. But ignoring feedback may be an important error for relatively large programs.

There is one problem that I haven't heard mentioned with regard to synthetic samples, or indeed in any use of statistical relations to map a distribution into fewer dimensions. This is the fact that the information used is essentially a set of correlations observed in historical data. But if it is a policy change that is being analyzed, it should be admitted that the change may affect the correlations being used. The synthetic sample is drawn from a particular set of conditions, let's say a particular legal structure, and its statistical properties will change with a change in conditions. For example, the correlation between capital gains and income could easily be changed by economic reactions to changes in the tax law.

Why Micromodels?

There has been an increasing demand for detailed micromodels stemming, in my judgment, from several entirely distinct sources.

The really big impulse has not been scientific curiosity or the demand for better models but the need for a kind of answer that simply didn't come out of the existing macromodels. Input-output analysis was supported at various stages, if not originated, for similar reasons. It was developed to answer the question: What happens to any specific industry? Similarly, the current work on microsimulation is not merely designed to yield better answers for aggregate questions but to yield answers to questions at the microlevel. The form of the models reflects the form of the answers sought. When discussing income maintenance, for instance, we want to know what happens to particular income groups, because the purpose of the whole exercise is to improve the distribution of income—maybe the size distribution of income; maybe the distribution of income by region or by other criteria (which, as an economist, I find less interesting than the size distribution). But, whatever it is, there is some socially compelling reason for a distributive question, the answer to which must be stated in distributive terms. It is no use knowing that a large transfer program presumably doesn't affect aggregates at all to a first approximation and that, if it does have an effect, it is probably negative. The question is: Is the program being targeted to an appropriate group? The need for answering this question was recognized by the President's Commission on Income Maintenance, back in the late 1960s.

Closely related to the need for disaggregated answers is the fact that appropriate data are now available from various surveys—particularly special-purpose surveys like the Survey of Income and Education, or the Survey of Economic Opportunity—that didn't exist before. The timing of the development of data appropriate for micromodel building is not a coincidence but came from the same perceived need for detailed answers.

A second motive for microsimulation modeling is the belief that the technique results in better models. One reason for this belief is implicit in what has already been said; disaggregated relations are simpler and more transparent than aggregated relations. This may have been one of the reasons, years ago, behind Orcutt's work (chapter 3 in Volume 1). Our aggregated relations conceal distributional assumptions of some kind. Therefore, there is a need for variables that are not decision-making variables but reflect, in some way, the aggregation procedure. If these variables are not introduced, the aggregation implicitly and illegitimately assumes a vast mass of identical individuals. The error is especially striking if the individual relations are nonlinear. Even if the individual relations are linear, there are aggregation problems; each one may be linear but in a variable specific to that individual. Thus, my consumption depends on my income, and somebody else's consumption depends on his income; even if each individual relationship is linear, there is an aggregation problem if the propensities to consume differ among individuals. If the model deals with the individual level, or some relatively fine level of disaggregation, the relationships should be much simpler and our understanding much better than at the aggregate level.

A third motive, less completely accepted, is the view that values of some of the parameters can be deduced directly from the detailed observations. In other words, by disaggregating to small parts of the economy which we understand better, we can get—by direct questionnaires or by relatively simple observations— estimates of parameters whose meanings are murky in the system as a whole. There can be differences of opinion on this question. One problem is that observations in the individual sectors, though easily obtained, may not aggregate well. There are also comparability questions. On the aggregation question, it seems to have been taken as axiomatic that a complete model of the entire economy should be consistent with national income accounting. That may not, however, be right. Since we happen to have a large number of national income statistics, there are obvious reasons for seeking consistency. But it may be that, in terms of behavioral manifestations at the individual level, the national concepts as we have them now are not in fact useful.

All these reasons behind the recently increasing demand for detailed micromodels seem to lead to the conclusion that models built up from individual behavior should yield better predictions even of aggregates. More information is being poured into the system because it is capable of absorbing individual information that conventional models cannot absorb.

Methodological Issues

The development of microanalytic simulation models also raises methodological issues, which may not be totally new but certainly appear in new versions. The first one I want to mention is the problem of estimation. As I have already mentioned, one key methodological hope for microanalytic models is that parameters can be estimated "directly," in some sense. But strictly speaking all parameters are parameters of statistical relations, and the general principles of statistical inference should apply. No matter how detailed the observations in a particular sector are, there is still a statistical inference of some kind to arrive at the estimate of a parameter. It is very important, in particular, to know that parameters are estimated with uncertainty. Unfortunately, as far as I can see, in all uses of models for policy purposes (including those at this conference) there is no confidence or error band.

What is done is to predict on the basis of many different alternative policy assumptions (the purpose, of course, of the exercise). Sometimes model builders do get so far as to present the consequences of alternative assumptions about the model. But rarely have I seen statistical theory used to generate a confidence band. And yet the statistical theory itself—the very statistical calculations performed—will provide, as a by-product, confidence bands on forecasts. Now, I suppose somebody will tell me that the fault lies with the consumers; they do not understand error. Of course, they know the analyst is very probably wrong, but they don't want to see a standard error. Cochrane's recent article (1975, p. 203) discussed the famous guidepost formulation in the middle 1960s of 3.2% per annum wage increase. The Council of Economic Advisors was aware that the basis of that figure was shaky. But they said it was impossible to present this uncertainty to President Johnson. To him a "range" was a place where you kept cattle.

It may be a common characteristic of decision makers, of people who actually have to do something, to dislike a reminder of uncertainty. But since uncertainty is real, it does seem that we should recognize and quantify it, however crudely. In some cases, as in input-output models such as that of Haveman et al. (chapter 4 in this volume) and that of Dresch and Updegrove (chapter 6 in this volume) or in the model presented by Fullerton et al. (chapter 3 in this volume), there is only one observation. In those cases it is impossible to get any estimate of variance at all. There is no way of deriving a confidence band from a single measurement. But we know that no model is correct. It couldn't be; there are so many factors omitted, even under ideal circumstances. Estimates based on a single observation, therefore, must also be unreliable, even though we cannot obtain measures of their unreliability. What is needed is replication, repeated observations within a time series or a cross-section context (although the latter has other difficulites). So it has to be understood that even direct observation should be tested by repeated observations, at several points in time or for several individuals.

There is one example I know of in which system parameters were obtained with very low error by direct questioning. It concerned pricing rules. The idea of replacing maximization models by assuming that economic agents follow simple rules of thumb in matters like pricing is probably very old, but it was certainly pushed hard by Herbert Simon and his disciples at Carnegie-Mellon University. In particular, Richard Cyert and James March (1963) went to a department store and learned from the management what pricing rules were being followed. A department store, assuming it has any monopoly power at all, should be worried about the cross-elasticities of demand between any two of its products and the demand for them. But instead of using a complex set of rules incorporating all this information, it turned out the store classified all items into three categories with the same markup on all items in the same category; for example, the markup on an item in the "standard" category was two-thirds over purchase price (subject to a round-off). There were also rules for markdowns when an item didn't sell. (Remember that these operating rules were found by simply asking the management.) They then priced the commodities, and the fit was fantastic. For 188 out of 197 cases, the error was *zero*. This is not ordinary economics.

But what is more striking is that a number of years later, William Baumol and Maco Stewart (1971) went to another department store and checked the Cyert-March rules. Of course, they didn't fit perfectly. The markups tended to be higher and less uniform. But in virtually all cases, the markup was between 67% (the Cyert-March rule) and 82%—indeed, 60% of the items had exactly an 82% markup. Now, that's the kind of prediction economists don't find very often. But somehow, nobody paid any attention to these results, as far as I can make out. One research problem, of course, is cost. In this case, for instance, one would have to go to every department store to find the rules. It might be hoped that, after a while, some pattern would emerge. But this line of research has not been much pursued. I think the main reason is that the theory and the observation are not far enough apart to be interesting. These studies do, in any case, exemplify the argument that information about system parameters can be obtained by direct questioning if the system is sufficiently disaggregated. It is hard to know how to assess the parameter values statistically, although the fit is so good that one might not worry about that problem.

An alternative approach to estimating in these models, and one that was suggested by Bennett and Bergmann (chapter 1 of this volume) among others, is to guess the parameters and then fit the model; if the fit is poor, then change the estimates. To some degree, this method is logically not that different from statistical estimation. The statistical properties of the Bennett-Bergmann estimates cannot be derived from statistical theory. They can, however, be derived by simulation. For a given set of parameter values, the model can be simulated with random shocks. By repeating this operation often enough all the desired estimates of statistical reliability, whether confidence intervals or tests of hypotheses, can be obtained. Deriving statistical properties this way is not cheap computationally; but in view of current prices, that may not be a very serious obstacle. That the usual apparatus of normal distributions cannot be used merely illustrates the perfectly good argument that so many have referred to today, that you can use computers instead of mathematics. Computers are, after all, a form of mathematical calculation; and, ever since it has been established that four colors are enough for coloring a map, even relatively pure mathematics has been invaded by the computer.

Let me turn to one concern about large models of any kind (and models may get to be much larger than the largest macroeconometric models used today), the danger of rigidity. It becomes harder and harder to see through them.

Suppose a model is not doing very well at prediction or plausibility. It may become difficult to see what is wrong. It is possible to spot a particular relation that isn't fitting very well. But, more often, what is needed for improved prediction is not just putting one new variable in and taking one away but rethinking the model more comprehensively. If what is needed is a change in concepts, for example, definitional changes will be needed everywhere in the model. In effect, scrapping a large intellectual investment is called for, and this gets harder and harder the larger and more complex the model.

In this context, the demands for consistency of data voiced at the conference worry me. It is a very attractive idea. It is frustrating, on the one hand, to find that data from different sources cannot be amalgamated because the definitions are not identical. On the other hand, the analytic community can get locked into a consistency which becomes harder and harder to change. This is the old argument about individualism and laissez-faire. There is a loss through lack of coordination; and the argument for coordination, for direct interference, is pretty strong. But the fear that innovation will be inhibited has got to be taken care of.

It might be argued that the supply of innovative ideas will be insured by the fact that nobody can make a reputation except by being different. But it must be kept in mind that these are rather costly new ideas. As I mentioned earlier, the demand for microanalytic simulation models was not generated within the field of scholars but outside. The interest in innovation must be financed by the consumer.

I would like to raise still another question. This conference had as its topic microsimulation for policy analysis. But, of course, someone like myself is interested in the fact that new knowledge should have scientific usefulness. "Scientific" signifies, if you like, the generalizability of the knowledge as a basis for a great many different policy analyses. Perhaps it is also relevant that it be interesting for its own sake. Finally, scientific study explains the policy analysis to theorists, which is important because that's where the next generation of policy research is going to come from anyway. But regardless of how I try to defend my curiosity, I just want to understand the relations better. Now, many of the hypotheses used here are basically familiar, and the emphasis has been rather on their empirical implementation. But, a few of the analytic structures implied somewhat unconventional approaches—most strikingly in the models of the entire economy where markup pricing was used. Markup pricing still represents a challenge to orthodox thinking;

determination of whether a market-equilibrating price is a better or worse fit to the data than a markup price would be most important. Of course, the markup price theory in itself conceals a rather wide variety of possibilities; two distinctly different ones have been presented in the conference papers.

With respect to this point, one trouble is that the large macroeconometric models have, I think, gotten beyond the point of being scientifically useful. They are very important for prediction and policy purposes; but if we want a new idea about a consumption function or about investment demand, the context of a large macroeconometric model is probably a poor environment for developing it. Most of the equations in the macromodels did not originate, in my judgment, from earlier models but from somebody just studying that particular relationship.

Whether or not these remarks are fair, they lead to the questions of validation. How do we validate these relationships?

One possibility is to use the model for forecasting for a different period. This criterion was mentioned in the discussion of the Ozanne and Vanski housing model (chapter 5 of this volume). One of the comments was that conditions had changed entirely, which, unfortunately, is true. The model is complete enough; the factors that have changed so much are in the model—if only as exogenous variables. Presumably the model should have been capable of generating conditional forecasts. One could calibrate the world as of 1970 and take the exogenous variables as they were in 1960. The model would generate a prediction, which might be termed a "hindcast." Hindcasting is an alternative technique which at least has the virtue that it can be done rapidly. You don't have to wait a year for verification. I think some of the macroeconomic models proposed in this conference could be profitably run back in time, to see how well they would have performed. That provides some kind of validation.

Forecasting or hindcasting is a way of validating a whole system. One would like, really, to be able to validate individual relations as well because, if the whole system doesn't work well, it is necessary to know where the repair job is needed. This problem requires a methodological discussion which I have not yet seen.

As a small side remark on the relation between scientific as against policy or predictive uses of models, I wonder about the treatment of consumption. The hypotheses about consumption that have had the most success have been based on dynamic considerations, the permanent income or life-cycle hypotheses. A number of the models deal with processes extended in time. But it seems to me, unless I missed something, that none of the consumption hypotheses used in any of the models had any permanent income component. I wonder why that was the case when, presumably, a dynamic model would enable one to use the permanent income hypothesis more fruitfully than is usually done.

Let me conclude with a few remarks on the policy applications. The presentation of results is, I suppose, to some extent imposed by the user. Nevertheless, some more extensive use of welfare-economic concepts should be made. As was pointed out in discussion, we are interested in two aspects, equity and efficiency. We want some idea of aggregate benefits and losses, and we want some idea of the distributional aspects. But the equity aspects should take account of all effects, not merely the financial.

Consider, for example, the study of the effects of alternative energy policies. there is certainly going to be some restrictive policy on gasoline—say in the form of a tax on gasoline consumption. To measure the welfare effects, it is not enough merely to look at individuals' taxes. One pattern seems to be first to look at the financial burden; the tax has behavioral effects, in lowering of the consumption of energy, which will partly offset the initial tax. Then the tax burden or the after-tax energy consumption is measured. But that is an underestimate of the welfare loss; it neglects the fact that the individual is forced to reduce his or her consumption. Something parallel has occurred in a number of case studies.

Now, it is true that the alternative of calculating the tax on the initial consumption, not correcting for behavioral effects, would overestimate the welfare loss. The truth lies between the two.

The trouble here is that, instead of looking at equity and efficiency as the economist's measure, there is a tendency to look at budgetary costs. Now, theoretically, the only justification for even considering budgetary costs as such is that they are financed by taxes, which have their own distortionary significance. The financial cost may be a rough way to at least remind the user of the problems. But there is no harm in supplying, in addition to the asked-for information, some measures of benefits and costs calculated along economically more interesting lines. Typically, the informational raw material for the welfare measures consists of calculations already made.

Reference was made, in discussion, to the inherent difficulty introduced by the fact that really big changes are unpredictable. Big shifts in fertility are the classic examples given. Although there are various economic hypotheses about such changes, I do not think they have stood up very well. We do have changes; and, I suppose, detailed consumption categories, rather than just total consumption, are subject to major shifts. Even aggregate consumption has shown unpredicted changes, such as the rise in the savings ratio in the last few years. This shift may be explicable somehow, but I don't think anyone actually predicted it. A cynic might thus ask, "What's the use of talking about policy at all, when the conditions on which you base your forecast can change abruptly?" The answer is that these changes typically are not all that rapid. These models and the policy responses based on them must be thought of as, to some extent, adaptive mechanisms that respond to these changes. The really long-run consequences of a policy may not be that important, because we can hope that remedial steps will be undertaken if in fact the policies being implemented turn out badly.

I heard at the conference the familiar complaint against all quantitative analysis: that the nonmeasurable magnitudes have been omitted; that there is a tendency to exaggerate the importance of measurable as opposed to nonmeasurable magnitudes.

The charge is true. But it is also true that the situation is not in any way improved by not doing measurements. Many examples can be given from, say, the field of water resources—where exactly the same cry is heard all the time—to suggest that, on the whole, the analysis based on the quantitative work is an improvement and does not necessarily lead to biased results. It is of course incumbent upon the analyst to make sure that the relevant factors are accounted for, to the extent that this is possible. And as a matter of fact, the general approach represented at this conference does introduce many factors not brought in before. Those are just the repercussions that one can take account of.

Finally, I noticed severe complaints about the quality of the data, the workmanship, and so forth. This is a very encouraging sign. If one thing is clear in any dynamic branch of scientific activity, it is that the ratio of complaints to accomplishment is roughly a constant. Therefore, you may even use the volume of complaints as some measure of the amount of accomplishment.

REFERENCES

Aaron, H. J. 1978. *Politics and the professors*. Washington, D.C.: The Brookings Institution.

Aaron, H. J., and Todd, J. 1978. The use of income maintenance experiment findings in public policy 1977-1978. Paper presented at the American Economics Association meeting. Chicago, August.

Adelman, I., and Robinson, S. 1977. *Income redistribution policies in developing countries: A case study of Korea*. Stanford, Calif.: Stanford University Press.

Ahlstrom L. 1978. The market oriented interindustry stock and flow aggregation scheme used in MOSES. In G. Eliasson (Ed.), *A micro-to-macro model of the Swedish economy*. Stockholm: Industrial Institute for Economic and Social Research.

Albrecht, J. 1978a. Expectations, cyclical fluctuation and growth—experiments on the Swedish model. In G. Eliasson (Ed.), *A micro-to-macro model of the Swedish economy*. Stockholm: Industrial Institute for Economic and Social Research.

Albrecht, J. 1978b. Capacity utilization in Swedish industry 1975-76. *Industrikonjunkturen*, Spring, pp. 234-244.

Allen, J. T., and Hollister, R. G. 1975. Food stamps: Out of control. *Washington Post*. October 5, p. A7.

Altman, S. H. 1971. *Present and future supply of registered nurses*. HEW Publication No. (NIH) 72-34. Washington, D.C.: U.S. Government Printing Office.

American Hospital Association. 1967. *Hospitals*, Guide Issue, *41*, Part 2.

American Hospital Association. 1970. *Hospitals*, Guide Issue, *44*, Part 2.

American Hospital Association. 1971. *Hospitals*, Guide Issue, *45*, Part 2.

American Hospital Association. 1977. *Hospital statistics*. Chicago: American Hospital Association.

American Medical Association. 1968. *Medical school alumni 1967*, by C. N. Theodore, G. E. Sutter, and J. N. Haug. Chicago: American Medical Association.

American Medical Association. 1971. *Foreign medical graduates in the United States 1970*. Chicago: American Medical Association.

American Medical Association. 1977. *Physician distribution and medical licensure in the United States 1976*. Chicago: American Medical Association.

Andreassi, M., and MacRae, C. D. 1978. Metropolitan housing and the income tax. Working Paper No. 253-4. Washington, D.C.: The Urban Institute.

Armington, C., and Odle, M. 1975. Research on microdata files based on field surveys and tax returns; creating the MERGE-70 file: Data folding and linking. Working paper. Washington, D.C.: The Brookings Institution.

Arthur D. Little, Inc. 1975. *Energy conservation in new building design: An impact assessment of ASHRAE standard 90-75*. Final report to the Federal Energy Administration. Washington, D. C.: U.S. Government Printing Office.

Bailey, M. J. 1959. A note on the economics of residential zoning and urban renewal. *Land Economics, 25*, 288-290.

Bailey, M. J. 1969. Capital prices and income taxation. In A. C. Harberger and M. J. Bailey (Eds.), *The taxation of income from capital*. Washington, D.C.: The Brookings Institution.

Bailey, M. J. 1974. Progressivity and investment yields under U.S. income taxation. *Journal of Political Economy*, November-December, pp. 1157-1175.

Barr, R. S., Glover, F., and Klingman, D. 1977. The alternating basis algorithm for assignment problems. *Mathematical Programming, 13*, 1-13.

Barr, R. S., and Turner, J. S. 1978. A new linear programming approach to microdata file merging. In *1977 Compendium of tax research*, sponsored by U.S. Department of the Treasury, Office of Tax Analysis. Washington, D.C.: U.S. Government Printing Office.

Baumol, W. J., and Stewart, M. 1971. On the behavioral theory of the firm. In R. L. Marris and A. Wood (Eds.), *The corporate economy: Growth, competition and innovative potential*. Cambridge, Mass.: Harvard University Press.

Beebout, H. 1977a. Reporting of transfer income on the Survey of Income and Education: Initial correction of the microdata for underreporting. Discussion Paper No. 7335-001. Washington, D.C.: Mathematica Policy Research.

Beebout, H. 1977b. *Microsimulation as a policy tool: The MATH model*. Policy Analysis Series No. 14. Washington, D.C.: Mathematica Policy Research.

Beebout, H., and Bonina, P. 1973. TRIM: A microsimulation model for evaluating transfer income policy. Working Paper No. 971-4. Washington, D.C.: The Urban Institute.

Beebout, H., Doyle, P., and Kendall, A. 1976. *Estimation of food stamp participation and cost for 1977: A microsimulation approach*. Working Paper No. E48. Washington, D.C.: Mathematica Policy Research.

Beebout, H., leMat, M. F., and Kendall, A. 1976. *Estimates of food stamp eligibility including the impact of the resources test and survey income underreporting factors*. Project Report No. 76-10. Report submitted to USDA. Washington, D.C.: Mathematica Policy Research.

Bendt, D. 1975. *The effects of changes in the AFDC program on effective benefit reduction rates and the probability of working*. Project Report No. 76-13. Washington, D.C.: Mathematica Policy Research.

Bennett, R. L., and Bergmann, B. R. 1978. A microsimulated Transactions Model of the United States economy. Working Paper No. 79-4, Department of Economics, University of Maryland, College Park. Mimeographed.

Bergsman, A., and leMat, M. F. (Eds.). 1977. *MATH users guide*. Reference Series. Washington, D.C.: The Hendrickson Corporation.

Berndt, E. R., and Christensen, L. R. 1974. Testing for the existence of a consistent aggregate index of labor inputs. *American Economic Review, 64*, 391-404.

Berndt, E. R., Darrough, M. N., and Diewert, W. E. 1977. Flexible functional forms and expenditure distributions: An application to Canadian consumer demand functions. *International Economic Review, 18*, 651-675.

Betson, D., Greenberg, D., and Kasten, R. In preparation. A simulation analysis of the economic efficiency and distributional effects of alternative program structures: The negative income tax versus the credit income tax. In I. Garfinkel (Ed.), *Universal versus income-tested transfer programs*. Book in preparation, Institute for Research on Poverty, Madison, Wis., 1979.

Bickel, G., and MacDonald, M. 1975. Participation rates in the food stamp program: Estimated levels, by state. Institute for Research on Poverty Discussion Paper No. 253-75. Madison, Wis.: Institute for Research on Poverty.

Bischoff, C. W. 1971a. In G. Fromm (Ed.), *Tax incentives and capital spending*. Washington, D.C.: The Brookings Institution.

Bischoff, C. W. 1971b. Business investment in the 1970s: A comparison of models. *Brookings Papers on Economic Activity*, *1*, 13-63.

Blackorby, C., Primont, D., and Russell, R. R. 1978. *Duality, separability, and functional structure: Theory and economic applications*. New York: North-Holland.

Blumberg, M. S. 1971. *Trends and projections of physicians in the United States 1967-2002*. Berkeley, Calif.: Carnegie Commission on Higher Education.

Boland, B. 1973. *Participation in the Aid to Families with Dependent Children Program*. Studies in Public Welfare, No. 12, Part 1. Washington, D.C.: U.S. Congress, Joint Economic Committee.

Boskin, M. J. 1978. Taxation, saving, and the rate of interest. *Journal of Political Economy*, *86*, S3-S27.

Brannon, G. 1976. Prices and incomes: The dilemma of energy policy. *Harvard Journal of Legislation*, *13*, 445-478.

Brazer, H. 1968. Tax policy and children's allowances. In E. M. Burns (Ed.), *Children's allowances and the economic welfare of children*. New York: Citizens' Committee for Children of New York, Inc.

Break, G. F., and Pechman, J. A. 1975. *Federal tax reform: The impossible dream?* Washington, D.C.: The Brookings Institution.

Brewer, G. D. 1973. *Politicians, bureaucrats and the consultant: A critique of urban problem solving*. New York: Basic Books.

Brinner, R. 1973. Inflation, deferral and the neutral taxation of capital gains. *National Tax Journal*, *26*, 565-573.

Brittain, J. A. 1966. *Corporate dividend policy*. Washington, D.C.: The Brookings Institution.

Brittain, J. A. 1972. The incidence of social security payroll taxes. *American Economic Review*, *62*, 739-742.

Budd, E. C. 1971. The creation of a microdata file for estimating the size distribution of income. *Review of Income and Wealth*, *17*, 317-334.

Budd, E. C. 1972. Comments. *Annals of Economic and Social Measurement*, *1*, 349-354.

Burtless, G., and Hausman, J. 1978. The effect of taxation on labor supply: Evaluating the Gary negative income tax experiment. *Journal of Political Economy*, *86*, 1103-1130.

Butter, I. 1971. The migratory flow of doctors to and from the United States. *Medical Care*, *9*, 17-31.

Caddy, V. 1976. Empirical estimation of the elasticity of substitution: A review. Preliminary Working Paper OP-09, IMPACT Project. Melbourne, Australia: Industrial Assistance Commission.

Cagan, P. 1974. Common stock values and inflation—The historical record of many countries. *National Bureau Report Supplement*, No. 13 (March), pp. 1-10. New York: National Bureau of Economic Research.

Carlson, M. D. 1974. The 1972-73 Consumer Expenditure Survey. *Monthly Labor Review*, *97*, 16-23.

Carter, A., and Everett, C. 1974. A partially closed input-output model. Brandeis Economic Research Center, Brandeis University, Waltham, Mass. Mimeographed.

Citro, C. F., and Bendt, D. L. 1975. *Developing a 1970 census state public assistance cost estimator*, vol. 1, *Description and evaluation of the SPACE sample*. Final report submitted to HEW, Office of the Secretary, and the Social and Rehabilitation Service. Washington, D.C.: Mathematica, Inc.

Cochrane, J. L. 1975. The Johnson administration: Moral suasion goes to war. In C. D. Goodwin (Ed.), *Exhortation and controls: The search for a wage-price policy, 1945-1971*. Washington, D.C.: The Brookings Institution.

Coen, R. M. 1971. In G. Fromm (Ed.), *Tax incentives and capital spending*. Washington, D.C.: The Brookings Institution.

Coen, R. M. 1976. Alternative measures of capital and its rate of return in U.S. manufacturing.

Department of Economics, Northwestern University, Evanston, Illinois. Mimeographed.

Cogan, J. F. 1977. Labor supply with time and money of participation. Rand Report R-2044-HEW. Santa Monica: Rand Corporation.

Crecine, J., Davis, O. A., and Jackson, J. 1967. Urban property markets: Some empirical results and their implications for municipal zoning. *Journal of Law and Economics, 10*, 79-99.

Cyert, R. M., and March, J. G. 1963. *A behavioral theory of the firm*. Englewood Cliffs, N. J.: Prentice-Hall.

Dahlberg, L., and Jakobsson, U. 1977. On the effects of different patterns of public consumption expenditures. *The Review of Income and Wealth, 4*, 385-395.

Dahlman, C. J., and Klevmarken, A. 1971. *Den privata konsumtionen 1931-1975*. Stockholm, Sweden: Industrial Institute for Economic and Social Research.

Data Resources, Inc. 1975. *The Data Resources U.S. long-term review*. Summer. Lexington, Mass.: DRI.

Davis, K., and Russell, L. B. 1972. The substitution of hospital outpatient care for inpatient care. *Review of Economics and Statistics, 54*, 109-120.

Deane, R. T. 1977. An alternative specification for participation rates. *Applied Economics, 9*, 1-7.

Deane, R. T., and Yett, D. E. 1979. Nurse market policy simulations using an econometric model. In *Research in health economics: An annual compilation of research*, vol. 1. Greenwich, Conn.: JAI Press.

de Leeuw, F., and Struyk, R. J. 1975. *The web of urban housing: Analyzing policy with a market simulation model*. Washington, D.C.: The Urban Institute.

Denton, F. T., and Spencer, B. G. 1975. Health-care costs when the population changes. *Canadian Journal of Economics, 8*, 34-48.

DeSalvo, J. S. 1975. Benefits and costs of New York City's middle-income housing program. *Journal of Political Economy, 83*, 791-805.

Dhrymes, P. J., Howrey, E. P., Hymans, S. H., et al. 1972. Criteria for evaluation of econometric models. *Annals of Economic and Social Measurement, 2*, 291-324.

Difiglio, C., and Kulash, D. 1976. *Marketing and mobility*. Report of a panel of the Interagency Task Force on Motor Vehicle Goals beyond 1980. Washington, D.C.: U.S. Department of Transportation.

Doyle, P., and Beebout, H. (Eds.). 1977. *MATH technical description*. Washington, D.C.: Mathematica Policy Research.

Doyle, P., and Beebout, H. (Eds.). 1978. *MATH technical description*. (An update.) Washington, D.C.: Mathematica Policy Research.

Doyle, P., Beebout, H., and Penland, J. (Eds.). 1978. *MATH codebook*. Reference Series 7271-006. Washington, D.C.: Mathematica Policy Research.

Dresch, S. P. 1972. Disarmament: Economic consequences and developmental potential. Report to the United Nations, Department of Economic and Social Affairs, Center for Development Planning, Projects and Policies, New York. December.

Dresch, S. P., and Goldberg, R. D. 1973. IDIOM: An inter-industry, national-regional policy evaluation model. *Annals of Economic and Social Measurement, 2*, 323-356.

Eaton, B. C., and Lipsey, R. 1976. The non-uniqueness of equilibrium in the Loschian Location Model. *American Economic Review, 66*, 77-93.

Eckaus, R. S., and Parikh, K. S. 1968. *Planning for growth: Multisectoral intertemporal models applied to India*. Cambridge, Mass.: MIT press.

Edson, D. 1978. Better jobs and income cost and caseload estimates based on the JOBS model and the March 1975 Current Population Survey. Discussion Series No. 7287-005. Washington, D.C.: Mathematica Policy Research.

Eliasson, G. 1969. *The credit market investment planning and monetary policy*. Stockholm: Industrial Institute for Economic and Social Research.

Eliasson, G. 1976a. *Business economic planning—Theory, practice and comparison*. New York: John Wiley and Sons.

Eliasson, G. (with the assistance of G. Olavi and M. Heiman). 1976b. A micro-macro interactive simulation model of the Swedish economy. Preliminary Documentation. Working Paper No. 7. Stockholm: Industrial Institute for Economic and Social Research.

Eliasson, G. 1977. Competition and market processes in a simulation model of the Swedish economy. *American Economic Review, 67*, 277-281.

Eliasson, G. 1978. A micro simulation model of a national economy; How does inflation affect growth? In G. Eliasson (Ed.), *A micro-to-macro model of the Swedish economy*. Stockholm: Industrial Institute for Economic and Social Research.

Eliasson, G., and Olavi, G. 1978. Stepwise parameter estimation of a micro-simulation model. In G. Eliasson (Ed.), *A micro-to-macro model of the Swedish economy*. Stockholm: Industrial Institute for Economic and Social Research.

Evans, R. G. 1974. Supplier-induced demand: Some empirical evidence and implications. In M. Perlman (Ed.), *Economics of health and medical care*. New York: John Wiley and Sons.

Fair, R. C. and Jaffee, D. M. 1972. Methods of estimation for market in disequilibrium. *Econometrica, 40*, 497-514.

Feldstein, M. S. 1971. Hospital cost inflation: A study of nonprofit price dynamics. *American Economic Review, 61*, 853-872.

Feldstein, M. S. 1974. Econometric studies in health economics. In M. D. Intriligator and D. A. Kendrick (Eds.), *Frontiers of quantitative economics*, vol. 2. Amsterdam: North-Holland.

Feldstein, M. S. 1976. Quality change and the demand for hospital care. Harvard Institute of Economic Research Discussion Paper Series No. 475. Cambridge, Mass.: Harvard Institute of Economic Research.

Feldstein, M. S. 1977. The high cost of hospitals—And what to do about it. *Public Interest*, Summer, pp. 40-54.

Feldstein, M. S., and Friedman, B. 1976. The effect of national health insurance on the price and quantity of medical care. In R. Rosett (Ed.), *The role of health insurance in the health services sector*. New York: National Bureau of Economic Research.

Feldstein, M. S., and Fane, G. 1973. Taxes, corporate dividend policy and personal savings: The British postwar experience. *Review of Economics and Statistics, 55*, 399-411.

Feldstein, P. J. 1964. The demand for medical care. In *Report of the Commission on the Cost of Medical Care*, vol. 1. Prepared by the American Medical Association. Chicago: American Medical Association.

Fisher, W. H., and Chilton, C. H. 1971. An *ex ante* capital matrix for the United States, 1970-1975. Final report to the *Scientific American*, Battelle Memorial Institute, Columbus, Ohio.

Friedman, M. 1977. Inflation and unemployment. (Nobel lecture.) *Journal of Political Economy, 85*, 451-472.

Friend, I., and Jones, R. 1966. *Proceedings of the Conference on Consumption and Saving*, vol. 2. Philadelphia: University of Pennsylvania Press.

Fuchs, V., and Kramer, M. 1972. Determinants of expenditures for physicians' service in the United States, 1948-1968. Occasional Paper No. 117. New York: National Bureau of Economic Research.

Fullerton, D., Shoven, J. B., and Whalley, J. 1978. General equilibrium analysis of U.S. taxation policy. In Department of the Treasury, Office of Tax Analysis, *1978 compendium of tax research*. Washington, D.C.: U.S. Government Printing Office.

Genberg, H. 1974. *World inflation and the small open economy*. Federation of Swedish Industries Research Report No. 17. Stockholm: Swedish Industrial Publishers.

Goldfeld, S. M., and Quandt, R. E. 1973. The estimation of structural shifts by switching regressions. *Annals of Economic and Social Measurement, 2*, 475-486.

Golladay, F., and Haveman, R. 1977. *The economic impacts of tax-transfer policy*. New York: Academic Press.

Gordon, N. M. 1978. The treatment of women in the public pension systems of five countries. Working Paper No. 5069-1. Washington, D.C.: The Urban Institute.

Greenberg, D. 1978. Participation in guaranteed employment programs: An exploratory simulation. In J. Palmer (Ed.), *Creating jobs: Public employment programs and wage subsidies*. Washington, D.C.: The Brookings Institution.

Greenberg, D., and Kosters, M. 1973. Income guarantees and the working poor: The effect of income-maintenance programs on the hours of work of male family heads. In G. G. Cain and H. W. Watts (Eds.), *Income maintenance and labor supply*. New York: Academic Press.

Greenberger, M., Creeson, M., and Crissey, B. 1976. *Models in the policy process: Public decision making in the computer era*. New York: Russell Sage Foundation.

Grunfeld, Y., and Grilliches, Z. 1960. Is aggregation necessarily bad? *Review of Economics and Statistics*, *42*, 1-13.

Hall, R. E., and Jorgenson, D. W. 1971. In G. Fromm (Ed.), *Tax incentives and capital spending*. Washington, D.C.: The Brookings Institution.

Halsey, H., Kurz, M., Spiegelman, R., and Waksberg, A. 1977. *The reporting of income to welfare*. Research Memorandum No. 42. Menlo Park, Calif.: Stanford Research Institute.

Hamermesh, D. S. 1976. Econometric studies of labor demand and their application to policy analysis. *Journal of Human Resources*, *11*, 507-525.

Handbook of public income transfer programs. 1972. Studies in Public Welfare, No. 2. Washington, D.C.: U.S. Congress, Joint Economic Committee.

Harberger, A. C. 1959. The corporation income tax: An empirical appraisal. In U.S. Congress, House Committee on Ways and Means, *Tax revision compendium*, vol. 1. Washington, D.C.: U.S. Government Printing Office.

Harberger, A. C. 1962. The incidence of the corporation income tax. *Journal of Political Economy*, *70*, 215-240.

Harberger, A. C. 1966. Efficiency effects of taxes on income from capital. In M. Krzyzaniak (Ed.), *Effects of corporation income tax*. Detroit: Wayne State University Press.

Harberger, A. C., and Bailey, M. J. (Eds.). 1969. *The taxation of income from capital*. Washington, D.C.: The Brookings Institution.

Hausman, J. A. 1975. Project Independence report: An appraisal of U.S. energy needs up to 1985. *Bell Journal of Economics*, *6*, 517-551.

Haveman, R., and Krutilla, J. V. 1968. *Unemployment, idle capacity, and the evaluation of the public expenditures*. Baltimore: Johns Hopkins Press.

Haveman, R., and Smolensky, E. 1978. The Program for Better Jobs and Income—An analysis of costs and distributional effects. U.S. Congress, Joint Economic Committee, Joint Committee Print, February.

Heckman, J. 1974. Effect of child-care programs on women's work effort. *Journal of Political Economy*, *82*, 491-518.

Heckman, J. 1976. The common structure of statistical models of truncation, sample selection and limited dependent variable and a simple estimator for such models. *Annals of Economic and Social Measurements*, *5*, 475-492.

Hellinger, F. J. 1976. The effect of certificate-of-need legislation on hospital investment. *Inquiry*, *13*, 187-193.

Hendricks, G., and Holden, R. 1976a. A report on the variance in simulated earnings histories produced by DYNASIM. Working Paper No. 5075-1. Washington, D.C.: The Urban Institute.

Hendricks, G., and Holden, R. 1976b. The role of microanalytic simulation models in projecting OASDI costs. *1976 proceedings of the business and economic statistics section of the American Statistical Association*. Washington, D.C.: The American Statistical Association.

Hendricks, G., Holden, R., and Johnson, J. 1976. A file of simulated family and earnings histories through the year 2000: Contents and documentation. Working Paper No. 985-3. Washington, D.C.: The Urban Institute.

Herriot, R. A., and Spiers, E. F. 1975. Measuring the impact on income statistics of reporting differences between current population survey and administration sources. In U.S. Department of Commerce, Bureau of the Census, *Some preliminary results from the 1973 CPS-IRS-SSA exact match study*. Washington, D.C.: U.S. Government Printing Office.

Holahan, J. 1975. *Financing health care for the poor: The Medicaid experience*. Lexington, Mass.: Lexington Books.

Holahan, J., and Stuart, B. 1977. *Controlling Medicaid utilization patterns.* Paper No. 17900. Washington, D.C.: The Urban Institute.

Holahan, J., and Wilensky, G. R. 1972. *National health insurance: Costs and distributional effects.* Paper No. 70008. Washington, D.C.: The Urban Institute.

Holden, R. 1977. Components of variation in longitudinal earnings histories. Working Paper No. 5075-2. Washington, D.C.: The Urban Institute.

Hollenbeck, K. 1977. *The comparative static work experience data adjustment algorithm (CSWORK).* Project Report No. 78-13. Washington, D.C.: Mathematica Policy Research.

Housing and Development Reporter, Reference File. 1977. Washington, D.C.: Bureau of National Affairs.

Husby, R. D. 1971. A nonlinear consumption function estimated from time-series and cross-section data. *Review of Economics and Statistics, 53*, 76-79.

Industrial Institute for Economic and Social Research (IUI). 1978. Current research project report (Annual report). Stockholm: IUI.

Industrikonjunkturen. 1974. (Journal of the Federation of Swedish Industries.) Spring, pp. 51-54.

International Research and Technology Corporation. 1970. *Effects of technological change on, and environmental implications of, an input-output analysis for the United States, 1967-2020.* Report No. IRT-229-R/I. Washington, D.C.: IRT.

Intriligator, M. D. 1976. Comments on M. Feldstein and B. Friedman, "The effect of national health insurance on the price and quantity of medical care." In R. Rosett (Ed.) *The role of health insurance in the health service sector.* New York: National Bureau of Economic Research.

Intriligator, M. D., and Kehrer, B. H. 1972. A simultaneous equations model of ancillary personnel employed in physicians' offices. Paper presented at the Econometric Society Meetings, Toronto, December.

Intriligator, M. D., and Kehrer, B. H. 1974. Allied health personnel in physicians' offices: An econometric approach. In M. Perlman (Ed.), *Economics of health and medical care.* New York: John Wiley and Sons.

Jack Faucett Associates. 1976. *Automobile sector forecasting model: User's guide.* Final report to the Federal Energy Administration. Chevy Chase, Md.: Jack Faucett Associates.

Jakobsson, U., and Normann, G. 1974. *Inkomstbeskattningen i den ekonomiska politiken.* Stockholm: Industrial Institute for Economic and Social Research.

Jencks, C., Smith, M., Aaland, N., et al. 1972. *Inequality: A reassessment of the effects of family and schooling in America.* New York: Basic Books.

Johnston, H. N. 1974. A note on the estimation and prediction inefficiency of "dynamic" estimators. *International Economic Review, 15*, 251-255.

Kadane, J. 1975. Statistical problems of merged data files. OTA Paper No. 6. Washington, D.C.: U.S. Department of the Treasury, Office of Tax Analysis.

Kadane, J. 1978. Some statistical problems in merging data files. In *1977 compendium of tax research*, sponsored by the U.S. Department of the Treasury, Office of Tax Analysis. Washington, D.C.: U.S. Government Printing Office.

Kain, J., and Quigley, J. 1975. *Housing markets and racial discrimination.* New York: Columbia University Press.

Kalachek, E., Raines, F., and Larson, D. 1979. The determination of labor supply: A dynamic model. *Industrial and Labor Relations Review, 32*, 367-377.

Keeley, M. C., Robins, P. K., Spiegelman, R. G., and West, R. W. 1977a. *The labor supply effects and costs of alternative negative income tax programs: Evidence from the Seattle and Denver Income Maintenance Experiment, Part 1: The labor supply response function.* Research Memorandum 38. Menlo Park, Calif.: Stanford Research Institute.

Keeley, M. C., Robins, P. K., Spiegelman, R. G., and West, R. W. 1977b. *The labor supply effects and costs of alternative negative income tax programs: Evidence from the Seattle and Denver Income Maintenance Experiment, Part 2: National predictions using the labor supply response function.* Research Memorandum 39. Menlo Park, Calif.: Stanford Research Institute.

Kendrick, J. 1976. *The national wealth of the United States: By major sectors and industry.* New York: The Conference Board.

Kesselman, J. R., Williamson, S. H., and Berndt, E. R. 1977. Tax credits for employment rather than investment. *American Economic Review, 67*, 339-349.

Kimbell, L. J., and Lorant, J. H. 1972. Production functions for physicians' services. Paper presented at the Econometric Society Meetings, Toronto, December.

Kimbell, L. J., and Lorant, J. H. 1977. Physician productivity and returns to scale. *Health Services Research, 12*, 367-379.

Kimbell, L. J., and Yett, D. E. 1975. *An evaluation of policy related research on the effects of alternative health care reimbursement systems.* Springfield, Va.: National Technical Information Service.

King, A. T. 1979. Estimation of a linear expenditure system for the United States in 1973. *Journal of Economics and Business, 31*, 190-195.

King, A. T., and Mieszkowski, P. M. 1973. Racial discrimination, segregation, and the price of housing. *Journal of Political Economy, 81*, 590-606.

King, J. A. 1975. *The impact of energy price increases on low income families.* Final report to the Federal Energy Administration. Washington, D.C.: Mathematica, Inc.

King, J. A. 1977. *The distributional impact of energy policies: Development and application of the Phase I Comprehensive Human Resources Data System.* Final report to the Federal Energy Administration. Washington, D.C.: Mathematica Policy Research.

King, J. A. 1978. *Estimating household energy expenditures in the Phase I Comprehensive Human Resources Data System.* Final report to the Department of Energy. Washington, D.C.: Mathematica Policy Research.

King, J. A., Beebout, H., and Doyle, P. 1977. Technical specifications: Phase I Comprehensive Human Resources Data System. Discussion Paper No. 7141-006. Final report to the Federal Energy Administration. Washington, D.C.: Mathematica Policy Research.

King, M. A. 1974. Taxation and the cost of capital. *Review of Economic Studies, 41*, 21-36.

Klein, L. R., and Taubman, P. J. 1971. In G. Fromm (Ed.), *Tax incentives and capital spending.* Washington, D.C.: The Brookings Institution.

Kolodrubetz, W. W., and Landay, D. M. 1973. Coverage and vesting of full-time employees under private retirement plans. *Social Security Bulletin*, November, pp. 20-36.

Krzyzaniak, M., and Musgrave, R. A. 1963. *The shifting of the corporation income tax.* Baltimore: Johns Hopkins Press.

Lave, J., Lave, L., and Leinhardt, S. 1974. Modeling the delivery of medical services. In M. Perlman (Ed.), *Economics of health and medical care.* New York: John Wiley and Sons.

Lee, M. L., and Wallace, R. L. 1969. Demand, supply and the distribution of physicians. Paper presented at the Western Economic Association Meetings, Long Beach, Calif., August.

Leontief, W. 1951. *The structure of American economy, 1919-1939.* New York: Oxford University Press.

Leontief, W., Chenery, H. B., Clark, P. G., et al. 1953. *Studies in the structure of the American economy.* New York: Oxford University Press.

Leontief, W., Morgan, A., Polenske, K., et al. 1965. The economic impact—Industrial and regional—Of an arms cut. *Review of Economics and Statistics, 47*, 217-241.

Leontief, W., and Petri, P. A. 1971. Impact of disarmament on strategic raw materials demand. Report to the United Nations, Department of Political and Security Council Affairs, New York. July.

Leuthold, J. H. 1975. The incidence of the payroll tax in the United States. *Public Finance Quarterly, 3*, 3-13.

Lowenstein, R. 1971. Early effects of Medicare on health care of the aged. *Social Security Bulletin*, April, pp. 3-20.

Lubick, D. C. 1978. Testimony before the U.S. Congress, House Committee on Government Operations. 95th Congress, second session, March 9.

MacDonald, M. 1978. *Food, stamps, and income maintenance.* New York: Academic Press.

MacRae, C. D. 1978. Urban housing in discrete structures. Working Paper No. 253-3. Washington, D.C.: The Urban Institute.

Manka, P. T. 1977. *Technical documentation: 1976 Survey of Income and Education computer microdata file*. Washington, D.C.: U.S. Department of Commerce, Bureau of the Census.

Maxfield, M., Jr. 1977. *Estimating the impact of labor supply adjustments on transfer program costs: A microsimulation methodology*. Project Report No. 77-11. Washington, D.C.: Mathematica Policy Research.

May, J. J. 1975. Utilization of health services and the availability of resources. In R. Andersen, J. Kravits, and O. W. Anderson (Eds.), *Equity in health services*. Cambridge, Mass.: Ballinger Publishing Co.

McClung, N. 1970. Estimates of income transfer program direct effects. In *The President's Commission on Income Maintenance Programs, technical studies*. Washington, D.C.: U.S. Government Printing Office.

McClung, N. 1973. Editing census microdata files for income and wealth. *Annals of Economic and Social Measurement*, *2*, 201-208.

McClung, N., Moeller, J., and Siguel, E. 1971. *Transfer income program evaluation*. Paper No. 950-3. Washington, D.C.: The Urban Institute.

Mead, G. H. 1934. *Mind, self, and society* (C. W. Morris, Ed.). Chicago: University of Chicago Press.

Merrill, O. H. 1972. Applications and extensions of an algorithm that computes fixed points of certain upper semi-continuous point to set mappings. Unpublished doctoral dissertation. University of Michigan, Ann Arbor.

Meyer, J., and Kuh, E. 1957. *The investment decision—An empirical study*. Cambridge, Mass.: Harvard University Press.

Midwest Research Institute. 1975. *Energy conservation implications of master metering*. Final report to the Federal Energy Administration. Kansas City, Mo.: Midwest Research Institute.

Minarik, J. J. 1977. Appendix: The yield of a comprehensive income tax. In J. A. Pechman (Ed.), *Comprehensive income taxation*. Washington, D.C.: The Brookings Institution.

Modigliani, F., and Cohen, K. J. 1961. *The role of anticipations and plans in economic behavior and their use in economic analysis and forecasting*. Urbana, Ill.: University of Illinois Press.

Moeller, J. F. 1970. Household budget responses to negative income tax simulations. Unpublished doctoral dissertation. University of Wisconsin, Madison.

Moeller, J. F. 1973. Development of a microsimulation model for evaluating economic implications of income transfer and tax policies. *Annals of Economic and Social Measurement*, *2*, 183-187.

Moynihan, D. P. 1973. *The politics of a guaranteed income: The Nixon administration and the Family Assistance Plan*. New York: Random House.

Murray, M. P. 1975. The distribution of tenant benefits in public housing. *Econometrica*, *43*, 771-788.

Musgrave, R., Heller, P., and Peterson, G. E. 1970. Cost effectiveness of alternative income maintenance schemes. *National Tax Journal*, *23*, 140-156.

Muth, R. F. 1960. The demand for nonfarm housing. In A. C. Harberger (Ed.), *The demand for durable goods*. Chicago: University of Chicago Press.

Muth, R. F. 1978. The Allocation of Households to Dwellings. *The Journal of Regional Science*, *18*, 159-178.

Newhouse, J. P., and Phelps, C. E. 1974. Price and income elasticities for medical care services. In M. Perlman (Ed.), *Economics of health and medical care*. New York: John Wiley and Sons.

Normann, G., and Södersten, J. 1978. *Skattepolitisk resursstyrning och in-komstutjämning*. Stockholm: Industrial Institute for Economic and Social Research.

Okner, B. A. 1972a. Constructing a new data base from existing microdata sets: The 1966 MERGE file. *Annals of Economic and Social Measurement*, *1*, 325-342.

Okner, B. A. 1972b. Reply and comments. *Annals of Economic and Social Measurement*, *1*, 359-362.

Olsen, E. O. 1972. An econometric analysis of rent control. *Journal of Political Economy*, *80*, 1081-1100.

Orcutt, G. 1957. A new type of socio-economic system. *Review of Economics and Statistics*, *58*, 773-797.

Orcutt, G. 1960. Simulation of economic systems. *American Economic Review*, *50*, 893-907.

Orcutt, G., Caldwell, S., and Wertheimer, R., II. 1976. *Policy exploration through microanalytic simulation*. Washington, D.C.: The Urban Institute.

Orcutt, G., Greenberger, M., Korbel, J., and Rivlin, A. 1961. *Microanalysis of socioeconomic systems: A simulation study*. New York: Harper and Row.

Ozanne, L. 1977. Calculating benefit/cost ratios with the Urban Institute model. Working Paper No. 235-3. Washington, D.C.: The Urban Institute.

Packer, A. 1973. Categorical public employment guarantees: A proposed solution to the poverty program. In *Concepts in welfare design*. Studies in Public Welfare, No. 9, Part 1. Washington, D.C.: U.S. Congress, Joint Economic Committee.

Pechman, J. A. 1965a. A new tax model for revenue estimating. In *Proceedings of a symposium on federal taxation*. Washington, D.C.: American Bankers' Association.

Pechman, J. A. 1965b. A new tax model for revenue estimating. In A. T. Peacock and G. Hauser (Eds.), *Government finance and economic development*. Paris: Organization for Economic Co-operation and Development.

Pechman, J. A. (Ed.). 1977. *Comprehensive income taxation*. Washington, D.C.: The Brookings Institution.

Pechman, J. A., and Okner, B. A. 1972. Individual income tax erosion by income classes. In U.S. Congress, Joint Economic Committee, *The economics of federal subsidy programs*, Part 1, 92 Cong., 2 Sess. Washington, D.C.: U.S. Government Printing Office.

Pechman, J. A., and Okner, B. A. 1974. *Who bears the tax burden*. Washington, D.C.: The Brookings Institution.

Pechman, J. A., and Timpane, P. M. (Eds.). 1975. *Work incentives and income guarantees*. Washington, D.C.: The Brookings Institution.

Peck, J. K. 1972. Comments. *Annals of Economic and Social Measurement*, *1*, 347-348.

Penner, R. 1977. Statement. In *Recycling energy tax revenues*. Hearings before the Subcommittee on Administration, Committee on Finance, U.S. Senate. June 6 and 27. Washington, D.C.: U.S. Government Printing Office.

Pesando, J. E., and Rea, S. A., Jr. 1977. *Public and private pensions in Canada: An economic analysis*. Toronto: University of Toronto Press.

Piggott, J. R., and Whalley, J. 1976. General equilibrium investigations of U.K. tax subsidy policy: A progress report. In M. J. Artis and A. R. Nobay (Eds.), *Studies in modern economic analysis*. Oxford: Blackwell.

Piggott, J. R., and Whalley, J. 1977. Parameterizing Walrasian policy models. Department of Economics, University of Western Ontario, London, Ontario. Mimeographed.

Platt, D., and Hollenbeck, K. 1978. *Proposed strategies for constructing a CHRDS data base*. Report to the U.S. Department of Energy. Washington, D.C.: Mathematica Policy Research.

Polenske, K. 1972. The implementation of a multiregional input-output model for the United States. In A. Brody and A. P. Carter (Eds.), *Input-output techniques*. Amsterdam: North-Holland.

Polenske, K. 1974. *State estimates of technology, 1963*. Lexington, Mass.: Lexington Books.

Polenske, K. 1975. *The United States multi-regional input-output model*. Lexington, Mass.: Lexington Books.

Pratten, C. F. 1976. *A comparison of the performance of Swedish and UK companies*. Cambridge: Cambridge University Press.

Pugh, R., Hendrickson, A., and Caldwell, G. 1977. Updating statistical samples: Conceptual development and an empirical case study. Washington, D.C.: The Hendrickson Corporation. Memorandum.

Raduchel, W. J. 1971. A general equilibrium model for development planning. Unpublished doctoral dissertation. Harvard University, Cambridge, Mass.

Rand Corporation. 1978. *Fourth annual report of the Housing Assistance Supply Experiment.* R-2302-HUD. Santa Monica, Calif.: Rand Corporation.

Reid, M. 1962. *Housing and income.* Chicago: University of Chicago Press.

Reifler, R. F. 1973. Interregional input-output: A state of the arts survey. In G. G. Judge and T. Takayama (Eds.), *Studies in economic planning over space and time.* Amsterdam: North-Holland.

Reinhardt, U. E. 1978. Parkinson's Law and the demand for physicians' services: Comment on paper presented by Sloan and Feldman. In W. Greenberg (Ed.), *Competition in the health care sector: Past, present, and future: Proceedings of a conference sponsored by Bureau of Economics, Federal Trade Commission.* Washington, D.C.: U.S. Government Printing Office.

Revised deflators of new construction, 1947-73. 1974. *Survey of Current Business, 54,* 18-27.

Rivlin, A. M. 1971. *Systematic thinking for social action.* Washington, D.C.: The Brookings Institution.

Rodgers, J. M. 1972. *State estimates of outputs, employment and payrolls, 1947, 1958, 1963.* Lexington, Mass.: Lexington Books.

Rodgers, J. M. 1973. *State estimates of commodity trade flows, 1963.* Lexington, Mass.: Lexington Books.

Rosenberg, L. C. 1969. Taxation of income from capital, by industry group. In A. C. Harberger and M. J. Bailey (Eds.), *The taxation of income from capital.* Washington, D.C.: The Brookings Institution.

Ruggles, N., and Ruggles, R. 1974. A strategy for merging and matching microdata sets. *Annals of Economic and Social Measurement, 3,* 353-371.

Ruggles, N., Ruggles, R., and Wolfe, E. 1977. Merging microdata: Rationale, practice and testing. *Annals of Economic and Social Measurement, 6,* 407-428.

Russell, L. B. 1979. *Technology in hospitals: Medical advances and their diffusion.* Washington, D.C.: The Brookings Institution.

Sadowsky, G. 1976. *MASH, a computer system for microanalytic simulation for policy exploration.* Washington, D.C.: The Urban Institute.

Salkever, D. S., and Bice, T. W. 1976a. *Impact of state certificate-of-need laws on health care costs and utilization.* Final report on contract HRA-106-74-57, National Center for Health Services Research, HEW. Springfield, Va.: National Technical Information Service.

Salkever, D. S., and Bice, T. W. 1976b. The impact of certificate-of-need controls on hospital investment. *Health and Society, 54,* 185-214.

Scarf, H. E. (with T. Hansen). 1973. *The computation of economic equilibria.* New Haven, Conn.: Yale University Press.

Shoven, J. B. 1976. The incidence and efficiency effects of taxes on income from capital. *Journal of Political Economy, 84,* 1261-1283.

Shoven, J. B., and Whalley, J. 1972. A general equilibrium calculation of the effects of differential taxation of income from capital in the U.S. *Journal of Public Economics, 1,* 281-321.

Shoven, J. B., and Whalley, J. 1977. Equal yield tax alternatives: General equilibrium computational techniques. *Journal of Public Economics, 8,* 211-224.

Simon, H. 1959. Theories of decision-making in economics and behavioral science. *American Economic Review, 49,* 253-283.

Sims, C. 1972. Comments. *Annals of Economic and Social Measurement, 1,* 343-346.

Skolnik, A. M. 1976a. Private pension plans, 1950-1974. *Social Security Bulletin,* June, pp. 3-15.

Skolnik, A. M. 1976b. Twenty-five years of employee benefit plans. *Social Security Bulletin,* September, pp. 3-21.

Slitor, R. E. 1966. Corporate tax incidence: Economic adjustments to differentials under a two-tier tax structure. In M. Krzyzaniak (Ed.), *Effects of corporate income tax.* Detroit: Wayne State University Press.

Sloan, F. A. 1974. A microanalysis of physicians' hours of work decision. In M. Perlman (Ed.), *Economics of health and medical care*. New York: John Wiley and Sons.

Sloan, F. A., and Feldman, R. 1978. Competition among physicians [presented as "monopolistic elements in the market for physicians' services"]. In W. Greenberg (Ed.), *Competition in the health care sector: Past, present, and future: Proceedings of a conference sponsored by Bureau of Economics, Federal Trade Commission*. Washington, D.C.: U.S. Government Printing Office.

Smith, R. E. 1977a. A simulation model of the demographic composition of employment, unemployment, and labor force participation. In R. G. Ehrenberg (Ed.), *Research in labor economics*, vol. 1. Greenwich, Conn.: JAI Press.

Smith, R. E. 1977b. *The impact of macroeconomic conditions on employment opportunities for women*. U. S. Congress, Joint Economic Committee Print. Washington, D.C.: U.S. Government Printing Office.

Smith, R. E. (Ed.). 1979. *The subtle revolution: Women at work*. Washington, D.C.: The Urban Institute.

Smith, R. E., Vanski, J. E., and Holt, C. C. 1974. Recession and the employment of demographic groups. *Brookings Papers on Economic Activity, 3*, 737-760.

Spitz, B., and Holahan, J. 1977. *Modifying Medicaid eligibility and benefits*. Paper No. 12800. Washington, D.C.: The Urban Institute.

Statistical Abstract of the United States. 1972. Washington, D.C.: U.S. Government Printing Office.

Stiglitz, J. E. 1973. Taxation, corporate financial policy and the cost of capital. *Journal of Public Economics, 2*, 1-34.

Stiglitz, J. E. 1976. The corporation tax. *Journal of Public Economics, 5*, 303-311.

Stone, R. 1954. Linear expenditure systems and demand analysis—An application to the pattern of British demand. *Economic Journal, 64*, 511-527.

Struyk, R. J., Marshall, S., and Ozanne, L. 1978. *Housing policies for the urban poor: A case for local diversity in federal programs*. Washington, D.C.: The Urban Institute.

Sudovar, S. G., Jr., and Sullivan, K. 1977. *National health insurance issues: The unprotected population*. Vienna, Va.: Pracon, Inc.

Sunley, E. M., Jr. 1977. Employee benefits and transfer payments. In J. A. Pechman (Ed.), *Comprehensive income taxation*. Washington, D.C.: The Brookings Institution.

Teigen, R. 1976. *Financial development and stabilization policy*. Federation of Swedish Industries Research Report No. 19. Stockholm: Swedish Industrial Publishers.

Thompson, L. H. 1976. Intracohort redistribution in the social security retirement program. In *1976 Proceedings of the business and economics statistics section of the American Statistical Association*. Washington, D.C.: American Statistical Association.

Thornton, C. 1978. *Zoning, apartments, and land use interactions*. Unpublished doctoral dissertation. Johns Hopkins University, Baltimore.

Turner, J. S., and Gilliam, G. B. 1975. Reducing and merging microdata files. OTA Paper No. 7. Washington, D.C.: U.S. Department of the Treasury, Office of Tax Analysis.

United Nations. 1972. *Disarmament and Development*. Report of the Group of Experts on the economic and social consequences of disarmament. New York: United Nations.

U.S. Congress (Joint Economic Committee). 1977a. *1976 tax expenditures*. Washington, D.C.: U.S. Government Printing Office.

U.S. Congress (Senate). 1977b. *Arms transfer policy: Report to Congress for use of the Committee on Foreign Relations*, Annex 2, Study of the economic effects of restraint in arms transfers. Washington, D.C.: U.S. Government Printing Office.

U.S. Congressional Budget Office. 1976. *Five-year budget projections: Fiscal years 1978-1982*. Washington, D.C.: U.S. Government Printing Office.

U.S. Congressional Budget Office. 1977. *President Carter's energy proposals: A perspective*. Staff working paper. Washington, D.C.: U.S. Government Printing Office.

U.S. Department of Agriculture (Food and Nutrition Service). 1975. Report on the Food Stamp Program: Response to Senate Resolution 58.

U.S. Department of Agriculture (Food and Nutrition Service). 1977a. *Characteristics of food stamp households, September 1976*. FNS 168. Washington, D.C.: USDA.

U.S. Department of Agriculture (Food and Nutrition Service, Food Stamp Program). 1977b. Statistical summary of operations for June 1977.

U.S. Department of Commerce (Office of Business Economics). 1954. *National Income, 1954 edition*. Washington, D.C.: U.S. Government Printing Office.

U.S. Department of Commerce (Office of Business Economics). 1958. *U.S. income and output*. Washington, D.C.: U.S. Government Printing Office.

U.S. Department of Commerce (Bureau of the Census). 1968. 1967 Survey of Economic Opportunity codebook. Looseleaf.

U.S. Department of Commerce (Bureau of the Census). 1971. Projections of the population of the United States, by age and sex: 1970 to 2020. *Current Population Reports*, Series P-25, No. 470. Washington, D.C.: U.S. Government Printing Office.

U.S. Department of Commerce (Bureau of the Census). 1972a. *Public use samples of basic records from the 1970 census*. Washington, D.C.: Department of Commerce.

U.S. Department of Commerce (Bureau of the Census). 1972b. *United States census of population*, vol. 1, *Characteristics of the population, 1970*. Final report PC(1)-B1. Washington, D.C.: U.S. Government Printing Office.

U.S. Department of Commerce (Bureau of the Census). 1972c. *Census of housing: 1970*. Metropolitan housing characteristics, final report HC(2), the United States and regions. Washington, D.C.: U.S. Government Printing Office.

U.S. Department of Commerce. 1973. *Price index of new one-family houses sold*. Report No. C27-73-2, November. Washington, D.C.: U.S. Government Printing Office.

U.S. Department of Commerce (Bureau of Economic Analysis). 1975. *Summary input-output tables of the U.S. economy 1968, 69, 70*. BEA Staff Paper No. 27 (BEA-SP 75-207). Washington, D.C.: Department of Commerce.

U.S. Department of Commerce (Bureau of the Census). 1976a. Characteristics of households purchasing food stamps. *Current population reports*, Series P-23, No. 61. Washington, D.C.: U.S. Government Printing Office.

U.S. Department of Commerce (Bureau of the Census). 1976b. Money income in 1974 of families and persons in the United States. *Current population reports*, Series P-60, No. 101. Washington, D.C.: U.S. Government Printing Office.

U.S. Department of Commerce (Bureau of the Census). 1976c. Selected data from the 1973 and 1974 surveys of purchases and ownership. Mimeographed.

U.S. Department of Commerce (Bureau of Economic Analysis). 1976d. *Survey of current business*, July. Washington, D.C.: U.S. Government Printing Office.

U.S. Department of Commerce (Bureau of the Census). 1978a. Money income and poverty status in 1975 of families and persons in the United States and the northeast region by divisions and states. *Current population reports*, Series P-60, No. 110. Washington, D.C.: U.S. Government Printing Office.

U.S. Department of Commerce (Bureau of the Census). 1978b. *The Current Population Survey: Design and methodology*. Technical Paper No. 40. Washington, D.C.: U.S. Government Printing Office.

U.S. Department of Commerce (Bureau of the Census). 1978c. Money income in 1977 of households in the United States. *Current population reports, consumer income*, Series P-60, No. 117. Appendix A. Washington, D.C.: U.S. Government Printing Office.

U.S. Department of Health, Education, and Welfare (Office of the Assistant Secretary for Program Coordination). 1966a. *Selected human investment programs*. Program analysis 1966-10. Washington, D.C.: HEW.

U.S. Department of Health, Education, and Welfare (Office of the Assistant Secretary for Program Coordination). 1966b. *Income and benefit programs*. Program analysis 1966-2. Washington, D.C.: HEW.

U.S. Department of Health, Education, and Welfare (Public Health Service, Bureau of Health Manpower). 1969. Manpower supply and educational statistics for selected health occupations. *Health Manpower Source Book*. PHS Publication No. 263, Section 20. Washington, D.C.: U.S. Government Printing Office.

U.S. Department of Health, Education, and Welfare (Bureau of Health Manpower Education). 1970. *Health manpower in hospitals*, by G. L. Losee and M. E. Altenderfer. DMI Report No. 1. Washington, D.C.: U.S. Government Printing Office.

U.S. Department of Health, Education, and Welfare (National Center for Health Statistics). 1971a. *Vital statistics of the United States, 1968*, vol. 2, *Mortality*. Section 5, "Life Tables." Washington, D.C.: U.S. Government Printing Office.

U.S. Department of Health, Education, and Welfare (National Center for Health Statistics). 1971b. Current estimates from the Health Interview Survey United States—1969, by G. E. Blanken. In *Vital and health statistics*, Series 10, No. 63. PHS Publication No. 1000. Washington, D.C.: U.S. Government Printing Office.

U.S. Department of Health, Education, and Welfare (National Center for Health Statistics). 1972. Utilization of short-stay hospitals summary of nonmedical statistics United States—1967, by A. L. Ranofsky. *Vital and health statistics*, Series 13, No. 9. HEW Publication No. (HSM) 72-1058. Washington, D.C.: U.S. Government Printing Office.

U.S. Department of Health, Education, and Welfare (Social Security Administration). 1973a. *Studies from interagency data linkages*, Report No. 1. Washington, D.C.: U.S. Government Printing Office.

U.S. Department of Health, Education, and Welfare (Social Security Administration, Office of Research and Statistics). 1973b. *Compendium of national health expenditures data*, by B. S. Cooper, N. L. Worthington, and M. F. McGee. HEW Publication No. (SSA) 73-11903. Washington, D.C.: U.S. Government Printing Office.

U.S. Department of Health, Education, and Welfare (Public Health Service, Bureau of Health Resources Development). 1974. *The Supply of Health Manpower: 1970 Profiles and Projection to 1990*, by H. V. Stambler and P. Schwab, et al. HEW Publication No. (HRA) 75-38. Washington, D.C.: U.S. Government Printing Office.

U.S. Department of Health, Education, and Welfare (Social Security Administration, Office of Research and Statistics). 1975. *1973 Current Population Survey—Summary earnings record exact match file codebook*. Studies from interagency data linkages. Washington, D.C.: U.S. Government Printing Office.

U.S. Department of Health, Education, and Welfare (Bureau of Health Manpower) and the American Hospital Association. 1967. *Manpower resources in hospitals—1966*. Report G297. Chicago: American Hospital Association.

U.S. Department of Labor (Bureau of Labor Statistics). 1967. *Industry wage survey: Hospitals July 1966*. Bulletin No. 1553. Washington, D.C.: U.S. Government Printing Office.

U.S. Department of Labor (Bureau of Labor Statistics). 1969. *Tomorrow's manpower needs*, vol. 4, Bulletin No. 1606. Washington, D.C.: U.S. Government Printing Office.

U.S. Department of Labor (Bureau of Labor Statistics). 1971. *Industry wage survey: Hospitals March 1969*. Bulletin No. 1688. Washington, D.C.: U.S. Government Printing Office.

U.S. Department of Labor (Bureau of Labor Statistics). 1977. *Handbook of labor statistics*. Washington, D.C.: U.S. Government Printing Office.

U.S. Department of the Treasury (Internal Revenue Service). 1976. *Statistics of income, 1973: Individual income tax returns*. Washington, D.C.: U.S. Government Printing Office.

U.S. Department of the Treasury. 1977a. *Blueprints for basic tax reform*. Washington, D.C.: U.S. Government Printing Office.

U.S. Department of the Treasury (Internal Revenue Service). 1977b. *Statistics of income 1973: Business income tax returns and corporation income tax returns*. Washington, D.C.: U.S. Government Printing Office.

U.S. Environmental Protection Agency (Office of Research and Development). 1974. *A guide to models in governmental planning and operations* (S. Gass and R. Sisson, Eds.). Washington, D.C.: Environmental Protection Agency.

U.S. Executive Office of the President (Energy Policy and Planning). 1977. *The National Energy Plan*. Washington, D.C.: U.S. Government Printing Office.

U.S. Federal Energy Administration (now Department of Energy). 1976. *1976 National energy outlook*. Washington, D.C.: U.S. Government Printing Office.

U.S. Federal Energy Administration (now Department of Energy). 1977. *Lifestyles and household energy use: 1973 and 1975 national surveys. Codebook and processing guide*. Washington, D.C.: Federal Energy Administration.

U.S. Library of Congress (Congressional Research Service, Education and Public Welfare Division). 1975. *Estimating the population eligible for food stamps*, by H. Beebout. No. 75-49ED. Washington, D.C.: Congressional Research Service.

U.S. Office of Management and Budget. 1972. *Special analyses: Budget of the United States Government, fiscal year 1973*. Washington, D.C.: U.S. Government Printing Office.

U.S. Office of Management and Budget. 1976a. *Current service estimates for the fiscal year 1978*. Washington, D.C.: U.S. Government Printing Office.

U.S. Office of Management and Budget. 1976b. *Special analyses: Budget of the United States Government, fiscal year 1977*. Washington, D.C.: U.S. Government Printing Office.

University of Michigan. 1978. A panel study of income dynamics. Ann Arbor: Institute for Social Research.

van der Gaag, J. 1978. *An econometric analysis of the Dutch health care system*. Doctoral dissertation. Leiden University, The Netherlands.

Vroman, W. 1974. Payroll tax incidence: Empirical tests with cross country data. *Public Finance, 29*, 185-199.

Weisbrod, B. 1977. Is health care different? Institute for Research on Poverty, Notes and Comments, Madison, Wis.

Weitenberg, J. 1969. The incidence of social security taxes. *Public Finance, 24*, 193-208.

Wertheimer, R., II, and Zedlewski, S. R. 1976. The impact of demographic change on the distribution of earned income and the AFDC Program: 1975-1985. Working Paper No. 985-1. Washington, D.C.: The Urban Institute.

Wertheimer, R., II, and Zedlewski, S. R. 1978. The elderly in 1990. Working Paper No. 1224-1. Washington, D.C.: The Urban Institute.

Wilensky, R. G. 1970. An income transfer computational model. In *The President's Commission on Income Maintenance Programs, technical studies*. Washington, D.C.: U.S. Government Printing Office.

Wold, H. 1959. Ends and means in econometric model building: Basic considerations reviewed. In U. Grenander (Ed.), *Probability and statistics: The Harald Cramér Volume*. Stockholm: Almqvist and Wiksell; New York: John Wiley and Sons.

Wright, C. 1969. Savings and the rate of interest. In A. C. Harberger and M. J. Bailey (Eds.), *The taxation of income from capital*. Washington, D.C.: The Brookings Institution.

Yett, D. E. 1965. The supply of nurses: An economist's view. *Hospital Progress, 46*, 88-102.

Yett, D. E. 1970a. Causes and consequences of salary differentials in nursing. *Inquiry, 7*, 78-99.

Yett, D. E. 1970b. The chronic shortage of nurses: A public policy dilemma. In H. E. Klarman (Ed.), *Empirical studies in health economics*. Baltimore: Johns Hopkins Press.

Yett, D. E. 1974. *Data source book for an economic analysis of nursing supply and demand*. Springfield, Va.: National Technical Information Service.

Yett, D. E. 1975. *An economic analysis of the nurse shortage*. Lexington, Mass.: Lexington Books.

Yett, D. E. 1978. Facts versus folklore concerning the market for physicians' services: Comment on paper presented by Sloan and Feldman. In W. Greenberg (Ed.), *Competition in the health care sector: Past, present, and future: Proceedings of a conference sponsored by Bureau of Economics, Federal Trade Commission*. Washington, D.C.: U.S. Government Printing Office.

Yett, D. E., Drabek, L., Ernst, R. L., and Greenlees, J. S. 1976. Estimation testing, and implementation of a basic model to predict impacts of state-level policies to influence physicians' specialty and practice location choices: Preliminary proposal. In *Final report on grant No. 2051 from the Robert Wood Johnson Foundation*. Los Angeles: Human Resources Research Center.

Yett, D. E., Drabek, L., Intriligator, M. D., and Kimbell, L. J. 1970. The development of a microsimulation model of health manpower demand and supply. *Proceedings and report of conference on a health manpower simulation model, Aug. 31-Sept. 1, 1970*, vol. 1. Washington, D.C.: U.S. Government Printing Office.

Yett, D. E., Drabek, L., Intriligator, M. D., and Kimbell, L. J. 1972. Health manpower planning: An econometric approach. *Health Services Research*, 7, 134-147.

Yett, D. E., Drabek, L., Intriligator, M. D., and Kimbell, L. J. 1974. Econometric forecasts of health services and health manpower. In M. Perlman (Ed.), *Economics of health and medical care*. New York: John Wiley and Sons.

Yett, D. E., Drabek, L., Intriligator, M. D., and Kimbell, L. J. 1977. A macroeconometric model of the production and distribution of physician, hospital, and other health care services. In D. D. Venedictov (Ed.), *Health system modeling and the information system for the coordination of research in oncology*. Luxemburg, Austria: International Institute for Applied Systems Analysis.

Yett, D. E., Drabek, L., Intriligator, M. D., and Kimbell, L. J. 1979. *A forecasting and policy simulation model of the health care sector: The HRRC Prototype Microeconometric Model*. Lexington, Mass.: Lexington Books.

Yuskavage, R., Hirschberg, D., and Scheuren, F. 1977. The impact on personal and family income of adjusting the CPS for undercoverage. *1977 proceedings of the social statistics section of the American Statistical Association*. Washington, D.C.: American Statistical Association.

Zabrowski, E. K. 1974. IDIOM: An aid to national and regional policy making. In *Reports*. Office of Economic Research, Economic Development Administration, U.S. Department of Commerce. Washington, D.C.: Department of Commerce.

Zabrowski, E. K., and Krueger, P. K. 1974. Contingent projections to 1980: Output, employment, occupations, capital, effluents and raw materials. Systems Analysis Group, Bureau of Domestic Commerce, Domestic and International Business Administration, U.S. Department of Commerce. Washington, D.C.: Department of Commerce.

Zedlewski, S. R. 1977. Distributional impact of two macroeconomic scenarios and a negative income tax program. Working Paper No. 5075-5. Washington, D.C.: The Urban Institute.

INDEX*

A

Aid to Families with Dependent Children (AFDC)
and IDIOM, 248
and PBJI, 140-141, 142, 160, 161-162

B

Bailey's racial-boundary model, 205
Baumol and Stewart study, 261
Bennett and Bergmann model, *see* Transactions Model
Bureau of the Census, *see* Census Bureau
Bureau of Economic Analysis (BEA)
as data source for general equilibrium model, 107, 110
as data source for IDIOM, 219
Bureau of Labor Statistics, *see also* Survey of Consumer Expenditures
and microeconomic simulation model, 158 n*11*
and Transactions Model, 36

C

Carter administration, *see also* Program for Better Jobs and Income
and IDIOM, 224
urban policies of, 171, 210
Census Bureau, *see also* Current Population Survey; Survey of Economic Opportunity; Survey of Income and Education
as source of data for microeconomic simulation model, 140, 158 n*12*, 159 n*15*
as source of data for Urban Institute Housing Model, 180, 181, 209
Census of Population and Housing, *see* Census Bureau
Chase Econometrics, quarterly forecasting model, 44, 47
Cobb-Douglas functions, and general equilibrium model, 103, 105, 107, 112, 119, 129
Cochrane article, 260
Coen study, 109
Congressional Budget Control and Impoundment Act of 1974, 44
Constant Elasticity of Substitution (CES) function, and general equilibrium model, 103, 105, 112, 129
Consumer Expenditure Survey, *see* Survey of Consumer Expenditures
Corporate and personal tax integration, 97-133
Council of Economic Advisors, 260
Crecine study, 205
Current Population Reports, as data source for Transactions Model, 4
Current Population Survey, 138
Cyert and March study, 261

*Acronyms, agencies, surveys, and studies.

D

Data Resources, Inc. (DRI), quarterly forecasting model, 44, 46-47
Dresch and Updegrove model, *see* IDIOM
Dynamic Simulation of Income Model, *see* DYNASIM
DYNASIM, and IDIOM, 245

E

Eckaus and Parikh model, 255
Eliasson model, *see* Swedish micro to macro model
Earned Income Tax Credit (EITC), and PBJI, 141
Experimental Housing Allowance Program, and Urban Institute Housing Model, 179, 212

F

Federal Housing Administration (FHA), as data source for Urban Institute Housing Model, 175, 183
Federal Reserve System
    and general equilibrium model, 108 n*11*
    and Transactions Model, 31
Federation of Swedish Industries, and Swedish micro to macro model, 66
Food Stamp Program, and PBJI, 141, 161-162
Fullerton model, *see* General equilibrium model

G

General equilibrium model, 260
    and corporate and personal tax integration, 97-133
General equilibrium theory, model applications of, 254-255, 257-258

H

Haveman model, *see* Microeconomic simulation model
Housing Allowance Supply Experiment, *see* Experimental Housing Allowance Program
Human Resources Research Center (HRRC), Prototype Microeconomic Model, 256

I

IDIOM, 213-249, 260

Income Determination Input-Output Model, *see* IDIOM
Industrial Institute for Economic and Social Research (IUI), and Swedish micro to macro model, 66, 68 n*21*, 70 n*25*, 71 n*26*
Input-Output Table, and Transactions Model, 11
Internal Revenue Service (IRS), and general equilibrium model, 108 n*11*, *see also* *Statistics of Income*

J

Jencks, C., study, 256
Johnston, H. N., study, 46

K

Keynesian models, 69, 90, 254, *see also* Leontief-Keynesian model
    and IDIOM, 214, 219, 233, 246
    and microeconomic simulation model, 152, 164

L

Laspeyres measures, and general equilibrium model, 116, 119, 123
Leontief functions
    and general equilibrium model, 129
    and microeconomic simulation model, 152, 156-157
Leontief-Keynesian model, and Swedish micro to macro model, 50, 71 n*26*, 90
Linear Expenditure System (LES) functions, and general equilibrium model, 112, 119, 129

M

MATH model, 258
    and IDIOM, 245
Mead, George, 254
MERGE file, 256
Merged Tax File, as data source for general equilibrium model, 107, 111, 113, 114
Micro Analysis of Transfer to Households model, *see* MATH model
Microeconomic simulation model, 260
    and analysis of tax-transfer policies, 138-170
Minarik, Joseph, and MERGE file, 256-257
MRIO model
    and IDIOM, 217

and microeconomic simulation model, 156-157, 158 n*11*, 163-166

Multi-Regional Input-Output Model, *see* MRIO model

N

National Income Division (NID), as data source for general equilibrium model, 107, 108-110

O

Office of Tax Analysis, and general equilibrium model, 116, *see also* Merged Tax File

Ozanne and Vanski model, *see* Urban Institute Housing Model

P

Paasche measures, and general equilibrium model, 119, 123

Panel Study of Income Dynamics (PSID), 138, 257

PBJI, *see* Program for Better Jobs and Income

Pratten, C. F., study, 75

President's Commission on Income Maintenance, 259

Program for Better Jobs and Income, and microeconomic simulation model, 140-151, 159-162, 165, 168-170

S

Section 8 Housing Rehabilitation Program, and Urban Institute Housing Model, 171, 176, 186, 189-190, 200-203, 210

Section 312 Rehabilitation Loan Program, and Urban Institute Housing Model, 171, 186, 187-203, 209-210, 211

Simon, Herbert, 261

Standard and Poor's as data source for Transactions Model, 4-5

Statistics of Income
and general equilibrium theory, 109
and Transactions Model, 5 n*2*

Supplemental Security Income (SSI), and PBJI, 141, 142 n*4*, 160, 162

Survey of Consumer Expenditures (SCE), 138
as data source for general equilibrium model, 105, 107, 111
as data source for microeconomic simulation model, 139, 151, 154 n*5*, 155 n*6*

Survey of Current Business (SCB), as data source for general equilibrium model, 107, 108-111

Survey of Economic Opportunity (SEO), 138, 259

Survey of Income and Education (SIE), 138, 259, as data source for microeconomic simulation model, 139, 153, 154

Survey Research Center of University of Michigan, *see* Panel Study of Income Dynamics

Swedish Central Bureau of Statistics, and Swedish micro to macro model, 49

Swedish micro to macro model, 49-95, 255

T

Tax-transfer policies, and microeconomic simulation model, 137-170

Thornton, C., study, 205

Transactions Model, 3-48, 255, 261

Transfer Income Model, *see* TRIM

TRIM, and IDIOM, 245

U

U.S. Department of Commerce, *see also* Bureau of Economic Analysis; National Income Division
as data source for Urban Institute Housing Model, 187 n*20* and IDIOM, 224

U.S. Department of Housing and Urban Development (HUD), and Urban Institute Housing Model, 186-187, 190 n*24*

U.S. Department of Labor, and industrial-occupation matrix, 140, *see also* Survey of Consumer Expenditures

U.S. Treasury Department, and IDIOM, 224, *see also* Merged Tax File; Office of Tax Analysis

Urban Institute, *see* DYNASIM

Urban Institute Housing Model, 171-212, 256, 263

W

Wharton Econometric Forecasting Associates, quarterly forecasting model, 44

Wald, Herman, 255

Y

Yett model, *see* Human Resources Research Center Prototype Microeconomic Model

Institute for Research on Poverty
Monograph Series

Robert H. Haveman and Kevin Hollenbeck, Editors, *Microeconomic Simulation Models for Public Policy Analysis, Volume 1: Distributional Impacts, Volume 2: Sectoral, Regional, and General Equilibrium Models.* 1980

Peter K. Eisinger, *The Politics of Displacement: Racial and Ethnic Transition in Three American Cities.* 1980

Erik Olin Wright, *Class Structure and Income Determination.* 1979

Joel F. Handler, *Social Movements and the Legal System: A Theory of Law Reform and Social Change.* 1979

Duane E. Leigh, *An Analysis of the Determinants of Occupational Upgrading.* 1978

Stanley H. Masters and Irwin Garfinkel, *Estimating the Labor Supply Effects of Income Maintenance Alternatives.* 1978

Irwin Garfinkel and Robert H. Haveman, with the assistance of David Betson, *Earnings Capacity, Poverty, and Inequality.* 1977

Harold W. Watts and Albert Rees, Editors, *The New Jersey Income—Maintenance Experiment, Volume III: Expenditures, Health, and Social Behavior; and the Quality of the Evidence.* 1977

Murray Edelman, *Political Language: Words That Succeed and Policies That Fail.* 1977

Marilyn Moon and Eugene Smolensky, Editors, *Improving Measures of Economic Well-Being.* 1977

Harold W. Watts and Albert Rees, Editors, *The New Jersey Income—Maintenance Experiment, Volume II: Labor-Supply Responses.* 1977

Marilyn Moon, *The Measurement of Economic Welfare: Its Application to the Aged Poor.* 1977

Morgan Reynolds and Eugene Smolensky, *Public Expenditures, Taxes, and the Distribution of Income: The United States, 1950, 1961, 1970.* 1977

Fredrick L. Golladay and Robert H. Haveman, with the assistance of Kevin Hollenbeck, *The Economic Impacts of Tax—Transfer Policy: Regional and Distributional Effects.* 1977

David Kershaw and Jerilyn Fair, *The New Jersey Income-Maintenance Experiment, Volume I: Operations, Surveys, and Administration.* 1976

Peter K. Eisinger, *Patterns of Interracial Politics: Conflict and Cooperation in the City.* 1976

Irene Lurie, Editor, *Integrating Income Maintenance Programs.* 1975

Stanley H. Masters, *Black—White Income Differentials: Empirical Studies and Policy Implications.* 1975

Larry L. Orr, *Income, Employment, and Urban Residential Location.* 1975

Joel F. Handler, *The Coercive Social Worker: British Lessons for American Social Services.* 1973

Glen G. Cain and Harold W. Watts, Editors, *Income Maintenance and Labor Supply: Econometric Studies.* 1973

Charles E. Metcalf, *An Econometric Model of Income Distribution.* 1972

Larry L. Orr, Robinson G. Hollister, and Myron J. Lefcowitz, Editors, with the assistance of Karen Hester, *Income Maintenance: Interdisciplinary Approaches to Research.* 1971

Robert J. Lampman, *Ends and Means of Reducing Income Poverty.* 1971

Joel F. Handler and Ellen Jane Hollingsworth, *"The Deserving Poor": A Study of Welfare Administration.* 1971

Murray Edelman, *Politics as Symbolic Action: Mass Arousal and Quiescence.* 1971

Frederick Williams, Editor, *Language and Poverty: Perspectives on a Theme.* 1970

Vernon L. Allen, Editor, *Psychological Factors in Poverty.* 1970